Smart Devices, Applications, and Protocols for the IoT

Joel J.P.C. Rodrigues
National Institute of Telecommunications (Inatel), Brazil

Amjad Gawanmeh
Khalifa University, UAE

Kashif Saleem
King Saud University, Saudi Arabia

Sazia Parvin
Melbourne Polytechnic, Australia

A volume in the Advances in
Multimedia and Interactive
Technologies (AMIT) Book Series

Published in the United States of America by
IGI Global
Engineering Science Reference (an imprint of IGI Global)
701 E. Chocolate Avenue
Hershey PA, USA 17033
Tel: 717-533-8845
Fax: 717-533-8661
E-mail: cust@igi-global.com
Web site: http://www.igi-global.com

Library of Congress Cataloging-in-Publication Data

Names: Rodrigues, Joel Jose P. C., editor.
Title: Smart devices, applications, and protocols for the IoT / Joel J.P.C.
   Rodrigues, Amjad Gawanmeh, Kashif Saleem, and Sazia Parvin, editors.
Description: Hershey, PA : Engineering Science Reference, [2019] | Includes
   bibliographical references.
Identifiers: LCCN 2018036348| ISBN 9781522578116 (h/c) | ISBN 9781522578123
   (eISBN)
Subjects: LCSH: Internet of things. | Intelligent control systems. | Computer
   network protocols.
Classification: LCC TK5105.8857 .S59 2019 | DDC 004.678/8--dc23 LC record available at https://
lccn.loc.gov/2018036348

This book is published in the IGI Global book series Advances in Multimedia and Interactive Technologies (AMIT) (ISSN: 2327-929X; eISSN: 2327-9303)

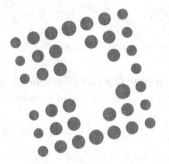

Advances in Multimedia and Interactive Technologies (AMIT) Book Series

ISSN:2327-929X
EISSN:2327-9303

Editor-in-Chief: Joel J.P.C. Rodrigues, National Institute of Telecommunications (Inatel), Brazil & Instituto de Telecomunicações, University of Beira Interior, Portugal

MISSION

Traditional forms of media communications are continuously being challenged. The emergence of user-friendly web-based applications such as social media and Web 2.0 has expanded into everyday society, providing an interactive structure to media content such as images, audio, video, and text.

The **Advances in Multimedia and Interactive Technologies (AMIT) Book Series** investigates the relationship between multimedia technology and the usability of web applications. This series aims to highlight evolving research on interactive communication systems, tools, applications, and techniques to provide researchers, practitioners, and students of information technology, communication science, media studies, and many more with a comprehensive examination of these multimedia technology trends.

COVERAGE

- Multimedia Streaming
- Digital Games
- Digital Images
- Digital Technology
- Mobile Learning
- Internet Technologies
- Digital Communications
- Gaming Media
- Digital Watermarking
- Multimedia Services

IGI Global is currently accepting manuscripts for publication within this series. To submit a proposal for a volume in this series, please contact our Acquisition Editors at Acquisitions@igi-global.com or visit: http://www.igi-global.com/publish/.

Titles in this Series

701 East Chocolate Avenue, Hershey, PA 17033, USA
Tel: 717-533-8845 x100 • Fax: 717-533-8661
E-Mail: cust@igi-global.com • www.igi-global.com

Table of Contents

Detailed Table of Contents

The present power grid is going through a substantial and radical transformation process. Unification of existing electrical infrastructure with information and communication network is an unavoidable requirement of smart grid deployment and operation. The key characteristics of smart grid technology are full duplex communication, advanced metering infrastructure, integration of renewable and alternative energy resources, distribution automation and complete monitoring, as well as control of entire power grid. Smart grid communication infrastructure consists of varied and hierarchical communication networks. Application of smart grid can be realized in the various the facets of energy utilization. Internet of things also plays a pivotal role in smart grid infrastructure as it provides a ubiquitous communication network. This chapter describes an implementation of internet of things (IoT)-based wireless energy management system for smart microgrid communication infrastructure.

Traffic is an inevitable problem for metro cities around the globe. Intelligent traffic management system helps to improve the traffic flow by detecting congestions or incidents and suggesting appropriate actions on traffic routing. A new and dynamic internet-based decision-making tool for traffic management system was proposed and implemented in authors' previous works. The tool needs weather, road, and vehicle-related integrated information from different data repositories. Several online web portals host real-time weather data streams. However, road and vehicle information are missing in those portals. In addition, their coverage is limited to city-level congregate information but precise road segment-based information is necessary for real-time TMS decision. Internet of things (IoT)-based online sensors can be a solution for this circumstance. As a consequence, in this chapter, an IoT-based framework is proposed and implemented with several remote mobile agents. Agents are securely interconnected to the cloud, and able to collect and exchange data through wireless communication.

Chapter 3

The internet of things (IoT) is a complex system of heterogeneous devices connected to a network. While IoT can significantly add value to people's everyday activities around the world, there are numerous security risks and privacy breaches imposed by the IoT landscape. Traditional security solutions are not applicable for the IoT as they require high-end processing capacity. The objective of this chapter is two-fold. Firstly, it provides a comprehensive summary of the recent advancements in the IoT and identifies their vulnerabilities. Secondly, it proposes the paradigm of self-learning as an intelligent and sustainable mechanism that is capable of automatically detecting suspicious activities in the IoT. Overall, this chapter presents a contemporary coverage of the recent developments in the IoT scene, the security and privacy challenges confronting the security experts, a proposal of a self-learning framework for performing health check of the IoT environment, and finally a set of high-level implementation guidelines and conclusions.

Chapter 4

Surveillance is the process of close observation of a person, place, or object to avoid and minimize the risk of any undesired dangerous situations or suspicious activities to maintain normalcy. However, manual surveillance techniques have certain constraints including unavailability of trained manpower and erroneous observation triggering tricky situations. The proliferation of the use of information and communication technologies (ICT) have increased the levels automation and have made it a part of surveillance application. The aspects of automation have greatly reduced human intervention and have made systems more reliable and efficient. The new advancements in internet of things (IoT) and artificial intelligence (AI) have made automation in surveillance security even more convenient and efficient. It has been found that the application of IoT and AI-based learning mechanism have made significant performance improvement for automated surveillance purpose. Here, the authors discuss some of the recent trends and challenges faced by all pervasive surveillance systems.

Chapter 5

The underlying vision of the internet of things (IoT) is to create a world where the real and the virtual realms are converging to create smart environments that makes energy, transport, cities, and many other areas more intelligent. With the IoT, the physical world is being interfaced through the things to the virtual world in heterogeneous environment. In heterogeneous environment, privacy and security are the major challenges. The secure information exchange is most critical pitfall to ensure the system security. This chapter gives a detailed analysis of cryptographic algorithms in IoT. A comparison of lightweight cryptography algorithms on basis of block size, key size, gate equivalents, and throughput is given. Moreover, the various security issues in IoT are discussed along with possible solution.

Chapter 6

The two objectives of the smart accident detection and prevention system (SADPS) are 1) accident prevention and 2) accident detection. Based on the survey, 1.3 million people die every year due to roadway accidents. The main reason for this type of accident is speeding. So, the proposed SADPS focused on finding the speed parameters of each vehicle and giving notification to speeding vehicles through SMS that can be used to prevent accidents. The second objective is accident detection. For this task, each vehicle accelerometer values will be taken by the SADPS system. When an accident occurs, the location as well as the related details are sent to the SADPS system. This proposed system takes the immediate remedy by alerting the nearby police station and hospitals. Proposed SADPS also acts as a video surveillance and monitoring system. Automatic background subtraction and object tracking is done with the help of novel approaches.

Chapter 7

Ramgopal Kashyap, Amity University Chhattisgarh, India

Today, IoT in therapeutic administrations has ended up being more productive in light of the fact that the correspondence among authorities and patients has been improved with versatile applications. These applications are made by the associations with the objective that the pros can screen the patient's prosperity. If any issue has hopped out at the patient, the authority approaches the patient and gives the correct treatment. In this proposition, particular focus is given to infant human administrations, in light of the fact that the greatest fear of gatekeepers is that they would lose their infant kids at whatever point. Therefore, a business contraption has been recognized which screens consistent information about the infant's heart rate, oxygen levels, resting position. In case anything happens to the infant, the information will get to the adaptable application which has been made by an association and is mechanically available by finishing a representation field test for the kid.

Chapter 8

Olga Berenice Mora, Universidad de Guadalajara, Mexico
Elsa Julieta Cedillo-Elias, Universidad de Guadalajara, Mexico
Emmanuel Aceves, Universidad de Guadalajara, Mexico
Victor M. Larios, Universidad de Guadalajara, Mexico

Most of the work to develop a smart city is how to connect physical urban infrastructure to the digital world to use it as a solution space for citizens and authorities to make best decisions to reach the best quality of life every day. Every city as a complex system needs to adequately manage their different dimensions. This chapter proposes the second approach with a top-down architecture identifying a set of information technologies linked in processes that every city service needs as part of their digital transformation process in their urban space. Hence, this chapter introduces six technological layers in a workflow pipeline that are explained as an approach to develop every smart system of a city. However, in the proposed workflow of technologies to implement, the authors give a central focus to the IoT infrastructure as the base to build information of quality, to have reliable services even after getting insights from analytics to come back to the IoT with their connected actuators to take actions.

Chapter 9

Rahul Singh Chowhan, Agriculture University Jodhpur, India
Purva Dayya, MPUAT, India

Modern technologies are revolutionizing the way humans have lived. The world's population is expected to reach 9.6 billion by year 2050 and to serve this much population, the agricultural industries and layman farmers need to embrace IoT and e-agriculture or ICT in agriculture. Feeding the global population is the biggest problem of the world. The terminology has advanced from IIoT (Industrial Internet of Things), IoFT (Internet of Farm Things), IoSFT (Internet of Smart Farming Things), etc. The agriculture industries are open for ideas, advances, and technically trained workforce to help sustain ever increasing needs of food and allocate better choices of resources. Smart farming is less labor intensive and more capital intensive. Smart farming is furthering the Third Green Revolution around the globe by using various ICT technologies in agriculture.

Chapter 10

The radio frequency idtentification (RFID) is a wireless technology that enable automatic identification and extraction of stored information from any tagged object within a supply chain environment. A simple RFID system uses radio waves to collect and transfer data from a tag attached to an object linked to an RFID reader for identifying, tracking, and data capturing. However, RFID-based systems have numerous security- and privacy-related threats for the deployment of such technology in supply chain automation purpose. This chapter explains the technical fundamentals of RFID systems and its security threats. It also classifies the existing security and privacy threats into those which target the RFID components such as the tag, the communication channel, and the overall system threats. Finally, the chapter discusses the open research challenges that need further investigation, especially with the rapid introduction of diverse RFID applications in supply chain management (SCM).

Preface

The new paradigms and tremendous advances in computing, communications and control have provided and supported wide range of applications in all domains of live, in particular, bridging the physical components and the cyber space leading to the smart Internet of Things (IoT). As a result, several smart protocols and algorithms are needed to communicate IoT devices and exchange data between them. Smart communication protocols and algorithms make use of several methods and techniques in order to achieve reliable and efficient communication in several recent applications. This include, machine learning, decision making, knowledge representation, network management, network optimization, problem solution techniques, adaptive methods, and smart algorithms and protocols. Smart protocols and algorithms are usually used in order to perform adaptive decisions and take smart actions based on learning form the environment of operation. The notion of IoT has extraordinary significance for the future of several industrial domains and hence, it is expected that the complexity in the design of IoT applications will continue to increase due to the integration of several cyber components with physical and industrial systems. This book will present a comprehensive reference on the state of the art and recent advances in this area, given the recent amount of publications in this topic.

Chapter 1 presents smart energy system through IoT based management of smart microgrid. The present power grid is going through a substantial and radical transformation process. Unification of existing electrical infrastructure with information and communication network is an unavoidable requirement of Smart Grid deployment and operation. The key characteristics of Smart Grid technology are full duplex communication, advanced metering infrastructure, integration of renewable and alternative energy resources, distribution automation and complete monitoring as well as control of entire power grid. Smart grid communication infrastructure consists of varied and hierarchical communication networks. Application of Smart grid can be realized in the various the facets of energy utilization. Internet of Things also plays a pivotal role in Smart grid infrastructure as provides a ubiquitous communication network. This chapter describes an implementation of Internet of Things (IoT) based wireless energy management system for Smart microgrid communication infrastructure.

Chapter 2 discuss Cloud IoT based Mobile Agent Framework for real-time traffic information acquisition, storage and retrieval. Traffic is an inevitable problem for metro cities around the globe. Intelligent Traffic Management System helps to improve the traffic flow by detecting congestions or incidents and suggesting appropriate actions on traffic routing. A new and dynamic internet-based-decision-making tool for traffic management system was proposed and implemented in the authors' previous work. The tool needs weather, road, and vehicle related integrated information from different data repositories. Several online web portals host real-time weather data streams. However, road and vehicle information are missing in those portals. In addition, their coverage is limited to city level congregate information but precise road segment-based information is necessary for real-time TMS decision. Internet of Things (IoT) based online sensors can be a solution for this circumstance. As a consequence, in this chapter, an IoT-based framework is proposed and implemented with several remote mobile agents. Agents are securely interconnected to the cloud, and able to collect and exchange data through wireless communication.

Chapter 3 proposes a Self-Learning Framework for the IoT Security. The Internet of Things (IoT) is a complex system of heterogeneous devices connected to a network. While IoT can significantly add value to everyday activities for everyone around the world, there are numerous security risks and privacy breaches imposed by the IoT landscape. Traditional security solutions are not applicable for the IoT as they required high-end processing capacity. The objective of this chapter is two-fold. Firstly, it provides a comprehensive summary of the recent advancements in the IoT and identifies their vulnerabilities. Secondly, it proposes the paradigm of self-learning as an intelligent and sustainable mechanism that is capable of automatically detecting suspicious activities in the IoT. Overall, this chapter presents a contemporary coverage of the recent developments in the IoT scene, the security and privacy challenges confronting the security experts, a proposal of a self-learning framework for performing health check of the IoT environment, and finally a set of high-level implementation guidelines and conclusions.

All Pervasive Surveillance Techniques and AI Based Applications is discussed in Chapter 4. Surveillance is the process of close observation of a person, place or object to avoid and minimize the risk of any undesired dangerous situations or suspicious activities to maintain normalcy. However, manual surveillance techniques have certain constraints including unavailability of trained manpower and erroneous observation triggering tricky situations. The proliferation of the use of information and communication technologies (ICT) have increased the levels automation and have made it a part of surveillance application. The aspects of automation have greatly reduced human intervention and have made systems more reliable and efficient.

The new advancements in Internet of Things (IoT) and artificial intelligence (AI) have made automation in surveillance security even more convenient and efficient. It has been found that the application of IoT and AI based learning mechanism have made significant performance improvement for automated surveillance purpose. Here we discuss some of the recent trends and challenges faced by all pervasive surveillance systems.

An analysis of cryptographic algorithms in IoT is presented in Chapter 5. The underlying vision of the Internet of Things (IoT) is create a world where the real and the virtual realms are converging to create smart environments that makes energy, transport, cities and many other areas more intelligent. With the IoT, the physical world is being interfaced through the things to the virtual world in heterogeneous environment. In heterogeneous environment privacy and security are the major challenges. The secure information exchange is most critical pitfall to ensure the system security. This study gives a detailed analysis of cryptographic algorithms in IoT. A comparison of lightweight cryptography algorithms on basis of block size, key size, gate equivalents, and throughput is given. Moreover, the various security issues in IoT are discussed along with possible solution.

The main two objectives of the Smart Accident Detection and Prevention System (SADPS) is analyzed in Chapter 6: i) Accident Prevention ii) Accident Detection. Based on the survey, 1.3 million people died every year in the road way accidents. The main reason for this type of accident is the over speeding of the vehicles. So, the proposed SADPS focused on finding the speed parameters of each vehicles and give the notification to the over speeding vehicles to its corresponding owners threw sms that can be used to prevent accidents. The second objective is accident detection. For this task, each vehicle accelerometer values will be taken for communication to the SADPS system. When an accident occurs, the location as well as the related details is sending to the SADPS system. This proposed system takes the immediate remedy by give the alert to the nearby police station and hospitals.

Chapter 7 presents the miracles of Healthcare with Internet of Things. Today, IoT in therapeutic administrations has ended up being more productive in light of the fact that the correspondence among authority's and patients has been improved with versatile applications. These applications are made by the associations with the objective that the pros can screen the patient's prosperity. If any issue has hopped out at the patient, by then the authority approaches the patient and gives the correct treatment. In this proposition, particular focus is given to infant human administrations, in light of the fact that the greatest fear of gatekeepers is that they would lose their infant kids at whatever point. Therefore, in this part a business contraption has been recognized which screens the consistent information about the infant's heart rate, oxygen levels, resting position. In case anything happens to the tyke, the information will get to the adaptable application which has starting at now been made by an association and is mechanically available by finishing a representation field test for the kid, the information which is recorded is examined.

Chapter 8 presents the relevance of Technologies for Smart Cities. Most of the work to develop a Smart City is how to connect physical urban infrastructure to the digital world to use it as a solution space for citizens and authorities to take best decisions to reach the best quality of life every day. Every city as a complex system needs to adequately manage their different dimensions. In this chapter, is propose the second approach with a top-down architecture identifying a set of Information Technologies linked in processes that every city service need as part of their Digital Transformation process in their urban space. Hence, this chapter introduce six technological layers in a work-flow pipe line that are explain as an approach to develop every smart system of a city. However, in the proposed workflow of technologies to implement, we give a central focus to the IoT infrastructure as the base to build information of quality, to have reliable services even after getting insights from analytics to come back to the IoT with their connected actuators to take actions.

Chapter 9 presents sustainable Smart Farming for Masses using Modern Ways of Internet of Things (IoT) into Agriculture. Modern technologies are revolutionizing the way humans have lived ever. The world's population is expected to reach 9.6 billion by year 2050 and to serve this much population, the agricultural industries and layman farmers need to embrace IoT and e-agriculture or ICT in agriculture. Feeding the global population has been rising as a biggest problem of world. The terminology has advanced from IIoT (Industrial Internet of Things), IoFT (Internet of Farm Things), IoSFT (Internet of Smart Farming Things) etc. The agriculture industries are open for ideas, advances and technically trained workforce to help sustain ever increasing needs of food and allocate better choices of resources. Smart farming is less labor intensive and more capital intensive, advanced cutting-edge technology to imperishable and incessant cultivation. Smart farming is Third Green Revolution around the globe by using various ICT technologies in agriculture.

Radio Frequency Identification Systems Security Challenges in Supply Chain Management is discussed in Chapter 10. The Radio Frequency IDentification (RFID) is a wireless technology that enable automatic identification and extraction of stored information from any tag object within a supply chain management (SCM) environment. A simple RFID system uses radio waves to collect and transfer data from an RFID tag attached to an object linked to an RFID reader for the purpose of identifying, tracking, and data capturing. However, RFID based systems are challenged by numerous security and privacy threats for the deployment of such technology for supply chain automation purpose. This chapter explains the technical fundamentals of RFID systems, and its security threats. It also classifies the existing security and privacy threats into those which target the RFID components such as the tag, the communication channel, and the overall system threats. Finally, the chapter discusses the open research challenges that need further investigation, especially with the rapid introduction of diverse RFID applications in SCM.

This book will provide current researchers and students in the area of IoT with a comprehensive reference for recent and up-to-date technologies in smart communications, protocols, and algorithms in IoT.

We hope this book will shed a light recent on advancements in smart devices, applications, and protocols for the IoT in next generation networks.

Joel J. P. C. Rodrigues
National Institute of Telecommunications (Inatel), Brazil & Instituto de
Telecomunicações, Portugal & Federal University of Piauí (UFPI), Brazil

Amjad Gawanmeh
Khalifa University, UAE

Sazia Parvin
Melbourne Polytechnic, Australia

Kashif Saleem
King Saud University, Saudi Arabia

Chapter 1
IoT-Based Management of Smart Microgrid:
Smart Energy System

Lipi Chhaya
UPES, India

ABSTRACT

The present power grid is going through a substantial and radical transformation process. Unification of existing electrical infrastructure with information and communication network is an unavoidable requirement of smart grid deployment and operation. The key characteristics of smart grid technology are full duplex communication, advanced metering infrastructure, integration of renewable and alternative energy resources, distribution automation and complete monitoring, as well as control of entire power grid. Smart grid communication infrastructure consists of varied and hierarchical communication networks. Application of smart grid can be realized in the various the facets of energy utilization. Internet of things also plays a pivotal role in smart grid infrastructure as it provides a ubiquitous communication network. This chapter describes an implementation of internet of things (IoT)-based wireless energy management system for smart microgrid communication infrastructure.

DOI: 10.4018/978-1-5225-7811-6.ch001

INTRODUCTION

The power 'Grid' is a generation, transmission and distribution network that carries electrical energy from power plants to customer premises. Smart grid technology is an innovatory move toward improvisation in an existing power grid. It can be envisioned as ''Technology for all and everything''. Smart Grid is an automated and largely distributed energy generation, transmission and distribution network. It is characterized by full duplex network with bidirectional flow of electricity and information (Farooq & Jung, 2014). It is a close loop system for monitoring, control and response. Smart Grid network integrates an electrical distribution system with information and communication networks (Mahmood et al., 2015). Smart grid technology ensures consistent, proficient, resilient and advanced energy distribution system with enormous features. Integration of renewable energy resources will lead to reduced carbon footprint and emissions. It can be defined in various ways as per its functional, technological or beneficial aspects. As per the definition given by U.S. department of energy, "A smart grid uses digital technology to improve reliability, security, and efficiency (both economic and energy) of the electric system from large generation, through the delivery systems to electricity consumers and a growing number of distributed-generation and storage resources" (United States Department of Energy, 2009). Various layers of Smart Grid deployment involve diverse set of wired and wireless communication standards. The scope of Smart grid is from electrification to web of all things. Internet of things is an unavoidable component of ubiquitous Smart grid communication infrastructure. IoT is a convergence of various communication protocols for web based monitoring and controlling applications. It comprises of interconnected and heterogeneous entities. Smart grid technology is intelligent in terms of automation and control (Saputro et al., 2012). Apart from these brainy features, clean and green energy generation is the most striking aspect of Smart grid technology. Diminution of carbon emissions through distributed generation using renewable energy resources is the central purpose of Microgrid. Consumers can monitor their energy consumption statistics, take decisions based on priorities and prices, control their appliances and generate revenue by selling extra energy to energy service provider through renewable energy generation. Energy usage statistics is communicated to central home monitor and regulator which is a part of AMI and it further communicates this statistics to main grid through various intermediate networks for billing, fault diagnosis, control and management of generation, transmission and distribution of energy. This makes the process of generation and consumption of energy transparent and reliable. Smart microgrid is intended to expedite the usage of renewable energy sources. An intermittent and non dispatchable nature of renewable energy sources necessitates consistent monitoring and control. This paper explores web based monitoring and control of smart home area network. Wireless sensor networks can accomplish the sensing and measurement requirements of home area networks (Erol-Kantarci et al., 2011). Tiny sensor nodes placed at various locations measure and communicate the load current. This data is used for remote monitoring and control of home area network. This chapter describes an experimental investigation of smart home using smart grid communication infrastructure. A graphical user interface and dedicated website is designed for real-time execution of the developed prototype. A web server is developed for implementation of prototype. The energy statistics are collected on a local web server and the same data is made available on website using port forwarding method. The client can request for developed website and the local server information is displayed on the wide area network. The prototype is working successfully using dynamic DNS and port forwarding technologies. Home area network ranges for few hundreds of meters. Various communication standards such as Bluetooth, Zigbee, WLAN, Ethernet, Z-Wave, WiMAX etc. can be used for real time monitoring, control, operation and management of smart power system. The prototype can also be developed using IEEE 802.15 based standards (Chen et al., 2006).

BACKGROUND

Smart grid is an amalgamation of communication and power infrastructures. Smart grid communication infrastructure consists of hierarchical networks such as home area network, neighborhood area network and wide area network. Home area network is suitable for smart home and home automation applications. Integration of home area network is called neighborhood area network. It forwards energy statistics of home area networks to wide area network for different purposes such as monitoring, management, control, billing, fault finding and diagnosis (Sun et al., 2009). Some of the key components of smart grid are advanced metering infrastructure, microgrid, Internet of things, smart meter and wireless sensor network (Patel et al., 2011). All these components function on varied set of communication standards (Chhaya et al., 2017). Microgrid is the most promising component of Smart grid technology as it leads towards green energy system. It is a novel approach to overcome various challenges such as aging of power plants, GHG emissions, non dispatchable and unreliable nature of renewable energy resources and unelectrified villages. It integrates various renewable energy sources with main grid (Xu et al., 2014). Smart microgrid is technically, environmentally and economically beneficial for every stakeholder. A Microgrid can be categorized as AC Microgrid or DC microgrid. DC microgrid is considered in this chapter for prototype development. Consumers can participate in the process of energy generation and also sell the extra power back to grid to earn a waiver in their energy utilization metering and billing. Internet of things is an integral technology for realization of smart grid technology. This chapter illustrates IoT based implementation of smart microgrid prototype. The developed system works in both local as well as wide area network. A dedicated server is developed for real-time monitoring and control of smart home energy system. Three power sources are used in prototype. A user can monitor and shift the load on any of the three systems. The prototype illustrates the manifestation of remote wireless monitoring and control of smart microgrid system for home area network.

IMPLEMENTATION OF IoT BASED SMART MICROGRID ENERGY SYSTEM

Microgrid comprises of renewable energy sources as well as backup power supply module such as battery. The developed prototype is designed to manifest DC microgrid. Three power sources are considered namely grid, battery and solar photovoltaic. ACS 712 hall effect analog current sensors are used for monitoring of load current. ACS 712, 30 Amp Hall effect Sensor Output Voltage = analog Read (sensor Pin)*5.0/1023.0

At zero current, Sensor Output Voltage = 2.5 V

Sensitivity= 66 mv/A, (Sensitivity: Output voltage proportional to AC or DC currents)

Sensor Output Voltage = 66 mv/A*Current + 2.5 V

Current = (Sensor Output Voltage – 2.5)/ 66 mv/A

User can shift the load on the basis of observed value of current. Figure 1 shows the block diagram of developed prototype. Figure 2 shows the flow chart of monitoring system for IoT based smart microgrid system. Figure 3 shows the flow chart of controlling system.

A graphical user interface is developed for monitoring and control of smart energy system. The monitoring and control system is developed using IEEE 802.11 and IEEE 802.3 standards. The IoT based smart microgrid system works successfully in both local as well as wide area network. Arduino Uno and Ethernet shield are used for implementation of web server which serves the client request for the developed website. The current sensors are connected to the input pins of controller. ATMEGA328P controller is used for energy management. The values of sensed current are visible on the developed graphical user interface. An HTML webpage

Figure 1. Block diagram of the developed prototype

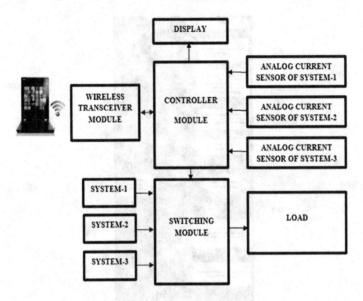

Figure 2. Flowchart of monitoring of prototype

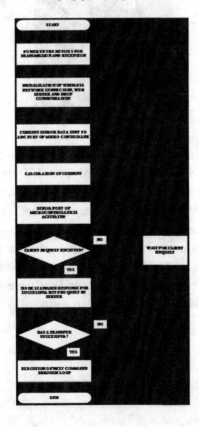

Figure 3. Flowchart of controlling of prototype

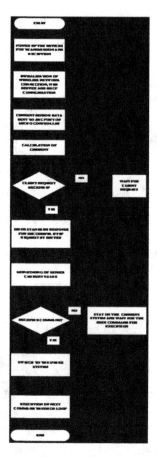

is used for graphical user interface. HTML buttons are also provided for controlling purpose. Dynamic Host Configuration Protocol (DHCP) is used for assignment of IP addresses to devices. This protocol enables the web server to automatically assign IP address to various devices when they are connected to the network. The web server is assigned an IP address of 192.168.1.177. Figure 4 shows the snapshot of monitoring and control of prototype in local area network. Figure 5 shows that the system 1 is activated and load is served through grid. The value of sensed current is shown in the figure. CoolTerm serial terminal software is used to fetch the real time stamped data. The snapshot of CoolTerm software is shown in Figure 6.

Figure 4. Snapshot of remote wireless monitoring and control of smart power system through HTML webpage

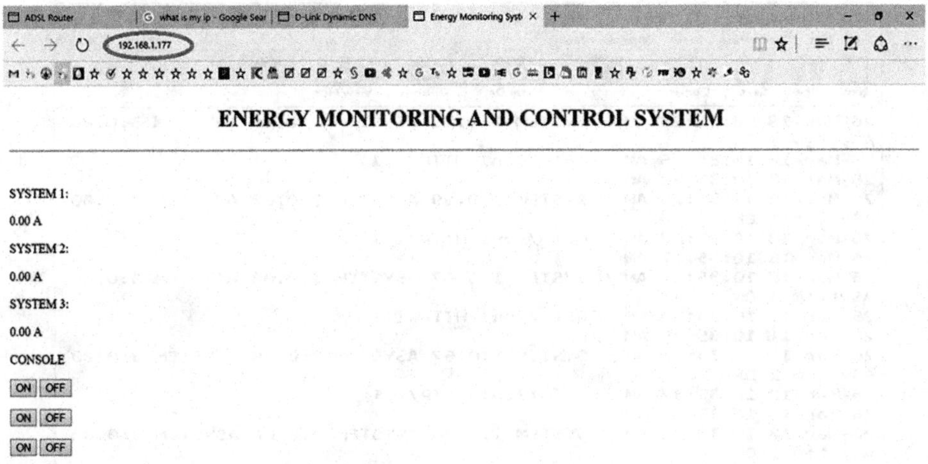

Figure 5. Snapshot of remote wireless monitoring and control of smart power system through HTML webpage

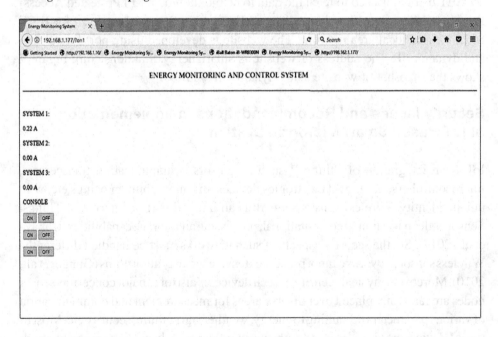

Figure 6. Snapshot of remote wireless monitoring and control of smart power system on serial terminal program

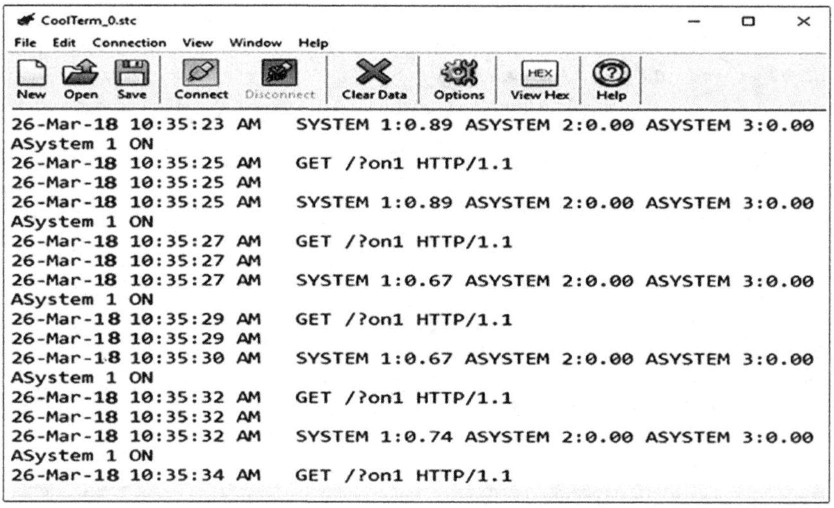

GET method is used to fetch the data to be monitored. Wi-Fi Protected Access-Pre Shared Key algorithm and Advanced Encryption Standard are used for IEEE 802.11 based local area network. The website is developed using port forwarding and dynamic IP. The address of website is smartenergy.dlinkddns.com. Figure 7 shows the snapshot of website using dynamic IP address.

Security Issues and Recommendations in Implementation of IoT Based Smart Microgrid System

IoT is an integration of ''things'' such as sensors, communication transceivers, microcontrollers, intelligent electronics devices, machines, human beings etc. with unique identity. Wireless sensor network is an integral part of Internet of Things. Sensor nodes have limited computational, processing and storage capabilities (Chhaya et al., 2017). So, the security aspects of such networks must be handled differently. Wireless sensor networks cannot process extensive security algorithms (Gungor et al., 2010). Moreover, physical security of such devices is also of a major concern as sensor nodes are randomly placed over diverse areas for measurement and communication of various parameters pertaining to energy, weather, agriculture, security etc. Most of the IoT devices are placed in hostile, uncontrolled and complicated environment which

Figure 7. Snapshot of remote wireless monitoring and control of smart power system through HTML webpage in Wide Area Network

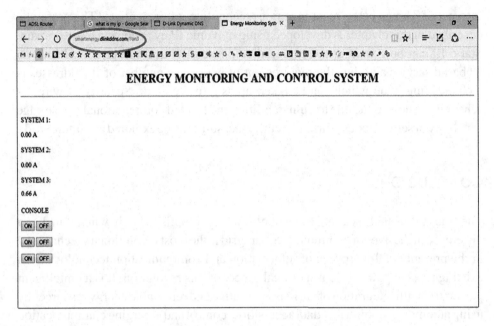

impose numerous challenges such as device updating, authentication, authorization, security, data privacy and integrity. Most of the IoT devices function on battery and thus need to operate on low power. This type of devices cannot perform complex encryption and decryption tasks. Furthermore they are vulnerable to side channel attacks such as power analysis attack. This type of devices requires lightweight security algorithms and manifold layers of security mechanism. Identification and authorization of devices is also a crucial issue for security of IoT devices. Updating of software and firmware is a crucial and complex issue as all IoT devices might not support automatic update over radio interface and require physical interface. Device management solutions can be implemented in such cases for secured network. It is recommended that multilayer security can be developed for attack prone IoT network. Segregation of security resources such as firewalls can be implemented for better network security. IoT is an IP based network. MAC filtering can be done for restricted information access. WPA2 and AES based devices can be used for IEEE 802.11 based IoT network.

FUTURE RESEARCH DIRECTIONS

Internet of Things is the most ingenious technology of present era. The prototype described in this chapter is developed using dynamic IP by acquiring a sub domain. Static IP can be acquired and explored as a future work. Furthermore, IoT is an IP based service and thus the requirement of enormous number of IP addresses is a challenging issue which can be taken up as a future work. Security of wireless sensor is a crucial issue due to vulnerabilities and limited computational and storage capability of sensor nodes. Various security measures can be explored as a future work.

CONCLUSION

The true and factual meaning of technology is accomplished only when it makes a difference in the lives of community. Smart grid is the most revolutionary technology in the present era. Integration of information and communication technology with existing passive power grid is a critical aspect of this revolution. It is an intelligent power grid with integration of various alternative and renewable energy resources by using automated monitoring, data acquisition, control and emerging communication technologies. Smart grid is envisioned as a technology for empowerment and progress. The most crucial requirement of empowerment is energy. Energy is an essential commodity in present era. Smart grid assures reliable and stable electricity. It includes distinctive elements from tiny sensor node to gigantic web of things. This paper explores an application of smart grid technology in energy management. The chapter depicts an experimental investigation of web based monitoring and control of smart home using smart microgrid information and communication infrastructure. The prototype is developed for local area network as well as wide area network. It describes an implementation of smart microgrid for smart energy. An experimental investigation of various hierarchical network layers of Smart grid communication infrastructure is implemented in this chapter. IoT is an integral component of Smart grid infrastructure. It facilitates web connectivity of various components of Smart grid network for real time operation and management. The prototypes are designed and verified to validate the conceptual aspects of Smart grid architecture. The prototypes are designed for Home area network using IEEE 802.15.1 and Wide area network using IEEE 802.3 and IEEE 802.11 standards. An integrated development environment (IDE) 1.6.11 is used as a source code editor and debugger. An HTML based webserver and GUI are developed for HAN and WAN. An independent web server works on an address "192.168.1.177". The prototypes are verified using serial monitor as well as HTML based GUI. IDE serial monitor and CoolTerm software are used to monitor, capture and store the real time data. The real time data with time stamps is captured for graphical representation of acquired results. The GUI is developed using HTML-5. GUI is meant for remote wireless monitoring and control of designed prototype. A website for IoT exploration is developed and can be accessed on URL "smartenergy.dlinkddns.com". The website is developed for dynamic IP using port forwarding method. The applications of smart grid are enormous and limitless in various areas as it can be anticipated as a technology for all and everything.

ACKNOWLEDGMENT

This research received no specific grant from any funding agency in the public, commercial, or not-for-profit sectors.

REFERENCES

Chen, B., Wu, M., Yao, S., & Ni, B. (2006). ZigBee Technology and Its Application on Wireless Meter-reading System. In *IEEE International Conference on Industrial Informatics (INDIN 06)*. IEEE Press. 10.1109/INDIN.2006.275820

Chhaya, L., Sharma, P., Bhagwatikar, G., & Kumar, A. (2017). Communication theories and protocols for smart grid hierarchical network. *Journal of Electrical and Electronics Engineering (Oradea)*, *10*(1), 43–48.

Chhaya, L., Sharma, P., Bhagwatikar, G., & Kumar, A. (2017). Wireless Sensor Network Based Smart Grid Communications: Cyber Attacks, Intrusion Detection System and Topology Control. *Electronics (Basel)*, *6*(1), 5. doi:10.3390/electronics6010005

Erol-Kantarci, M., & Mouftah, H. (2011). Wireless multimedia sensor and actor networks for the next generation power grid. *Ad Hoc Networks*, *9*(4), 542–551. doi:10.1016/j.adhoc.2010.08.005

Farooq, H., & Jung, L. (2014). Choices available for implementing Smart Grid communication network. In *Computer and Information Sciences* (Vol. 5). Kuala Lumpur: ICCOINS.

Gungor, V., Lu, B., & Hancke, G. (2010). Opportunities and Challenges of Wireless Sensor Networks in Smart Grid. *IEEE Transactions on Industrial Electronics, 57*(10), 3557–3564. doi:10.1109/TIE.2009.2039455

Mahmood, A., Javaid, N., & Razzaq, S. (2015). A review of wireless communications for smart grid. *Renewable & Sustainable Energy Reviews, 41*, 248–260. doi:10.1016/j.rser.2014.08.036

Patel, A., Aparicio, J., Tas, N., Loiacono, M., & Rosca, J. (2011). *Assessing communications technology options for Smart Grid applications.* IEEE Press. doi:10.1109/SmartGridComm.2011.6102303

Saputro, N., Akkaya, K., & Uludag, S. (2012). A survey of routing protocols for smart grid communications. *Computer Networks, 56*(11), 2742–2771. doi:10.1016/j.comnet.2012.03.027

Sun, Z., Zhao, T., & Che, N. (2009). Design of electric power monitoring system based on ZigBee and GPRS. In *1st International Symposium on Computer Network and Multimedia Technology (CNMT 2009)*. IEEE Press. 10.1109/CNMT.2009.5374624

U.S. Department of Energy. (2009). *Smart Grid System Report*. Author.

Xu, Z., Xue, Y., & Wong, K. (2014). Recent Advancements on Smart Grids in China. *Electric Power Components and Systems, 42*(3-4), 251–261. doi:10.1080/15325008.2013.862327

ADDITIONAL READING

Andreadou, N., Guardiola, M., & Fulli, G. (2016). Telecommunication Technologies for Smart Grid Projects with Focus on Smart Metering Applications. *Energies, 9*(5), 375. doi:10.3390/en9050375

Asad, O., Erol-Kantarci, M., & Mouftah, H. (2013). A Survey of Sensor Web Services for the Smart Grid. *Journal of Sensor and Actuator Networks, 2*(1), 98–108. doi:10.3390/jsan2010098

ITU. (2005, November). The Internet of Things. International Telecommunication Union. Retrieved from https://www.itu.int/net/wsis/tunis/newsroom/stats/The-Internet-of-Things-2005.pdf

Khalifa, T., Abdrabou, A., Shaban, K., & Gaouda, A. (2018). Heterogeneous Wireless Networks for Smart Grid Distribution Systems: Advantages and Limitations. *Sensors (Basel)*, *18*(5), 1517. doi:10.339018051517 PMID:29751633

Madakam, S., Ramaswamy, R., & Tripathi, S. (2015). Internet of Things (IoT): A literature review. *Journal of Computer and Communications*, *3*(5), 164–173. doi:10.4236/jcc.2015.35021

Ruiz-Garcia, L., Lunadei, L., Barreiro, P., & Robla, I. (2009). A review of wireless sensor technologies and applications in agriculture and food industry: State of the art and current trends. *Sensors (Basel)*, *9*(6), 4728–4750. doi:10.339090604728 PMID:22408551

Ruiz-Garcia, L., Lunadei, L., Barreiro, P., & Robla, I. (2009). A review of wireless sensor technologies and applications in agriculture and food industry: State of the art and current trends. *Sensors (Basel)*, *9*(6), 4728–4750. doi:10.339090604728 PMID:22408551

Zanella, A., Bui, N., Castellani, A., Vangelista, L., & Zorzi, M. (2014). Internet of things for smart cities. IEEE Internet of Things journal, 1(1), 22-32.

Zhang, J., Hasandka, A., Wei, J., Alam, S., Elgindy, T., Florita, A., & Hodge, B.-M. (2018). Hybrid Communication Architectures for Distributed Smart Grid Applications. *Energies*, *11*(4), 871. doi:10.3390/en11040871

KEY TERMS AND DEFINITIONS

Internet of Things: Internet of things is an IP-based network consisting of interconnection of sensors, actuators, communication transceivers, intelligent electronic devices, actuators, machines, etc.

Smart Grid: An electrical grid with an integration of power as well as information and communication infrastructure. It is characterized by bidirectional flow of energy and information, advanced metering infrastructure, renewable energy resources, self-healing, active involvement of consumers, and Internet of things.

Wireless Sensor Network: A network comprising of sensor, communication transceivers, memory, processing unit and power supply. Wireless sensor network is useful to convey various parameters such as current, temperature, humidity, etc. to the remote monitoring and control unit by using wireless communication technology.

Chapter 2
Cloud IoT–Based Mobile Agent Framework for Real–Time Traffic Information Acquisition, Storage, and Retrieval

Md Abdullah al Forhad
East West University, Bangladesh

Md Nadim
East West University, Bangladesh

Md. Rahatur Rahman
ⓘ https://orcid.org/0000-0002-0620-961X
Simplexhub Ltd., Bangladesh

Shamim Akhter
East West University, Bangladesh

ABSTRACT

Traffic is an inevitable problem for metro cities around the globe. Intelligent traffic management system helps to improve the traffic flow by detecting congestions or incidents and suggesting appropriate actions on traffic routing. A new and dynamic internet-based decision-making tool for traffic management system was proposed and implemented in authors' previous works. The tool needs weather, road, and vehicle-related integrated information from different data repositories. Several online web portals host real-time weather data streams. However, road and vehicle information are missing in those portals. In addition, their coverage is limited to city-level congregate information but precise road segment-based information is necessary for real-time TMS decision. Internet of things (IoT)-based online sensors can be a solution for this circumstance. As a consequence, in this chapter, an IoT-based framework is proposed and implemented with several remote mobile agents. Agents are securely interconnected to the cloud, and able to collect and exchange data through wireless communication.

DOI: 10.4018/978-1-5225-7811-6.ch002

INTRODUCTION

An internet based real time bi-directional traffic management support system was proposed and implemented in Rahman and Akhter (2015,2016), Nawrin et al. (2017) and Akhter et al. (2016) with the integration of different modules including traffic monitoring, road weight updating, forecasting, congestion management, and optimum route planning decision. The decision making of that system requires different environmental attributes including rainfall, temperature, wind, and humidity, and other road and vehicle-related decision attributes- peak hour, speed, road status, road accident status to calculate the road weights in real time and thus able to recognize current/future traffic operation(s) and traffic flow conditions. Therefore, the system can precisely administrate, monitor and control moving vehicles. The values of the environmental attributes are intelligently crawled by search engine, with meta-data indexing (title, description, keyword etc.), directly from the multiple data feeds (like website, RSS feeds, web service etc.). However, their coverage is limited to the city level. In addition, location/area based congregate information at an instant is necessary for accurate TMS decision-making system. In addition, there is no availability of real-time road and vehicle-related information. Embedded devices/ sensors are required to collect information from the mobile vehicles. Moreover, devices need to communicate among themselves and transfer the acquired information to the TMS system. Subsequently, TMS decision-making system will make routing related decision from those data.

Internet of Things (IoT) is a network, where remote agents are interconnected and able to communicate with each other (sensor enable communication), can be a solution for this circumstance. IoT in traffic system needs to collect and integrate real-time traffic information, process and analysis them automatically, and makes the system more self-reliable and intelligent. The aim of this chapter is to present a secure IoT-based framework for real-time traffic related information acquisition with monitoring architecture, and to implement it with several remote agents utilizing wireless communication (GSM/GPRS/Bluetooth). Each agent is an embedded device with integrated sensors (including DHT11, Raindrops Sensor Module), Arduino microcontroller and GSM/GPRS/GPS Bluetooth enable modules.

There are many models for IoT-based TMS. The solutions are varying in respect to their applied technologies. As an example, Radio Frequency Identification (RFID) based IoT, which is suited best for smaller spaces, where the infrastructure is already in place to use it. RFID requires specialized scanners to read data, and specific receivers to transmit data.

The proposed agents are securely interconnected with an authenticated cloud server (AWS) using GSM/GPRS based HTTP protocol, and able to collect or exchange encrypted TMS data among themselves through GSM/GPRS/Bluetooth wireless communication. Agents can collect specific data with a degree of autonomy and interact with the cloud server (without human intervention). In addition, the agents have fault tolerance systems as they are capable to communicate (sending or receiving data) with the cloud server even the failure of GSM signal. They do this by connecting another nearby agent or authenticated mobile phone (GSM enable and has signal) using Bluetooth communication channel and request him (agent/phone) to communicate with the cloud server. In addition, AES 128 CBC encryption and/or decryption algorithms are used to secure the data transmission.

BACKGROUND

IoT Architecture

Internet of Things (IoT) refers to a set of devices which are interconnected to the Internet and able to perform communication between them. There is no uniform standard for IoT architecture. However, Lu (2017) and Sethi and Sarangi (2017) proposed the requirements for an IoT framework and the key requirements are as follows:

Figure 1. Demonstrates the proposed IoT framework for Traffic Management System (TMS)

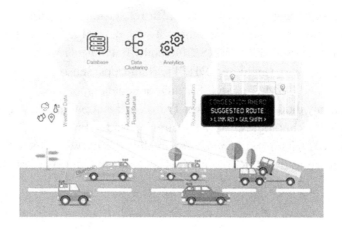

- Diverse modes of connection (wired and wireless) including ANT+, Bluetooth, EDGE, GPRS, IrDA, LTE, NFC, RFID, Weightless, WLAN, ZigBee, and Z-Wave.
- Automation capabilities between software and middleware applications and need to reduce costs but increase efficiency and improve regulatory compliance.
- Manage a range of devices including sensors to gather information in their vicinity and actuators to perform specific tasks.
- Devices are able to generate/transmit massive amounts of data.
- Require powerful analytics to translate a significant amount of data into meaningful and actionable insights.
- Should offer robust security in all levels of communication from data collection to storage.

Table 1 provides the detail explanation of each level and figure 2 illustrates the formulation of an IoT reference model.

Cloud Computing

According to what is cloud computing? (2017), cloud computing reflects-"the delivery of computer services, including servers, storage, databases, networking, software, analytics and more, over the internet". There are many reasons to consider cloud computing over general server based computing, few of the reasons are cost efficiency, high speed, global scale, productivity, performance, reliability, and etc

Figure 2. Formulation of an IoT Reference Model

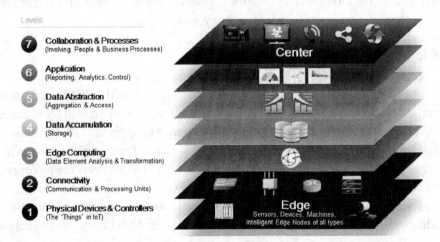

Table 1. IoT Reference Model

Level No	Level Name	Description
7	Collaboration and Processes	Involving people and business processes: providing real-time insights, decision support and collaboration options to other areas in the business.
6	Application	Reporting, analytics control: diagnostic, predictive and prescriptive analytics (preferably autonomous) to control IoT devices. Accounting, usage, state on IoT devices and applications (service).
5	Data Abstraction	Aggregation and access: aggregation of data to reports (required usage) and access of data (interface) for applications.
4	Data Accumulation	Storage: event persistence, filtering, sampling events, event-based rules, event aggregation and complex event processing.
3	Edge (Fog) Computing	Data element analyses and transformation: filtering, cleaning and aggregating data, generating events and alarms.
2	Connectivity	Communication and processing units: providing security, reliable networking, protocol translation, switching and routing.
1	Physical Devices and Controllers	The IoT devices: generating data (analogue/digital) and events queried and controlled over the net.

(Aceto et al.,2013). Mell and Grance (2011) in NIST (National Institute of Standards and Technology) defined three (3) standard models to provide cloud services including Software as a Service (SaaS), Platform as a Service (PaaS), and Infrastructure as a Service (IaaS). Figure 3 demonstrates the service models of cloud computing. The details of the service models are given in What is iaas? (2017). There are four (4) ways to deploy cloud computing resources including public cloud, private cloud, hybrid cloud and community cloud as defined by Mell and Grance (2011). Our proposed application is ported in Amazon Web Service (AWS) cloud computing as it provides a secure cloud services platform, offering higher compute power, bigger database storage, and instant content delivery services.

Traffic Management System

A new low cost, flexible, maintainable, and secure internet-based traffic management system with real-time bi-directional communication was implemented by Rahman and Akhter (2015,2016), Nawrin et al. (2017) and Akhter et al. (2016) to assist and reduce the traffic congestion. And, A new version of road weight measuring technique was implemented by Sumit and Akhter (2018) using deep-neuro-fuzzy c -mean clustering. The route is divided with equal segment size and their dynamic weights are calculated from current road, vehicle and environmental situations including- rainfall, temperature, wind, humidity, peak hour, speed, construction

Figure 3. Service Models of Cloud Computing

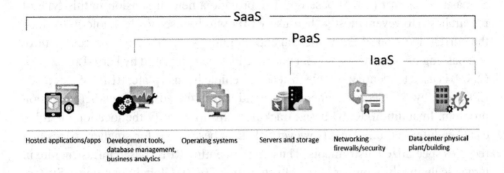

status, damaged status, accident status, traffic status, environmental disaster status, and etc. The values of the statuses/attributes are intelligently crawled by search engine from the multiple data feeds (like website, RSS feeds, web service etc.). Crawled data (city/province) are simplified (structured) and stored in a historic table. Initially, decision tree (DT) based logic was implemented over the simplified data to adjust the route weights in the database. Thereafter, Artificial Neural Network (ANN) was used to adjust the route weights in the database and provide more accurate classification result. Dijkstra algorithm is applied to calculate the optimal path/route using the calculated dynamic route weights from each segment. In addition, Weighted Moving Average algorithm is used on stored data to provide route prediction services including future weights calculation and optimal route generation. So far, the TMS model calculates road weights from the values of the environmental attributes that are intelligently crawled by the search engine. There is no availability of real-time information regarding road status, maintenance and road accident information of the particular study area. Simulated data is formulated to set these attributes values. However, making an analytical decision on optimum route planning requires real time road segment weight calculation from continuous data, in different time domains, for everyday in a year. Thus, TMS is suffering from real time data collection from a specific location, in a specific time.

RELATED WORKS

At present, intelligent traffic monitoring system depends on automatic vehicle identification technologies including image and vehicle license plate recognition systems (Messelodi and Modena, 1999; Fernandez-Caballero et al.,2008; Tai et al.,2004; Zhu et al., 2000). However, adverse weather and low recognition rates are the main bottlenecks for them. Technologies proposed by Sherly and Somasundareswari (2015) based on IoT provide a new dimension in this type of researches. However, mostly they use RFID wireless sensor technology to track the current location of the vehicle/agent, monitor the traffic flow, process control and parking managements. Global unique EPC code proposed by Peris-Lopez et al. (2009) is used to identify vehicle instead of vehicle license plate. RFID reader reads EPC code by RF electromagnetic wave and solves the adverse weather operation problem. In addition, RFID based tracking helps to identify the location of stolen car (Tendulkar et al.,2016). However, RFID is best suited for smaller spaces and requires specialized instruments. Thus, implementing RFID based infrastructure in larger scale involves higher cost (Allychevalier, 2017). Global Positioning System (GPS) works different than RFID. It uses radio waves from satellites to transmit data. GPS is better to trace accurate location in longitude and latitude form, and able to navigate data. For RFID technology, scanners are needed to set up almost in every route to get an accurate result, but GPS is easier to locate and collect data from any location and process them. Global Systems for Mobile Communications (GSM) is the standard protocol for communication between mobile devices. General Packet Radio Service (GPRS) is an extension to the GSM technology, provides high-speed wireless IP services for mobile devices, and supports TCP/IP data communication.

The TMS research of Nawrin et al. (2017) used weather data to analyze road weight. Vehicle and road related data are used as simulated features. In addition, they crawled data from an open website and the data cover average city level spatial and day level temporal values. However, TMS needs each road segment data and is missing in the prior researches (Rahman and Akhter, 2015, 2016). Collection of continuous data from each road segment is a complex task, and needs for real time road segment weight calculation, in different time domains, for every day in a year. Later the road weights help to make an analytical decision on optimum route planning.

Real time distributed data collection needs to store them in a secure place and retrieve them on demand. IoT and cloud were integrated together in many recent researches (Yu X et al.,2012; Qin E et al.,2013; Lumpkins, 2013). We use cloud computing for global access, faster access, better security and low-cost storage platform. IoT is used for traffic system automation. Our designed TMS is not yet ported to the cloud based service oriented platform. This is the first step to direct the TMS research to service oriented domain. Thus, IoT based mobile agents help to collect real time road segment weather, road, and vehicle associated data and store them securely into AWS cloud based architecture using GPRS communication system. Later, TMS retrieves those data as a service to make proper traffic connected analytical decisions.

MAIN FOCUS OF THE CHAPTER

Agents for Intelligent Traffic Management System

Congestions and accidents have a direct impact on the road traffic system as they are the reason for the waste of time, fuel consumption, property damage and environmental pollution (emission of greenhouse gases). Many projects related to traffic congestion detections and solutions were implemented by different organizations however still it is one of the major concerning issues around the globe. The aim of this chapter is to present a secure IoT-based framework for real-time traffic-related information acquisition and monitoring architecture and also implement it with several remote agents utilizing wireless communication.

Secure IoT

As IoT agents are always connected to internet the main challenge is to make secure IoT. So, another focus of this chapter is to secure IoT agents. And many security measures will be implemented on those agents to make communication error-free and secure data collection.

SOLUTIONS AND RECOMMENDATIONS

Flowchart of agent working approach is presented in Figure 4. Rest of this section is going to present an elaborate explanation for each sub modules and their construction strategies to formulate the proposed IoT framework.

Agent Configuration and Setup

Cost efficient, reliable and user-friendly components are considered during the agent building phase. Arduino microcontroller UNO R3 ("Arduino Board Uno,"2017), GSM/GPRS/GPS/Bluetooth SIM808 Shield ("GPRS GSM GPS Bluetooth All in one SIM808 Shield for Arduino Roboticsbd,"2017), DHT11 Sensor (TemperatureandhumiditymoduleDHT11ProductManualakizukidenshi,"2017) and Rain drop sensor modules (Arduino Rain Sensor Module Guide and Tutorial capnfatz",2017) are chosen and integrated together to formulate the targeted agent device. GSM/GPRS/GPS/Bluetooth SIM808 Shield is Arduino compatible and easy to assemble on it. Figure 5 provides a schematic diagram of the proposed agent.

Figure 4. Flow chart of Agent work

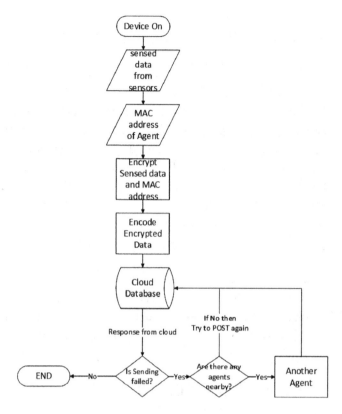

To achieve serial port mode communication between SIM808 Shield with Arduino, a jumper cap connects 900_R to U_R and 900_T to U_T pins in the Serial Port Mode Selection Interface (P1). RX=10 and TX=11 port numbers are also used for serial communication. A jumper cap is used to connect GND pin of the control interface (J2) with PWK Pin to power on the SIM808 Shield automatically.

DTH11 sensor has four (4) pins but three (3) of them are used for VCC, Signal, and GND. Signal pin is used to transfer sensor data digitally to Arduino and connects via pin number 2. VCC and GND pins are connected to 5V pin and GND pin respectively. There is a 10K Ohm pull-up resistor connected from the Signal line to 5V to guarantee signal level high by default. Raindrop sensor has four (4) pins, A0 (Analog Output), D0 (Digital Output), GND and VCC. VCC and GND pins are connected to 5V pin and GND pin respectively and Pin A0 is connected to A0 pin of Arduino board. D0 is used as connectionless. A push button is used to turn on the built-in LED of Arduino at port 13 and the LED is used to reflect the Bluetooth communication is ON/OFF. A wire from digital pin 4 connects with one leg of the push button. That same leg of the button connects through the pull-down resistor (here 10K Ohm) to GND and the other leg of the button connects to the 5V supply of Arduino. When the push button is opened (unpressed), there is no connection between the two legs of the push button, so the pin is connected to GND (through the pull-down resistor) and a LOW voltage is READ. When the button is closed (pressed), it makes a connection between its two legs, connecting the pin to 5V, and a HIGH is READ. GSM/GPRS/GPS/Bluetooth SIM808 Shield and Arduino UNO board both are powered by 12V battery power.

Figure 6 contains the setup of the proposed agent. Arduino IDE programming platform is used and installed on a Windows 10 OS based computer.

Data Format

Agent acquires Temperature data in Celsius, Relative Humidity in percentage, location in latitude, longitude and the velocity in Km/H. However, rain sensor module captures analog values within range 0 to 1024. We have formatted the rain data into different ranges to match it with the TMS decision making input system. The formulae of converting sensor data to ITMS format is-

Figure 5. Schematic diagram of the proposed agent

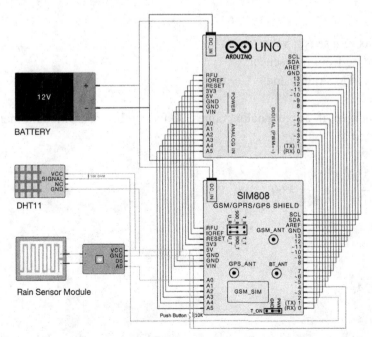

Figure 6. Actual picture of the proposed agent

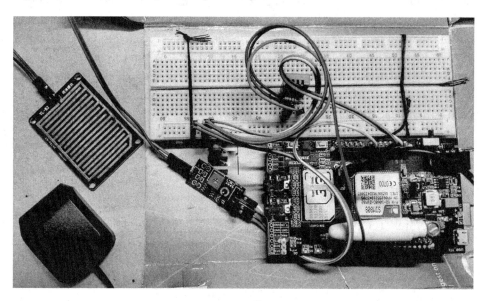

$$\left| \frac{\left(MA - RE \right) * IM}{MA} \right|$$

where,

MA = Max rain sensor value,
RE= Reading from rain sensor,
IM = Max ITMS rain value.

For example, if we get analog value 500 from rain sensor module then it will be converted to

$$\left| \frac{\left(1024 - 500 \right) * 118}{1024} \right| = 60$$

where,

MA = 1024,
RE= 500,

Table 2. Rain Sensor data

Range	Meaning
0 to 10	No rain
10 to 45	Moderate rain
45 to 118	Heavy rain

IM = 118

Cloud Server Configuration

A cloud server is a logical server that is built, hosted and delivered through a cloud computing platform over the Internet. For the proposed IoT system, Amazon's cloud service called Amazon Web Services (AWS) is used. AWS provides both storage and server facility through Amazon RDS and Amazon EC2 instance services.

Setting Up AWS

Amazon Web Services (AWS) is a secure cloud service platform, offering variety of services including compute power, database storage, content delivery and other functionalities to help businesses scale and grow. Amazon EC2 and Amazon RDS instances are used to port the TMS into cloud-based system. Amazon Elastic Compute Cloud (EC2) is a web service that provides secure, resizable compute capacity in the cloud. A Linux based virtual server- Ubuntu server 14.04 LTS (HVM) -is installed to manage MySQL database, and then Amazon Relational Database Service (RDS) is installed. After successful configuration, both EC2 and RDS instances are capable to run as cloud instances.

Database Configuration

Database needs to configure to store agent data. A phpMyAdmin application is setup to configure the MySQL database. There are three (3) tables: Login, Device and Sensor. Login table stores the username and passwords, Device table stores the Mac address of the agent and an ID to identify the agent and distinguish it's acquiring data. Sensor table stores all the data sent from the agent including its fixed Media Access Control (MAC) address. The device table cross matches that MAC address and finds the corresponding agent id. Agent id is used to fetch agent data and display them in web. Figure 7 shows the structure of the sensor table.

There are nine (9) attributes in the table (figure 7) where the Time is the primary key. Other attributes are: Did (device/agent id), Temperature, Humidity, Rain, Lon (Longitude), Lat (Latitude), Vel (Velocity) and Wt (Weight).

Security Integration

User Authentication for Login

Each user has to go through a login page to access the website. Login table is stored in the secure database with username and password pair. After input the username

Table 3. Description of columns with an example of data visualization on web

Name	Description	Example Data
Device ID	The Identification number of the device, data sent from	02
Time	Time and Date of the data update	2017-03-27 15:54:17
Temperature	Shows the temperature data in Celsius	30.00
Humidity	Quantity of humid	46.00
Rainfall	Rainfall reading from the sensor.	6.56
Velocity	Velocity of the vehicle in km per hour	16.74 km/h
Location Longitude) (Latitude,	The combined value of Latitude and Longitude to get the exact location	23.742133, 90.363860
Weight	Calculated road weight value	2
Delete	Deletes the entire record of that time	Data has been deleted.

Figure 7. Structure of the sensor table

Figure 8. Screenshot of data visualization on the web

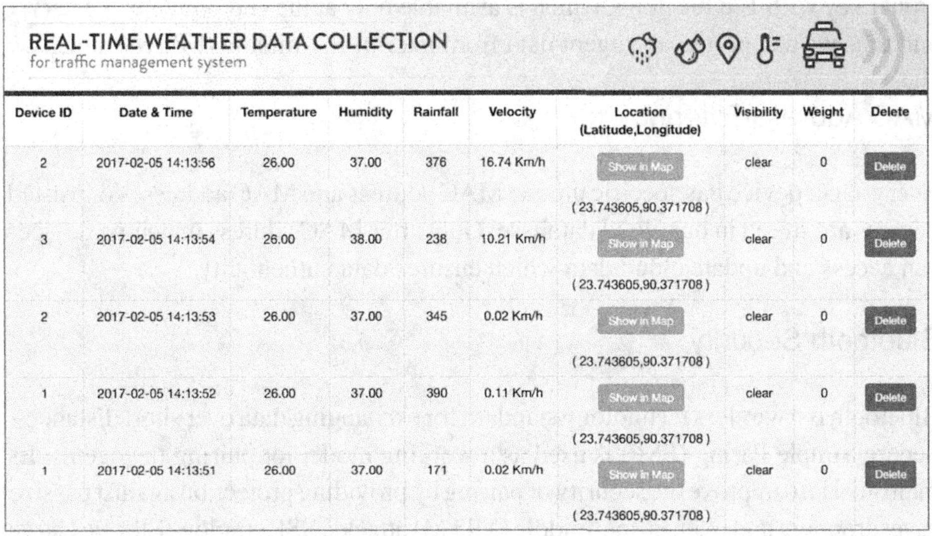

Device ID	Date & Time	Temperature	Humidity	Rainfall	Velocity	Location (Latitude,Longitude)	Visibility	Weight	Delete
2	2017-02-05 14:13:56	26.00	37.00	376	16.74 Km/h	Show in Map (23.743605,90.371708)	clear	0	Delete
3	2017-02-05 14:13:54	26.00	38.00	238	10.21 Km/h	Show in Map (23.743605,90.371708)	clear	0	Delete
2	2017-02-05 14:13:53	26.00	37.00	345	0.02 Km/h	Show in Map (23.743605,90.371708)	clear	0	Delete
1	2017-02-05 14:13:52	26.00	37.00	390	0.11 Km/h	Show in Map (23.743605,90.371708)	clear	0	Delete
1	2017-02-05 14:13:51	26.00	37.00	171	0.02 Km/h	Show in Map (23.743605,90.371708)	clear	0	Delete

and password, the user inputs are matched with the pre-fetched data from the database and if they are matched, the system will login for the user, and start a fresh new session. Only correct authentication enables the data to load on the site.

Session Security

A session can be defined as server-side storage of information and it is desired to persist throughout the user's interaction with the web site or web application. Instead of storing large and constantly changing information via cookies in the user's browser, only a unique identifier is stored on the client side (called 'session id'). This session id is passed to the web server every time the browser makes an HTTP request. The web application pairs this session id with its internal database and retrieves the stored variables for the requested page. Session security protocol is added into the login and index pages. After arriving the login page, the user session starts by session_start();phpscript method. It automatically creates a session id and puts it in the browser as a cookie. If the user logs out, the session id will expire and a new one will be generated for each new login session.

End-to-End Communication Security

End-to-end security is needed for the communication between agent to server, or vice-versa in the proposed IoT system. Advanced Encryption Standard (AES) encryption

(2001) is used to provide true end-to-end data security. AES encryption works with a cipher key with 128 bits long, which is available only at the end point device/server and thus we can protect the agent data from man-in-the-middle (MITM) attacks.

MAC Address Filtering

Every agent device has specific unique MAC address and MAC addresses of trusted devices are stored in our cloud database. Only after MAC address matching devices can access and update cloud data which ensures data authenticity.

Bluetooth Security

Bluetooth is a wireless technology standard for exchanging data over short distances. Secure Simple Paring (SSP) is used as a working model for pairing the agents. Its main goal is to improve the security of pairing by providing protection against passive eavesdropping and man-in-the-middle (MITM) attacks. SSP employs Elliptic Curve Diffie Hellman (ECDH) public-key cryptography for building the link keys (Padgette et al., 2012). SSP simple removes the passive eavesdropping by using a private key with approximately 95 bits of entropy. It is currently considered to be infeasible to run an exhaustive search on 95 bits entropy in a short period of time. We choose Just Works association model as it was designed for the situation where at least one of the pairing devices has neither a display nor a keyboard for entering digits. Because in the proposed model user/agent is not asked to perform any operation on numbers; instead, the agent may simply ask the user/agent to accept the connection request.

The Operational IoT and Cloud Framework

The proposed IoT framework for Traffic Management System (TMS) including data collection, storage and retrieval strategies are successfully implemented with AWS cloud environment. HTML table is being used to visualize the data on web. The columns are 'Agent ID', 'Date & Time', 'Temperature', 'Humidity', 'Rainfall', 'Velocity', 'Location (Latitude, Longitude)', 'Weight' and 'Delete'. Data are fetched from the database and presented in their corresponding matching columns.

Figure 8 illustrates the web view of the data. Three (3) different levels of security architecture are implemented to secure the IoT framework. Figure 9 shows all applied security protocol regions within the IoT based framework. In addition, the implemented IoT architecture covers all seven (7) required layers according to the reference model (presented in figure 2). Thus, we can express the proposed IoT implication as a complete and reliable framework for TMS data exploitation. Later the sensor data will be retrieved from the cloud server and will able to calculate the

Figure 9. Security integration in proposed IoT framework

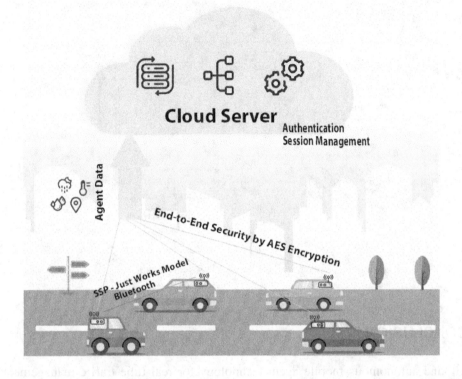

road segment weight. An intelligent decision module has been developed to calculate the road weights. The decision module was trained using an integrated fuzzy logic and deep neural network-based procedure. Figure 10 describes the road segment weight calculation process.

FUTURE RESEARCH DIRECTIONS

So far, we successfully implemented the data collection part. In near future, we will integrate the data collection with other data processing TMS modules. We will also improve the data communication method using SMS and mobile app based notification, voice routing suggestion etc. On the web based routing suggestion, we will use Google Maps API to suggest the optimized route directly on the map in case of any congestion detect. The detection will be automatically done by user's current position. User will be able to attain the service by visiting our website. Enhanced security protocol will be included in near future.

Figure 10. Process flow of road weight calculation

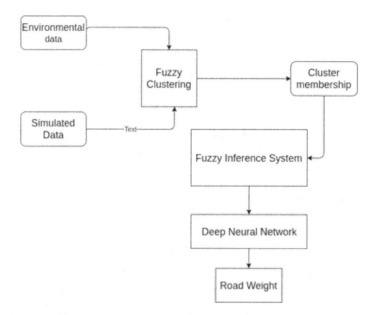

CONCLUSION

IoT and autonomous mobile agent technology for real time traffic management data collection, storage and retrieval is successfully implemented with an active AWS cloud server and its API and fulfils all the requirements to be an IoT based framework. The designed agents are capable to sense and collect the required data and send them securely to the database stored in the cloud server. In case of GSM connection failure from a specific agent, a secondary option is included to transfer device data through Bluetooth to its neighborhood agent or mobile device, and ensures easy data exchange with reduction of potential data lost. Web based real time data visualization makes it convenient to see all the data in a clean, formatted and user-friendly way.

ACKNOWLEDGMENT

This research received no specific grant from any funding agency in the public, commercial, or not-for-profit sectors.

REFERENCES

Aceto, G., Botta, A., Donato, W., & Pescape, A. (2013). Cloud monitoring: A survey. *Computer Networks*, *57*(9), 2093–2115. doi:10.1016/j.comnet.2013.04.001

Advanced Encryption Standard (AES). (2017). *Federal Information Processing Standards Publications (FIPSPUBS)*. doi:10.6028/NIST.FIPS.197

Akhter, S., Rahman, R., & Islam, A. (2016). Neural network nn based route weight computation for bi-directional traffic management system. *International Journal of Applied Evolutionary Computation*, 45–59.

Allychevalier. (2017). *What is the Difference Between GPS and RFID Tracking?* Retrieved from http://www.brighthub.com/electronics/gps/articles/60599.aspx

Arduino Board Uno. (2017). Retrieved from https://www.arduino.cc/en/Main/ArduinoBoardUno

Arduino Rain Sensor Module Guide and Tutorial capnfatz. (n.d.). Retrieved from https://henrysbench.capnfatz.com/henrys-bench/arduino-sensors-and-input/arduino-rain-sensor-module-guide-and-tutorial/

Fernandez-Caballero, A., Gomez, F. J., & Lopez-Lopez, J. (2008). Road-traffic monitoring by knowledge-driven static and dynamic image analysis. *Expert Systems with Applications*, *35*(3), 701–719. doi:10.1016/j.eswa.2007.07.017

GPRS GSM GPS Bluetooth All in one SIM808 Shield for Arduino. (n.d.). Retrieved from https://store.roboticsbd.com/arduino-shield/322-gprs-gsm-gps-bluetooth-all-in-one-sim808-shield-for-arduino.html

Lu, L. (2017). *Wise-paas introduction Advantech*. Retrieved from http://www2.advantech.com.tw/embcore/promotions/whitepaper/WISE-PaaS

Lumpkins, W. (2013). The internet of things meets cloud computing. *IEEE Consumer Electronics Magazine*, *2*(2), 47–51. doi:10.1109/MCE.2013.2240615

Mell, P., & Grance, T. (2011). The NIST Definition of Cloud Computing. *NIST Special Publication*, 800-145. Retrieved from https://csrc.nist.gov/publications/detail/sp/800-145/final

Messelodi, S., & Modena, C. (1999). Automatic identification and skew estimation of text lines in real scene images. *Pattern Recognition*, *32*(5), 791–810. doi:10.1016/S0031-3203(98)00108-3

Nawrin, S., Rahman, M. R., & Akhter, S. (2017). Exploreing k-means with internal validity indexes for data clustering in traffic management system. *International Journal of Advanced Computer Science and Applications*, *8*(3), 264–268. doi:10.14569/IJACSA.2017.080337

Padgette, J., Bahr, J., & Batra, M. (2012). *Guide to bluetooth security*. NIST Special Publication, 800-121. 1 doi:0.6028/NIST.SP.800-121r2

Peris-Lopez, P., Hernandez-Castro, J. C., Estevez-Tapiador, J. M., & Ribagorda, A. (2009). Cryptanalysis of a novel authentication protocol conforming to epc-c1g2 standard. *Computer Standards & Interfaces*, *31*(2), 372–380. doi:10.1016/j. csi.2008.05.012

Qin, E., Long, Y., Zhang, C., & Huang L. (2013). Human Interface and the Management of Information. *Information and Interaction for Health, Safety, Mobility and Complex Environments*, 173-180.

Rahman, M. R., & Akhter, S. (2015). Real Time Bi-directional Traffic Management Support System with GPS and WebSocket. *2015 IEEE International Conference on Computer and Information Technology; Ubiquitous Computing and Communications; Dependable, Autonomic and Secure Computing; Pervasive Intelligence and Computing*, 959-964.

Rahman, M. R., & Akhter, S. (2015). Bi-directional traffic management support system with decision tree based dynamic routing. *2015 10th International Conference for Internet Technology and Secured Transactions (ICITST)*, 170-178.

Rahman, M. R., & Akhter, S. (2016). Bi-directional traffic management with multiple data feeds for dynamic route computation and prediction system. *International Journal of Intelligent Computing Research*, *7*(2), 720–727. doi:10.20533/ ijicr.2042.4655.2016.0088

Sethi, P., & Sarangi, S. R. (2017). Internet of Things: Architectures, Protocols, and Applications. *Journal of Electrical and Computer Engineering*, *2017*, 1–25. doi:10.1155/2017/9324035

Sherly, J., & Somasundareswari, D. (2015). Internet of things based smart transportation systems. *International Research Journal of Engineering and Technology*, *2*(7), 1207–1210.

Sumit, S. H., & Akhter, S. (2018). C-means clustering and deep-neuro-fuzzy classification for road weight measurement in traffic management system. Soft Computing [Internet]. Springer Nature; 2018 Feb 21; Available from: http://dx.doi. org/10.1007/s00500-018-3086-0.

Tai, J., Tseng, S., Lin, C., & Song, K. (2004). Real-time image tracking for automatic traffic monitoring and enforcement applications. *Image and Vision Computing*, *22*(6), 485–501. doi:10.1016/j.imavis.2003.12.001

Tendulkar, N., Sonawane, K., Vakte, D., Pujari, D., & Dhomase, G. (2016). A review of traffic management system using IoT. *International Journal of Modern Trends in Engineering and Research*, 247-249.

What is Cloud Computing? (2017). Retrieved from https://azure.microsoft.com/en-in/overview/what-is-cloud-computing/

What is iaas? (2017). Retrieved from https://azure.microsoft.com/en-us/overview/what-is-iaas/

Yu, X., Sun, F., & Cheng, X. (2012). Intelligent urban traffic management system based on cloud computing and internet of things. *2012 International Conference on Computer Science and Service System*, *31*(2), 2169-2172. 10.1109/CSSS.2012.539

Zhu, Z., Xu, G., Yang, B., Shi, D., & Lin, X. (2000). Visatram: a real-time vision system for automatic traffic monitoring. *Image and Vision Computing*, *18*(10), 781-794.

Chapter 3
A Self–Learning Framework for the IoT Security

Sitalakshmi Venkatraman

https://orcid.org/0000-0002-2772-133X

Melbourne Polytechnic, Australia

ABSTRACT

The internet of things (IoT) is a complex system of heterogeneous devices connected to a network. While IoT can significantly add value to people's everyday activities around the world, there are numerous security risks and privacy breaches imposed by the IoT landscape. Traditional security solutions are not applicable for the IoT as they require high-end processing capacity. The objective of this chapter is two-fold. Firstly, it provides a comprehensive summary of the recent advancements in the IoT and identifies their vulnerabilities. Secondly, it proposes the paradigm of self-learning as an intelligent and sustainable mechanism that is capable of automatically detecting suspicious activities in the IoT. Overall, this chapter presents a contemporary coverage of the recent developments in the IoT scene, the security and privacy challenges confronting the security experts, a proposal of a self-learning framework for performing health check of the IoT environment, and finally a set of high-level implementation guidelines and conclusions.

DOI: 10.4018/978-1-5225-7811-6.ch003

INTRODUCTION

In the past decade, we witnessed the deployment of a large number of sensors and devices for various applications ranging from monitoring of specific health conditions to tracking of shipments or even living things, and this has resulted in the Internet of Things (IoT) (Evans, 2011; Hung, 2018). The IoT provides a new connectivity paradigm by integrating heterogeneous devices of the physical world with the online computing world via the computer networks and applications (apps) (Al-Fuqaha et al, 2015; EMC & IDC, 2014). IoT is offering a new paradigm of opportunities to solve some of the world's most challenging problems in every industry, such as construction, healthcare, agriculture, energy and retail in the development of smart environment (Grindovall et al, 2012; Parvin et al, 2018). On one hand, the IoT promises a smarter world with intelligent systems leveraging on Big Data that facilitates the management of both personal and business activities more efficiently (Guo et al, 2013; Bovet et al, 2014). On the other hand, the effective use of IoT can only be possible with a continuous monitoring of such a complex device infrastructure in the deployed environment and the collection of large volumes of data that need to be processed by specialised apps (Kumar et al, 2014; FTC, 2015). Such apps warrant utmost privacy and security measures to be in place for robust performance of the IoT. For instance, it is growingly becoming common to use wearable devices for monitoring one's health via smartphones that can access the health data collected from these devices. In such scenarios, privacy and information leakage are key aspects that required to be addressed sufficiently well (FTC, 2015).

Unlike computer peripheral connectivity, in the IoT scenario, more and more smaller devices are getting connected to the network every day on an ad hoc basis, and one cannot expect them in reality to work automatically when plugged in. Currently, they require human intervention for setup, connectivity and security configurations (Liu et al, 2017; Maene et al, 2017). In addition, for an effective use of the IoT system, software apps and upgrades need to be installed from time to time. All these requirements and inherent parameters of the IoT make privacy and security mechanisms to be of high priority for the correct functioning of the devices. A typical IoT consisting of several communication technologies such as radio frequency identifications (RFIDs), Bluetooth, wireless sensor networks (WSNs), and cloud computing, IoT systems are more vulnerable to malicious attacks such as intrusions, jamming, eavesdropping, malwares, spoofing attacks, denial of service (DoS). attacks and distributed denial of service (DDoS). attacks (Li et al, 2016; Han et al, 2017).

Traditionally, much research has been conducted for several decades to arrive at security protocols and best practices for servers, personal computers, and smartphones. While these are well-understood and are reaching a maturity stage, privacy and security for IoT devices are still at the infancy stage. It is estimated that in the next 5 years, 50 billion new devices would be connected online and security is earmarked as the foremost challenge for the future of IoT (Hung, 2018).

This chapter presents the state-of-the-art advancements in the IoT systems and identifies their vulnerabilities that succumb to different malicious attacks. It further proposes a self-learning framework as a possible solution to address these security challenges. The chapter describes how the concept of self-learning derived from the autonomic computing paradigm could be adopted for the future IoT systems in achieving the desired privacy and security goals.

The organisation of the chapter is as follows. The next section describes IoT state-of-the-art with definition of IoT, key attributes and background details from literature. The need for an adaptive and intelligent IoT security framework is explained. Following this, a self-learning security framework for the IoT landscape is proposed and a set of high-level implementation guidelines. Finally, the conclusions and future work are presented.

IoT STATE-OF-THE-ART

The idea of connected devices has been there more than four decades ago and is more referred to as). embedded internet" or). pervasive computing" (Shelbyand et al, 2009). However, a variation of this term more recently used is 'Internet of Things' (IoT). which was coined by Kevin Ashton while working on a new technology called RFID in 1999. According to him,). IoT connects devices such as everyday consumer objects and industrial equipment onto the network, enabling information gathering and management of these devices via software to increase efficiency, enable new services, or achieve other health, safety, or environmental benefits". With the massive growth of mobile and embedded devices and communication technologies recently, this term has attracted more attention. Today, the major technology shift is centered around IoT and has impacted our lives in both visible and invisible ways. This term has now emerged to be of technical, social, and economic significance (Alsheikh et al, 2014).

Definition of IoT

A basic and succinct definition of IoT is: 'a network of physical objects'. IoT includes devices of all types and sizes, consumer products, durable goods, medical instruments, industrial and utility components, sensors, and other everyday objects such as cars and trucks, smart phones, home appliances, toys, cameras, etc that are being combined with Internet connectivity and powerful data analytic capabilities (Alsheikh et al, 2014). The definition of IoT has evolved with the development of enabling technologies such as nanoelectronics, communications, sensors, smartphones, embedded systems, cloud networking, network virtualization and software as the need grows in providing the capability and support for the devices to be connected all the time everywhere (Vermesan et al, 2014). With this vision of IoT to become part of bigger systems in a world of). systems of systems", Figure 1 provides a concise definition of IoT that is expected to be realised in the future.

According to this definition, the IoT is seen as a dynamic global network connecting, communicating and controlling through sharing of information related to physical and virtual thinks such as vehicles, industrial systems, animals, people, buildings, etc that promise to transform the way we work and operate our lives (Rose et al, 2015). The key factors enabling the IoT to deliver on its vision is in bridging the gap between cyber space and the physical world of real things to achieve a smarter world (Roman et al, 2018).

Key Attributes of IoT

Historically, the first wave of the fixed line Internet resulted in the advancements of common software applications like Microsoft Windows and Google. With the second

Figure 1. Definition of IoT
Source: Vermesan et al, 2014

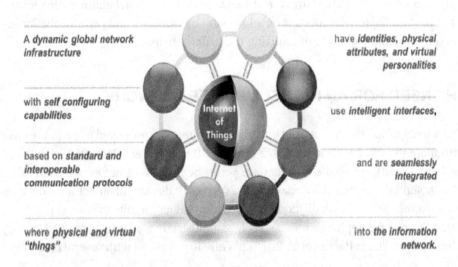

wave of the mobile Internet, development in wireless platforms such as Apple's iOS and Google's Android systems enabled communication anywhere and anytime. The current third wave of the IoT leverages on developments from previous waves of the Internet, and further possesses attributes that distinguish it from the). regular" Internet. IoT connects billions of things that include computing devices, software, people and many other living things across the world (Serrano et al, 2015; Shi et al, 2017). Two main trends observed that lead to the inherent attributes of IoT are:

1.   With increasing network connectivity, more and more smaller devices with specialised embedded technologies get connected in an ad-hoc basis, and
2.   With sophisticated software extensibility provided by third parties supporting device manufacturers, IoT is becoming an infrastructure where numerous software apps get installed and run processes generating huge data.

Some of the key attributes of the IoT that make sense of such mega trends are proposed through the S-E-N-S-E framework: Sensing, Efficient, Networked, Specialized, Everywhere (Goldman Sachs, 2014). From the point of view of the impact of IoT on businesses, the key attributes of IoT are identified as the three Cs namely, Communication, Control and automation, and Cost savings (Lopez, 2013). With these new wave inherent attributes of IoT, we are into a world of interesting devices and software applications ranging from implanted medical devises to smart home applications and programmable sensor networks. These attributes of IoT also pose a significant security threat. Recently incidents on malware attacks are on the rise and researchers have confirmed that code injection attacks against embedded devices could even lead to self-propagating worms (Xu et al, 2015; Xiao et al, 2017). Hence, in realising the vision of the future IoT systems, the four key characteristics that are associated with the 'smarter' IoT ecosystem are: faster, healthier, cleaner and safer. In this chapter, the focus is on addressing the security and privacy challenges faced by IoT in the context of realising the 'safer' attribute.

THE NEED FOR AN IOT SECURITY FRAMEWORK

The impact of IoT on the Internet and global economy is projected to be impressive with more than $11 trillion by (2025 (Hung, 2018; EMC & IDC, 2014). However, there are significant challenges that are yet to be addressed before we can realise IoT's potential benefits (Lamaazil et al, 2014). IoT device manufacturers develop incompatible devices with different sensor technologies, architectures and protocols suited to specific application areas such as industrial, e-health, home and energy (Granjal et al, 2015; Parvan et al, 2018).. While IoT is posed with several challenges such as interoperability and standardisation of policies, architectures, data transfer protocols and reliable power, recent security breaches are of major concern for the future of IoT (Andrea et al, 2015). In the past one year, hacking of the IoT and weaponisng Internet-connected devices for malware attacks of other internet-based services have been reported in the media (Xiao et al, 2016). Poorly designed devices that allow for weak passwords in smart home devices and other security flaws are exploited by the hackers to affect several other devices that are interconnected resulting in DDoS attacks. Today, both non-IP-enabled and IP-enabled devices communicate via IoT leading to rising security concerns and privacy fears among the public (Dujovne et al, 2014).

Overall, the following constraints and challenges in the IoT environment have been identified as the main basis to propose an IoT security framework:

1. With the IoT-GSI Global Standards Initiative IoT devices, there is a requirement to follow standards for privacy, security, architecture and protocols so that greater interoperability can be leveraged;
2. Prolonged supply of power is required to securely connect sensors and devices deployed in remote locations;
3. Automatic allocation of unique identification and naming of the IoT devices and objects is required using schemes such as 6LoWPAN to obtain unique IPV6 address for each node;
4. Dynamic and intelligent management of a huge variety of devices is needed to provide services for protecting user privacy and the IoT environment from several attacks such as spoofing, denial of service (DoS). attacks, distributed denial of service (DDoS). attacks, jamming, eavesdropping, and malwares;
5. New challenges are emerging around technology as well as relating to new policy, legal and development issues in the IoT landscape that warrant a more adaptable and intelligent security framework.

In summary, all the challenges of IoT, coming from technical, social and behavioural viewpoints fall under the prime concerns of privacy and security (Yan et al, 2014). These challenges are classified here under three main dimensions: People, Process and Data, as shown in Figure 2.

-   **People:** The 'People' dimension involves connecting the right people to the right device using secure authentication and by providing access to only relevant data that are valuable and timely within the IoT ecosystem.
-   **Process:** The 'Process' dimension involves validating the actions performed by the IoT, which requires interoperability among devices using Apps and middleware tools,, and at the same time enforcing the privacy and security

policies and industry standards. It is important for the process to analyse data and anomalies in the IoT and take the right actions.

- **Data:** The 'Data' dimension involves provision of the right data of the IoT, about the devices, the people, the processes, the environment, events, etc. Apart from maintain the integrity of data, it requires appropriate encryption and decryption as well as backup and recovery mechanisms associated with the different types of data collected and analysed in the IoT.

PROPOSED SELF-LEARNING SECURITY FRAMEWORK FOR THE IoT LANDSCAPE

The IoT ecosystem is revolutionising with new products, interfaces and services being introduces with the recent developments in enabling technologies such as sensors/actuators, nano-electronics, cyber-physical systems, network infrastructure, cloud/fog computing and software solutions. With high-end devices connected in the IoT, such as laptops, desktops, servers and even smart phones, the security and privacy challenges are well-understood and are being addressed with sophisticated security solutions. However, for the low-end, resource-constrained devices, such traditional security solutions cannot be adopted. They lack high processing and memory management capabilities (Raza et al, 2013). In addition, firewalls that are effective to protect computing resources within an organisation's network are irrelevant for IoT in the absence of a boundary or perimeter. Typically, IoT security requires protecting systems and data with a heterogeneous mix of security protocols in a de-perimeterised landscape. This calls for a self-protection without relying

Figure 2. Dimensions of IoT challenges

much on the network protection mechanisms such as firewalls and other standard security solutions. In recent years, researchers have been exploring more intelligent security solutions and alternate IoT security architectures for low-end networked devices than just supporting high-end processors. This chapter proposes a generic security framework for IoT systems using self-learning concepts.

The framework builds on linking IoT security concepts with self-learning features of autonomic computing, which is capable of self-managing and self-adapting in a proactive manner (Tennehouse, 2001; Rieck, 2011). This feature is particularly beneficial in systems with diverse distributed data service requirements on the Internet (Rieck, 2011; Ashraf et al, 2015). Context-dependent agents could be designed to possess the self-learning capability of autonomic systems (Ganek et al, 2003; Venkatraman et al, 2017). Such agents could be adapted for the IoT landscape to continuously monitor any security threat in the networked IoT devices.

Self-Learning Security Health Check for IoT Landscape

The proposed architecture described in this section leverages on autonomic agent capabilities: context-dependent agents that are designed to learn automatically and change their behaviour based on previous experiences to be able to self-manage and adapt intelligently. Context-dependent agents could be designed to perform IoT security health check by continuously monitoring the network connected devices to detect anomalies using a policy engine and a self-learning engine as shown in Figure 3. The proposed self-learning framework for IoT security helps to perform a health check in a continuous monitoring system with the aid of collaborative agents. It consists of the Self Learning Engine and the Anomaly Detection Policy Engine.

Self-Learning Engine

The Self-Learning Engine is made up of the following key components and adopts an autonomic self-learning using machine learning techniques:

- **Training Component:** The collaborative agents learn the normal and anomalous behaviors found in the IoT ecosystem using this component. Initially supervised learning (training phase). is conducted followed by unsupervised learning (self-learning phase). Here, machine learning techniques are adopted for IoT devices to be trained in choosing the right defense policy by determining the security protocol parameters that are suitable for their context of dynamic and heterogeneous networks. The normal behavior of the system is provided through instances of the state of the network in different situations. For example, an organization may deploy

41

Figure 3. Proposed self-learning framework for IoT security

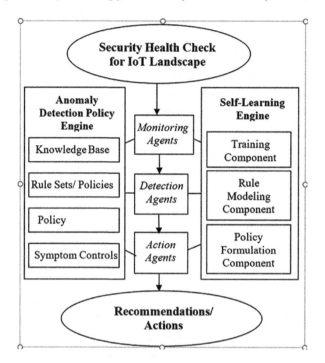

weather sensors to collect data about humidity, wind, rainfall, etc. and send them to their server or even a cloud storage for processing at a later stage. Details about each managed IoT device and environment information about the normal network activities such as traffic parameters, logging data paths, authentication, storage used, etc. are collected. Useful patterns are extracted and the training component not only learns about the environment, but also predicts future situations.

- **Rule Modelling Component:** This component builds a knowledge base of detection rules under two categories: i). Known Knowledge and ii). Unknown Knowledge.
  - ○ **Known Knowledge:** This consists of information gathered about IoT device configuration, services, device profile, system controls, nodes and gateways. All the existing context privacy variations, anonymity of IoT end nodes, firmware status, etc. are used to create the rule-base. For example, staff at various levels may have access to different device data based on their roles. All the normal system parameters, user and device profiles are formulated as facts and rules in the Rule Modelling

Component. It should make sure that the devices will run only authorized software.

◦ **Unknown Knowledge:** Constant monitoring of the environment and system states is required to arrive at any anomalous behavior patterns that could be associated with unknown attacks and this forms a self-learning process. by having a check on the following:

▪ **System Anomalies:** Device behaviour is compared with normal behaviour of other typical devices for detecting any fake behaviour patterns, privacy/security breaches, system performances, storage accesses, etc (Rieck et al, 2011).

▪ **Abnormalities of Traffic:** A distance measure is used to see the deviation of system parameters of the network profile from normal traffic, sniffing of data (Venkatraman et al, 2017).

▪ **Functional Change Analysis:** Detecting configuration changes, syntactic as well as semantic analysis involves detection of network address dependencies, repeated collisions, network availability, manipulations and device faults (Liu et al, 2013; Aref et al, 2017).

• **Policy Formulation Component:** This component assigns priorities to events by using high-level policies to execute the most efficient options for carrying out the anomaly detection tasks and to arrive at recommendations and further actions to perform. Context-dependent policy parameters for IoT are formulated and prioritised. The key policy parameters of different devices associated with a possible breach depend upon the following:

◦ Interoperability standards,
◦ Channel frequencies and bandwidth,
◦ Individual's privacy and confidentiality,
◦ Anonymity and non-linkability,
◦ Infrastructure failure,
◦ International governance,
◦ Data sharing,
◦ Unauthorised access and eavesdropping,
◦ Payload functions used,
◦ End-to-end encryption,
◦ Recovery, and
◦ Self-protection measures

Anomaly Detection Policy Engine

The system learns from the normal and anomalous behaviour patterns during the training and self-learning phases. Initially it learns from examples of). normal" behavior and formulates). *rules*". For instance, the normal traffic or environment state is fed into the system and it subsequently learns by identifying the patterns from time to time. It creates a profile of statistics of different system parameters. A distance vector of the observed traffic to the profile would help to raise an alarm if there is a huge deviation from the norm. The). *knowledge-base*" is developed using facts of the IoT environment status and rules formulated in the training phase. After this initial training phase, new system instances are inputted and the system is taught to detect anomalies accurately in real-time based on the standard). *policy parameters*" assigned to the IoT landscape. The system collects the necessary statistics of using collaborative agents to determine thresholds or). *symptom controls*". These symptom controls, in combination with the security and system policies, help the agents in raising an alarm. Machine learning takes place through mining of the collected data. Data mining methods along with statistical classifiers such as Bayesian or support vector machines (SVM). are used to automatically discover and learn new patterns from a large amount of data for anomaly detection or possible future threats or security risks/vulnerabilities that are found in the IoT landscape.

The knowledge base of the Anomaly Detection Engine also includes fuzzy logic to handle false alarms. Supervised learning, unsupervised learning, and reinforcement learning techniques help in self-learning, by introducing additional new rules that would trigger reevaluation of the existing rules for authentication, access control, anti-jamming offloading and malware detections. Similarly, predefined symptom controls that determine whether to raise alarm or not would get modified as the system goes through the self-learning phase.

Monitoring Agents

The main purpose of these agents is to monitor behavioural properties IoT services characterised by their mobility, bandwidth and their sensitivity to latency, data transfer destination addresses, resource usage, process authentication, packet attributes, connection types, etc. Thus, these agents operate collaboratively at various levels to capture behaviour patterns at user, system, process and even packet levels. Their role is to search for anomalies or suspicious activities by communicating with the policy engine that supplies the knowledge and policies of known intrusion behavioural properties and thresholds (Venkatraman, 2010). These agents function simultaneously by roaming the IoT network with specific tasks, some of them targeted at capturing data with regard to known intrusion parameters and some others pertaining to unknown intrusion behaviours. Such observed behaviour properties captured in consultation with the Policy Engine are passed on to the detection agents for further scrutiny. These behaviour properties also form a new dataset for the Self-Learning Engine.

Detection Agents

The detection agents apply the rules and policies from the Policy Engine to the observed behaviour properties captured by the monitoring agents that look at points of attack or vulnerabilities connected to IoT. The main points of attack could be when communication take place with an IoT device or between IoT devices or with a gateway. The detection agents analyse the data (collected from both the IoT network and the host machines). in a collaborative fashion and arrive at conclusions about intrusions, if any. The expert rule-based deductions and results would serve as meaningful inputs to the Self-Learning Engine for refining the rule-base and policies. These agents also serve as a vehicle to perform updates in the Policy Engine. Typically new knowledge is gained if polymorphic behaviour or completely new behaviour is observed in an IoT environment. However, there are instances when the Policy Engine updates are made by the system administrator and as the Self-Learning Engine matures through machine learning. For example, during genuine IoT network downloads, there could be additional conditions or parameter constraints set by the administrator or discovered by the Self-Learning Engine to avoid possible declaration of a worm which could actually be a False Positive (FP).

Action Agents

The action agents perform the final resulting tasks as suggested by the detection agents in a collaborative manner. If malicious activity has been identified, the follow up actions are undertaken. For example, based on the descriptive, predictive and prescriptive data-analysis of the observed behavioural properties in the host as well as the IoT network, the action agents may not allow a third party to update the profile of the owner of a device. In consultation with the Policy Engine, decision rules are executed and actions such as shutting down the server or closing a host process or disconnecting / blocking a remote connection to IoT devices or sending e-mail alerts etc. would be performed. In practice, the action agents communicate the decision actions or recommendations to the system administrator who could make the final decision. The action agents would then keep track of any deviations made from these recommendations as part of the learning process for updating the relevant knowledge of the IoT environment into the Self-Learning Engine. The action agent may also perform preventive actions dynamically such as in deciding suitable light-weight encryption of data or channel frequency or on the addition of noise to the data so that attackers are unable to reverse engineer any sniffed data.

The working of the proposed self-learning security framework for the IoT landscape depends much on how tightly the different agents collaborate and communicate. If the final result gives rise to new knowledge (related to fuzzy weights of rules, threshold values, malware feature measures, etc.), the action agents collaboratively perform the necessary updates to the Policy Engine and the Self-Learning Engine with new knowledge gained through the continuous health check of the IoT environment. The next section provides a summary of the implementation guidelines.

HIGH-LEVEL IMPLEMENTATION GUIDELINES

A set of high-level implementation guidelines for the proposed self-learning security framework in an IoT environment is given below:

1. The proposed security framework should facilitate in the deployment of new IoT devices and objects seamlessly by enforcing their own authentication schemes and security policy levels (specific to the context of the devices, network access, apps and users). The security health check mechanism of the self-learning framework should be able to suggest the appropriate security policy levels for them even in an untrusted IoT environment. To avoid leakage of privacy or localisation information of the IoT devices, the proximity-based authentication such as non-parameteric Bayesian method and other trust-based authentication of nodes could be deployed that helps in detecting spoofers outside the proximity range (Ashraf et al, 2014; Parvin et al, 2018).
2. Software on the nodes should be able to communicate with modules in IoT devices only through predefined entry points. External software should not be allowed to read or write the run time state or update the code of a module/app without IoT authentication and end-to-end security in the application layer protocol (Raza et al, 2012). Software providers could also check while updating a software if the modules loaded are unmodified maliciously. Detection agents should check for secure linking between software modules and monitor any anomalous behaviour in the runtime interactions between software modules in the IoT environment.
3. The implementation system should have the capability of representing and storing data, expert knowledge and the rule sets pertaining to virus signatures and typical anomalous behaviour patterns in a platform-independent IoT environment that supports interoperability and portability. It should possess the capability of performing dynamic filtering of policy parameters and

anomalous symptom matching for a continuous security health check of the IoT environment intelligently. Since this would be computation-intensive, secure offloading techniques should be adopted for IoT devices to use the computing and storage resources of the servers and edge devices in order to manage such latency-sensitive tasks.

4. In the proposed framework, IoT devices estimate the state of the network and possible malware attacks through machine learning. This self-learning process would enable in updating the thresholds or symptom controls that are more appropriate to the security and privacy policy levels for the different IoT resources. Data mining approaches could help in accelerating the learning speed so that any security mishap due to a wrong estimate or bad policy could be avoided (Buczak et al, 2015).

5. A distributed network environment would typically have different protection strategies at various layers of the network protocol, and adaptive cross-layer symptom and policy parameter extraction is required.

6. Any anomaly detection in the IoT landscape requires negotiations within the knowledge base and rule sets or established policies of the policy engine as these could pose conflicts. These conflicts need to be addressed automatically based on the context and adaptive policy parameters in the policy engine. Hence, the implementation modules in the self-learning security framework for IoT should support and leverage on context-dependent agents to follow policies from an adaptive policy engine.

7. Configuration changes in the distributed environment should be updated by dynamically propagating state changes, thereby offering an automated deployment and reconfiguration service for IoT devices. Similarly, new malware information is used to reconfigure the policy engine as a self-learning process.

8. Backup security mechanisms should be provided to protect light-weight IoT systems with restricted computation, memory, radio band width, and battery resource from security attacks or privacy leakage due to their higher risks of adopting a bad defense policy at the beginning of the self-learning process. New machine learning techniques with less computation and communication overheads is recommended for reliable IoT services. If any malicious intrusion is detected in the IoT environment, the best recovery tools should be adopted to revert back to the original clean state by adopting self-recovery procedures.

Overall, the implementation of the proposed self-learning security framework for IoT should facilitate in delivering the right information to the right person or device at the right time using simple, scalable, and easy to manage privacy and security mechanisms.

CONCLUSION AND FUTURE WORK

The IoT facilitates devices, people and services to communicate many different types of information with one another contributing towards a shared knowledge and a platform of Internet of Everything accessible from anywhere and anytime. While IoT can fuel technology innovations to create a new ecosystem with promising increased revenues, there are several challenges to be addressed before it can be considered as a successful enabling technology.

This chapter has described the current state-of-the-art developments of IoT and the underlying constraints. The key privacy and security challenges that surround the IoT landscape have been identified under three dimensions of people, process and data that warrant an innovative security framework to address the challenges. This chapter has taken a step further to propose a security framework for IoT that can apply self-learning techniques on the IoT data, people and processes. The proposed self-learning security framework has adopted collaborative agent-based mechanisms to perform the security health check of the IoT landscape by continuously monitoring its behaviour patterns using machine learning for detecting any privacy or security intrusions. The chapter has described the important functional modules such as, i). training, ii). rule modelling and iii). policy formulation components of the self-learning engine of the framework. The proposed method of developing collaborative agents that perform monitoring, detection and follow-up action in consultation with the Anomaly Detection Policy Engine and Self-Learning Engine have been described. In addition, high-level implementation guidelines of the proposed security framework have been presented. With the revolution of IoT and the increasing diversity of heterogeneous things connected over the internet the IoT is prone to malicious attacks, and a self-learning security framework provides promising ground for an effective defence mechanism for the IoT. Overall, this chapter takes a positive step towards triggering future research for the successful adoption of IoT in establishing smarter environments.

REFERENCES

Abu Alsheikh, M., Lin, S., Niyato, D., & Tan, H. P. (2014). Machine learning in wireless sensor networks: Algorithms, strategies, and applications. *IEEE Communications Surveys and Tutorials*, *16*(4), 1996–2018. doi:10.1109/COMST.2014.2320099

Al-Fuqaha, A., Guizani, M., Mohammadi, M., Aledhari, M., & Ayyash, M. (2015). Internet of things: A survey on enabling technologies, protocols and applications. *IEEE Communications Surveys and Tutorials*, *17*(4), 2347–2376. doi:10.1109/COMST.2015.2444095

Andrea, I., Chrysostomou, C., & Hadjichristofi, G. (2015). Internet of Things: Security vulnerabilities and challenges. *IEEE Symposium on Computers and Communications*, 180–187. 10.1109/ISCC.2015.7405513

Aref, M. A., Jayaweera, S. K., & Machuzak, S. (2017). Multi-agent reinforcement learning based cognitive anti jamming. *IEEE Wireless Communication and Networking Conference*, 1–6. 10.1109/WCNC.2017.7925694

Ashraf, Q. M., & Habaebi, M. H. (2015). Autonomic schemes for threat mitigation in Internet of Things, *Elsevier. Journal of Network and Computer Applications*, *49*(1), 112–127. doi:10.1016/j.jnca.2014.11.011

Ashraf, Q. M., Habaebi, M. H., Sinniah, G. R., & Chebil, J. (2014). Broadcast based registration technique for heterogenous nodes in the IoT. *International Conference on Control, Engineering, and Information Technology*.

Bovet, G., Ridi, A., & Hennebert, J. (2014). Toward Web Enhanced Building Automation System, in Eds. N. Bessis & C. Dobre - Big Data and Internet of Things: A Roadmap for Smart Environments. *Studies in Computational Intelligence*, *546*, 259–283.

Buczak, A. L., & Guven, E. (2015). A survey of data mining and machine learning methods for cyber security intrusion detection. *IEEE Communications Surveys and Tutorials*, *18*(2), 1153–1176. doi:10.1109/COMST.2015.2494502

Dujovne, D., Watteyne, T., Vilajosana, X., & Thubert, P. (2014). 6TiSCH: Deterministic IP-enabled industrial internet (of things). *IEEE Communications Magazine*, *52*(12), 36-41.

EMC & IDC. (2014). *The Internet of Things: Data from embedded systems will account for 10% of the digital universe by 2020: In The digital universe of opportunities: rich data and increasing value of the Internet of Things*. EMC & IDC White Paper.

Evans, D. (2011). *The Internet of Things - How the Next Evolution of the Internet Is Changing Everything*. CISCO White Paper.

Federal Trade Commission (FTC). (2015). *Internet of Things Privacy & Security in a Connected World*. FTC White Paper.

Ganek, A. G. & Corbi, T. A. (2003). The dawning of the autonomic computing era. *IBM Systems Journal, 42*(1), 5-18.

Goldman Sachs. (2014). *Making sense of the next mega-trend.* Goldman Sachs Global Investment Research Report.

Granjal, J., Monteiro, E., & Sa Silva, J. (2015). Security for the internet of things: A survey of existing protocols and open research issues. *IEEE Communications Surveys and Tutorials, 17*(3), 1294–1312. doi:10.1109/COMST.2015.2388550

Grindvoll, H., Vermesan, O., Crosbie, T., Bahr, R., Dawood, N., & Revel, G. M. (2012). A wireless sensor network for intelligent building energy management based on multi communication standards – a case study. *ITcon, 17*, 43–62.

Guo, X., Wang, Z., & Zhao, L. (2013). Intelligent Industrial Park based on Internet of Things. *Advanced Materials Research, 722*, 486–490. doi:10.4028/www.scientific.net/AMR.722.486

Han, G., Xiao, L., & Poor, H. V. (2017). Two-dimensional anti-jamming communication based on deep reinforcement learning. *IEEE Int'l Conf. Acoustics, Speech and Signal Processing*, 2087–2091. 10.1109/ICASSP.2017.7952524

Hung, M. (2018). *Leading the IoT.* Gartner White Paper.

Kephart, J., & Chess, D. (2003). The vision of autonomic computing. *Computer, 36*(1), 41–50. doi:10.1109/MC.2003.1160055

Kumar, J. S. & Patel, D. R. (2014). A Survey on Internet of Things: Security and Privacy Issues. *International Journal of Computer Applications, 90*(11), 20-25.

Lamaazi, H., Benamar, N., Jara, A. J., Ladid, L., & El Ouadghiri, D. (2014). Challenges of the Internet of Things: IPv6 and Network Management. *Eighth International Conference on Innovative Mobile and Internet Services in Ubiquitous Computing.*

Li, Y., Quevedo, D., Dey, E. S., & Shi, L. (2016). SINR-based DoS attack on remote state estimation: A game-theoretic approach, *IEEE Trans. Control of Network Systems, 4*(3), 632–642. doi:10.1109/TCNS.2016.2549640

Liu, G. X., Xu, J. L., & Hong, X. B. (2013). Internet of Things Sensor Node Information Scheduling Model and Energy Saving Strategy. *Advanced Materials Research, 773*, 215–220. doi:10.4028/www.scientific.net/AMR.773.215

Liu, X., Zhao, M., Li, S., Zhang, F., & Trappe, W. (2017). A security framework for the Internet of Things in the future Internet architecture. *Future Internet, 9*(3), 1–28. doi:10.3390/fi9030027

Lopez. (2013). *An Introduction to the Internet of Things (IoT)*. Lopez Research Report.

Maene, P., Gotzfried, J., de Clercq, R., M¨uller, T., Freiling, F., & Verbauwhede, I. (2017). Hardware-Based Trusted Computing Architectures for Isolation and Attestation. *IEEE Transactions on Computers, 67*(3), 361–374. doi:10.1109/TC.2017.2647955

Parvin, S., Gawanmeh, A., & Venkatraman, S. (2018). Optimised Sensor Based Smart System for Efficient Monitoring of Grain Storage. *IEEE International Conference on Communications Workshops*. 10.1109/ICCW.2018.8403537

Parvin, S., Gawanmeh, A., Venkatraman, S., Alwadi, A., & Al-Karak, J. (2018). Trust-based Authentication Framework for Enhanced Security of WPAN/WBAN Networks, Forthcoming paper. *Journal of Communications and Networks (Seoul)*.

Parvin, S., Gawanmeh, A., Venkatraman, S., Alwadi, A., & Al-Karak, J. (2018). Efficient Lightweight Mechanism for Node Authentication in WBSN. Advances in Engineering Technology & Sciences Multi-Conferences.

Raza, S., Shafagh, H., Hewage, R., Hummen, K., & Voigt, T. (2013). Lithe: Lightweight Secure CoAP for the Internet of Things. *Sensors Journal, IEEE, 13*(10), 3711–3720. doi:10.1109/JSEN.2013.2277656

Raza, S., Trabalza, D., & Voigt, T. (2012). 6LoWPAN compressed DTLS for CoAP. *IEEE 8th International Conference on Distributed Computing in Sensor Systems*, 287–289.

Rieck, K. (2011). Self-Learning Network Intrusion Detection. *Information Technology, 53*(3), 152-156.

Rieck, K., Trinius, P., Willems, C., & Holz, T. (2011). Automatic analysis of malware behavior using machine learning. *Journal of Computer Security, 19*(4), 639–668. doi:10.3233/JCS-2010-0410

Roman, R., Lopez, J., & Mambo, M. (2018). Mobile edge computing, Fog et al.: A survey and analysis of security threats and challenges. *Future Generation Computer Systems, 78*(3), 680–698. doi:10.1016/j.future.2016.11.009

Rose, K., Eldridge, S., & Chapin, L. (2015). *The Internet of Things: An Overview Understanding the Issues and Challenges of a More Connected World*. ISOC.

Serrano, M., Barnaghi, P., Carrez, F., Cousin, P., Vermesan, O., & Friess, P. (2015). Internet of Things Semantic Interoperability: Research Challenges, Best Practices, Recommendations and Next Steps. In European research cluster on the internet of things. IERC.

Shelbyand, Z., & Bormann, C. (2009). *6LoWPAN: The Wireless Embedded Internet*. Wiley. doi:10.1002/9780470686218

Shi, C., Liu, J., Liu, H., & Chen, Y. (2017). Smart user authentication through actuation of daily activities leveraging WiFi-enabled IoT. *ACM Int Symposium on Mobile Ad Hoc Networking and Computing*, 1–10. 10.1145/3084041.3084061

Tennenhouse, D. (2001). Proactive computing. *Communications of the ACM*, *43*(5), 43–50. doi:10.1145/332833.332837

Venkatraman, S. (2010). Self-Learning framework for intrusion detection. *International Congress on Computer Applications and Computational Science (CACS)*.

Venkatraman, S. (2017). Autonomic Framework for IT Security Governance. *International Journal of Managing Information Technology*, *9*(3), 1–14. doi:10.5121/ijmit.2017.9301

Venkatraman, S., & Alazab, M. (2017). Classification of Malware Using Visualisation of Similarity Matrices, IEEE Xplore. *Cybersecurity and Cyberforensics Conference*, 21-23.

Vermesan, O., & Friess, P. (2014). Internet of Things Strategic Research and Innovation Agenda. In O. Vermesan & P. Friess (Eds.), *Internet of Things–From Research and Innovation to Market Deployment* (pp. 7–122). River Publishers Series in Communications.

Xiao, L., Li, Y., Han, G., Liu, G. & Zhuang, W. (2016). PHY-layer spoofing detection with reinforcement learning in wireless networks. *IEEE Trans. Vehicular Technology*, *65*(12), 10037–10047.

Xiao, L., Li, Y., Huang, X., & Du, X. J. (2017). Cloud-based malware detection game for mobile devices with offloading. *IEEE Transactions on Mobile Computing*, *16*(10), 2742–2750. doi:10.1109/TMC.2017.2687918

Xu, Y., Cui, W., & Peinado, M. (2015). Controlled-channel attacks: Deterministic side channels for untrusted operating systems. In *IEEE Symposium on Security and Privacy*. IEEE.

Yan, Z., Zhang, P., & Vasilakos, A. V. (2014). A survey on trust management for Internet of Things. *Journal of Network and Computer Applications*, *42*(3), 120–134. doi:10.1016/j.jnca.2014.01.014

Zhou, J., Cao, Z., Dong, X., & Vasilakos, A. V. (2017). Security and privacy for cloud-based IoT: Challenges. *IEEE Communications Magazine*, *55*(1), 26–33. doi:10.1109/MCOM.2017.1600363CM

Chapter 4

All Pervasive Surveillance Techniques and AI- Based Applications:
Current Trends and Challenges

Jutika Borah
Gauhati University, India

Kandarpa Kumar Sarma
https://orcid.org/0000-0002-6236-0461
Gauhati University, India

Pulak Jyoti Gohain
Gauhati University, India

ABSTRACT

Surveillance is the process of close observation of a person, place, or object to avoid and minimize the risk of any undesired dangerous situations or suspicious activities to maintain normalcy. However, manual surveillance techniques have certain constraints including unavailability of trained manpower and erroneous observation triggering tricky situations. The proliferation of the use of information and communication technologies (ICT) have increased the levels automation and have made it a part of surveillance application. The aspects of automation have greatly reduced human intervention and have made systems more reliable and efficient. The new advancements in internet of things (IoT) and artificial intelligence (AI) have made automation in surveillance security even more convenient and efficient. It has been found that the application of IoT and AI-based learning mechanism have made significant performance improvement for automated surveillance purpose. Here, the authors discuss some of the recent trends and challenges faced by all pervasive surveillance systems.

DOI: 10.4018/978-1-5225-7811-6.ch004

INTRODUCTION

Over the years, a number of surveillance systems have been developed that have helped in managing security task, limiting the chances of intrusion or unauthorized access. The act of surveillance conducted for various reasons by different individuals, organisations, institutions etc. can be covert or overt depending on the requirement and intensity of applications. Security being the main issue today, protecting the life and property of the human has become a prominent matter of concern of the world today. The concept of security from manual door lock and key mechanism has now transformed into using more sophisticated security devices such as cameras, motion detection sensors, proximity sensors, alarms etc. In security surveillance system while maintaining the redundancy, the concept of total security is unavoidable such that the system continuously tracks the identity, location and activity of objects within the monitored space. A surveillance system typically focuses on tracking location and activity, while biometrics systems focuses on identifying individuals (Hampapur, Brown, Connell, Pankanti, Senior and Tian, 2004). The ability to recognise objects and humans, to describe their actions and interactions from information acquired by sensors is essential for automated visual surveillance (Valera and Velastin, 2004). The increasing need for intelligent visual surveillance in commercial, law enforcement and military applications makes automated visual surveillance systems one of the main current application domains in computer vision (Valera and Velastin, 2004).

With the advent of technologies and services, the facilities of interaction between human and machine has increased to a great extent. It is an often observed phenomenon of increasing the use of innovative security-aids with the rise in information and communication technology (ICT) and proliferation of human habitation. The user friendly nature and the facility to access to information has made automation a significant part of ICT systems. The automation has triggered many changes in the existing technologies. The security systems are designed taking into consideration the safety of the person or objects. Thus, providing security lies in factors such as equipment or technology and people. Taking into account the various issues related to security such as ease of access, lack of intrusion detection alert, inefficient monitoring method (Ansari, Sedkyl, Sharma and Tyagi, 2015), the different methods employed in monitoring is the key to prevent dangerous situations. This involves resorting an automated approach of monitoring and controlling once deployed. The ability of the network devices to connect to various other devices involves collection of a large amount of data from around the world and sharing that data over the internet, a host of application has been evolving, making revolution in technology. A part of such a technology and mechanism lies in continuous monitoring of the sensitive areas like home or areas such as an office, institutions, traffic point, airport entrance, defence installations, hospitals, roadsides, buildings, elevators, commercial organisations etc.

which involves real-time monitoring, capturing, hundreds and thousands of images each day. It has become a prominent part of the world today to make security an important aspect for the safety of life and property of person. The world is now entering into the era of Artificial intelligence (AI) and Internet of Things (IoT) which has been evolving at a great extent. This rise in the evolution of new connected devices and learning mechanism has brought about fundamental changes to the society. IoT which is a new leap in technology of network and connected device started with work on radio RFID tags and has expanded to connected sensors and actuators, along with many other technologies designed for different purposes (e.g., ZigBee, NFC, Bluetooth) including communication technology. With its impact in larger domain in the near future (Kolias, Voas, Bojanova and Kuhn, 2016) IoT devices will become the mainstream ranging from healthcare to retail to transportation. From the literature it has been found that a considerable amount of work has been done in surveillance systems over the past decades. The paper reports the work related to the integration of devices for physical intrusion detection and throws light on the means of increasing the level of security in sensitive areas.

The blocks in Figure 1 gives the representation of the surveillance system.

The architecture shown in Figure 2 is the general architecture of the video-based surveillance system.

Figure 1. Block representation of a surveillance system

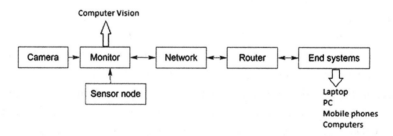

Figure 2. General architecture of a video-based surveillance system

BASIC CONSIDERATIONS

In order to get a proper understanding of the surveillance systems, it is necessary to study the basic theoretical considerations of surveillance applications and other such related topics. This section provides a brief overview of the basic theoretical considerations related to surveillance, various applied methods and techniques.

The task of surveillance security systems includes identifying an intruder or unauthorised person who might be trying to gain access to the home or any sensitive areas thereby alerting the owner of the sensitive area or in charge about that intruder or intrusion attempt, that might prevent from a dangerous situation from happening by collecting and gathering evidences about the real situation. An increase in processing power of newly-designed processors and the considerable reduction in power consumption, cost, and size of new electronics devices enables people to know and control every aspect. It is because of the advance in computing power, availability of large-capacity storage devices and high-speed network infrastructure, that we find inexpensive multi sensor video surveillance systems. Research tends to improve image processing tasks by generating more accurate and robust algorithms in object detection and recognition, tracking human activity recognition, database and tracking performance evaluation tools (Valera and Velastin, 2004). The creation of a distributed automatic surveillance system by developing multi-camera or multi-sensor surveillance systems, and fusion of information obtained across cameras, or by creating an integrated system is also an active area of research (Valera and Velastin, 2004).

Surveillance techniques is one of the burgeoning topic in image processing field, it has increased considerably from last few decades as security and safety has become a critical concept limited not only to public areas but also for private assets to remotely monitor activity across large environments. (Foresti, Micheloni, Snidaro, Remagnino and Ellis, 2005) It employs real-time image analysis techniques for efficient image transmission, color image analysis, event-based attention focusing, and model-based sequence understanding. Most of the time the primary sensor or pickup device used for surveillance and monitoring is the camera which may be placed at different locations.

A typical configuration of processing modules with different approaches is illustrated in Figure 3. For any distributed surveillance system these modules constitute the necessary building blocks necessary (Valera and Velastin, 2004). The figure outlines the most popular image processing techniques used in each of these modules.

The process flow in Figure 3 shows the traditional processing flow in visual surveillance system with different approaches.

Figure 3. Traditional processing flow in visual surveillance system with different approaches

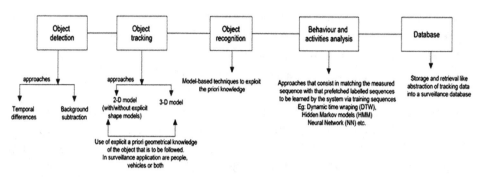

Figure 4. System architecture for intelligence task performance in surveillance

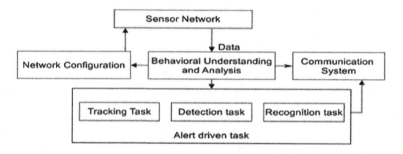

The architecture diagram in Figure 4 represents the system architecture used for intelligence task performance in surveillance.

The total security anywhere at any place is ensured with the facility that it requires systems that can perpetually track the identity, location and activity of people and vehicles within the monitored space (Hampapur, Brown, Connell, Pankanti, Senior and Tian, 2004). Accordingly, the existing surveillance technology should be capable of monitoring and sensing every single person loitering around near a high security building on multiple occasions. Such perpetual tracking can be the basis for very high levels of security (Hampapur, Brown, Connell, Pankanti, Senior and Tian, 2004). Typically, surveillance systems have focused on tracking location and activity, while biometrics systems have focused on identifying individuals. As smart surveillance technologies mature (Hampapur, Brown, Connell, Pankanti, Senior and Tian, 2004), it becomes possible to address all these three key challenges in a single unified frame work giving rise to, joint location identity and activity awareness, which when combined with the application context becomes the basis for situation awareness (Hampapur, Brown, Connell, Pankanti, Senior and Tian, 2004). The continuous monitoring and reliable vigilance is an inevitable part of the automated surveillance system that determines its QoS. The surveillance system connected to the networking devices shares the amount of data generated with the connected devices to generate the alert based task depending on the type of operation being performed.

Human behaviour analysis in a video surveillance is based on motion feature extraction and recognition, many information is hidden behind gesture, sudden motion and walking, many research works tried to model and then recognize human behaviour through motion analysis (Jaouedi, Zaghbani, Boujnah, and Bouhlel, 2017). In real world applications face recognition system is a complex image-processing technique with complex effects of illumination, occlusion, and imaging condition on the live images and a combination of face detection and recognition in image analyses (Gürel and Erden, 2012). The detection mechanism used in the system is applied to find the positions of the faces in an image through camera.

Recognition algorithm is used to classify given images with known structured properties, which are used commonly in most of the computer vision applications, at the same time recognition applications use standard images, and detection algorithms detect the faces and extract face images that include eyes, eyebrows, nose, mouth etc. (Gürel and Erden, 2012).

Another important aspect of a surveillance system is object detection and motion tracking. Most of the work on object detection relies heavily on the assumption of a static camera (Hampapur, Brown, Connell, Pankanti, Senior and Tian, 2004). There is some work which has looked at detecting independent motion in moving camera images where the camera motion is well modelled (Hampapur, Brown, Connell, Pankanti, Senior and Tian, 2004). In surveillance applications tracking of moving objects offers a significant benefit. In an intelligence application of surveillance, a task lies in detecting and tracking of moving object in video. Numerous approaches have been found to track moving objects in image or video sequence (Singh, Dunga, Mandal, Shekhar and Vohra, 2010).

Various Techniques Applied in Surveillance

There exist certain techniques that has been employed over the years by different individuals, researchers, technological manufacturing companies etc. for internal and outdoor environment monitoring surveillance applications, some of which has been discussed below.

Automation in Surveillance System

Automation is the set of method, systems or processes used for replacement of humans with technology or machines. Automation in a broader sense can be said as a technological creation that enables a system, process to perform various task on its own once deployed from manual control which requires workforce i.e. replace human role with machine driven processing. Automation has started to impacts the day-to-day lives, influencing each aspect of the daily life of the common man in a barely noticeable way. The world during the last few decades has witnessed a major leap in AI and robotics that are an essential part of automation industry today. The three components towards which the world is taking a turn to intelligent automation Machine Vision, a computer based mechanism that is used to understand visual input. Natural Language Processing (NLP) viz. Microsoft Cortana, Apple's Siri, Amazon Alexa etc. is a set of mechanism that is used to understand human voice and text inputs. Machine Learning enable machines to learn from the surrounding, retain the learning and use it subsequently to make intelligent decisions. These three aspects have immensely helped in designing automation system and automated intelligent surveillance system.

Many automated intelligent surveillance systems are designed to work on face recognition principles. These are based on a DSS which executes process control using the knowhow acquired from a set of faces held in a database. Certain systems are trained to detect suspicious behaviour. Popular video surveillance systems have one noticeable common feature i.e. these require human intervention. Further, the vigilance of the person deployed is largely responsible for the working of the system. Moreover, the areas under surveillance and number of cameras that can be used is dependent on the personnel count which in certain cases may turn out to be undesirable. At many situations the user may seek to avoid such a situation. To reduce these dependencies, the combination of computer vision, NLP and machine learning have emerged as an alternative for automated intelligent surveillance.

Wireless Sensor Network (WSN) Technology in Surveillance System

As surveillance has become an indispensable part for protecting the life and assets the advanced development in wireless sensor technology can be employed in surveillance applications. The significant impact of rapid development in wireless technologies has facilitated the collection of information from the physical world. A sensor with the ability to sense any parameters such as temperature, object detection, humidity, pressure, motion detection etc. can be integrated to certain processing unit facilitate the ability of making certain decision. A wireless sensor network (WSN) which is scattered in a region is meant to collect data through its sensor nodes where the sensor nodes are imagined as small computers which are equipped with basic capacities in terms of their interfaces and components (Gama and Gaber, 2007). In technological development, sensor network has profound impact being one of the highly accepted research areas for future technology. The wireless network with different sensors technology thus collect the information of the targeted object or any irregularities in sensing environment to be applicable in cases such as surveillance, emergency alarm, remote monitoring, biological detection, health and agricultural monitoring etc. Wireless monitoring with number of surveillances devices connected in wireless network for home surveillance application based on ZigBee technology, GSM or GPRS network are developed for real-time monitoring. The system will have capabilities of receiving and sending messages, images, warning messages, remote instructions etc. The advances in wireless sensor network technologies with large number of low cost and low power sensor node has reduced the cost of installing data acquisition and control systems with collection and dissemination of environmental data. The conventional methods of microwave and satellite used for transmission of real time video signal in surveillance from remote location has certain limitations such as installation having an integral satellite dish, setup limitations and accessibility limitations in transmission etc.

The WSN technology offers endless possibilities for multi-disciplinary task from electrical and computer engineering such as sensor technology, wireless communication, signal processing etc. with some of the subjects related t computer science such as routing, data processing, artificial intelligence, machine learning etc. to other potential fields such as medicine, environmental science, agriculture etc. (Gama and Gaber, 2007). WSN and video surveillance systems have characteristics complementary to each other such that intelligent WSNs provide an opportunity to significantly improve the quality and robustness of surveillance systems, making them more powerful and providing more information and services about environmental observation (Maddalena and Petrosino, 2008).

The variety of sensors and the enhancement of system's reliability guaranteed that the intelligent remote monitoring system can be responsible for home security. WSN can assist in object recognition, intrusion recognition and identification (Arampatzis, Lygeros and Manesis, 2005).

The rise in sensor network applications is due to certain factors as given below:

- The urge for a sophisticated, portable and cost effective technology that is justifiable for capturing, transmission of real time monitoring data from remote to base station location that has the ability to transmit these over computer network, or other network to multiple users in diverse geographical locations.

- It is due to rise in the technology of Microelectromechanical Systems (MEMS) that has made possible to develop sensors of smaller sizes.
- Due to the smaller sizes of the sensor it has made possible to install it in smaller volume and less production cost.
- Can be deployed in diverse environment to sense and collect data and periodically transmit to remote stations and receive data at the base station for surveillance applications.

Sensor networks like other networks, under heavy traffic face congestion problems (Khemapech, Duncan and Miller, 2014). Data delivery in sensor networks may be frequently light but may be very heavy under a specific event, for example, during a disaster or an attack (Khemapech, Duncan and Miller, 2014). Each sensor has limited resources including memory (Khemapech, Duncan and Miller, 2014). Moreover, radio signals may vary with interference due to concurrent data transmission from different nodes. Some research is focused on this issue (Khemapech, Duncan and Miller, 2014).

Bluetooth Technology in Surveillance System

With the advancement of wireless technology, various other techniques of connections have been introduced which includes GSM, Wi-Fi, ZigBee and Bluetooth, facilitating wireless connectivity (Ramlee, Leong, Singh, Ismail, Othman, Sulaiman, Misran, Meor, 2013). Bluetooth, a short-range wireless technology enables wireless communication between diverse devices (Yen, 2002), having a greater impact in global third generation (3G) wireless scheme, health/safety issues, and business implications (Yen, 2002). With the facility of short range wireless communication between devices convenient for users it eliminates the need for messy cables (Rhodes, 2006). With the facility to communicate with each other, synchronization of data with the ability to connect to the internet at a high speed wirelessly it has been widely used in home automation systems and surveillance applications. Bluetooth technology uses frequency-hopping spread-spectrum (FHSS) communication in the 2.4-GHz industrial, scientific, and medical (ISM) band, in which unlicensed devices are permitted to communicate in most countries of the world (Erasala and Yen, 2002). Bluetooth with 2.4 GHz ISM band is now found in a vast array of products such as input devices, printers, medical devices, VoIP (Voice over IP) phones, whiteboards, and surveillance cameras (Rhodes, 2006).

When Bluetooth-capable devices come within range of one another, an electronic conversation determines whether they have data to share or whether one needs to control the other (Erasala and Yen, 2002). The electronic conversation occurs automatically and there is no need for the users to press a button or give a command.

Once the conversation has initiated, the devices, whether part of a computer system or a stereo, form a network (Rhodes, 2006). Bluetooth can almost connect to any device, that can be used to form an ad hoc network of several upto an eight devices called the piconets (Rhodes, 2006). Data is transmitted between Bluetooth devices in packets across the physical channel that is subdivided into time units known as slots (Rhodes, 2006). With the range of personal devices using Bluetooth, the possibility arises to locate and track the movements of objects (Opoku, 2011). Bluetooth has become an emerging technology for determining indoor and sometimes outdoor position of a communicating device (Opoku, 2011). Although there is no specific support for positioning service in Bluetooth technology yet the predominant technology used are signal strength measurement, link quality and bit error rate which rely on the services of the Host Controller Interface (Opoku, 2011).

Bluetooth also face security issues like other wireless technology. Whenever a device attempts to connect to another device, user has to decide if it wants to allow other device to connect or not (Nasim, 2012). When two devices attempt to pair up, a key is generated which is based on the PIN number entered on both devices (Nasim, 2012). A stream cipher is used for encrypting packets (Nasim, 2012).

Internet of Things (IoT) in Surveillance System

The Internet of Things, IoT, is a new concept in which all sensing objects can be connected to the internet to have remote and constant access to its measurements (data) (Castro, Coral, Rodriguez, Cabra and Colorado, 2017). IoT aims in creating a network between objects embedded with sensors, that can store, analyse, communicate and exchange data together over the internet. This leads to efficient industry, manufacturing, efficient energy management, resource management, accurate health care, smarter business decisions based on analysed data, safer driving through smart cars that are able to communicate together, smart home automation and countless more applications (Erasala and Yen, 2002). The deployment of IoT security solution in all premises facilitates continuous vigil regarding entry, exit and activity in real-time, consistently regulate and check the working of the facility conditions from remote location with round the clock access, initiate corrective measures in case of an emergency.

Large-scale, real time video based monitoring arrangements have become indispensable for safety of human lives and assets. Such a system requires continuously growing transmission data rate and storage requirements. Such a demand can be fulfilled by designing and deploying a multi-layer mechanism which combines various technologies and provides required support. If the pick-up devices in such a framework are the video cameras these become "the things" which continuously stream video feed to a central unit where storage and decision making take place.

It can be cloud based connected via Internet. Lately, the devices connected in such arrangements prefer wireless links which adds to the efficiency while most of the wired connections are discarded as these create inconveniences at times and require dedicated support. As a result, the security and surveillance industry has grown in leaps and bounds as demands for such systems are increasing each day. Present day solutions have evolved from the rudimentary alarm based surveillance to more sophisticated IoT aided monitoring with decision support and process control. Live video streaming and related remote security mechanisms have enhanced the reliability of such systems for which these are preferred by organizations for protection of human life, assets, and premises. The IoT is enabling the creation of safer homes, communities, neighbourhoods and cities by ensuring round the clock monitoring to securely and remotely secure facilities and public spaces. Some of the major benefits derived by the use of IoT in security and surveillance systems by real estate managers, institutes, business concerns and security concerns are regulation of surveillance with remote management for monitoring every attribute of a set-up, facilitate AI driven decision support for ensuring real-time process control, ensure greater safety to personnel and assets especially in case of law enforcement, saving of time and money while providing security cover, improvement of the capabilities of the system with continuous analysis.

Review of Recent Works

Various works have been done around the globe during the last few decades which deals with remote monitoring, controlling and accessing and also provides analysis and categorization of security and surveillance systems. A few of the related works are included here. These are related to the present work and are expected to form the background of the study.

Review of previous work done on security and surveillance system with Arduino, Raspberry Pi, Bluetooth, ZigBee, GSM technology, wireless technology, wireless sensor network technology, Internet of Things (IoT) etc.

The following section provides a detailed survey on the study of the literature related to the work with surveillance and security system.

1. Basyal, Kaushal and Singh (2018). The authors have reported their work on voice recognition technology in single voice command that could perform a real world operation. They have reported that the conversion of input voice signal to its corresponding text through an android application could be dealt by the voice recognition and that the text message is transmitted through Bluetooth. The authors have discussed on the concept of real-time surveillance and automation.

2. Ayed, Elkosantini and Abid (2017). The authors have demonstrated their work of a specific System on Chip architecture for surveillance system based on Multi-Processor (MPSOC) and hardware accelerator. They have aimed at accelerating the processing and obtain reliable and an accelerated suspicious behaviour of recognition. The implementation of a specific architecture based on MPSOC in a single chip is accomplished by FPGA.

3. A (2017), The author has described the application of IoT in developing reliable and dependable home security system and for industrial security as well. The author mentioned that the system informs the owner about any unauthorized access by sending notification to the user. The author states that the developed system is not only restricted to the sensitive areas.

4. Kodali, Boppana and Jain (2016). The authors have reported their work on IoT connected remotely and monitoring real world objects or things through the Internet. Their work is focused on building a smart wireless home security system that sends alerts to the owner by using Internet in case of any trespass and raises an alarm optionally. The microcontroller used in the system is the TI-CC3200 Launchpad board with an embedded micro-controller and an onboard Wi-Fi shield.

5. Chuimurkar and Bagdi (2016). The authors have demonstrated their work on implementation and the results of smart surveillance monitoring system using Raspberry pi and PIR sensor for mobile devices. They have discussed on the increased use of mobile technology that provide essential security to home and for other control operation. Their work on home security system that captures information and transmits that via a 3G Dongle to a Smart phone using web application.

6. Venugopal and Pattewale (2016). The authors have discussed their work on focuses on developing a home automation and security system based on IoT. They have discussed home automation systems that has remote controlled switches for machines, systems based on GSM networked devices to comprehensive home server for monitoring and control of domestic environment.

7. Moubara and Desouky (2016). The authors have presented their work focused on smart home automation i.e. increasing home security using Internet of Things (IoT), integrating that with computer vision, web services and cross-platform mobile services. The authors have worked on areas such as sending data and receiving instructions by sensors, cameras and servo motors, to and from the end user.

8. Bashal, Jilani and Arun (2016) presented an intelligent door system using IoT that notifies intrusion by sending out email notification to the owner. In the system the changes in the motion of the door is detected by ADXL345 accelerometer

and the raspberry pi read the sensor intrusion data and communicate to the Amazon Web Service Internet of Things (AWS IoT) console.

9. Shaik and D. (2016) have presented a system with door accessibility and voice alerting through Smart Phone and have received captured image of visitor at door as alert message through email. The system uses a PIR motion sensor with camera module for the detection of motion and captures images to make the security system alive. The user can monitor and control the door accessibility on active SSH (Secure Shell) page designed on android platform and enhanced with JavaScript.

10. S. and G. (2016). The authors have presented their work on the design of a smart surveillance system, monitored by owner remotely. The system utilizes IOT technology and whenever an intrusion is detected inside the room the notification is sent. The authorized user who knows the details can access to their monitoring system remotely.

11. Bhatkule, Shinde and Zanwar (2016) have focused on the design and implementation of an affordable, flexible and fast monitoring home security system using Raspberry Pi with GSM technology. With different sensors installed at different locations, the USB camera and the PIR sensor interfaced to the Raspberry Pi designed system detect burglary, the image of the person captured by the camera.

12. Vigneswari, V., R., A. and J. (2015). The authors have reported the vast implementation of home security and automation. They through their developed system have provided a high level security and automation of appliances. The user is alerted simultaneously by sending an SMS with the link using GSM modem.

13. Nagarajan and Surendran (2015). The authors have reported their work on the design and implementation of an automated security system that would facilitate a healthy, flexible, comfortable and a secure environment to the residents. Their designed system incorporates a SIRC (Sony Infrared Remote Control) protocol based infrared remote controller for the wireless operation and control of electrical appliances. The appliances on the other hand are monitored and controlled via a laptop using a GUI (Graphical User Interface) application.

14. Darbari, Yagyasen, and Tiwari (2015). The authors have described their work on IoT based monitoring system that controls the traffic due to sudden rise in the use of vehicles that have raised due to rise in population. The authors have highlighted the different issue of Intelligent Traffic monitoring system using the technologies like IoT, Multi Agent system and Semantic Web. They have also stated the connection between IoT sensors using ZigBee protocol.

15. Sugapriya and Amsavalli (2015) report the security and authentication for individuals especially bank lockers. The work used techniques like pattern recognition comparing these existing traits, there is still need for considerable computer vision. Image processing is used and keypad password is needed for another level of security.

16. Reddy, Reddy, Reddy, Ramaiah, Nanda (2015) have reported how to control and monitor home appliances using android application over internet. The main feature of the system is to control the voltage levels of home appliance in home like speed of fan based on temperature, intensity of light based on light intensity etc. In this design android application has developed by using Android. Wi-Fi technology capable solution has proved to be controlled remotely, provide home security.

17. Ansari\Sedky, Sharma and Tyagi (2015). The authors have described their work on a security alarm system that is based on IoT in which they have used low processing power chips. They system through its camera performs the monitoring operation and on detecting any motion the alarm gets activated.

18. Widyantara and Sastra (2015). The authors have presented their work on the design and implementation of IoT for intelligent traffic monitoring system (ITMS) in the Denpasar city, Bali, Indonesia. The goal of their work was to develop a monitoring system that would be capable enough to visualize the traffic on the Web-based GPS/GPRS. The authors have discussed on the implementation of the work of IoT.

19. Pathari and Bojewar (2014). The authors have reported their work on monitoring and recording suspicious movement in a company during the closing hours of the company. They have reported the work of computer vision technology, intelligent video surveillance architecture to protect personnel and infrastructure to automate the process of watching web cam. They have implemented motion detection algorithm that acted as the security tool.

20. Kharat and Kharat (2014). The authors have reported the development of a system that makes the traditional way of fencing to avoid filtration better. The system consists of IR transceiver for continuous surveillance of the enclosure. The images and video captured by the camera on intrusion is sent to the central control station through the dual radio board for the authorities to take efficient action.

21. Kharik, Chaudhuri and Bhambare (2014) have reported the design of a communication based security system that provides enhanced security as a when a signal from the sensor is received, generates a text message to desired phone number to take necessary action and is based on GSM technology.

22. Domadia and Mehta (2014). The authors have reported their work on automated video surveillance systems in the field of security, the task that depends on detecting moving objects in surveillance area. They have mentioned that in video surveillance, detection of moving objects from a video is necessary for object classification, target tracking, activity recognition, as well as behavior understanding. The idea of their work revolves in developing human motion detection algorithm using image for which they have applied methods: Gaussian Mixture Modeling & Optical flow.

23. Ramlee, Leong, Singh, Othman, H., Misran and Meor (2013) have demonstrated an overall design of Home Automation System (HAS) with low cost and wireless remote control. The main control system implements wireless Bluetooth technology to provide remote access from PC/laptop or smart phone. The connected GUIs are synchronized to the control board.

24. Mandrupkar, Kumari and Mane (2013) have focused on smart video transfer and capture and have described mobile based remote control and surveillance architecture, suitable for remote bank monitoring etc. The set-up of a computer terminal equipped with a GSM modem at banks that can be used to transmit or receive videos or photos and/or commands to and from the administrator or the owner. They have detected the intrusion using image comparison technique i.e. Euclidean Distance Method.

25. ElShafee and Hamed (2012). The authors have presented their work on the design and prototype implementation of home automation system using Wi-Fi technology as a network infrastructure connecting its parts. The authors have mentioned that the system supports a wide range of home automation devices like power management components, and security components. The software of their work on home automation system is divided into server application software, and Microcontroller (Arduino) firmware.

26. Chiu, Ku and Wang (2010). The authors have reported the design of a real-time traffic surveillance system for the detection, recognition, and tracking of multiple vehicles in roadway images. They have implemented the moving object segmentation method that automatically separates the moving vehicles from the image sequences. The system integrates image capture, an object segmentation algorithm, an occlusive vehicle segmentation method, a vehicle recognition method, and a vehicle tracking method.

27. Kumari, Goel and Reddy (2009). The authors have presented a system that is specially designed for deaf and hearing impairment people. The stand-alone device notified the doorbell ringing for people who live alone in the house. The system is based on Raspberry Pi which include camera, sensor, vibrator, wireless GSM and Bluetooth.

28. Oludele, Avodele, Oladele and Olurotimi (2009), the paper suggests a means of increasing the level of security in an enclosed area with the use three of the four security layers necessary for optimum security. The work illustrates the implementation of an enclosed area whose security level kept high at all times.

Some of the relevant works depicting the use of IoT, wireless technology, WSN technology, Bluetooth technology, computer vision, image processing as well as Biometrics etc. is summarized in Table 1. It also highlights the various techniques used, the task performed by the different systems with their features for performing the task of surveillance.

Table 1 shows a brief summary of some previous work done on surveillance applications using various techniques.

AI in Surveillance System

Security whether it be in industry or government or any other sensitive areas including home or personal assets has a myriads of context ranging from individuals to nation-wide. AI and machine learning (ML) technologies are now being widely employed and developed across the spectrum of security are an unavoidable and important matter of concern of the world. Artificial Neural Network (ANN) finds application in different task due to its efficiency by learning complex input output mappings (Sharma and Sarma, 2016). The training procedures that is applied and theoretical properties of ANN are of utmost importance for its performance. For a large variety of classification task which can be enhanced by discriminative property, has shown reliable and good performances. The parameters of the system are estimated by the training algorithms. For the purpose of identification of unknown process or factors can be done by training the network to predict the sequences originated from the sources. The perception of human motion is one of the most important skills people possess and the visualization system of the people provides rich information. Human motion analysis has received much attention in last few decades due to the plethora of its applications. The immense amount of video data being recorded and collected everyday from surveillance security cameras it has become an essential task to automatically analyse and understand the contents. The ANN with the large number interconnected nodes demonstrates the ability to learn and generalize from training pattern. ANN integrated with systems like fuzzy logic control/ decision systems, are excellent at developing human-made system that can perform the same type of information processing that our brain performs []. The face recognition in some mobile devices, Facebook etc. analyses images, extracts attributes and then places them as per classes which facilitates recognition.

Table 1. Summary of the previously done work in tabular format using various technologies for the surveillance application on various domains

Year	Author/s	Techniques/Algorithm used	Task performed	Features
2004	Bodor, Morlok and Papanikolopoulos	Camera coupled with a computer-controlled pan/tilt/zoom-lens camera, image processing	Monitoring of indoor and outdoor environments and activity recognition tasks.	Error compensation
2008	Chen, Chen, Lee and Huang	Wireless Sensor Network (WSN)	Real-time video surveillance	Can be implemented for fire emergency, surveillance system and smart home.
2011	Opoku	Bluetooth communication technology	Tracking the movement of indoor object	Powerful system capable of handling computations effectively and efficiently.
2012	Vishwakarma and Agarwall	Image processing	Human activity recognition and behaviour understanding	Automatic Video surveillance
2012	Park, Choi, Park, Hong and Kim	Chirp Spread Spectrum (CSS) method	Resolving the object tracking problem on the video security surveillance system	Improvement of video quality and increase of valid video information in multiple object environment.
2014	Spadacini, Savazzi and Nicoli	WSN technology	Monitoring, detecting possible risky situations and response triggering.	Surveillance and home automation
2014	Frejlichowski, Gosciewska, Forczma´nsk, Hofman	Visual content analysis(VCA),Gaussian Mixture model, Mean Shit tracking, Haar and Histogram of Oriented gradient (HOG)	Protection against unauthorised intrusion, crime detection or supervision over ill person	Effective detection, classification, and tracking of moving objects.
2015	Ko and Le	YCbCr color model with pant/tilt system	Detection of a moving human face from the stereo image sequences captured by the stereo camera system	Implementation on a real-time intelligent surveillance system for robust detection and tracking.

continued on following page

Table 1. Continued

Year	Author/s	Techniques/Algorithm used	Task performed	Features
2016	Damodhar, Vanathi and Shanmugam	Wi-Fi network technology	Video monitoring, capturing of image and storing of video frames in SD (Secure Digital) memory mounted on the robot for further verification.	Home security and surveillance
2016	Monbarak	IoT with computer vision, web services and cross platforms mobile services	Home security	Monitoring, controlling, surveillance, detection
2016	Rajeswari.E and Subramanian.R	AMMFCA with hidden markov mode	Detecting and evaluating abnormal and clustering situations induced by pedestrians, vehicle drivers as well as unattended objects	Smart video surveillance security system
2016	Isa, Sklavos	GSM mobile communication	Security, enables the alert messages transmission to both mobile devices of end users, and central security offices.	Smart home automation
2017	Rathod, Vatti, Nandre and Yenare	Bluetooth technology	Door security	Ability of controlling from anywhere within a range application. It's easy and allows communication with set up without wired connection.
2017	Negi, Gupta and Khurana	Embedded systems and Biometrics	Recognition, Authentication, Alarm	Provides an optimal solution for saving/protecting from the hassle of stolen/lost key or an unauthorized entry.
2017	Honawad	Motion detection technique and GSM / GPRS network	Intelligent remote monitoring system	Implement real-time surveillance of the home security

Figure 5. Process flow in AI

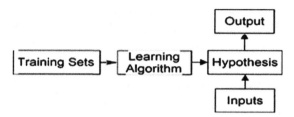

The blocks in Figure 5 represents the process flow in AI.

ML is a new concept in the field of AI that has been grown out of the works in learning based systems. Machine learning improves the efficiency of decision making. The future is expected to be filled with more spectacular developments which shall contribute towards transforming of the ways and means of doing work around the world. ML is about the machines, how they improve decision making from knowledge, experience, data and interaction. Two of the widely accepted definition of ML given by Arthur Samuel and Tom Mitchell is that ML is the field which involves the study of the ability of the computer to learn without explicitly programmed and in more precise form, machine learning involves a computer program that learn from experience E w.r.t. some class of tasks T and performance measure P, if its performance at task in T, as measured by P, improves with experience E respectively. It is where investigation is performed on how the computer agents can improve their perception, cognition and action with experience. With the development of science and technology new technological fields are evolving that are making greater impact on life and society compared to older traditional methods. One such is the intelligent surveillance systems that are making life more safe and secured as compared to other manual based technical systems. Intelligent surveillance systems based on learning falls under the AI research that can make intelligent analysis for real time surveillance without human intervention (Yu, Zheng, Liu and Li, 2011). In ML approach the system by itself learns what to do, what not do through the different training sets fed into the system by using certain algorithm. The learning involves supervised learning, unsupervised learning etc. These involves the system performance after feeding some data sets learns how to make the correct decision or predict the correct decision or output. The various fields in intelligent video surveillance technology involves image processing, image analysis, pattern recognition, machine vision, AI. With development of these fields have facilitated using the soft computational techniques in various domains such as detection, classification, tracking and behavioural analysis. The present day work on surveillance involve work on learning based system that automatically learn through its training sets, data and experience to take decisions. Many of studies have been made in the past few decades to address the problems of representation, recognition and learning human activities from videos and related applications (Turaga and Chellappa, 2008).

The variety of techniques that the machine learning utilizes to intelligently handle large and complex amount of information is built upon many disciplines. That includes:

1. Statistics
2. Computer System
3. Planning and control
4. Causal inference
5. Knowledge representation
6. Machine Vision
7. Natural Language Processing

The blocks in Figure 6 represents the machine learning process. This is the generalised block used for its representation.

In the last few years works have been done in developing intelligence systems in surveillance utilizing machine learning techniques to make robust, efficient, sound and reliable systems for maintaining security and peace.

Figure 6. Machine Learning process block representation

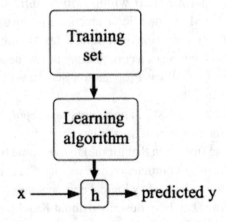

REVIEW OF VARIOUS WORKS DONE IN THE FIELD OF AI IN SURVEILLANCE APPLICATIONS USING LEARNING AND SOFT COMPUTATIONAL TECHNIQUES

Review of previous work done on surveillance security system in the field of artificial intelligence using computer vision techniques, unsupervised techniques, ANN, Modified Probabilistic Neural Network (MPNN), ML, Probabilistic Decision based Neural Network (PDBNN), Convolutional Neural Network (CNN) etc. in surveillance applications.

The following section provides a detailed survey on the study of the literature related to the work that deals with learning technique.

1. Saini, Ahir and Ganatra (2016). The authors have presented their work on an intelligent control system for real-time detection of an abnormal behaviour of the system to predict. Here the authors have used the technique of anomaly detection of camera control system. The authors have used Supervised learning, Unsupervised learning and a priori knowledge application learning methods in soft computing for anomaly detection. They have discussed the various soft computing techniques that can be implemented for anomaly detection including the Neural Network, ANN, SVM, Fuzzy Logic, clustering etc. that can discriminate between normal abnormal behaviour.

2. Ondrej, Vollmer and Milos (2009). The authors have discussed on the resiliency and security in control systems in the world of hackers and malware and the computer systems that are used within critical infrastructures. They have presented an IDS-NNM i.e. Intrusion Detection System using Neural Network based Modeling, the construction of training dataset using randomly generated intrusion vectors and the use of a combination of two neural network learning algorithms i.e. the Error-Back Propagation and Levenberg- Marquardt, for normal behaviour modeling.

3. Shah, Omar and Khurram (2007). The authors have reported their work on using video cameras for monitoring and surveillance which is common in both federal agencies and private firms. On that ground to overcome those limitations they have reported the use of computer vision and artificial intelligence. In their work they have introduced the key logical components of a general automated surveillance system. They have described about Knight, a monitoring system that have been developed and used in a number of surveillance related scenarios.

4. Babu and Makur (2006), the author here presents their work on video compression system which is object based. For applications as archival and transmission of surveillance video they have used foreground motion compensation. They have first segmented object from the background, obtaining the foreground object motion between the frames. They have used the SA-DCT procedure for errors from object-based motion compensation.

5. Jan (2004). The author has discussed on the reliable detection of suspicious human behaviour by automated visual surveillance systems. The author has mentioned about the conventional classifiers that have shown performance inadequately due to unpredictable nature of human behaviour. The author here has used the Modified Probabilistic Neural Network (MPNN). In their work, they have worked on the detection of suspicious behaviour and have evaluated the use of ANN based classifiers for assessment of abnormal or suspicious behaviours in an automated visual surveillance application.

6. Teschioni, Oberti and Regazzoni (1999). The authors have described about the need of real time solution of outdoor environment monitoring system for complex computer vision problems. The authors have discussed about the advanced visual surveillance systems for detecting, tracking of moving objects and interpretation of their behavioural pattern. They have presented a method based on neural networks for classification of moving tracked objects. They have focused on the surveillance system that could detect moving objects, localize and recognize them and interpret their behaviour such that a dangerous situation could be prevented.

7. Lin and Kung (1997). The authors have presented a face recognition system based on probabilistic decision based neural networks (PDBNN). The authors have described about their work on PDBNN face recognition system that has three modules namely a face detector, an eye localizer and the third module a face recognizer. They have also presented automatic face recognition that performed human face detection, eye localization, and face recognition. They have applied the PDBNN which is a probabilistic variant of the decision based neural network to implement the major modules of their work.

8. Moghaddam and Pentland (1995). The authors have presented an unsupervised technique for visual learning that is based on density estimation in high dimensional spaces using an Eigen space decomposition. The authors have derived two types of density estimates for modeling the training data i.e. a multivariate Gaussian and a multivariate Mixture of Gaussians model, whose probabilities are then used to formulate a maximum likelihood for visual search and target detection for automatic object recognition. The authors have described a density estimation technique for unsupervised visual learning.

Table 2. Summary of the previously done works on soft computation using learning methods

Year	Author/s	Techniques/Algorithm Used	Task Performed	Features
1991	Turk and Pentland	Neural Network	Localization, tracking, face recognition	Ability to learn, recognize new faces in an unsupervised manner
1991	Teschioni, Oberti and Regazzoni	Neural Network	Tracking of moving objects and interpretation of behavioural pattern	Classification and discrimination of object recognition
1997	Lin and Kung	Probabilistic Decision Based Neural Network (PDBNN)	Face recognition, tracking, interpretation	High performance automatic techniques or biometric recognition
2004	Jan	Modified Probabilistic Neural Network (MPNN)	Detection of suspicious human behavior	Automatic Visual surveillance applications
2008	Maddalena and Petrosino	Artificial Neural Network (ANN) based self-organising approach	Detection of moving objects	Handles scene in containing moving background, gradual illumination variation, camouflage, robust detection
2012	Kushwaka, Sharma, Khare, Srivastava and Khare	Machine Learning and particle filter creation	Detection and tracking of human in video	Automatic tracking and detection of human on a number of videos
2014	Kuklyte	Machine learning, classification approach, computer vision	Unusual event detection	Real world visual monitoring application
2016	Saini, Ahir and Ganatra	Supervised learning, Unsupervised learning and a priori knowledge application	Anomaly Detection	Detection and processing of anomaly in surveillance systems
2017	Hsia and Guo	Fuzzy-AHP algorithms	Disaster prevention and detection	Reduction in false positive events, provides for the early detection of the possible failure of a security system module.
2017	Castro, Coral, Rodriguez, Cabra and Colorado	Machine learning	Human activity recognition using an IoT approach	Remote visualization and programmable alarms
2017	Radovic, Adarkwa, Wang	Convolution Neural Network (CNN)	Object recognition	Real time tracking, detection and classification

The summary that provides a detailed survey on the study of the literature related to the work that deals with learning technique based on ANN, CNN, MPNN, PDBNN etc. in surveillance application with various techniques and algorithm used, task performed and the features related to the systems is given in Table 2.

Table 2 shows some previous work done on surveillance applications using various soft computational techniques.

CONCLUSION

Over the years many surveillance methods have been developed due to technological advancement. Different techniques have been evolved which have led to more sophisticated devices and systems making life at ease and safe. Different methods have been applied in design and implementation of such systems but the prime concern, the efficacy and aspect of security to maintain the normalcy is an unavoidable task for any researcher or individual concerned. Researches in these areas of the technologies has evolved many fields from traffic monitoring and automated surveillance system to biometrics to artificial Intelligence to Machine Learning. This has led to the significant advances in behavioural analysis, motion and object detection, face detection and recognition, tracking etc. For any higher intelligence system based on vision it is required to maintain the efficiency of any task performed detection, recognition or tracking etc.

REFERENCES

Ahmed, Ramana, & Gajanand. (2015). *Smart Surveillance Image Transmission Using Raspberry PI*. doi:10.4010/2015.480

Ansari, Sedkyl, Sharma, & Tyagi. (2015). An internet of things approach for motion detection using raspberry Pi. In *International conference on intelligent computing and internet of things (ICIT)*. IEEE.

Arampatzis & Manesis. (2005). A Survey of Applications of Wireless Sensors and Wireless Sensor Networks. *Proceedings of the 2005 IEEE International Symposium on, Mediterrean Conference on Control and Automation Intelligent Control, 2005*. 10.1109/.2005.1467103

Ayed, Elkosantini, & Abid. (2017). An Automated Surveillance System based on Multi-Processor System-On-Chip and Hardware Accelerator. *International Journal of Advanced Computer Science and Applications.*, 8(9), 59.

Bashal, Jilani, & Arun. (2016). An Intelligent Door System using Raspberry Pi and Amazon Web Services IoT. *International Journal of Engineering Trends and Technology.*

Basyal, Kaushal, & Singh. (2018). Voice Recognition Robot with Real Time Surveillance and Automation. *International Journal of Creative Research Thoughts, 6*(1), 2320–2882.

Bharanialankar & ManikandaBabu. (2014). Intelligent Home Appliance Status Intimation Control and System Using GSM. *International Journal of Advanced Research in Computer Science and Software Engineering, 4*(4).

Bhatkule, Shinde, & Zanwar. (2016). Home Based Security Control System using Raspberry Pi and GSM. *International Journal of Innovative Research in Computer and Communication Engineering, 4*(9).

Castro, C., & Rodriguez, C. (2017). Wearable-Based Human Activity Recognition Using an IoT Approach. *Journal Sensor and Actuator Networks, 6*(28).

Chiu, Ku, & Wang. (2010). Automatic Traffic Surveillance System for Vision-Based Vehicle Recognition and Tracking. *Journal of Information Science and Engineering, 26*, 611–629.

Domadia & Mehta. (2014). Automated Video Surveillance System for Human Motion Detection with Face Detection. *International Journal of Advance Engineering and Research Development, 1*(5).

Erasala, N., & Yen, D. C. (2002). Bluetooth technology: A strategic analysis of its role in global 3G wireless communication era. *Computer Standards & Interfaces, 24*(3), 193–206. doi:10.1016/S0920-5489(02)00018-1

Erasala & Yen. (2002). Bluetooth technology: A strategic analysis of its role in global 3G wireless communication era. *Article in Computer Standards & Interfaces.* doi:10.1016/S0920-5489(02)00018-1

Evans, D. (2011). *The Internet of Things How the Next Evolution of the Internet Is Changing Everything.* Cisco.

Foresti, M., & Snidaro, R. (2005). Active video-based surveillance system: The low-level image and video processing techniques needed for implementation. *IEEE Signal Processing Magazine, 22*(2), 25–37. doi:10.1109/MSP.2005.1406473

Gama & Gaber. (2007). *Learning from Data Streams Processing Techniques in Sensor Networks.* Springer.

Gunge, Y. (2016). Smart Home Automation: A Literature Review. *International Journal of Computer Applications.*

Gürel & Erden (2012). Design of Face Recognition System. In The 15th International Conference on Machine Design and Production, Pamukkale, Denizli, Turkey.

Hampapur, B., & Connell, P. (2004). Smart Surveillance: Applications, Technologies and Implications. *ETP '04 Proceedings of the 2004 ACM SIGMM workshop on Effective telepresence*, 59-62.

Hsia, K.-H., & Gu, J.-H. (2017). Fusion-Algorithm-Based Security System with Multiple Sensors. *Sensors and Materials*, 29(7), 1069–1080.

Jan. (2004). Neural Network Based Threat Assessment for Automated Visual Surveillance. *Neural Networks, 2004. Proceedings. 2004 IEEE International Joint Conference on.* Doi:10.1109/IJCNN.2004.1380133

Jaouedi, Zaghbani, Boujnah, & Bouhlel. (2017). Human Motion Detection and Tracking. *Proceedings Ninth International Conference on Machine Vision.*

Kadu, Dekhane, Dhanwala, & Awate. (2015). Real Time Monitoring and Controlling System. *International Journal of Engineering and Science*, 4(2), 15-18.

Kechao, Xiangmin, Zhifei, Zongfu, & Jingwei (2011). Design and implementation of embedded network video monitoring terminal. In *IEEE conference on computer science and automation engineering (CSAE).* IEEE.

Kharat, Kharat, & Kharat. (2014). Wireless Intrusion Detection System Using Wireless Sensor Network: A Conceptual Framework. *International Journal of Electronics and Electrical Engineering*, 2(2).

Kharik, Chaudhuri, & Bhambare. (2014). A Smart Home Security System Based On Arm7 Processor. *International Journal of Engineering and Computer Science*, 3(4), 5283-5287.

Khemapech, Duncan, & Miller. (2014). *A Survey of Wireless Sensor Network Technology.* Academic Press.

Khurana. (2017). IoT Based Safety and Security System. *International Journal of Advance Research, Ideas and Innovations in Technology, 3*(3).

Ko & Lee. (2015). Stereo Camera-based Intelligence Surveillance System. *Journal of Automation and Control Engineering, 3*(3), 2015. doi:10.12720/joace.3.3.253-257

Kodali, Bose, & Boppana. (2016). IoT Based Smart Security and Home Automation System. *In: International Conference on Computing, Communication and Automation (ICCCA2016).*

Kolias, V., Stavrou, A., Voas, J., Bojanova, I., & Kuhn, R. (2016). Learning Internet-of-Things Security "Hands-On". *IEEE Security and Privacy, 14*(1), 37–46. doi:10.1109/MSP.2016.4

Kumar, S., & Sharma, P. (2007). Home Automation System Using Android via Bluetooth. *International Journal of Advanced Research in Electrical Electronics and Instrumentation Engineering, 6*(4), 3297.

Kumari, G., & Reddy (2009). PiCam: IoT based Wireless Alert System for Deaf and Hard of Hearing. *International Conference on Advanced Computing and Communication.*

Lin & Kung. (1997). Face Recognition/Detection by Probabilistic Decision-Based Neural Network. *IEEE Transactions on Neural Networks, 8*(1), 1045–9227. PMID:18255615

Lynggaard, P. (2017). *Artificial intelligence and Internet of Things in a "smart home" context: A Distributed System Architecture.* Retrieved from vbn.aau.dk

Maddalena & Petrosino. (2008). A Self-Organizing Approach to Background Subtraction for Visual Surveillance Applications. *IEEE Transactions on Image Processing, 17*(7), 2008. PMID:18586624

Mandrupkar & Mane. (2013). Smart Video Security Surveillance with Mobile Remote Control. *International Journal of Advanced Research in Computer Science and Software Engineering Research Paper, 3*(3).

Moghaddam & Pentland. (1995). Probabilistic Visual Learning for Object Detection. *IEEE Transactions on Pattern Analysis and Machine Intelligence, 19*(7).

Nagarajan & Surendran. (2015). A High End Building Automation and Online Video Surveillance Security System. *International Journal of Engineering and Technology, 7*(1).

Nasim. (2012). Security Threats Analysis. *International Journal of Network Security & Its Applications, 4*(3). doi: 41 doi:10.5121/ijnsa.2012.4303

Nguyen, Loan, & Huh. (2017). Low Cost Real-Time System Monitoring Using Raspberry Pi. *Innovations in Electronics and Communication Engineering.*

Oludele, Avodele, Oladele, & Olurotimi. (2009). Design of an Automated Intrusion Detection System incorporating an Alarm. *Journal of Computers, 1*(1), 2151–9617.

Ondrej, T., & Milos. (2009). Neural Network Based Intrusion Detection System for Critical Infrastructures. *Proceedings of International Joint Conference on Neural Networks.*

Opoku. (2011). *An Indoor Tracking System Based On Bluetooth Technology.* Academic Press.

Patel, Vallabhbhai, & Choksi, Bhaskaracharya, & Jadhav. (2016). Smart Motion Detection System using Raspberry Pi. *International Journal of Applied Information Systems. Foundation of Computer Science, 10.*

Ramlee, L., Singh, I., Othman, S., & Misran, M. (2013). Bluetooth Remote Home Automation System Using Android Application. *International Journal of Engineering and Science, 1,* 149-153.

Rao, S.K. (2015). Raspberry pi home automation with wireless sensors using smart phone. *International Journal of Computer Science and Mobile Computing, 4,* 797 – 803.

Rhodes. (2006). *Bluetooth Security.* Retrieved from www.infosecwriters.com

Russell, S. J., & Norvig, P. (1995). *Artificial Intelligence a Modern Approach.* Prentice Hall.

S., & G. (2016). Motion Detection Using IoT and Embedded System Concepts. *International Journal of Advanced Research in Electrical, Electronics and Instrumentation, 5*(10).

Shah, Omar, & Khurram. (2007). Automated Visual Surveillance in realistic Scenarios. *IEEE Computer Society.*

Shaik & D. (2016). IoT based Smart Home Security System with Alert and Door Access Control using Smart Phone. *International Journal of Engineering Research & Technology, 5*(12).

Sharma & Sarma. (2016). Soft-Computational Techniques and Spectro-Temporal Features for Telephonic Speech Recognition: An Overview and Review of Current State of the Art. Handbook of Research on Advanced Hybrid Intelligent Techniques and Applications.

Sharma & Tiwari. (2016). A review paper on "IOT" & It's Smart Applications. *International Journal of Science, Engineering and Technology Research*, *5*(2).

Singh, D., & Mandal, S. (2010). Moving Object Tracking Using Object Segmentation. *International Conference on Advances in Information and Communication Technologies ICT 2010: Information and Communication Technologies*, 691-694.

Singh & Verma. (2012). Tracking of Moving object in Video scene using Neural Network. *International Journal of Advanced Research in Computer Engineering & Technology*, *1*(10), 2278–1323.

Teschioni, Oberti, & Regazzoni. (1991). *A Neural-Network Approach for Moving Objects Recognition in Color Image Sequences for Surveillance Applications.* Academic Press.

Turaga & Chellappa. (2008). Machine Recognition of Human Activities. *Survey (London, England).*

Tuscano, L., & Machado, R. (2013). Smart Web Cam Detection Surveillance System. *International Journal of Modern Engineering Research*, *3*(2), 1169-1171.

Valera & Velastin. (2004). Intelligent distributed surveillance systems: a review. *Intelligent Distributed Surveillance Systems, IEEE Proceedings.* doi: 10.1049/ip-vis:20041147

Yeole, Bramhankar, & Gaikward, Bansod, & Borade. (2015). RTOS Based Home Automation System Using ATMEGA. *International Journal of Innovative Research in Computer and Communication Engineering*, *3*(2).

Yu, Liu, & Li. (2011). Review of Intelligent Video Surveillance Technology Research. *International Conference on Electronic & Mechanical Engineering and Information Technology.*

Chapter 5
An Analysis of Cryptographic Algorithms in IoT

Samed Bajrić
Jožef Stefan Institute, Slovenia

ABSTRACT

The underlying vision of the internet of things (IoT) is to create a world where the real and the virtual realms are converging to create smart environments that makes energy, transport, cities, and many other areas more intelligent. With the IoT, the physical world is being interfaced through the things to the virtual world in heterogeneous environment. In heterogeneous environment, privacy and security are the major challenges. The secure information exchange is most critical pitfall to ensure the system security. This chapter gives a detailed analysis of cryptographic algorithms in IoT. A comparison of lightweight cryptography algorithms on basis of block size, key size, gate equivalents, and throughput is given. Moreover, the various security issues in IoT are discussed along with possible solution.

DOI: 10.4018/978-1-5225-7811-6.ch005

INTRODUCTION

The internet as we know it is always evolving, and in recent years an enormous increase in number of devices connected to the internet has occurred. It is estimated that by 2020, there will be 50 to 100 billion devices connected to Internet (Perera, Zaslavsky, Christen, & Georakopoulus, 2013). Now, ordinary objects like TVs, watches and smoke detectors are given the feature to connect to the Internet. From a sensor that enables us to configure the heating of our house when driving back home to devices that are placed inside our garden to measure the amount of rain. This is what we call the Internet of Things (IoT). The concept of IoT gives a new chapter in the history of the Internet giving the possibilities for cars, cameras, medical equipment to communicate through wired or wireless medium. With more and more devices being connected to the Internet, it can be expected that many of our day to day tasks will be aided by small connected computers, and probably be executed without any human intervention. While the technology itself might not be brand new, now is the time when it can be implemented in almost any object to create a network of things. Some of these devices use powerful processors and can be expected to use the same cryptographic algorithms as standard desktop computers.

The distributed nature of IoT necessitates secure communication with and between billions of devices. This relies on cryptography, whether for authenticating devices, protecting confidentiality and integrity of communications or for distributing digitally signed firmware updates. Many applications, such as smart cars and industrial control, require very high levels of security, as a successful attack could endanger not only sensitive data but human life. However, many of them use very low power micro controllers which can only afford to devote a small fraction of their computing power to security. For instance, sensor networks are intended to connect vast amount of very simple sensors to a central hub. These sensors would run on batteries and generate their own energy using for example solar panels. Cryptographic algorithms must be used on the messages sent by sensors to their hub in order to secure them and provide their authenticity and integrity. Because of their very low energy, the cryptographic algorithms have to be as 'small' as possible. On the other hand, the general method for ensuring the confidentiality of information is through the use of cryptography but most cryptographic mechanisms require a significant amount in terms of processing power and energy. This is quite a challenging issue to overcome and has received a lot of attention in the academic community.

Similarly, Radio Frequency Identification (RFID) technology uses radio waves to automatically identify objects, people and perhaps other information on a microchip that is attached to an antenna. The antenna enables the chip to transmit the identification information to a reader. In order to prevent an eavesdropper from learning the identification to a chip, this information has to be encrypted. Because of the very small number of logical gates and very little energy available, specially designed algorithms are necessary. Hence, the conventional cryptographic algorithms may perform well in computers, servers, and some mobile phones, but might not be suited for low-resource smart devices. It is well-known that the 1024 bit RSA algorithm cannot be implemented in RFID tags. Therefore, security is a significant issue in constrained devices. The number of commercial IoT systems deployed without adequate security mechanisms is growing exponentially. The large number of devices with relatively high computational power makes them an attractive target for attackers seeking to compromise these devices and use them to create large scale botnets. For instance, in 2017 thousands of insecure IoT devices were infected by malware and controlled for use in a massive Distributed Denial of Service (DDoS) attack (Jerkins, 2017). These insecurities have lead to a lack of trust in IoT in some spheres, somewhat limiting confident growth in the industry. Moreover, the tight constraints inherent the mass developments of smart devices that impeding the requirements of developing a new cryptographic algorithm, which performs strong security mechanism, encryption and decryption, with low power applications and other functionalities for the pervasive computing.

This new research area is referred as lightweight cryptography, and there are two main reasons for adopting it. The first one is efficiency of end to end communications where some smart devices have an implementation of a lightweight symmetric key algorithm. The second one is adoptability in low resources smart devices where for instance the footprint of lightweight cryptographic primitives is smaller than the conventional cryptographic ones. Many researchers have proposed lightweight symmetric (Hatzivasilis, Fysarakisloannis, Papaefstathiou, & Manifavas, 2018) and asymmetric security algorithms (Kumar & Singh, 2016) for IoT. Symmetric algorithms provide confidentiality and integrity, have small key size and are less complex, but they do not offer authenticity and distribution of keys in them is a challenging task. On the other hand, asymmetric algorithms provide confidentiality, integrity and authenticity, but their key size is too large which make them more complex for constrained devices. It is imperative that research in security keeps up with the fast-paced ongoing developments in other aspects of IoT. In this work we try to contribute towards better understanding of security lightweight encryption algorithms that can be implemented on IoT devices. Further, we deeply review and compare some existing symmetric and asymmetric lightweight encryption algorithms based on security parameters.

BACKGROUND

The IoT has changed our world in the recent years in many aspects, including industrial components, cars, smart phones, TVs, and many other objects that have unique identities in which can be remotely available. IoT enables small resource constrained computational devices which have lower computational power, smaller memory size, smaller physical size, limited battery life, lower price to communicate, compute process and make decision in the communication network (Slama, Puhlmann, Morrish, & Bhatnagar, 2015). As the internet is growing day by day, more and more devices are getting connected to it. Some applications of IoTs are listed below.

- **Home Automation System:** Objects like smoke detectors, thermostats and light bulbs can be monitored and controlled for added functionality and convenience. Home automation is becoming highly attractive and more and more people see the benefits of connecting household objects to the internet. Common features include monitor security camera, remote control of lights and appliances and energy saving. An overview of home automation systems can be found in (Asadullah & Raza, 2016).
- **Intelligent Transportation System:** Traffic monitoring, accidents, traffic jams or violation of traffic rules can be reported to authorities. Intelligent transportation system is one of the major domains in a smart city which can be used to monitor and control the vehicular traffic in a smart way by using the different communication modes and networks. A survey of intelligent transportation system can be found in (Ghosh, Pragathi, Ullas, & Borra, 2017).
- **Health Care System:** Remote monitoring of patients, constant monitoring of health parameters and activities, support for independent living or monitoring medicines intake by the patient can be provided like a health care facility. Various applications of IoT in health care industries are discussed in (Pang, Chen, Tian, Zheng, & Dubrova, 2013).
- **Prediction of Natural Disasters:** Predicting the upcoming events and delivering an early warning to community through smart systems. Although IoT cannot prevent any disaster from happening, can definitely aid in efficient disaster preparedness. The most challenging and probably the most exhaustive job that follows any disastrous event is recovery and rescue. The IoT technology can be efficiently used for creating online systems that search missing people and even manage emergency funds. The significant contributions in the development of appropriate constructs for IoT Technology in the context of disaster management are presented in (Sinha, Kumar, Rana, Islam, & Dwivedi, 2017).

IoT Architectures

With the rapid development in the devices and their way of operating, it has been a difficult task to keep up standard ways of implementation and communication for IoT devices. Since IoT does not only establish a connection between other objects for information sharing, it also makes multiple decisions after network establishment. And of course, these decisions are taken in real time, which is established through the architecture of IoT. In the following lines various architectures of IoTs are discussed.

1. **Three-Layer Architecture:** The three-layer architecture was introduced in the early stages of the research (Mashal, et al., 2015; Said & Masud, 2013). The layers are called Physical layer, Network layer and Application layer from the bottom to top. The Physical layer defines the basic minimal things needed for devices to be connected to the internet. It contains RFID tags, sensors, cameras, etc. The Network layer contains all the software and hardware compositions of the network and is the management and information center. Its work it to transmit and process the information obtained from the Physical layer. The last layer of this architecture is the Application layer. The aim of this layer is to make a bridge between industrial technology and social needs of IoTs. Note that this architecture only gives basic level information and does not completely explain IoTs detailed structure and association. This is why, we have many more layered architectures proposed in the literature.

2. **Four-Layer Architecture:** Authors in (Bozdogan & Kara, 2015) are presented the four-layer architecture with Perception, Network, Transport and Application layer. The Perception layer is similar to the Physical layer. The Network layer provides the communication nodes have the different technologies and must use one of the IP protocols. Besides, the Transport layer provides implementation of quality of service, reliability and security rules. At the end the Application layer provides end-user operations and forms communication software.

3. **Five-Layer Architecture:** Rafiullah Khan et. al. (Khan, Khan, Zaheer, & Khan, 2012) have described the architecture of IoT as combination of five different layers. The Perception layer deals with physical objects. It identifies and collects the object specific information like location, temperature, motion, etc. The Transport layer is responsible for secure transmission of physical object data to processing system. In the middle, the Middleware layer stores the data in databases, performs information processing. The Application layer deal with the management of different applications. At the top, the Business layer is responsible for the analysis, and it determines the future actions.

4.   **Six-Layer Architecture:** The author in (Thingom, 2015) has proposed six-layer architecture. In addition to the Sensing, Networking, Services and Business layer, two more layers the MAC layer and Processing and storage layer have been introduced. The MAC layer is responsible for monitoring and control. It makes the devices to sleep in their idle time to save the energy. The Processing and storage layer is responsible for query processing, analysis and storage, and security.

Apart from above presented architectures, IoT architecture should be apt enough to support all the features for its best possible use. The architecture should be capable to provide application support, quality of service, security, reliability and have optimized performance. In Table 1, the key features of different architectures is given.

Security Goals in IoT

The fact that we use the Internet of Things in various areas such as banking, medicine or business, and the importance of the information exchanged in these areas as well as the importance of privacy for human beings has led to the increasing significance of security in IoT. In order to protect complete security to IoTs, security must be

Table 1. Overview of IoT architectures

Three-Layer Architecture	Four-Layer Architecture	Five-Layer Architecture	Six-Layer Architecture
Physical layer: Smart cards, RFID tags, sensors	**Perception layer:** RFID tags, sensors, NFC readers	**Perception layer:** RFID tags, sensors, barcode	**Sensing layer:** RFID tags, sensors, actuators
Network layer: 3G, WiFi, Bluetooth, ZigBee	**Network layer:** WiFi, GSM, ZigBee, WCDMA	**Transport layer:** WiFi, 3G, Bluetooth, ZigBee infrared	**MAC layer:** Quality of service, energy management
			Networking layer: 6LoWPAN
	Transport layer: Quality of service, Web service servers, management	**Middleware layer:** Ubiquitous computing, service management, decision unit	**Processing and storage layer:** Ubiquitous computing, cloud computing
Application layer: Smart applications and management	**Application layer:** Smart applications	**Application layer:** Smart applications	**Services layer:** Intelligent applications
		Business layer: Flow charts, graphs, business models	**Business layer:** Service charge, cost estimation and distribution

integrated into every node of system otherwise an insecure component in the network could be a point of attack and can make the whole system vulnerable. That is why security must be succeeded in every aspect of the design of IoT applications that will require a high level of security. Therefore, without any protective mechanism, the network could suffer from attacks or malfunctions that disrupt the services provided by the network (Deng, Han, & Mishra, 2006). When dealing with security in IoT, the following are some essential security requirements that are sometimes considered as the measures to compare the performance of various secured systems.

- **Confidentiality:** Confidentiality ensures that the data is secure and only available to authorized users. In IoT an authorized user can be human, machines and services, and internal objects. For instance, it is very important that sensors do not reveal the collected data to neighboring nodes (Farooq, Waseem, Khairi, & Mazhar, 2015). In addition, an eavesdropper should not be able to extract the content of a confidential message.
- **Integrity:** Integrity refers to prevent falsification or modification of data transmitted in the network by unauthorized users. The IoT is based on exchanging data between a lot of different devices, and therefore it is very important to ensure the integrity of data. For instance, the integrity data can be imposed by supporting end to end security in IoT communication.
- **Availability:** Availability ensures that unauthorized users or systems cannot deny access system resources to authorized users. The users of the IoT should have all the data available whenever they need it and only authorized users can access data, services and other available resources when requested.
- **Authenticity:** Each object in the IoT must be able to identify and authenticate other objects. However, this task is challenging because many entities are involved such as devices, people, services. Moreover, some objects may need to communicate with others for the first time (Roman, Zhou, & Lopez, 2013).
- **Freshness:** Freshness refers to ensure that unauthorized users cannot generate old messages in the system. This is very important, for instance, in smart home automation systems where sensors often sense and transmit time critical data such as someone's blood pressure and heart rates at certain times which should be in real time for ensuring the safety of lives.

LIGHTWEIGHT CRYPTOGRAPHIC ALGORITHMS

We see that the security of IoT poses a lot of challenges. Many of these can be directly tied to algorithms for encryption requiring too many resources. On the other hand, adding more powerful hardware to such limited space can be difficult without driving the cost of product up to an unreasonable level. Conventional cryptography algorithms do not fit perfectly in IoT environments because of numerous resource limitations and conditions such as power, limited battery, etc. Therefore, the main objective is to design and employ lightweight cryptographic algorithms that can be applied in IoT environments while proving desired security levels. The term lightweight should not be mistaken with weak in terms of cryptographic protection, but instead be interpreted as referring to a family of cryptographic algorithms with low energy consumption, low computational power which need to resolve both energy and security challenges. There are numerous examples of using lightweight cryptographic algorithms in IoT such as authentication schemes (Li, Liu, & Nepal, 2017) or device management (Jin, Tomoishi, & Yamai, 2017). Even though no strict criteria is defined for lightweight cryptography algorithms, the features usually includes one or more of the following factors.

- **Size:** Minimum size (circuit, ROM/RAM) required for hardware implementation. Size poses a challenge in the design of IoT devices, because some devices need to be as small as possible. This leaves little space for components, and as a result such devices have limitation in how fast they are and how much storage they have.
- **Low Computational Power:** Power is especially important with the RFID and energy harvesting devices. While the power provided by the battery may be sufficient to do its intended tasks, computing keys and encryption data can sometimes draw too much power.
- **Low Implementation Cost:** It is important to minimize the cost, but keeping the service useful. For example, a cheap and efficient chip may be vulnerable to side-channel attacks.
- **Processing Speed:** A high throughput is necessary for devices with large data transmissions such as a video camera or vibration sensor, while a low delay is important for real-time control processing of a car control system, etc.
- **Good Security:** A secure lightweight cryptographic algorithm is one of challenging issues in IoT, because it provides confidentiality, data integrity and authentication to IoT devices.

The designers of lightweight cryptographic algorithms have to manage with the trade-off between security, costs and performance. It is very difficult to optimize all the three design goals at the same time. Usually, two of three design goals such as security and low costs or security and performance or low costs and performance can be optimized easily. In addition, there is a requirement of the secure algorithm that will map best options of lightweight symmetric and asymmetric algorithms in such a way that can take optimum energy requirements with less execution time and will confirm all security services such as authenticity, confidentiality and integrity.

Symmetric Lightweight Algorithms for IoT

Symmetric algorithm uses only one key for both encryption and decryption of the secret message. Therefore, it is necessary for the sender and receiver to obtain a common secret key which only they know about. Symmetric key assures confidentiality and integrity of data, but do not guarantee authentication leading to attack on availability. This can affect real-time information collecting and processing which can lose the resources of IoT. Therefore, a secure algorithm for IoT with the guarantee of services like confidentiality, integrity and authentication in optimal time should be proposed. Advantage of symmetric algorithms is less number of keys required with less key size. Disadvantage is secret key distribution between both sender and receiver. The secret key can be unveiled in two possible ways: using brute force attack or discovering the key during the initial key agreement.

Symmetric ciphers can be classified as stream ciphers, block ciphers and hash functions. In the following we mention only a small selection of lightweight designs.

1. **Stream ciphers:** A stream cipher is a generalization of a one-time pad, where its security depends on pseudo randomness of the key stream generator. One of the major characteristics of a secure stream cipher regarding the implementation is the nonrepeatable key stream length. Another very important characteristic of a secure stream cipher is a bit length of the symmetric key used. Stream ciphers are typically executed at a higher speed than block ciphers and have lower hardware complexity.
    a. **Grain:** Grain is best described as a family of hardware-efficient synchronous stream ciphers. However, the design of the Grain family allows for an ingenious multiplication of throughput speed, though at the cost of minor increase in the space consumed (Hell, Johansson, & Meier, 2007). A new Grain stream cipher, Grain-128a, was proposed as strong version of the Grain family with 128 bit security in 2011 (Agren, Hell, Johansson, & Meier, 2011) and has been standardized for RFID devices.
    b. **MICKEY:** The family of stream ciphers MICKEY (Mutual Irregular Clocking KEY stream generator) is intended to have a low complexity in hardware, while providing a high level of security (Babbage & Dodd, 2008). It is well suited to applications where very low power or gate count are the primary requirements.

c.   **Trivium:** The Trivium algorithm is a hardware-efficient stream cipher designed to be compact and fast in applications that require a high throughput. In particular, the cipher's design is such that the basic throughput can be improved through parallelization, i.e. allowing computing 64 iteration at once, without increasing of the area required for its implementation (De Canniere & Preneel, Trivium specifications, 2008).

A comparison of these stream ciphers based on their key sizes, consumed area measured in gate equivalents (A gate equivalent (GE) stands for a unit of measure which allows specifying manufacturing-technology-independent complexity of digital electronic circuits, and corresponds to a silicon area for a dedicated manufacturing technology) and maximum clock frequency is given in Table 2.

2.   **Block ciphers:** The aim of block cipher is to provide a keyed pseudo-random permutation which is then used as the building block of more complex protocols. A good block cipher must be fast and secure, i.e. it must be impossible for an adversary with realistic computing power to retrieve the key used. There are two families of design for block ciphers: Substitution Permutation Network and Feistel Network. There are also specific constraints when designing lightweight block ciphers. For instance, memory is very expensive so that implementing S-boxes as look-up table can lead to a large hardware footprint. That is why these ciphers usually have no S-box at all (SIMON and SPECK) or very small ones, only four times four (PRESENT).

a.   **Advanced Encryption Standard (AES):** AES is a symmetric block cipher standardized by NIST (National Institute of Standards and Technology). It uses substitution permutation network (SPN) and works on four times four matrices having block size of 128 bits with keys of 128, 192 and 256 bits. Depending on the key length, AES performs encryption in 10, 12 or 14 rounds. Up to now there has not been proven any attack that can break AES. Side channel attack like differential power analysis is

Table 2. A comparison of stream ciphers

Algorithm	Key size (bits)	Area (GE)	Max. clock freq. (MHz)
Grain	128	1857	925.9
MICKEY	128	5039	413.2
Trivium	80	2599	358.4
Better is:		lower	higher

possible, but these do not target mathematical properties of AES, instead of rather a weakness in the way of implementation. It has been proved that it is quite difficult to make AES very adaptable to the constrained platforms since, for instance, implementation of AES with block size of 128 bits utilize 2400 gate equivalents which is quite big.

b.   **PRESENT:** Present is another block cipher designed to be used with limited computational power available (Bogdanov, et al., 2007). It is based on the AES and has very similar operations. The PRESENT is hardware efficient but permutation layer produces large cycles in software. It is one of the leanest lightweight algorithms and has the following features.

   i.   Low gate count and low memory;
   ii.   Level of security commensurate with a 64 bit block size and 80 bit key;
   iii. Implementation requirements similar to many compact stream ciphers.

c.   **RECTANGLE:** An improved version of PRESENT was proposed known as RECTANGLE cipher. The design of RECTANGLE makes use of the bit-slice technique in a lightweight manner, hence to achieve not only a very low cost in hardware but also a very competitive performance in software (Zhang, Bao, Lin, Rijmen, & Yang, 2014). It has the following features.

   i.   Extremely hardware-friendly;
   ii.   Very competitive software speed among the existing lightweight block ciphers due to its bit-slice style;
   iii. Very good security-performance trade off.

d.   **SIMON and SPECK:** These ciphers have been designed by the American National Security Agency (NSA) in June 2013. Both perform exceptionally well across the full spectrum of lightweight applications, but SIMON is tuned for optimal performance in hardware, and SPECK for optimal performance in software. They have advantages as:

   i.   Very simple design and efficient implementation;
   ii.   Open to analysis using the existing techniques.

Unlike all other ciphers' specification, there is no provided security analysis. The NSA has been pushing SIMON and SPECK really hard as standards, but it did not happen. The International Organization for Standardization (ISO) last year decided not to approve these ciphers after expressing concerns that NSA was able to crack the encryption techniques and would thus gain a back door into coded transmissions.

e. **SEA:** Scalable Encryption Algorithm (SEA) is designed for scalable software implementations on constrained devices, being parameterized in text, key and processor size (Standaert, Piret, Gershenfeld, & Quisquater, 2006). It has the following features.

    i. Low memory requirements;

    ii. Small code size;

    iii. Limited instruction set.

f. **KATAN and KTANTAN:** KATAN and KTANTAN are from a family of six block ciphers divided into two groups. The first one, KATAN, is composed of three block ciphers with 32, 48 and 64 bit block size. The second one, KTANTAN, is composed of other three block ciphers with the same block sizes. Besides that, the KTANTAN is more efficient in hardware where the key is burnt into the device and cannot be changed (De Canniere, Dunkelman, & Knezevic, 2009). They have the following features.

    i. Highly compact and minimal size;

    ii. Low power consumption.

A comparison of these block ciphers based on their key sizes, block sizes, consumed area measured in gate equivalents and throughput at 100 kHz (low RFID/WSN applications) is given in Table 3.

3. **Hash Functions:** Hash function is a mathematical algorithm that maps data of arbitrary length to a bit string (a hash) and is designed to be a one-way function, i.e., a function which is infeasible to invert. They can serve many different purposes, within applications ranging from digital signatures and message

Table 3. A comparison of block ciphers

Algorithm	Key size (bits)	Block size (bits)	Area (GE)	Tput at 100 kHz (kbps)
AES	128	128	2400	57
PRESENT	128	64	1339	12
RECTANGLE	128	64	1787	246
SIMON	128	128	1317	23
SPECK	128	128	1396	12
SEA	96	96	3758	103
KATAN	64	80	1054	25
KTANTAN	64	80	688	25
Better is:			lower	higher

authentication codes to secure passwords' storage, key derivation or forensics data identification. Lightweight cryptographic hash functions are responsible for appropriate security mechanisms in lightweight applications. There are a number of lightweight hash functions designed for different applications and requirements with varying security levels. Some of them are QUARK, PHOTON and SPONGENT.

a. **QUARK:** QUARK is a hash function that incorporates design methodologies from two exciting works, Grain – which is a stream cipher and KATAN – which is a block cipher. It uses a sponge construction in order to minimize memory requirements and can be used for message authentication, stream encryption or authenticated encryption. The construction and core algorithm are conformist to the hardware of chips. In addition, Aumasson et al. wanted to create a hash function that fulfills the security and hardware requirements of RFID applications as example for an IoT device (Aumasson, Henzen, Meier, & Naya-Plasencia, 2013).

b. **PHOTON:** PHOTON is a sponge-based, lightweight and hardware-oriented hash function. It is not very performant for big amounts of data because the bitrate is chosen to be very small in order to minimize the memory used. Its design is mostly meant to be used in RFID applications (Jian Guo, Peyrin, & Poschmann, 2011).

c. **SPONGENT:** SPONGENT is a sponge construction based on a wide present type permutation. A design goal for it is to follow hermetic sponge strategy, i.e., no structural distinguishes for the underlying permutation are allowed (Bogdanov, et al., 2011).

A comparison of these hash functions based on their output sizes, consumed area measured in gate equivalents and throughput at 100 kHz (low RFID/WSN applications) is given in Table 4.

Table 4. A comparison of hash functions

Algorithm	Output size (bits)	Area(GE)	Tput at 100 kHz (kbps)
QUARK	128	1379	1.47
PHOTON	80	865	2.82
SPONGENT	128	1060	0.34
Better is:		lower	higher

Asymmetric Lightweight Algorithms for IoT

Unlike symmetric cryptographic algorithms, asymmetric cryptographic algorithms or public key algorithms use a pair of public/private keys. Anyone can encrypt a message under the public key of another party. However, only this latter can decrypt the encrypted data. The major advantage of using public key algorithms is that they provide a secure communication between any two parties previously unknown to each other. Another advantage is that the sender can use its private key to ensure the recipient of his identity, i.e., data can be digitally signed. A disadvantage is the large size of the key which increases the complexity of an algorithm. The position of asymmetric algorithms is clear in conventional Internet. However, it is not the case in the context of IoT because of its expensive encryption and verification operations. In addition, the development and implementation of asymmetric algorithms in IoT have never been stopped. The most common algorithms that continue to reduce the cost of cryptographic operations for constrained environments are ECC and NTRU.

- **RSA:** Rivest-Shamir-Adleman (RSA) is an asymmetric algorithm which is widely used today for creating a secure way to transmit. It is the most common and well-known of all asymmetric algorithms. RSA was developed in 1977 (Rivest, Shamir, & Adleman, 1978). The algorithm is based upon the difficulty of finding the prime factors of a large number. RSA is embedded in the SSL/TLS protocol which is used for secure communication. The currently most used key sizes are 2048 and 4096 bits. Nevertheless, it has been proven that RSA remains inappropriate for constrained devices because they need to process large numbers and long keys to realize sufficient security. In addition, small computing devices will no longer be able to accommodate large keys since key generation, encryption and decryption operations demand high power consumption.
- **ECC:** Elliptic Curve Cryptography (ECC) is performed by doing operations on the algebraic structure of elliptic curves over finite fields. It has been shown that decryption and digital signing can be done significantly faster with ECC than with RSA, and therefore require less computational power. Therefore, to achieve the same level of security as long as the parameters are chosen correctly it requires a smaller key size. In addition, ECC can do the same job with less power. This is the excellent attribute, seeing as so many of the IoT devices have limitations in hardware. Difficulty of the elliptic curve discrete logarithm problem plays a major role in the security of ECC, and this problem can be resolved in exponential time (Koblitz, 1987). ECC is the most attractive family of asymmetric algorithms for embedded environments

attributable to its relatively lower computational requirements and smaller operand lengths.

- **NTRU:** Nth Degree Truncated Polynomial Ring Units (NTRU) is the first asymmetric algorithm not based on factorization or discrete logarithmic problems. It is a lattice-based alternative to RSA and ECC, and it is based on the shortest vector problem in a lattice. It was first presented in 1996 (Hoffstein, Pipher, & Silverman, 1998). The NTRU algorithm offers high speed key generation, encryption and decryption. Indeed, its cryptographic elementary operations require only polynomial multiplications, which are highly efficient and suitable for constrained devices. The security of NTRU is based on finding a short vector in a lattice of high dimension. This is a very hard problem, even in a quantum word. In addition, the NTRU is gaining interest in the electronics industry and makes a promising alternative for the future of asymmetric algorithms.

Checking how secure an algorithm is always required to review it with 'bits of security'. This determines a level of security to compare algorithms with varying key sizes. For instance, AES with 128 bit key length offers 128 bits of security. To achieve this level of security with RSA, ECC and NTRU, we need key sizes of 3072, 256 and 3501 bits respectively (see Table 5). The following table shows the comparison of the key sizes for RSA, ECC and NTRU. Note that the key sizes are also matched with the equivalent level of security symmetric key size.

From Table 5 we notice that ECC has the best key size. At lower security levels RSA has smaller key sizes than NTRU's. But as the security level increases the key size of RSA increases more than NTRU's. In addition, from key size point of view, ECC has the best results although for lower security levels RSA is better than NTRU.

Table 5. A comparison of asymmetric ciphers

Key size (bits)			Security level (bits)
RSA	**ECC**	**NTRU**	
1024	160	2008	80
2048	224	3033	112
3072	256	3501	128
4096	320	4383	160
7680	384	5193	192
15360	521	7690	256

Attacks on Lightweight Algorithms

Security of the any cipher is judged through cryptanalysis. Cryptanalysis aims at finding weaknesses in cryptographic algorithms to breach their security and access the content of any ciphertext. As discussed above, the main challenge in lightweight algorithms is how to balance between low resources requirements in constrained devices, performance and security. IoT is vulnerable to various types of security threats. Attacks are mainly categorized by two types: inside and outside attacks. In an inside attack an adversary consists of attacking nodes by running malicious code in them, while in an outside attack an adversary is not a participant of the network (Christin, Mogre, & Hollick, 2010). Among the attacks that can be mounted on such wireless systems, we have briefly elaborated on a few of them.

- **Physical Attack:** Physical attack deals with the ability of the attacker to gain physical access to the components of IoT device. It gives a number of attacks including destroying or stealing the nodes, removing them from their original locations, inserting malicious code. Tamper proof hardware is sometimes seen as a good option to protect the sensors, but this is expensive and may not be effective against an attacker.
- **Denial of Service (DoS):** Denial of Service attack occurs when attackers use computers to transmit signals in order to interfere with the radio frequencies being used by the network. It leads sensors to retransmit messages indefinitely and render them inoperative by exhausting battery power.
- **Eavesdropping:** Eavesdropping is an outside attack where intruder can choose to passively eavesdrop on the network communication and steal the data. So this is attack on confidentiality. In some cases, the intruder can use advanced techniques to send queries to see what is going on in the network or try to determine the content of the packets in order to gain more information (Anand, et al., 2006).
- **Man In The Middle (MITM):** The MITM is a dangerous attack where the attacker poses as the original sender. As the attacker has the original communication, they can trick the recipient into thinking they are still getting a legitimate message. For instance, we can imagine a scenario where a malicious party may want to fake temperature data from a monitoring device in order to force a piece of machinery to overheat, therefore ceasing production. Since IoT devices are being released with security vulnerabilities and poorly configured WiFi networks, devices will be more easily prone to MITM attacks. This is especially true if the product did not validate the HTTPS certificates of servers it connected to.

SECURITY CHALLENGES IN IOT

Ensuring adequate security in IoT is an ongoing challenge, especially in the area of privacy and confidentiality among heterogeneous management and network capacity constraints. Reliability, economy, efficiency and effectiveness of the security and privacy of IoT are essential for ensuring the fundamental elements of AIC triad: Availability, Integrity and Confidentiality. The IoT security can be classified in the following way.

1. **Security and Data Protection:** The IoT devices are typically connected through the wireless network and may be located in public places. Therefore, they can share sensitive information on the public network and become a target of malicious attacks. A key to ensuring information security in IoT is the using cryptographic algorithms. Unfortunately, many IoT devices are not powerful enough to robust encryption. In addition, the algorithm must not be so heavy that a device with limited computational power cannot run it. And it must also have a sufficient level of security to ensure confidentiality for the users.

2. **Authentication and Identification:** The IoT devices do not have the same role. For instance, in smart home, a security camera and bulbs both must be connected, but they do not have the same role and access specifications. This means that devices should be able to identify other devices and authenticate them. Identification can be either by being part of a certain class or by unique identification. Identification is important challenge in IoT. In addition, there are raised some questions such as: Should each device have an address every moment? What is the best scheme for identification all devices in IoT?

3. **Privacy:** The significant growth of the IoT has showed during recent years the fact that devices at the moment do not offer all desired warranties, especially user privacy. The privacy issue in IoT is wider than mere data protection since it encompasses the protection of a private sphere including important and sensitive data of an authorized user. On the other hand, collecting, transmitting and using the sensitive information increases the attack surface of privacy leak. Therefore, how to offers an attractive trade-off between sensitive information utility and privacy is a great challenge for the academic community.

CONCLUSION AND FUTURE RESEARCH DIRECTIONS

In this chapter we made an attempt to provide an analysis for cryptographic algorithms in IoT. Current cryptographic systems exploits the strengths of both symmetric and asymmetric algorithms. Symmetric algorithms are preferred when confidentiality is required because they are faster than asymmetric. Moreover, symmetric algorithms usually use smaller keys than asymmetric. On the other hand, asymmetric algorithms provide non-repudiation. Some cryptographic algorithms are vulnerable to some kinds of attack, which has been described in the chapter. It is very important to develop more secure and lightweight encryption algorithm that have a smaller key size, fast processing, smaller gate equivalents and higher throughput. In addition, implementations of lightweight algorithms should withstand all known forms of attacks since lightweight cryptography is not meant to be the weakest link in the security system. Nevertheless, there are remaining open questions we still need help to figure out

1.   Which type of network architecture is best suited for the future of IoT?
2.   Should the symmetric lightweight encryption algorithm PRESENT replace AES in such a setting?
3.   Is the asymmetric lightweight encryption algorithm ECC more suitable for IoT devices than RSA?

ACKNOWLEDGMENT

This research was supported by the Slovenian Research Agency (research program P2-0037).

REFERENCES

Agren, M., Hell, M., Johansson, T., & Meier, W. (2011). Grain-128a: A new version of Grain-128 with optional authentication. *International Journal of Wireless and Mobile Computing*, 5(1), 48–59. doi:10.1504/IJWMC.2011.044106

Anand, M., Cronin, E., Sherr, M., Blaze, M. A., Ives, Z. G., & Lee, I. (2006). Sensor network security: more interesting than you think. In *1st USENIX Workshop on Hot Topics in Security*. USENIX Association.

Asadullah, M., & Raza, A. (2016). An overview of home automation systems. In *2nd International Conference on Robotics and Artificial Intelligence (ICRAI)* (pp. 27-31). Rawalpindi, Pakistan: IEEE.

Aumasson, J. P., Henzen, L., Meier, W., & Naya-Plasencia, M. (2013). Quark: A lightweight hash. *Journal of Cryptology*, 26(2), 313–339. doi:10.100700145-012-9125-6

Babbage, S., & Dodd, M. (2008). The MICKEY stream ciphers. In M. Robshaw & O. Billet (Eds.), *New stream cipher designs*. Berlin: Springer. doi:10.1007/978-3-540-68351-3_15

Bogdanov, A., Knezevic, M., Leander, G., Toz, D., Varici, K., & Verbauwhede, I. (2011). SPONGENT: A lightweight hash function. In *International Workshop on Cryptographic Hardware and Embedded Systems* (pp. 312-325). Berlin: Springer.

Bogdanov, A., Knudsen, L., Leander, G., Paar, C., Poschmann, A., Robshaw, M., . . . Vikkelsoe, C. (2007). PRESENT: An ultra-lightweight block cipher. In *International Workshop on Cryptographic Hardware and Embedded Systems* (pp. 450-466). Vienna, Austria: Springer.

Bozdogan, Z., & Kara, R. (2015). Layered model architecture for internet of things. *Jouranl of Engineering Research and Applied Science*, *4*(1), 260–264.

Christin, D., Mogre, D. S., & Hollick, M. (2010). Survey on wireless sensor network technologies for industrial automation: The security and quality of service perspectives. *Future Internet*, *2*(2), 96–125. doi:10.3390/fi2020096

De Canniere, C., Dunkelman, O., & Knezevic, M. (2009). KATAN and KTANTAN - A family of small and efficient hardware-oriented block ciphers. In *International Workshop on Cryptographic Hardware and Embedded Systems* (pp. 272-288). Berlin: Springer. 10.1007/978-3-642-04138-9_20

De Canniere, C., & Preneel, B. (2008). Trivium specifications. In M. Robshaw, & O. Billet (Eds.), New Stream Cipher Designs. Springer.

Deng, J., Han, R., & Mishra, S. (2006). Countermeasures against traffic analysis attacks in wireless sensor networks. In *First International Conference on Security and Privacy for Emerging Areas in Communications Networks* (pp. 113-126). Athens, Greece: IEEE.

Farooq, M. U., Waseem, M., Khairi, A., & Mazhar, S. (2015). A critical analysis on the security concerns of Internet of Things. *International Journal of Computers and Applications*, *111*(7), 1–6. doi:10.5120/19547-1280

Ghosh, R., Pragathi, R., Ullas, S., & Borra, S. (2017). Intelligent transportation systems: A survey. In *International Conference on Circuits, Controls, and Communications* (pp. 160-165). Bangalore, India: IEEE.

Guo, J. J., Peyrin, T., & Poschmann, A. (2011). The PHOTON family of lightweight hash functions. In *Annual Cryptology Conference* (pp. 222-239). Berlin: Springer. 10.1007/978-3-642-22792-9_13

Hatzivasilis, G., Fysarakisloannis, K., Papaefstathiou, I., & Manifavas, C. (2018). A review of lightweight block ciphers. *Journal of Cryptographic Engineering, 8*(2), 141–184. doi:10.100713389-017-0160-y

Hell, M., Johansson, T., & Meier, W. (2007). Grain - A stream cipher for constrained environments. *International Journal of Wireless and Mobile Computing, 2*(1), 86–93. doi:10.1504/IJWMC.2007.013798

Hoffstein, J., Pipher, J., & Silverman, J. H. (1998). NTRU: A ring-based public key cryptosystem. In *International Algorithmic Number Theory Symposium* (pp. 267-288). Berlin: Springer-Verlag. 10.1007/BFb0054868

Jerkins, J. A. (2017). Motivating a market or regulatory solution to IoT insecurity with the Mirai botnet code. In *7th Annual Computing and Communication Workshop and Conference*. Las Vegas, NV: IEEE. 10.1109/CCWC.2017.7868464

Jin, Y., Tomoishi, M., & Yamai, N. (2017). A secure and lightweight IoT device remote monitoring and control mechanism using DNS. In *41st Annual Computer Software and Applications Conference* (pp. 282-283). Turin, Italy: IEEE. 10.1109/COMPSAC.2017.33

Khan, R., Khan, S. U., Zaheer, R., & Khan, S. (2012). Future Internet: The Internet of Things Architecture, Possible Applications and Key Challenges. In *10th International Conference on Frontiers of Information Technology* (pp. 257-260). Islamabad, India: IEEE. 10.1109/FIT.2012.53

Koblitz, N. (1987). Elliptic curve cryptosystems. *Mathematics of Computation, 48*(177), 203–209. doi:10.1090/S0025-5718-1987-0866109-5

Kumar, H., & Singh, A. (2016). Internet of Things: A comprehensive analysis and security implementation through elliptic curve cryptography. *International Journal of Current Engineering and Technology, 6*(2), 498–502.

Li, N., Liu, D., & Nepal, S. (2017). Lightweight mutual authentication for IoT and its applications. *IEEE Transactions on Sustainable Computing, 2*(4), 359–370. doi:10.1109/TSUSC.2017.2716953

Mashal, I., Alsaryrah, O., Chung, T. Y., Yang, C. Z., Kuo, W. H., & Agrawal, D. P. (2015). Choices for interaction with things on Internet and underlying isssues. *Ad Hoc Networks, 28*, 68–90. doi:10.1016/j.adhoc.2014.12.006

Pang, Z., Chen, O., Tian, J., Zheng, L., & Dubrova, E. (2013). Ecosystem analysis in the design of open platform-based in home healthcare terminals towards the internet-of-things. In *15th International Conference on Advanced Communications Technology* (pp. 529-534). PyeongChang, South Korea: IEEE.

Perera, C., Zaslavsky, A., Christen, P., & Georakopoulus, D. (2013). Context aware computing for the Internet of Things: A survey. *IEEE Communications Surveys and Tutorials, 16*(1), 414–454. doi:10.1109/SURV.2013.042313.00197

Rivest, R., Shamir, A., & Adleman, L. (1978). A method for obtaining digital signatures and public-key cryptosystems. *Communications of the ACM, 21*(2), 120–126. doi:10.1145/359340.359342

Roman, R., Zhou, J., & Lopez, J. (2013). On the features and challenges of security and privacy in distributed internet of things. *Computer Networks, 57*(10), 2266–2279. doi:10.1016/j.comnet.2012.12.018

Said, O., & Masud, M. (2013). Towards internet of things: Survey and future vision. *International Journal of Computer Networks, 5*(1), 1–17.

Sinha, A., Kumar, P., Rana, N., Islam, R., & Dwivedi, Y. (2017). Impact of internet of things (IoT) in disaster management: A task-technology fit perspective. *Annals of Operations Research*, 1–36.

Slama, D., Puhlmann, F., Morrish, J., & Bhatnagar, R. (2015). Enterprise IoT. Strategies and best practices for connected products and services. Sebastopol, CA: O'Reilly Media.

Standaert, F. X., Piret, G., Gershenfeld, N., & Quisquater, J. J. (2006). SEA: A scalable encryption algorithm for small embedded applications. In *International Conference on Smart Card Research and Advanced Applications* (pp. 222-236). Berlin: Springer. 10.1007/11733447_16

Thingom, I. (2015). Internet of Things: design of a new layered architecture and study of some exisiting issues. *IOSR Journal of Computer Engineering*, 26-30.

Zhang, W., Bao, Z., Lin, D., Rijmen, V., & Yang, B. (2014). RECTANGLE: A bit-slice ultra-lightweight block cipher suitable for multiple platforms. *Cryptology ePrint Archive*. Retrieved from https://eprint.iacr.org/2014/084.pdf

KEY TERMS AND DEFINITIONS

Cryptographic Algorithms: A cryptographic algorithm or cipher is a mathematical function used in the encryption and decryption process. Changing plaintext to ciphertext is known as encryption, whereas changing ciphertext to plaintext is known as decryption.

Heterogeneous Environment: Using hardware and system software from different vendors. Organizations often use computers, operating systems and databases from a variety of vendors.

IoT Architecture: An approach of how the various elements (such as sensors, actuators, gateways, mobility applications) should be designed and integrated to each other, so as to robustly deliver a service delivery network, which can serve the needs for future.

IoT Device: An IoT device is any nonstandard computing device that connects wirelessly to network and has the ability to transmit data.

Layer: In computer programming, layering is the organization of programming into separate functional components that interact in some sequential and hierarchical way such that each layer usually has the ability to interface only to the layer above it and the layer below it.

Non-Repudiation: Non-repudiation is the assurance that someone cannot deny the validity of something. In other words, it makes very difficult to successfully deny who (or where) a message came from as well as the authenticity of that message.

System Security: An objective of system security is the protection of information and property from theft, corruption and other types of damage, while allowing the information and property to remain accessible and productive. For instance, system security includes the use of a firewall, data encryption, passwords and biometrics.

Trade-Off: A trade-off is a situation in which the achieving of something you want involves the loss of something else which is also desirable, but less so.

Chapter 6
Smart Accident Detection and Prevention System (SADPS)

Jeyabharathi D.
Sri Krishna College of Technology, India

Kesavaraja D.
Dr. Sivanthi Aditanar College of Engineering, India

Sasireka D.
V. V. College of Engineering, India

Barkath Nisha S.
Sri Krishna College of Technology, India

ABSTRACT

The two objectives of the smart accident detection and prevention system (SADPS) are 1) accident prevention and 2) accident detection. Based on the survey, 1.3 million people die every year due to roadway accidents. The main reason for this type of accident is speeding. So, the proposed SADPS focused on finding the speed parameters of each vehicle and giving notification to speeding vehicles through SMS that can be used to prevent accidents. The second objective is accident detection. For this task, each vehicle accelerometer values will be taken by the SADPS system. When an accident occurs, the location as well as the related details are sent to the SADPS system. This proposed system takes the immediate remedy by alerting the nearby police station and hospitals. Proposed SADPS also acts as a video surveillance and monitoring system. Automatic background subtraction and object tracking is done with the help of novel approaches.

DOI: 10.4018/978-1-5225-7811-6.ch006

INTRODUCTION

IoT Based Accident Detection and Prevention

Due to traffic hazards and road accidents, the life of the people went under risk. This is because of the lack of best emergency facilities available in our country.

To improve this, there is a need for alert the emergency services to get the accident information as soon as possible when an accident is occurring. Overspeed of the vehicle is a main reason for accidents. To save people lives, IOT based accident detection and prevention is an essential one.

The Internet of Things (IoT) is an arrangement of interrelated computing gadgets, mechanical and digital machines, objects, animals or individuals that are given one kind of an identifiers and the capacity to exchange information over a system without requiring human to human or human.

Using IoT technique automatic accident detection and prevention system can be built. In the proposed system without using sensor automatic vehicle detection and tracking is done. For accident detection and prevention purpose IOT sensor is used.

Vision Based Vehicle Detection and Tracking

Background Subtraction (BS) plays an important role in video surveillance system because it provides a focus of attention for moving object detection. Even though numerous background subtraction algorithms have been proposed in the literature, the issue of distinguishing moving objects in challenging scenarios such as dynamic backgrounds and illumination variation is still far from being totally solved. The proposed background subtraction approaches create an accurate and adaptive background model with the help of key frame selection strategy and symmetry-based subspace construction process. So, it can handle the challenges prevailing with respect to background subtraction.

Object tracking is also one of the challenging tasks in the field of computer vision. Tracking can be defined as the problem of estimating the trajectory of an object in the image plane as it moves around the scene. The main problem prevailing even now in object tracking is occlusion handling. The proposed trackers utilize diagonal directional derivatives to extract unique features from each object capable of handling occlusion and partial occlusion successfully.

With respect to further analysis of the tracked object, in traffic video surveillance system, the speed of the vehicle has to be estimated. Vehicle speed measurement system uses sensors to measure the speed of the vehicles. It is more expensive. The proposed system estimates the speed of each vehicle from the video footage. Hence it provides a cheaper solution than other existing mechanisms and is well suited for real-time applications.

Objective

The main objective of the proposed system is twofold:

- The main objective is to identify the overspeeding vehicle as well to detect accident and find out the location for accident to take remedy.
- The secondary objective of the proposed system is to develop novel approaches for background subtraction and tracking. The objective of the proposed background subtraction approaches is to create an accurate and adaptive background model suitable for real-time environment.

Contribution of the Book Chapter

The following are the contribution of this book chapter:

- Raspberry Pi3 sensor and Arduino Uno sensor can be used to detect and prevent accident.
- Highlighted Point Tristate Pattern (HPTP) is proposed for both background subtraction and object tracking. Most highlighted point from each spatio-temporal block is taken to create an accurate background model. So the computational complexity is reduced greatly.
- Proposed invariant Tristate pattern can be used to give an accurate object detection process.

Outline of the Chapter

The rest of this thesis is organized as follows.

Section 2 discusses the previous works related to accident detection and prevention, background subtraction, feature extraction and object tracking. Section 3 discusses the working process of the proposed system. . Also it, gives details about the proposed feature descriptors HPTP. Section 4 presents the implementation of the proposed approach and the experimental results. Section 5 presents conclusion and also presents future directions for research.

RELATED WORKS

A detailed survey on previous works on Accident detection and prevention mechanism, object detection and tracking is made in this chapter, and the problems associated with these approaches are highlighted.

IoT Based Accident Detection and Prevention

IoT based accident detection is an enormous technology. White et al. focussed on utilizing the smart phone for accident discovery and notification (Chen et.al, 2009). Zhao et.al (2009) have proposed accident management system based on location awareness on cellular devices, and utilising this for smarter accident monitoring systems in cars.

Desima et al have proposed a tool that detect fire and collision. This tool make use of MQ-135 sensor detects smoke, the fire sensor detects a fire and push button detects a collision. In addition to this tool also features GSM SIM800L module to provide information to the security agency.

Hossain et al. have proposed drowsy detection system for the prevention of road accidents. The proposed system used the eye closure ratio as input parameter to detect the drowsiness of the driver. If the eye closure ratio deteriorates from the standard ratio, the driver is alerted with the help of a buzzer. For our system, a Pi camera is used to capture the images of the driver's eye and the entire system is incorporated using Raspberry-Pi.

Umetani et al have describes a method for the detection of changes in sleeping conditions using multipoint ambient sensing for safety and amenity in the sleep environment. This method continuously detects changes during sleep, such as the movements of the person and bedding based on the measurement of acceleration, temperature and humidity of the comforter. Through the measurement of these ambient conditions, this system improves sleep quality and prevents accidents, such as falling off the bed.

Background Subtraction, Feature Extraction and Object Tracking

Jeyabharathi et al. (2017) have proposed new feature descriptor for background subtraction named as Diagonal Hexadecimal Pattern (DHP). This proposed feature descriptors encodes the relationship between the center pixel and its neighbours based on the directional that are calculated using diagonal directive. To overcome the limitation in these feature descriptors, the work is extended with the help of symmetrical pattern as well as key frame. This extended feature descriptor is named as Extended Symmetrical-Diagonal Hexadecimal Pattern.

Jeyabharathi et al. (2018) have proposed Reflectional Symmetry Pattern (RSP) for background subtraction. RSP is based on the assumption that the geometric reflectional symmetrical pattern of each of the objects (person) is much lower than the surrounding background. Reflectional symmetrical texture pattern can be used to create a subspace from the result of frame differencing approach.

Jeyabharathi et al. (2018) have proposed cut set based dynamic key frame selection process to select the key frame accurately. Adaptively change the layer for each background model. So, accurate background model is created to improve the accuracy in object detection.

Object Tracking

Object tracking is a process of locating objects in each frame. The main difficult task in object tracking is the representation of object, to do this task different approaches are proposed such as color histogram, (Li 2008) image features (Collins and Liu 2001).

Pu et al. (2011) have uses sobel operator and color features to track the object. The main limitation for this approach is, this method fail to track objects at the time of occlusion.

Lu et al. (2012) have proposed an object tracking approach based on contours. The object rough area is discovered utilizing multi-feature fusion methodology. For precise and solid object contour tracking, they have removed the contours with the assistance of region-based object contour extraction. In their model, the object's rough area is gotten by color histogram and Harris corner features fusion method. In the molecule filer method, they have used the Harris corner feature fusion methodology. Their model of region-based transient differencing is associated in object contour detection step; furthermore, the resultant is the rough area tracking result.

Kim et al. (2011) have proposed the methods that are based on motion information in the background scenario. In this approach, motion direction is predicted based on the arrangement of points. That is named as Shape Control Points (SCPs). The main logic for this concept is, it consider similar objects have same motion direction.

Jeyabharathi et al. (2017, 2018) have proposed new feature descriptor for tracking. These new feature descriptors are based on diagonal derivative. Sixteen directional codes are generated using turning point texture features. These genuine turning point texture invariant features are more appropriate to preserve a statistical representation of the scene and can thus tolerate both global and local illumination changes. It is also more stable against noise because uniform patterns can be used to reduce the noise in DHP histogram as well as symmetrical patterns can be used to reduce noise in ES-DHP.

Feature-based tracking method for detecting vehicles can be used to track objects effectively under challenging conditions such as more congestion, shadows and lighting transition. Instead of tracking entire vehicles, vehicle features are tracked to make the method robust to partial occlusion. Under varying lighting conditions also the system is fully functional because most significant features are used for tracking purpose. So, the proposed system relies on feature-based tracking method.

Feature Extraction

In (Guyon & Elisseeff 2003), variable elimination strategies are extensively grouped into filter and wrapper techniques. Filter strategies go about as pre-processing to rank the features wherein the much positioned features are chosen and connected to the predictor. In wrapper techniques, the feature determination standard is the execution of the predictor, i.e. the predictor is wrapped on a hunt calculation which will discover a subset which gives the highest predictor execution. Embedded methods (Guyon & Elisseeff 2003), (Blum and Langley 1997) incorporate variable determination as a component of the preparation procedure without parting the information into preparing and testing sets. In this paper, supervised learning algorithms are used for feature selection.

Motivation

From the observation, immediate recovery when accident occur as well as accident prevention is more essential factor,

For this the chapter contributions are,

- Using accelerometer sensor the speed of the over speeding vehicles are calculated. Once overspeed is calculated then give the alert to the vehicle with the help of Arduino Uno sensor.
- Using Vibration sensor accidents are detected and with the help of Raspberry Pi3 immediate remedies are taken.

After reviewing the related literature of background subtraction and object tracking, it is observed that detecting the object in a video sequence and also tracking an object is a really challenging task. Object detection and tracking can be a time-consuming process due to the amount of data that is contained in the video.

From the literature survey it is found that the main issues with background subtraction and object tracking are:

- High computational complexity is reported for both object detection and tracking
- Background model should be adaptively changed due to scene variation so as to properly classify the foreground object and background thus removing false alarm.
- Background model should be adaptively changed to cope within the varying levels of illumination at different times of the day.
- In object tracking, occlusion is still a challenging task.

The proposed system is developed to address all these issues.

PROPOSED APPROACH

SADPS system has Three main steps i) Accident prevention and Accident detection ii) Object (vehicle) detection (iii) Object (vehicle) Tracking

Accident Prevention and Accident Detection

Both accident detection and prevention is achieved using IoT sensors. Accident detection is found out with the help of Raspberry Pi3 sensor and the overspeeding vehicle is determined with the help of Arduino Uno sensor.

Raspberry Pi3 Sensor for Accident Detection

Proposed SADPS system used Raspberry Pi3 sensor to detect accidents. If any obstacle is found then the vibration sensor sent interrupt to the SADPS system. SADPS system applies the algorithm to process the sensor signal and send the geographic location along with some ancillary information to the control room, indicating accident occurrence. The proposed architecture for accident detection is shown in Figure 1.

Arduino Uno Sensor for Accident Prevention

For accident prevention, over speeding vehicles are determined with the help of speed parameters and gps and give the alert to the driver to prevent accidents. Arduino Uno sensor is used to determine. Once over speeding vehicle is found then the immediate message is given to the corresponding owner of the vehicle. That can be used to avoid accidents. It is shown in Figure 2.

Figure 1. Accident detection

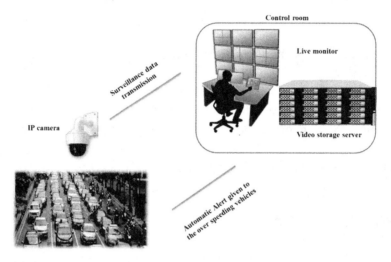

Figure 2. Accident Prevention

Working Process for Accident Detection

Vibration sensor which is a device that measures obstacle in the vehicle. Once obstacle is encountered then it will send the signal to Raspberry Pi3. Raspberry Pi3 is connected with GPRS (General Packet Radio Device), which is a packet oriented mobile data service on the 2G and 3G cellular communication system's global system for mobile communication. It is used to transfer the data to nearby police station or ambulance along with location of vehicle.

Working Process for Accident Prevention

The unlimited speed of vehicle is a main reason for traffic accidents. With the help of accelerometer sensor which is a device that measures the proper acceleration, that the sudden changes in the axes of the vehicle is detected. If the speed of the vehicle increases above the limited level, then it will send the signal to Arduino UNO. An interfacing circuit is connected between accelerometer sensor and Arduino to transfer the signal.

Object (Vehicle) Detection

Object detection is achieved using proposed feature descriptor: Highlighted Point Tristate Pattern (HPTP). For every two frames in a video, Highlighted Point Tristate Pattern (HPTP) has to be generated for each spatio-temporal block. Highlighted Point Tristate patterns are i) High Intensity pixel ii) Low Intensity pixel iii) Random pixel. Tristate patterns from each 4×4 size of spatio-temporal blocks are grouped, and then it is given to the input of Exponential Regression Model.

This model can be used to find out the similarity within the spatio-temporal blocks and the similarity between the spatio-temporal blocks. So, it predicts temporal relationship between the blocks in every two frames.

Finally, two parameters are created that are Appearance Similarity (AS), Temporal Coherence (TC). Grouping of those parameters in a spatio-temporal block is act as an initial background model.

Highlighted Point Tristate Pattern (HPTP)

Highlighted Point Tristate Pattern is generated for the first two 4×4 size of spatio-temporal blocks. The pattern takes high intensity pixel value, low intensity pixel value and one random value from each spatio-temporal block in the first two frames.

The comparison between high intensity value in the successinve two spatio-temporal blocks and low intensity value between successive two spatio-temporal blocks can be used to predict the accurate motion changes in background. The third point in the tristate pattern is random point selection so that also used to predict the intermediate motion changes in the two blocks. The accurate and invariant background model is achieved using these three points. That is the reason why this tristate pattern is taken for object detection.

Every three points in the spatio-temporal blocks are grouped together to form of the subspace. Exponential Regression Model is applied to the subspace. The output of the Exponential Regression Model have two parameters, one is used to denote the similarity within the spatio-temporal blocks that is named as Appearance Similarity

(AS) and another one parameter that can be used to find out the similarity between the spatio-temporal blocks that is named as Temporal Coherence (TC). This parameters can be used to find out the motion information between the successive frames.

These two parameters in every spatio-temporal block are grouped together that is called background model. This background model is act as a background model for the first two frames. Then the background model updating is done for every node.

Update Background Model

Background model updating is done using the parameters Temporal Coherence (TC).

There is no need for updating the parameter Appearance Similarity (AS).

Object (Vehicle) Tracking

Unique identification of target objects is necessary to track the vehicle in a video. Feature vector for every moving object is extracted using the proposed feature descriptor HPTP from the background subtracted video.

Each object in the first frame is considered as a target objects. Target object's location is predicted and its corresponding features are extracted using the proposed HPTP descriptor. That is each object is represented by it HPTP feature. In the subsequent frames, candidates are defined and are represented by their corresponding HPTP features. Tracking procedure starts with the calculation of distance between feature vector of the target objects and candidate objects in the next frame. Based on minimum distance each object is tracked.

EXPERIMENTAL RESULTS

The experimental analysis of both object detection and tracking in terms of qualitative and quantitative is given in below section.

Object Detection

In this section, a few trial comes about have been exhibited which can cover the efficiency and accuracy of the proposed background subtraction strategy. The execution of HPTP are assessed against five most generally utilized foundation subtraction procedures GMM, MOG, XCS-LBP, Bayesian Histogram, Sigma-Delta Z and in addition with a standout amongst the latest method CS-STLTP.

The F-Score value is high for HPTP when compared to other techniques. Results are arranged in Table 1. The observation from that, the proposed HPTP give the high F-score value because it exactly provide the accurate background model because tristate pattern is generated based on motion direction from every spatio-temporal blocks in each frame.

CONCLUSION

Proposed SADPS system is used to detect accident and prevent accident with the help of IOT sensors such as Arduino Uno sensor, Raspberry Pi3. Unlimited speed

Table 1. Performance analysis based on F-score

Sequences	GMM(Stauffer et.al, 1999)	MoG(Power et.al 2002)	XCS-LBP(Yan et.al, 2017)	Sigma-Delta Z	Bayesian Histogram	CS-STLTP (Jeyabharathi et.al, 2009)	Proposed method
PETS Dataset							
Seq 1:WS	0.3212	0.3908	0.4578	0.5691	0.6201	0.8809	0.8803
Seq 2:AF	0.3101	0.4673	0.4601	0.5200	0.6197	0.8471	0.8480
Seq 3:WC	0.3875	0.5009	0.5271	0.5826	0.6423	0.7502	0.8075
Seq 4:SM	0.3409	0.4998	0.5198	0.5421	0.5822	0.7623	0.7903
Seq 5:AP	0.3423	0.5291	0.5291	0.5312	0.5621	0.7509	0.8042
Seq 6:BS	0.2892	0.4712	0.4712	0.4821	0.5012	0.5712	0.5902
Seq 7: Loppy	0.2513	0.4527	0.3527	0.4011	0.4402	0.5829	0.6511
Seq 8: Restaurant	0.2791	0.4232	0.4502	0.4710	0.4900	0.6231	0.7011
Seq 9: Counter	0.3012	0.4110	0.4702	0.5019	0.5120	0.5900	0.6409
Seq 10: Forum	0.3912	0.3841	0.4832	0.5201	0.5300	0.6101	0.6398
Seq 11: ATM	0.4265	0.4701	0.4766	0.5545	0.5987	0.5871	0.6710
Seq 12: Lift	0.4109	0.4690	0.4912	0.5844	0.6011	0.6109	0.6956
BMC Dataset							
Seq _001	0.5278	0.6124	0.6324	0.5901	0.6276	0.8102	0.8656
Seq _002	0.5201	0.6301	0.6423	0.6302	0.6300	0.8012	0.8423
Seq _003	0.5400	0.6587	0.6587	0.6490	0.6512	0.8154	0.8477
Seq _004	0.5512	0.6623	0.6623	0.6499	0.6710	0.8423	0.8432
Seq 005	0.5730	0.6219	0.6420	0.6511	0.6932	0.8322	0.8300
1.1 Institut für Algorithmen und Kognitive Systeme Traffic sequence							
Seq 1:Durlacher-Tor	0.3890	0.4011	0.4200	0.6091	0.6299	0.6324	0.7634
Seq 2: Ettlinger-Tor	0.3912	0.4010	0.4512	0.5932	0.6300	0.6291	0.7723
Seq 3: Taxi	0.4210	0.4587	0.4635	0.5910	0.6012	0.6120	0.7532

is detected with the help of accelerometer sensor. That can be used to give an alert to the vehicles which are exceeded the normal speed. Using vibration sensor which is attached to Raspberry Pi3, that can be used to detect accidents and immediate remedies are taken.

This chapter also gives the full idea about object detection and tracking mechanism. A novel approach Highlighted Point Tristate Pattern (HPTP) is used to detect as well as track the vehicles. Accuracy of the proposed work is compared with other existing works in terms of F-score.

REFERENCES

Bouwmans, T. (2011). Recent Advanced Statistical Background Modeling for Foreground Detection: A Systematic Survey. *Recent Patents on Computer Science*, *4*(3), 147–176.

Brutze, S., Hoferlin, B., & Heidemann, G. (2011). Evaluation of background subtraction techniques for video surveillance. *IEEE Conference on Computer Vision and Pattern Recognition (CVPR)*, 1937–1944.

Burlina, P., & Chellappa, R. (1998). Temporal analysis of motion in video sequences through predictive operators. *International Journal of Computer Vision*, *28*(2), 175–192. doi:10.1023/A:1008067101494

Chen, Q., Sun, Q. S., Heng, P. A., & Xia, S. (2010). Two-Stage Object Tracking Method Based on Kernel and Active Contour. IEEE Transactions on Circuits and Systems for Video Technology, 605-609. doi:10.1109/TCSVT.2010.2041819

Chen, T. (2009). Object Tracking Based on Active Contour Model by Neural Fuzzy Network. *IITA International Conference on Control Automation and Systems Engineering*, 570-574. 10.1109/CASE.2009.165

Cheung, G. K. M., Kanade, T., Bouguet, J. Y., & Holler, M. (2000). *Real time system for robust 3 D voxel reconstruction of human motions*. CVPR. doi:10.1109/CVPR.2000.854944

Cheung, S. C., & Kamath, C. (2004). Robust techniques for background subtraction in urban traffic video. *Video Communications and Image Processing*, *5308*(1), 881–892.

Collins, R., & Liu, Y. (2001). Online Selection of Discriminative Tracking Feature. *IEEE Transactions on Pattern Analysis and Machine Intelligence*, *27*(10), 1631–1643. doi:10.1109/TPAMI.2005.205 PMID:16237997

Comaniciu, D., Ramesh, V., & Meer, P. (2000). Real time tracking of non-rigid objects using mean shift. *IEEE Conference on Computer Vision and Pattern Recognition (CVPR '00)*, 2, 142-149. 10.1109/CVPR.2000.854761

Comaniciu, D., Ramesh, V., & Meer, P. (2003). Kernal Based Object Tracking. *IEEE Transactions on Pattern Analysis and Machine Intelligence*, 25(5), 564–577. doi:10.1109/TPAMI.2003.1195991

Cucchiara, R., Grana, C., Neri, G., Piccardi, M., & Prati, A. (2001). The sakbot system for moving object detection and tracking. *European Workshop on Advanced Video-Based Surveillance Systems*, 171, 159.

Cucchiara, R., Grana, C., Piccardi, M., & Prati, A. (2003). Detecting moving objects, ghosts, and shadows in video streams. *IEEE Transactions on Pattern Analysis and Machine Intelligence*, 25(10), 1337–1347. doi:10.1109/TPAMI.2003.1233909

Danelljan, M., Khan, F. S., Felsberg, M., & Weijer, J. V. D. (2014). *Adaptive Color Attributes for Real-Time Visual Tracking*. CVPR. doi:10.1109/CVPR.2014.143

Desima, M., Ramli, P., Ramdani, D., & Rahman, S. (2017). Alarm system to detect the location of IOT-based public vehicle accidents. *International Conference on Computing, Engineering, and Design (ICCED)*, 1 – 5. 10.1109/CED.2017.8308118

Elgammal, A., Harwood, D., & Davis, L. (2000). Non-parametric Model for Background Subtraction. *European Conference on Computer Vision*, 2, 751-767.

Elgammal, A., Harwood, D., & Davis, L. (2004). *Non-parametric model for background subtraction* (Vol. 4). IEEE FRAME-RATE Workshop, Springe on Systems, Man and Cybernetics.

Hossain, M. D., & George, F. (2018). IOT Based Real-Time Drowsy Driving Detection System for the Prevention of Road Accidents. In International Conference on Intelligent Informatics and Biomedical Sciences (Vol. 3, pp. 190–195). ICIIBMS. http://i21www.ira.uka.de/image_sequences

James, M., Stephen, J., & Anthony, D. (2000). Visual surveillance for moving vehicles. *International Journal of Computer Vision*, 37(2), 187–197. doi:10.1023/A:1008155721192

Jeyabharathi, D., & Dejey, D (2016). A novel Rotational Symmetry Dynamic Texture (RSDT) based sub space construction and SCD (Similar-Congruent-Dissimilar) based scoring model for background subtraction in real time videos. *Multimedia Tools and Applications*, 75(16), 1-29. doi:). doi:10.100711042-016-3772-9

Jeyabharathi, D., & Dr Dejey, D. (2016). Vehicle Tracking and Speed Measurement System (VTSM) Based on Novel Feature Descriptor: Diagonal Hexadecimal Pattern (DHP). *International Journal of Visual Communication and Image Representation, 40*, 816–830. doi:10.1016/j.jvcir.2016.08.011

Jeyabharathi, D., & Dr Dejey, D. (2018). Cut set-based Dynamic Key frame selection and Adaptive Layer-based Background Modeling for Background Subtraction. *Journal of Visual Communication and Image Representation, 55*, 434–446. doi:10.1016/j.jvcir.2018.06.024

Jeyabharathi, D., & Dr Dejey, D. (2018). Efficient background subtraction for thermal images using reflectional symmetry pattern (RSP). *Multimedia Tools and Applications, 77*(17), 22567–22586. doi:10.100711042-018-6220-1

Kastrinaki, V., Zervakis, M., & Kalaitzakis, K. (2003). A survey of video processing techniques for traffic applications. *Image and Vision Computing, 21*(4), 359–381. doi:10.1016/S0262-8856(03)00004-0

Over, P., Awad, G., & Fiscus, J. (2009). *Goals, Tasks, Data, Evaluation Mechanisms and Metrics* (Vol. 16). TRECVID-NIST.

Power, P., & Schoonees, J. (2002). Understand background mixture models for foreground Segmentation. *Proc. Image and Vision Computing*, 267–271.

Stauffer & Grimson. (1999). Adaptive background mixture models for real-time tracking. *Proc. IEEE Conf. CVPR*, 2246–2252.

Takahashi, M., Kawai, Y., Fujii, M., Shibata, M., Babaguchi, N., & Satoh, S. (2009). *NHK STRL at TRECVID 2009: Surveillance Event Detection and High-Level Feature Extraction* (Vol. 17). TRECVID.

Umetani, T., Ishii, M., Tamura, Y., & Saiwaki, N. (2018). Change Detection of Sleeping Conditions based on Multipoint Ambient Sensing of Comforter on Bed. *40th Annual International Conference of the IEEE Engineering in Medicine and Biology Society (EMBC)*, 4997 - 5001. 10.1109/EMBC.2018.8513477

Yan, C., Xie, H., Yang, D., Yin, Y., & Zhang, Q. (2017). Supervised hash coding with deep neural network for environment perception of intelligent vehicles. *IEEE Transactions on Intelligent Transportation Systems*, 1–12.

Yokoi, K., & Watanabe. (2009). Surveillance Event Detection Task. *TRECVID, 17*.

Zhang, T., Ghanem, B., Liu, S., & Ahuja, N. (2013). Robust visual tracking vis structured multi-task spare learning. *International Journal of Computer Vision, 101*(2), 367–383. doi:10.100711263-012-0582-z

Zhao, G., Barnard, M., & Pietikainen, M. (2009). Lipreading with local spatial temporal descriptor. *IEEE Transactions on Multimedia, 11*(7), 1254–1265. doi:10.1109/TMM.2009.2030637

Zhao, T., & Nevatia, R. (2004). Tracking Multiple Humans in Crowed Environment. *IEEE Computer Society Conference on Computer Vision and Pattern Recognition (CVPR'04), 2, 406.*

Zhao, Y., Gong, H., Lin, L., & Jia, Y. (2008). *Spatio-temporal patches for night background modeling by subspace learning.* IEEE ICPR.

Zhong, W., Lu, H., & Yang, M. (2012). Robust Object Tracking via Sparsity-based Collaborative Model. *IEEE International Conference on Computer Vision and Pattern Recognition.* 10.1109/CVPR.2012.6247882

Zhou, H., Yuan, Y., & Shi, C. (2009). Object tracking using SIFT features and mean shift. *Computer Vision and Image Understanding, 113*(3), 345–352. doi:10.1016/j.cviu.2008.08.006

Chapter 7
Miracles of Healthcare With Internet of Things

Ramgopal Kashyap
(iD) https://orcid.org/0000-0002-5352-1286
Amity University Chhattisgarh, India

ABSTRACT

Today, IoT in therapeutic administrations has ended up being more productive in light of the fact that the correspondence among authorities and patients has been improved with versatile applications. These applications are made by the associations with the objective that the pros can screen the patient's prosperity. If any issue has hopped out at the patient, the authority approaches the patient and gives the correct treatment. In this proposition, particular focus is given to infant human administrations, in light of the fact that the greatest fear of gatekeepers is that they would lose their infant kids at whatever point. Therefore, a business contraption has been recognized which screens consistent information about the infant's heart rate, oxygen levels, resting position. In case anything happens to the infant, the information will get to the adaptable application which has been made by an association and is mechanically available by finishing a representation field test for the kid.

DOI: 10.4018/978-1-5225-7811-6.ch007

INTRODUCTION

The articulation "Web of Things" has started late ended up being outstanding in correspondence advancement. It has been made from various perspectives and is called as the accompanying backcountry. IoT is set to change various parts of our lives, it changes our existence. In the coming years, the quantity of IoT devices is required to grow altogether (Novo, 2018). The traverse of IoT is in excess of 12 billion devices that can right presently connect with the Internet; anyway by 2020 it is surveyed that there will be 26 times more connected things with the Internet than the overall public. Today, everything around us from family lights and unmistakable home machines to dispersing machines and cars can get on the web and speak with various machines. IoT implies devices or articles that can team up with the Internet by making usage of physical contraptions, sensors, microcontrollers, and framework arrange that enable these articles to accumulate and exchange data as showed up in Figure 1.

In order to accumulate the steady data dependably, every what's the entire more; every contraption has its unique identifier, which makes the correspondence possible basically like machine to machine (M2M) correspondence. An enormous measure of data is assembled from devices wherever all through the world which is secured in the cloud. Accordingly, structures will end up being more capable and all the more savvy. IoT makes sharp articles which constitute unavoidable building hinders in the difference in computerized physical shrewd comprehensive structures. It is

Figure 1. Interpretation of the research problem and solution with IoT

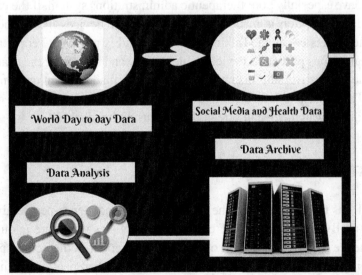

normal for billions of physical things or articles that will be furnished with different sorts of sensors and actuators that are joined by the Internet through arranged access frameworks helped by different developments, for instance, remote sensor frameworks, radio recurrence ID (RFID), ceaseless and semantic web organizations (Kumar and Chaurasiya, 2018).

To keeping every one of these things in considers, we to be an entire know a couple of utilization which have been made for IoT, in which each and every physical challenge is related through the Internet by using sensor contraptions. The correspondence is upheld through the sensors brought into the sharing devices ("Numerical Studies on the Electronic Gadgets in a Personal Computer Using CFD", 2016). Sensors accept a basic part in recognizing signals. Sensors are right now found in various applications, for instance, splendid contraption structures, air watching, mechanical control and therapeutic administrations. Starting late, IoT has ended up being more productive in the locale of therapeutic administration's systems. Specifically, IoT in the restorative administrations field combines sensors, microcontrollers et cetera. Consolidating the IoT features into remedial contraptions improves the quality and organization of watch over elderly patients and moreover for kids. IoT in human administrations could keep up a considerable number of patient's data which is electronic and urges the patients to get their data at whatever point. Various prosperity identifying sections have been delivered continuously that are smaller; this empowers the patients to wear them for checking. The prosperity watching device is related with the patient to such a degree, to the point that the pro can watch the patient's condition at whatever point. As IoT helped patients can be gotten to over the Internet, the prosperity state of the patient can be recognized at the ideal time so authentic move is made (Gao, 2016). By far most of the making countries have especially poor therapeutic administrations system. If the prosperity recognizing contraption is made to talk with smaller devices like propelled cell phones and tablets et cetera. Talking with the cloud is possible. People approach these advantageous particular devices which are by and by getting the chance to be pitiful. The restorative administrations industry has made patient care more tried and true. The consistent information of the patient data is researched and recorded, and the masters/watchmen can screen them by using handheld PCs.

MOTIVATION

Today, IoT has transformed into the most able correspondence perspective of the 21st century. By and by, in the IoT condition, all articles which are in our regular daily existence transform into a bit of the Web on account of their correspondence and enrolling capacities. By 2020, 90 percent of all the therapeutic administrations affiliations will have executed IoT development (Fattah, Sung, Ahn, Ryu and Yun, 2017). Upgrading the viability of social protection and the need of passing on quality care to patients is one of the testing things of current society. Some social protection affiliations don't make contrast data from related contraptions to various business shapes. Effective social protection depends upon speed besides, accuracy, supporting various people and a colossal extent of devices which are interfacing with IoT. Along these lines, IoT has ended up being more productive in the zone of restorative administrations systems. In the past couple of years, various awkward youngsters were kicking the pail or persevering with prosperity bothers. To deal with this issue, IoT has developed another advancement in social protection to improve the idea of regulate to babies.

PROBLEM STATEMENT

Prosperity support of each individual should be considered as fundamental in this day and age because of a climb in various therapeutic issues. In case there is a development in the amount of patients, by then this prompts a lessening in the relative number of masters. In this way, the diagnostics are deferred or a couple of patients are neglected. This makes patients more dependent on pros for their enlistment. Recollecting each one of these issues, human administrations structures have started connecting with IoT for keeping up the propelled identity of each and every patient. On account of no accessibility of authorities/parental figures and not having the ability to get to the human administrations structures, various therapeutic issues are getting undetected in the restorative administrations system. Of course, these IoT based human administrations systems have helped the patients and masters to always screen and easily dismember the patient data. Infant social protection is transforming into a noteworthy issue today. The greatest fear of any watchmen is that they would lose their infant youngster. Today the Sudden Infant Death Syndrome is a noteworthy issue (Berkowitz, 2012). The most generally perceived clarification behind the sudden going of infants is that they are having burden while they are unwinding. This sudden end happens without giving any signs. It may happen when the infant tyke is insignificant rest and beside when the baby is crying or engaging with some other issue. To avoid this issue, IoT has ensured the personalization of infant restorative administrations by keeping up the mechanized character of children each and every moment by influencing usage of IoT to sharp sensors, the infant kid prosperity can be watched, data can be assembled, and constant information of the children each and every moment can be sent to their people.

RESEARCH QUESTIONS

1.   In what capacity may we utilize IoT to improve the standard procedures for child human administrations?
2.   By what method may we utilize IoT to accumulate huge data to improve the care provided for infant kids what's more, cossets?
3.   In what way can IoT support social protection staff to upgrade their work capability?

AIM AND OBJECTIVES

IoT holds a magnificent potential to address the issues of therapeutic administrations. 1. The purpose of this hypothesis is to develop an application/building, which can do checking the soundness of infant youngsters. 2. It is being associated with upgrade the passageway to mind, to grow the idea of care, and to diminish the cost of care. 3. Screen the prosperity status of an infant kid by a sensor, which makes information that goes through a framework so it can be conferred or analyzed. Immediately, it has been started with separating the standard watch over infant youngsters and starts exploring the contraptions that can be put amid the time spent care to upgrade the precision of estimations and the response time for result examination. An infant screen can accumulate data likewise, send progressing information of the infant youngsters breathing stage, pulse, skin temperature, resting position and stomach related tract activity level. Advances in sensor and system development are empowering devices to accumulate record and separate data that was not open already; this infers having the ability to assemble basic data after some time that can be used to help enable preventive care.

VISION

To upgrade human prosperity and success is an authoritative goal of any fiscal, inventive and social headway. The quick rising and developing of people is one of the full scale controls that will change the world definitely, it has made magnificent weight sustenance supply and social protection systems wherever all through the world, and the rising advancement jump forward of the Internet-of-Things (IoT) is depended upon to offer promising game plans. Thusly the utilization of IoT developments for the sustenance creation organizes and in-home human administrations (IHH) have been regularly highlighted in the key research guides (Abrahamson et al., 2016). To develop basically usable advancements and plans of IoT for these two applications is the last focal point of this work. As a complex computerized physical system, the IoT facilitates an extensive variety of identifying, recognizing confirmation, correspondence, sorting out, and informatics contraptions and structures, and reliably relates each one of the all inclusive community and things upon interests, with the objective that anybody, at whatever point and wherever, through any device and media, would all be able to the all the more successfully get to the information of any dissent and any organization. The impact caused by the IoT to human life will be as enormous as the web has caused in the earlier decades, so the IoT is seen as "the accompanying of web". A bit of the engaging developments are sensors and actuators, Wireless Sensor Network (WSN) (Allegretti, 2014), Wise and Interactive Packaging (Kim and Mondal, 2016), steady embedded structure, Micro Electro Mechanical Systems (MEMS) (Te Lindert and Van Someren, 2013), versatile web get to, disseminated figuring, Radio Frequency Identification (RFID), Machine-to-Machine (M2M) correspondence, human machine correspondence (HMI), middleware, Service Oriented Architecture (SOA), Undertaking Information System, data mining, et cetera. With various portrayals from alternate points of view, the IoT has transformed into the new perspective of the progression of information and correspondence advancement.

RESEARCH SPACE

It is widely recognized that the headways and usages of IoT are both in front of calendar mastermind and distant from create. Research challenges are scattered in all parts of an answer, going from the enabling devices to the best level designs of activity. So the investigation space for a whole IoT course of action exhibits a cross-layer and multidisciplinary configuration as appeared in Figure 2. On one hand, the examinations should cover each one of the layers from the base contraption layer, through the medium frameworks organization and data planning layer, and application layer, up to the best business layer. The base layer of the course of action is a movement of innovative remote sensor contraptions (Yaghmaee Moghaddam and Leon-Garcia, 2018); the data from the devices are accumulated through specific sorting out traditions; the data is set up at different layers and composed into essential information to customers; and plan of activity and work process are sketched out at the best layer to grow the extra characteristics towards viable business.

Advancements are circled at all the layers, and cross-layer design and streamlining is required. Of course, to develop a whole response for a particular application, architects ought to in any occasion join multidisciplinary data of ICT, organization,

Figure 2. Healthcare challenges

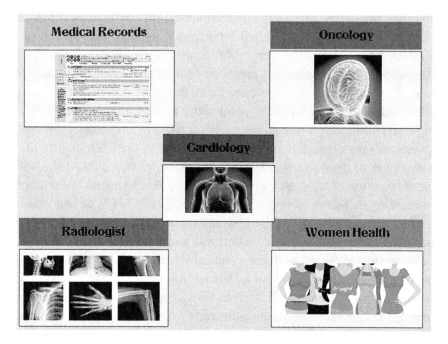

business association, and the goal application. Also, the specific learning of the target application every now and again covers distinctive instructs too. For example, in the utilization of sustenance stock system, to pick the regular parameters that the remote sensor devices should check, we need to examine the purposes behind sustenance hurts in the midst of the sustenance generation arrange. To pass on vital information to customers, e.g. to foresee time period of sensible ease of use, we need to abuse the importance of the massive measure of rough data. These works require a blend of capacity in sustenance planning, science, and agribusiness.

CHALLENGES

The IoT investigate is facing a central test: the course of action of enabling advancement and practical business necessities, by the day's end, there is an epic gap between the advancement headway and business improvement. The challenges of some gigantic exercises have avowed the essential troubles in business diagram of IoT advancements. For example, Wal-Mart's gathering of RFID has been deferred so much that a couple of savants even announced the "downfall" of RFID development and the mistake of Google Health is related to the unsuccessful regard chain establishment (Farris et al., 2017). We have examined many "positive conclusions" in creative papers on the credibility of such business, anyway really brutal! In particular, this gap achieves two significant obstructions for the progression of IoT grandstand. So it is earnest for commercialization attempts and in addition for engaging advancement change.

UGLY VALUE PROPOSITION

This is the basic limitation of mass volume determination for example, the RFID-based sustenance take after structure in which RFID names are used to record the chairmen and time over the creation arrange is a standout amongst the most typical IoT applications. It can reduce work cost and process time of sustenance vendors and retailers. Regardless, this extra regard isn't adequately speaking to drive the entire store organize. "The suppliers were reluctant to get the RFID in light of the fact that their basic theory cost, required by the untouchable coordination's firm, has conveyed the base level points of interest for themselves, which, therefore, fallingly affects the base level business benefits recognized by the outsider vital firm. Additionally, have in like manner watched that, in actuality most of the beneficial RFID applications today are out of the sorted out targets when this development was immediately made learning stream of shrewd administration is given in figure 3.

Basically, the nonattendance of huge worth chain charm furthermore exists in Health-IoT (Fosso Wamba, Barjis and Takeoka Chatfield, 2010). A significant part of existing game plans hasn't adequately offered opportunity to the basic human administrations advantage providers e.g. recuperating offices to get drew in with the regard chain. This has caused "the nonappearance of trust from patients and the nonattendance of budgetary assistance from open masters to such organizations". Along these lines, more added qualities should be passed on, and new functionalities and limits should be become clearly going for such new characteristics.

ABSENCE OF DEVICE AND SERVICE INTEGRATION

Various recognized advances have been made in continuous year for the two applications, covering about all the key segments of an answer. In any case, various reviews likewise our examination, have demonstrated the scattered case of the ebb and flow inquire about. That is, there are a mass of isolated headways and devices, yet there are few composed organizations (Alemdar, Durmus and Ersoy, 2010). Also "focused organizations for picked diseases won't not meet the honest to goodness essentials of multimorbid seniors; and along these lines, a mix of a couple of telehealth organizations might be judicious to help people in an all the more widely inclusive

Figure 3. Knowledge flow utilizing IoT for intelligent service

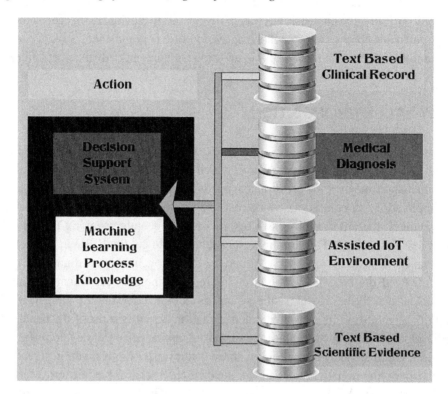

course; and to do this, an extensive measure of interdisciplinary work between all accomplices and the pros must be finished". The World Health Organization (WHO) furthermore includes this issue:

"A run of the mill case for the introduction of ICT and compact developments in countries is their entry to prosperity showcases in pockets, a mortar here or a swathe there, to settle a particular issue"; "the most understood result is a wealth of non-interoperable islands of ICT". Thusly, a widely inclusive arrangement structure is asked for to suitably join the scattered contraptions and advances into more productive organizations.

CHANGE OF RESEARCH MINDSET

Essentially, such opening is caused by the development driven research tradition or attitude. That is, advancement builds as often as possible make another development first and after that find what it could be used for. For the examination on a create application, the arrangement of activity what's more, application circumstance are clear and have recently been mapped into particular requirements. So the development originators essentially need to base on the advancement perspectives of particular functionalities or presentations. They don't generally need to invest much energy in business-related points of view. Regardless, unmistakably, if the advancement and application are both young, like the IoT, this is inefficient to the extent business-development course of action (Klumpp, 2018). There are an over the top number of potential results and vulnerabilities relatively, in plans of activity and application circumstances. One plan can never fit each one of these possible results. To decrease an opportunity to market and threat of disillusionment, business perspectives should be viewed as more than before to start with time of IoT development change. If the Trailblazers still hold the ordinary state of mind, the feedback from business sharpen is ordinarily past the final turning point for them to get by in the ruthless business world.

THE HEALTH IOT

In the coming decades, the movement model of restorative administrations will transform from the demonstrate specialist's office driven, through recuperating office home-balanced in 2020th, to the last homocentric in 2030th. The future human administrations system should be created in a layered structure, e.g. from low to high including the individual, home, organize, additionally, center layer; and the let layer has cut down work control and operational cost, higher repeat of utilization for unending affliction, and lower repeat of usage for extreme illness. So the in-home therapeutic administrations advantage engaged by the IoT development the assumed Health-IoT is promising for both regular human administrations industry and the ICT business (Duckett, 2016).

It is ubiquitous and modified what accomplishes more will quicken the difference in human administrations from calling headed to calm driven. A normal application circumstance of the Health-IoT is showed up in Figure 4. Typically, a Health-IoT plan consolidates the going with limits:

1. Following and checking. Controlled by the inescapable recognizing evidence, distinguishing, and correspondence restrict, each one of the things people, equipment, medication, et cetera can be taken after and checked by wearable WSN contraptions on an all the live long day start (Dhanalakshmi and Sam Leni, 2017).
2. Remote organization. Human administrations and help living organizations e.g. emergency revelation moreover, crisis treatment, stroke home and getting ready, dietary and pharmaceutical organization, telemedicine and remote

Figure 4. The health-IoT benefit

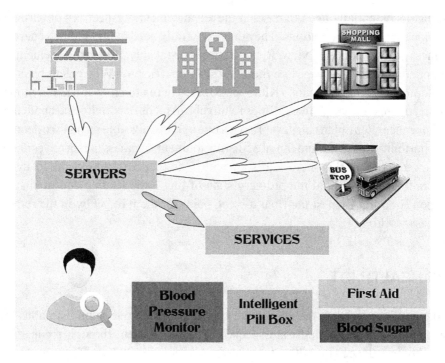

assurance, prosperity long range casual correspondence (Onyshchenko and Afanasieva, 2017) et cetera can be passed on remotely through the web and field contraptions.

3. Information organization. Engaged by the overall accessibility of the IoT, all the therapeutic administrations information (coordination, assurance, treatment, recovery, remedy, organization, back, and even step by step development (Siryani, Tanju and Eveleigh, 2017) can be accumulated, managed, and utilized all through the entire regard chain.

4. Cross-affiliation mix. The mending office information structures are extended to comprehension' home, and can be fused into greater scale therapeutic administrations system that may cover a system, city or even state (Gond, Cabantous and Krikorian, 2017).

PROBLEM

Our work starts from the action of the iPack VINN Excellence Center (iPack Focus) sponsored by the Swedish Governmental Agency for Innovation Systems, KTH, and mechanical assistance. The mission of iPack Center is "to make imaginative devices in vision of Internet-of-Things, through close joint exertion with industry, driving investigation centers, and early adopters all inclusive". At the moment that the work in this proposition was started, we had as of late some fundamental progressions (e.g. progressing introduced structure, RFID, WSN, utilitarian material), some fundamental business demands from current assistants, and a general vision. These business demands are generally around two target applications, 1) fresh sustenance following for sustenance stock system, and 2) understanding pharmaceutical organization and watching for in-home social protection. Thusly, the errand of this work when all is said in done is to make gainful and usable IoT answers for the FSC and IHH (Fuji and Abbott, 2014). To be short, in our work the IoT respond in due order regarding the use of FSC is called "Sustenance IoT", and the IoT respond in due order regarding the usage of IHH is called "Prosperity IoT". In particular, we hope to address the going with examination issues:

1. **WSN Structures:** As the articles in FSC and IHH are generally adaptable and for the most part dispersed, the WSN structure must encourage versatile and wide region course of action. Tried and true correspondence is furthermore anticipated that would work with poor radio banner causing through water-rich sustenance and human body (Bera, Misra, Roy and Obaidat, 2016). Furthermore, capable data weight is major to decrease the power use and moreover development stack especially for high data rate sensors. All these should be executed with sensible chips and meet the long life cycle need of current applications.

2. **Device Structures:** The more than two applications both require the WSN and I2Pack devices to arrange extraordinarily rich functionalities including different sensors, performing craftsmen, and limit (Hu, Wu and Wang, 2014). All these should be completed under keep purpose of restriction of vitality use.

3. **Structure Coordination Models:** These plans ought to enable the reliable joining of the proposed WSN and I2Pack devices in practical EIS. Capable information coordination counts are relied upon to pass on the most limited information for essential administration. Interoperability of devices and organizations from different suppliers, operational work process, and fitting security designs should fit in business sharpens ("Internet of Things – Integration and Semantic Interoperability of Sensor Data of Things in Heterogeneous Environments", 2016). Finally, the structures should be checked by executed models and preliminaries in field.

IOT SYSTEM FOR IN-HOME HEALTHCARE CHALLENGES

In this manner to the Food-IoT, the flow inquire about on Health-IoT are also unreasonably scattered and the opening between development progression and business application is obstruction towards real business. Convincing contraption and organization compromise is fundamental for the accomplishment of Health-IoT course of action. As a platform between the organization backend and the patients at home, an In-Home Healthcare Station (IHHS) is required to recognize such organization and device joining (Franckhauser, 2013) that is given in figure 5. The minimum complex kind of the current IHHS plans is unadulterated programming applications on an adaptable phone or PDA individual mechanized accomplice. Their handiness and included characteristics are limited by the hardware and designers ought to use more coherent information, sight and sound limits, relational associations, and even diversions in the prosperity intervention applications.

The second sort sustains the item applications by including outside sensors through nearby interfaces typically Bluetooth of the convenient terminal, yet the ideal sensors do bar various remedial ones; and sensor vendors and applications engineers need to participate to energize interoperability. The third sort, in like manner the most extraordinary, of game plans alters the IHHS together with biomedical contraptions,

Figure 5. eHealth application of IoT

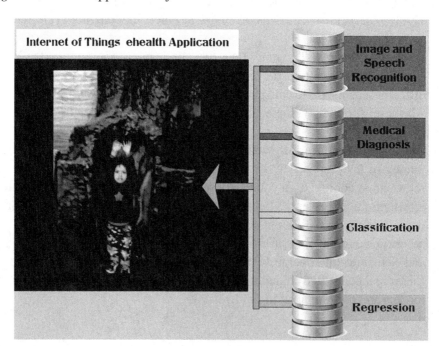

specific correspondence traditions, and complex application programming. These contraptions measure distinctive key signs, for instance, ECG, EEG, EMG, SpO2, glucose, cardiotocography, apnea, heart rate, beat, respiratory rate, act, et cetera. By then the data are transmitted to the IHHS through various remote body district orchestrate techniques. The IHHS partners with the organization backend through unavoidable preparing and correspondence conditions. This progress has asserted the probability of device and organization coordination through the IHHS. Regardless, the system is asking for a comprehensive framework to at the same time address both business issues and concentrated issues towards the productive joining in actuality, and "to do this, an extensive measure of interdisciplinary work between all accomplices and the modelers must be finished". Also, the trouble of business attempts, e.g. the failure of Google Health, has unequivocally exhibited the troubles to cross the opening between the scattered advances and sweeping business application. The "rehashing issues" that the development change is going up against: 1) starting at now settled budgetary structures direct down progression; 2) fundamental institutions for modernizing therapeutic administrations wait behind; 3) included social occasions are reluctant and take-up remains low; 4) development change based too unequivocally on outlining driven courses of action; 5) headways are passed on in a partitioned from and have poor adaptability; 6) the amount of accomplices and conditions cause versatile quality; 7) there is a nonappearance of cost-sufficiency considers; 8) investigate tends to base on finding clinical affirmation to the extent prosperity comes about, yet the influence advancement does not depend totally on clinical affirmation (Makushin and Martynov, 2018). These issues must be resolved by the best in class design of activity diagram. By the day's end, we should clearly answer "how to develop an accommodating business natural network and pass on enough included characteristics to all accomplices?" first when we develop the Health-IoT game plan.

eHEALTH SHIFT PARADIGM

The essential goal of Health Information Technology (HIT) is to change the restorative administrations zone to the necessities of the present world's inclinations towards globalism and versatility while broadening the scope of points of interest for the patient. Along these lines to ensure a patient-centered virtual world which enables more noteworthy flexibility through the availability of telehealth and telecare organizations, extended receptiveness to human administrations data over different land masterminds by ensuring interoperable EHR systems, overhauled data security and insurance, diminishment of threats by refraining from handwriting messes up by virtue of ePrescribing structures, automated help for specialists in clinical and pharmaceutical decisions, progress in therapeutic administrations research and direction by using the advances in data mining and fake cognizance fields, and some more. In addition, genuine eHealth structures are assuredly not essentially supplanting printed material with EHRs, smartcards, et cetera (Mittelstadt, 2017). However HIT in like manner engages therapeutic administrations to be modified. This makes meds more fruitful, and in addition it engages authorities to break down issues more quickly, and even predict them before they happen.

This move, from standard social protection paper-based records to a digitalized human administrations zone, plastically as eHealth move perspective, addresses the new point of convergence through which the therapeutic administrations see must be seen today (Kashyap, 2019b). In addition, the moving method everything considered isn't sufficient, given the extending enthusiasm for restorative administrations, developing people and decreasing human administrations workforce, also basic is the methods by which brisk and under which quality parameters it happens. It is related to the usability of the eHealth structure (Lake, Milito, Morrow and Vargheese, 2014). He considers that the accomplishment of crafted by these advances involves in giving a powerful arrangement to a human-PC interface. Additionally, "concerning the e-business change, e-prosperity is seen as an adjustment in standpoint from a specialist centered care system to a customer driven care structure. In a manner of speaking, e-prosperity systems put the e-clients rather than the parental figures at within".

FOUNDATIONS ON IOT IN HEALTHCARE

Healthcare and IoT

Advancement which is as of now in light of IoT has worked its heading onto various purchaser contraptions. Various people are foreseeing that it should half and half to therapeutic administrations. IoT development changes the way we live and work (Novo, 2018). Moreover, it could change various parts of our lives including social protection. Nowadays, various social protection applications are available which empowers the patients to design their plans through the applications on their phones, astute contraptions et cetera with no convincing motivation to make a call to the recuperating office and sit tight for long time for a game plan.

General IoT in Healthcare

IoT changes the therapeutic data into bits of information for all the more intelligent calm care therapeutic administrations are as of now more mechanically advanced and is tied in with interfacing things together (Kashyapn 2019a). Thusly, IoT is so basic in social protection. By using contraptions like related sensors and diverse sorts of things that people can wear every one of that information can be set in the cloud, and expert/watchman can without quite a bit of a stretch screen the constant information of the patient ("IoT Delegate: Smart Home Framework for Heterogeneous IoT Service Collaboration", 2016). IoT can reinforce life saving applications inside the social protection industry by get-together data from the bedside devices, seeing patient information, and diagnosing in continuous the entire course of action of the patient care see Figure 6.

Today, various restorative administrations contraptions work all through the world which transforms into an issue as it can cause data disaster and slip-ups in conclusion. To crush this data which is accumulated will be secured in cloud. The watchmen or experts can without quite a bit of a stretch screen and manage the patient prosperity moreover, can save significant minutes consistent. Without having to physically visit each patient, the parental figure/ace or expert can give a remote assurance and track the remedial assets. Using the sensors and Wi-Fi, the right division in the specialist's office can be found while recuperating extraordinary information.

Figure 6. Medical empowerment utilizing smart technology

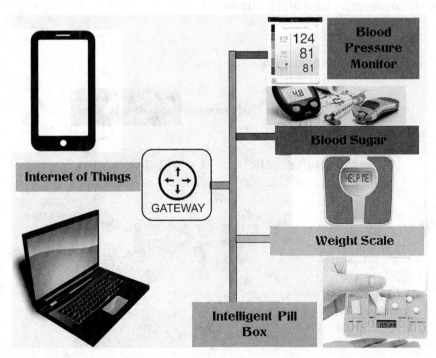

Clinical Care

Making use of IoT-driven sensor, the patient is constantly checked. The patient requires close thought due to their physiological status, which is a noninvasive watching. The tolerant status is seen by the sensor which accumulates the physiological information of the patient to be analyzed, making use of entryways (Namatame, Nakazawa and Tokuda, 2012). The procured information will be secured in the cloud. This information is then sent to the watchmen/experts remotely for help examination as showed up in Figure 7. This improves the idea of care and moreover diminishes the cost for the patient's.

Remote Monitoring

The general IoT in a remote prosperity checking systems tracks a patient's basic banners progressively and responds if there is an issue in calm prosperity. A contraption is joined to the patient as showed up in Figure 8. It transmits the data about the basic signs from where the tolerant is found. The transmitter is related through a telecom framework to amending focus. The specialist's office has a remote checking structure that scrutinizes about the patient's basic signs (Singh and Mittal, 2016). Similarly when the sensor is inserted into the patient's body, the data can be electronically transmitted. The information which is transmitted will be securely sent to human administrations providers/parental figures.

Figure 7. Clinical care frameworks

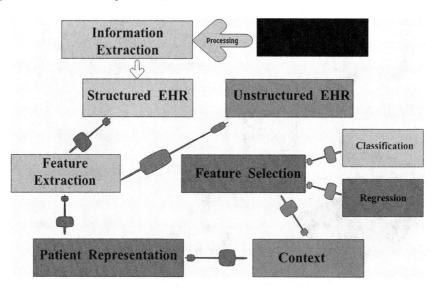

Figure 8. Remote wellbeing checking framework

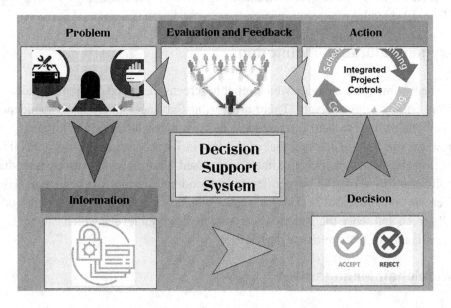

APPLICATIONS FOR IOT IN HEALTHCARE

Circulatory Strain Monitoring

Circulatory strain is a champion among the most basic physiological parameters of the human body. Secured and simple to use circulatory strain screens have ended up being general. With the headway in the restorative administrations system, the social protection equip/structure is related with an IoT device or sensors that make a basic correspondence between the patient's and masters/parental figures. An electronic circulatory strain screen is related with the IoT sensor that assembles the constant information of the patient BP levels (Mengden, Vetter, Tislér and Illyés, 2001).

Recovery System

A recuperation structure can overhaul and can restore the pragmatic limits and upgrades the individual fulfillment for the overall public who are persevering with a couple of ineptitudes to the extent alleviating issues that are associated with developing peoples and when there is an inadequacy of prosperity experts. There is a system based splendid rebuilding structure that gives a feasible treatment (Bisio, Delfino, Lavagetto and Sciarrone, 2016). A profitable acceptable association and allocation of remedial resources according to tenacious requirements ought to be conceivable by a power based mechanizing arranging methodology related with IoT-based splendid recuperation system.

Oxygen Saturation Monitoring

The beat oximeter is a device which reliably screens the blood oxygen submersion of the patient noninvasively. There are various advances in the correspondence development, i.e., remote frameworks, and restorative sensors are impacting at show days in light of the fact that of the low influence use and low mishap. The interminable watching pulse oximeters are used as a piece of various remedial applications to know the oxygen levels in blood and besides the heart rate (HR) (Wemple and Luks, 2012). The IoT sensor which is related with the patient body will screen and sense the patient's heart rate and oxygen levels, which can confine the patient development (Kashyap, 2019c).

Wheelchair Management

Wheelchairs are used by the overall public who are continuing with a physical sickness and they can't walk or some other physical inadequacies. Remote body area frameworks can connect quick articles with the Internet, to be used as a people-driven recognizing (sensor) device for wheelchair customers. There will be weight cushion which is a resistive weight sensor that will perceive when the human body is tumbling down from the wheelchair (Rahman and Hossain, 2017). A sharp wheelchair has another reviving operator sensor which perceives the falling of the wheelchair. The expert/parental figure can continually screen the patient's data from the center.

Medicinal Services Solutions Using Smart Phones

Mobile phones and human administrations applications give various focal points to social protection specialists. There are various remedial restorative administrations applications which are by and by open from multiple points of view and arranged to access, for instance, prosperity record, information and time, correspondence and guiding with authorities, diligent predictable checking and fitting clinical fundamental initiative. With the use of mobile phone applications and sensors, the reason for mind and besides the passage to mind has been extended and will reinforce the upgraded understanding outcomes (Salibian and Scholz, 2011).

Medicinal Services Applications Description

Calorie Counter Keeps on following the sustenance that we have exhausted and discovers the fat and moreover the weight and furthermore cholesterol appear in our body (Jepsen, 2014). It interminably screens the heart rate and assembles the related steady information. Circulatory strain Screen It accumulates the circulatory strain level of the patient inspects besides, records the data (Lamberts, Swart, Capostagno, Noakes and Lambert, 2009). It keeps following the body temperature and gives the information when the body temperature is extended. Pedometer is available in various mobile phones. It records the quantity of steps we have walked and gives the information of what number of calories is seared per a unit of time. Water Your Body Many of us use this application since it reminds us to drink water reliably and tracks our body water drinking affinities (Buiu, 2017).

Ontrack Diabetes and Other Areas

It keeps watching the blood glucose level and gives suitable remedy to supervise diabetes (Al-Taee, Al-Nuaimy, Muhsin and Al-Ataby, 2017). It keeps following the skin condition which enables us to perceive early if any skin issue happens. It screens the eyes vision and after that which is dismembered and attempted. Likewise, Log It screens nonstop information of the patient's asthma. It screens the cardiovascular recuperation which is done remotely reliably and accumulates the data. In the event that the patient fails to take a pill it reminds the patient arrangement times. It relentlessly screens the general population development levels and if any issues happen, it alerts us on falling.

IOT in Healthcare for Babies and Infants

For gatekeepers, nothing is more essential than keeping their kid happy and strong. Kids can't talk and tell if they are covetous or if it feels like hot, cold, and tired. By and by, IoT wearables can have a noteworthy impact. IoT has now been made for kids and infant youngsters to empower their people. Gatekeepers can screen their infant's prosperity remotely for example by methods for Bluetooth development, there are various IoT wearable's, devices and astute sensors which can constantly screen the baby's/infant youngsters fundamental signs and send that data directly to a flexible device. An infant tyke screen can assemble data and send steady information of the children each besides, consistently (Lingam M, 2017).

DIFFICULTIES FOR IOT IN HEALTHCARE

Security and security: There might have the capacity to various potential repercussions, with the objective that the devices which are related devices like mobile phones, sensors et cetera can be at a shot from software engineers or hacking. At whatever point there is transmission of data starting with one contraption then onto the next it must be mixed (Zhou and Piramuthu, 2017). Incorporating different contraptions and traditions inside the framework is another trying task for executing powerful IoT in therapeutic administrations. There are various mobile phones that are related with the framework which successfully accumulate data (Kashyap, 2019d). There are excessively unmistakable correspondence traditions that obfuscate the route toward gathering the information. Innovation gathering: Creating another application with imaginative contemplations that helps authorities and patients, this isn't adequate to pay for another development. The thing which is delivered should similarly be adjusted in the human administrations system.

ADVANTAGES OF IOT IN HEALTHCARE

Treatment for disorders is done before they escape hand, in light of the way that the patients are tenaciously watched and the watchmen or providers can get to the consistent data and improve the sickness organization. The robotized data and the sharp watching which are controlled by the devices related with the IoT and the decisions are made adequately in perspective of significant examination which diminishes botches. Persistent checking is done reliably, which basically slashes down the unnecessary expert visits and besides cleaves down the recuperating office remains (Vukovic, 2015). This can diminish the cost for patients. Associated restorative administrations enable the parental figures to pick up induction to constant information when the patient is unendingly checked and the decisions are taken truly (Shukla, Gupta, & Kashyap, 2019). This can help moreover; give advantageous care that upgrades the treatment comes about.

DISADVANTAGES OF IOT IN HEALTHCARE

There is a closeness issue for the IoT in human administrations, because starting at now there is no standard for naming and checking with the sensors. Protection and security is one of the immense issue with IoT in social protection, i.e., all the patient/

specialist data must be mixed. The programming can be hacked by various customers and the individual information is manhandled. These potential results are relentless in IoT. Progressing propels in social protection systems have opened up inconceivable open entryways for the utilization of canny circumstances and insightful restorative administrations (Tiwari, Gupta, & Kashyap, 2019). Especially in the prosperity and remedial field, a couple of sensors have been made to survey particular sorts of essential signs for instance, beat, body weight, temperature and oxygen levels. Researchers have kept an eye on a couple of issues in human administrations and IoT in social protection. This fragment delineates about research on therapeutic administrations structure using differing sensor frameworks (Zhou and Piramuthu, 2017). A sweeping overview on utilization of IoT in restorative administrations structure has been analyzed. In this section, they have kept an eye on a couple of strategies and things that are used as a piece of IoT in social protection systems, troubles of IoT in social protection. A system for the desire for perpetual disseminates from the wearable human administrations contraptions have been discussed to bring the savvy therapeutic administrations game plans wherever, which settles on the technique profitable for essential initiative. An IoT-based adroit rebuilding structure has been introduced. In this investigation, transcendentalism based mechanizing plan methodology for the splendid rebuilding structure using IoT development is displayed. The recuperation structure is developed through Wi-Fi and different progressions, for instance, RFID-based short-isolate radio correspondence advancement; unique identifier based conspicuous verification advancement, and overall arranging system development. Organization arranged designing is made which is used for delineating, executing, supervising and distinctive sorts of social protection organizations. In the wake of delineating and execution of the IoT recuperation structure, each and every patient will get awesome treatment and they are all around resolved to have the two recuperation methodology. This structure manages more than one patient.

A remote structure for remote checking of oxygen inundation and heart rate has been proposed and depicted. In this investigation, making use of the beat oximeters, the level of oxygen in the blood and besides the heart rate of the patient is evaluated. By then, this ponder data is traded to a central checking station through a WSN. The patient will be continually watched and the central checking station gets the information of the patient's oxygen submersion level and heart rate through the WSN. If any issue happens, an alert will be activated thusly. A graphical UI (GUI) is made to demonstrate the results and estimations (data) of the patients. An anchored IoT-based human administrations structure with body sensor frameworks works through BSN designing to achieve system and efficiency and intensity of transmission inside open IoT-based correspondence frameworks (Al-Turjman, Kirsal Ever, Ever, Nguyen and David, 2017). The utilization of great crypto-rough to manufacture two correspondence instruments, one is for ensuring transmission furtively and another is for giving the affirmation among the sharp questions, the adjacent taking care of unit and the backend sensor. The human administrations structure is completed with the Raspberry PI stage to demonstrate the presence of mind and moreover the feasibility of the parts.

A building an IoT-careful social protection checking system is exhibited. A model is shown for the utilization of an IoT-careful social protection checking structure, which will reduce the cost of restorative administrations and will extend the need of particular care. It alerts about the patient's prosperity condition ceaselessly, if any issue is experienced, and if the patient needs any restorative thought or hospitalization. In this paper, the makers also drew in and inspected about how to gather an extraordinarily selected extensible social protection watching structure in the midst of runtime by using negligible exertion remote sensors and starting at now existent IoT development as a correspondence organize. An arrangement of Infant prosperity condition check plan in light of a wearable contraption with mindset heading reference system has been talked about. The makers had proposed an arrangement for infant condition check respond in due order regarding lessen infant youngster mortality and incident rate by using a wearable device and camera. This arrangement has utilized the AHRS to measure the child's air, and they have used diverse biometric sensors to the information. In light of this, gatekeepers can watch the infant tyke's prosperity condition.

Fast and correct division of helpful pictures is up 'til now a testing issue in the PC vision and case affirmation. Active contour models (ACM) are the best frameworks for better regularization of the shape and better result. Dynamic shape models are named edge based, Region build and imperativeness based regarding which essentialness based models are grabbing unmistakable quality to the extent execution. The key purpose behind division is to assemble particular properties in the photos and perform better inside seeing Intensity inhomogeneity (Kashyap and Tiwari, 2018). The dynamic frame show is a strategy for arrangement of curve studied by inside and outside forces. Power inhomogeneity generally caused by the imperfect imaging devices or by factor edifications which as often as possible occur in therapeutic pictures and it causes misclassifications that think little of fairly passed on constraint. The Mumford-Shah (MS) show which accept that it gives smooth and subjective pictures in case of power inhomogeneity (Kashyap,Gautam and Tiwari, 2018). Chan and Vese (CV) began a level set system to restrain imperativeness term, yet stop term impacts the result since it doesn't depend upon the slant of the photo. In any case, the technique is responsive to the hidden shape, and the forming twist stuck into close-by minima (Kashyap and Piersson 2018a) has appeared in figure 9 utilizing distinctive strategy same information is giving diverse outcomes.

Figure 9. Comparison of energy construct method with traditional methods in light of same data

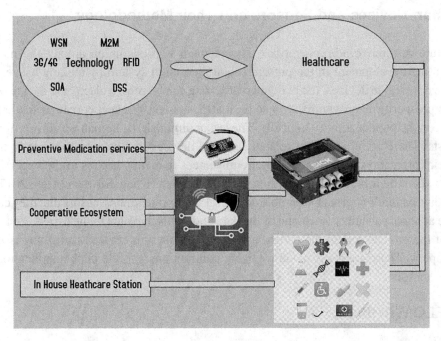

Also, the CV procedure isn't sensible for snappy programming due to powers of the shape figured in the each accentuation, which increment the CPU time profoundly. Locally real level set strategy uses Gaussian scattering and the changed space can be adaptively approximated by expanding an inclination field with the primary picture. In the level set technique with tendency cure, the imperativeness is restricted (Kashyap and Piersson, 2018b). The essentialness minimization is refined by an iterative system, where this methodology confines the imperativeness concerning each one of its elements. Neighborhood picture essentialness fitting technique relies upon partition limit and division regularize term that affirms the smoothness of the level set limit and moreover enlisting time and level set appraisal is decreased (Kashyap and Gautam, 2017). The level set limit is turned by improvement of fragmented differential condition and the variational level set model whose headway condition is imitated from the minimization issue of essentialness utilitarian.

SMART SENSORS AND DEVICES

Smart Devices and Sensors and Their Methodology

Astute restorative administrations advancement is a champion among the most creating development in the present social protection system by making usage of sharp wearable devices, the patient created data can be sent to electronic devices or any prosperity records with the objective that the masters/gatekeepers can particularly screen the patient activity logically. These can diminish the human administrations costs. There are a couple of related splendid devices that have been made in the social protection industry. In past circumstances' patient's had go to the expert to talk about their breathing issue, sugar levels et cetera (Khan, Silva and Han, 2017). Today, patient's approach wearable devices, PDA applications, sensors that they can use at home can amass each one of the data and sends that data to the expert, thusly, that the pro can screen the patient and gives a proper pharmaceutical if any issue happens. There are some made wearable contraptions, mobile phone applications and sensors.

HELO Wristband

A persistent prosperity checking device which screens the patient's prosperity without stopping for even a minute with an illness desire showed up. It can screen each and every moment in the body like work out, sentiments, circulatory strain, heart rate and electrocardiogram (ECG). This wristband has dynamic sensors that can distinguish your human body ("Sensor-installed wristband utilizes sweat to screen wearer's wellbeing", 2016). If you have any issue, you can send banner to your relatives, and they can thusly take after the GPS position of the tolerant. This will keep us in contact with phones.

Remote Blood Pressure Monitor

This device is used when the patient is suspected to have hypertension like hypertension. This remote circulatory strain screen is remotely connected with a phone application through Bluetooth. It screens the patient prosperity continuously and besides alerts the patient to take genuine remedy ("Progress on the advancement of the MediWatch wandering pulse screen and related gadgets", 2004).

Heart Monitor

This sharp sensor is affixed to the phone case as showed up in Figure 7. It is remotely connected with the wireless application; it assembles the ECG recording, and dismembers the data. In case there is any refinement in your ECG level, you should contact the specialist (Tsui, Liu and Lin, 2017).

Smart Devices and Sensors for Babies and Infants

Today, various newborn children are imagined awkward on the planet, some of them may kick the pail or some of them will encounter the evil impacts of physiological issues with loss of body water. The fear of the watchmen is about their infant youngster's prosperity condition. By and by, development has been made to improve the idea of restorative administrations. Splendid wearable contraptions and sensors are impacting in the present creating development. There are some splendid devices and sensors that would support the gatekeepers about not to worry over their infant youngsters (Khan, Silva and Han, 2017). The baby check is a wearable youngster screen; it lashes on to the kids arm successfully and tracks the tyke's body temperature and advancement see Figure 10. This baby check wearable device will coordinate with the parent's wireless application by methods for Bluetooth advancement. The data of the tyke can be seen in the application and prompts you in case anything happens.

It is a wearable sagacious contraption showed up in underneath Figure 9. It should be cut onto the two layers' of the diaper or to the pieces of clothing of the newborn child. The device is remotely connected with the phone application by methods for Bluetooth advancement. It can screen the body temperature and unwinding time of the newborn child and the examining will be appeared on the phone application. It alerts you at whatever point the readings are too low or too high. The adroit clothing sensor development is showed up in Figure 11.

It tracks the tyke while napping. The sensor is related with a home Wi-Fi composes remotely. It is related with the PDA application through Bluetooth. If there are any alterations in the newborn child's development, it will be revived to their people through the adaptable by methods for Bluetooth advancement. This Owlet Smart Sock 2 sensor screens the newborn child heart rate and oxygen levels constantly right when the baby is resting. It exhorts the watchmen through a wireless application, if the heart rate what's more, oxygen levels leaves preset zones (Dangerfield, Ward, Davidson and Adamian, 2017). This Smart Sock 2 sensor is used since it is one of the best sock sensors for the unseasoned guardians to feel perky about their newborn child see Figure 12.

Figure 10. Smart wearable infant screen

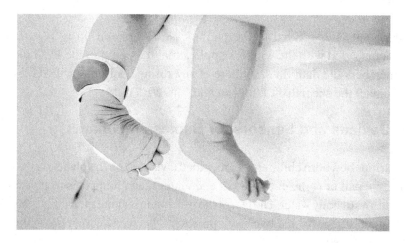

Figure 11. Baby monitor device

The clarification for picking this particular Smart Sock 2 is an immediate aftereffect of SIDS. The sudden passing happens when the newborn child is persisting with breathing issue and if the heart rate goes down. By using this Smart Sock 2, consistent information of the newborn child can be checked and we can watch the heart rate and oxygen levels of the kid when the baby is dozing, and moreover it prompts when the youngster is squirming and reinforcing. This contraption gives the readings when

Figure 12. Smart sock 2 for babies

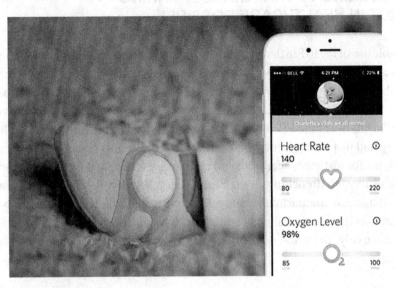

the tyke is supporting as well. By far most of exchange devices won't prompt the watchmen while the newborn child is empowering and the estimations like heart rate and oxygen levels both are not taken after using so to speak one splendid device or sensor. This Smart Sock 2 is remotely connected with the base station, and the base station will illuminate the gatekeepers through lights and sounds. It is like manner talks with the mobile phone application in the way that the base station remotely connects with the PDA application, and the application will caution the gatekeepers by giving takes note. A lone event tolerant server (like a privately settled server) is by and large an appalling layout as it epitomizes a lone point dissatisfaction that can't go ahead without genuine results. A multi-event quiet server is a more secure creates, and accuse tolerant, in any case, truly, slower than an utilitarian single case persistent server. The middle point discovers understanding data from a combination of sensors and securely stores it in the cloud, where it can be gotten to by those possessed with the patient's care. Data amassing contraptions like this will before long wind up run of the mill and won't simply assemble human administrations data yet also regulate other sensor masterminds inside the home (John Livingston and Umamakeswari, 2015). Freescale's second-age section directs data from splendid essentialness, buy equipment, and home computerization and security systems despite human administrations.

EMPOWERING TECHNOLOGIES: MAKING THE IOT IN HEALTHCARE POSSIBLE

The viable use of the IoT in the past human administrations representations relies upon a couple of engaging headways. Without these, it is hard to achieve the convenience, accessibility and limits required for applications in regions, for instance, prosperity watching. Sharp sensors, which join a sensor and a microcontroller, make it possible to handle the vitality of the IoT for human administrations by unequivocally evaluating, watching and inspecting a combination of prosperity status markers. These can join basic signs, for instance, heart rate and circulatory strain, and furthermore levels of glucose or oxygen drenching in the blood (Lee, 2015). Splendid sensors can even be joined into pill compartments and related with the framework to exhibit whether a tolerant has taken an arranged estimation of medication. For splendid sensors to work effectively, the microcontroller portions must breaker a couple of essential capacities:

Early Mediation/Avoidance

Solid, unique people can in like manner benefit by IoT-driven seeing of their consistently activities and flourishing. A senior living alone, for example, may need a watching device that can recognize a fall or other impedance in conventional development and report it to emergency responders or relatives. So far as that is concerned, a dynamic contender, for instance, a pioneer or biker could benefit by such an answer at any age, particularly if it's available as a touch of wearable advancement.

- Low-control assignment is essential to keeping contraption impression little and widening battery life, characteristics that help make IoT devices as usable as could be normal considering the present situation. Freescale, which has since a long time back offered low-control dealing with, is working by and by to enable absolutely sans battery devices that utilization imperativeness gathering frameworks utilizing ultra-low-control DC-DC converters.
- Integrated precision straightforward limits make it functional for sensors to achieve high exactness easily. Freescale offers this enabling development inside microcontrollers which contain basic parts, for instance, high-assurance easy to-cutting edge converters and low-control activity amps.
- Graphical UIs (GUIs) upgrade convenience by engaging show contraptions to pass on a great deal of information in particular detail and by making it easy to get to that information. Freescale's i.MX applications processors with high outlines taking care of execution support impelled GUI change.

Entries are the server farm focuses that assemble sensor data, research it and after that give it to the cloud by methods for wide locale mastermind headways. Gateways can be proposed for clinical or home settings; in the last said, they may be a bit of greater system resource that also manages imperativeness, diversion and distinctive structures in the home. The Freescale Home Wellbeing Hub reference organize fuses an entry part. Restorative contraption organizers can furthermore use the phase to influence remote to get to devices for remote checking.

IOT IN HEALTHCARE: THE TIME IS NOW

The since a long time back foreseen IoT change in social protection is starting at now in advance, as the cases in this paper clear up. Additionally, those are just the tip of the famous ice sheet, as new use cases continue rising to address the sincere prerequisite for direct, accessible care. Meanwhile, we are seeing the IoT building bits of computerization and machine-to-machine correspondence keep on being set up, with the extension of the organization layer completing the establishment. Freescale is anxious to be a bit of this revolt by offering end-to-end taking care of moreover, accessibility answers for IoT-driven social protection courses of action, advancing toward setting up standards for these game plans and enlivening progression for affiliations on edge to comprehend the upsides of the IoT in therapeutic administrations.

Smart Health

The IoT devices can enable remote prosperity watching nowadays, not only the customary splendid prosperity contraptions end up unmistakable in the market, yet there are similarly the wearable advancement devices, for instance, sharp watches, social protection devices, health GPS signals, baby and pregnancy wearable and even pet wearable. These sharp prosperity contraptions have the ability to get data from the sensors. Some unique contraptions support the UI or have appears and the remote framework accessibility, for instance, Bluetooth or flexible framework (Navya Teja, Vooha, Rohini Priya and V.K.Ramesh, 2018). The wearable development contraptions required features like low power use, life, quality, precision, faithful quality and security to guarantee the individual insurance.

ISSUE OF THE IOT SECURITY

The security issues drop the pace of the change of IoT. The attackers may use assorted systems in different layers to ambush the IoT sort out. As the IoT propels, digital assaults are all the all the more getting the chance to be physical perils. Data security has transformed into the need though for the illustrating of each IoT arranges systems. A couple of manufacturers don't have any security standard for their things; a couple of devices use its own acknowledged standard of security that don't impeccable with various makes things; some old adjustments of contraptions don't have any wellbeing exertion at all. PC controlled contraptions in automobiles, for instance, breakers, engines, locks and dashboards have been appeared to the defenseless against aggressors who approach the framework. Since the IoT is a rich wellspring of data it will constantly be feeble against refined ambushes (O'Neill, 2016). In diagram, there are number of security stresses from the end-customer point of view as recorded underneath: i) Inadequate physical security for interconnected contraptions ii) Insecure Web interfaces iii) Insecure programming/firmware iv) Insecure convenient interfaces v) Insecure framework organizations vi) Insecure transport and transmission vii) Inefficient endorsement and approval viii) Privacy and mystery concerns ix) Data uprightness concerns x) Distributed repudiation of-advantage perils. The security organization of the IoT masterminds structure is basic to the potential end-customers and framework providers.

IOT SECURITY MANAGEMENT SYSTEMS

The IoT security organization structure should be established on the building of the IoT compose system. There are five central security issues in the IoT sort out system; each one of them should be considered before the arrangement in the security organization structure. These security issues are that splendid sensors are definitely not hard to attack; security organization should support low-control sharp contraptions, assurance issues of the part layer devices, various Layers face with relative risks, and structure multifaceted nature and likeness issues (Kim, Kim and Seo, 2017). These necessities induce that we need to develop a security organization structure for the IoT condition that counters each and every evident hazard and be great with the IoT compose plan. Toward the day's end, since the IoT mastermind condition is arranged as four-layer structure building, it is extremely reasonable that the security organization of the framework be dealt with also as a layered plan. To execute this thought, we propose a four-layer security organization structure for the IoT condition like that used for the IPSec utilitarian plan. The IoT security organization structure (IoTSMS) has four utilitarian layers. The guidelines that were associated with meet up at four layers are according to the accompanying: (i) A layer of helpfulness is made where a substitute sort of security takes a shot at different level is required. (ii) Each layer plays out a particularly portrayed security work. (iii) The value of each layer is packed with thought toward adequately existing organized traditions. (iv) as far as possible are chosen to confine the data stream over the system interfaces. (v) The amount of layers is great with the IoT system layers to such an extent that specific security limits require not be through in a comparable layer. The exhibited security organization structure has three areas; on the left, we have shown the plan of the IoT orchestrate system which involves four layers. In the inside part is the IoTSMS, which has the four-layer as the security business approach organization, IoT security organizations organization, IoT security segments organization and IoT key security work. For instance, pseudorandom generator, multiplicative invert, estimated number juggling limit, et cetera. Each layer has its contrasting security organization convenience with give the data protection, data genuineness and data openness. On the right-50% of this outline is the IoT security organization information base.

FUNCTIONAL LAYERS OF SECURITY MANAGEMENT FOR IOT

There are four layers of security organization for IoT, has said already. They are IoT security business technique organization layer, IoT security advantage organization layer, IoT security segments organization layer and IoT basic security work layer. Each layer has its own ability to give the protection to the IoT security organization system.

IOT SECURITY BUSINESS POLICY MANAGEMENT REQUIREMENTS

The security business technique organization layer is stressed over the business customer essentials, for instance, shirking and acknowledgment of all ambushes from different reason for strikes, guaranteeing the security of each sagacious device and protecting the IoT structure from attacks and thwart the system frustration. Shows the IoT security business plan organization at any rate requirements. eHealth is a multidisciplinary zone that joins tremendous number of different intelligent what's more, development fields in programming building and arrangement. eHealth intends to the course of action of social protection organizations free of territory, customer versatility and time control. Started from an arrangement of electronic therapeutic kinds of apparatus, eHealth is at present a ubiquitous social protection perspective that spotlights on sickness balancing activity of an individual, proactive exercises and life quality change and, in particular cases, home-passed on emergency mind at the benefit place and flawless time if important.

In this outline, the makers proposed three sorts of components that solidly relate to each other: subjects, challenge and operational spaces. According to the makers, the whole outline bases on the patients. Subjects are through and through people including the patients, overwhelmingly pros and social protection specialists and furthermore the patient's relatives and friends. Articles are ICT objects that are being utilized to manage the patients. They address the whole watching system of the patients, for example wearable sensors, remedial sensors, body section, GPS contraptions, biosensors and setting careful sensors (Lake, Milito, Morrow and Vargheese, 2014). This system offers the progressing watching limit of the desired designing. Finally, the operational zone addresses the zone where the eHealth organizations are given, for instance, mending focuses, elderly care workplaces, focuses and especially the elderly people's own homes. The makers picked an eHealth telemonitoring organization as a show of the abnormal state designing said above. This organization is depended upon to offer capable care of an individual paying little regard to time, customer compactness, region and resource. The organization involves the going with capacities:

- Real-time invigorate and evaluation of the patient's prosperity conditions. This limit is depended upon to get the therapeutic and natural parameters from the patient's body additionally, review any movements happened
- Real-time invigorate of the patient's enveloping condition and activity. This limit is depended upon to pick upsetting information and see patient's activities.
- Dynamically encircling social affairs of sensible subjects (prosperity specialists, relatives, sustain, partners) in light of the patient's conditions and conditions. This limit relies upon the two past limits; the main picks the most sensible subjects in light of the data from the patient's profile while the second one instates the media transmission organize that partners the picked subjects.
- The making of information stream or possibly alerts to the reasonable subjects identified with the patient being checked.

The observing tele observing organization has the going with structure, with its four essential parts: smart home, widened entryway, application server and restorative administrations center. In the wise home, there are a couple of framework establishment, for instance, BAN, a remote individual area sort out and the WLAN that covers the whole home (Arbeille et al., 2016). The tiniest orchestrate, BAN, contains a couple of wearable sensors that reliably accumulate key body parameters from the patient and setting information from the enveloping condition. This information is gathered at the body section, which progresses the information to the WPAN. Finally, the WLAN sends data to the all inclusive community IP-based framework. The expanded entry will be in charge of giving architects of an eHealth remote watching organization with: the basic functionalities of a regulated ETSI/ Parlay structure, the instruments of sensor composes, the profiling parts and the security frameworks. This widened entryway is imperative in passing on an ensured, tweaked and setting careful remote prosperity watching organization.

STANDARDS FOR CONVEYING INDIVIDUAL TELEMEDICINE

Entering the grandstand requires a creative, usable contraption and in addition advance might be achievable with the strong condition. By condition I mean a broad establishment of different plans with sensational customer experience and support. Following parts could be a bit of the thing for therapeutic administrations conveyed in perspective of Internet of Things norms: Intelligent and related contraption itself, online gaining and support, Warranty administrations, Compatible frill, Social system. The web or flexible application for self-data examination, Environments for remedial experts, Hospital instruction, and Social protection advantage giving. Conveying such kind of course of action requires accessories and colleagues, as a lone association can't work such extensively beginning with no outside help. It infers that choice will depend upon models used (open standards are provoked), interoperability and closeness. These outlines the way that associations from remedial and social protection, devices, life sciences must pass on to introduce fitting human administrations Internet of Things, while segregate devices are just auto courses of action without astuteness.

INVESTIGATION OF POSITIVE COMMITMENT AND DANGERS

In this part pass on about possible threats of therapeutic administrations Internet of Things and their association with benefits for society. Already, an assortment of purposes of enthusiasm of telemedicine were shown, yet in this part I should need to dismember the peril scene behind awesome assurances of automated social protection, fathom the wellsprings of risk in display day orchestrated restorative devices and, finally, prepare recommendations for opening up a motivation to patients while constraining security threats starting from programming, gear, firmware and correspondence headways across finished individual helpful contraptions. The purpose of this part is to find the amicability between clear focal points and ability to guarantee the advancement and correspondence foundations of present day contraptions. The prizes of passing on Internet of Things to therapeutic administrations aren't so faultless, and it is making a couple of zones of concern. To appreciate the threats, I would immediately rapidly examine the assurance of automated restorative advancements yet again, to exhibit the basic establishments of security inconveniences. There are four essential sorts of telemedicine devices, showed up in Figure 15. I would focus on singular ones just, as they are the point of convergence of suggestion contemplate and because of the high difference of stationary remedial machines in applications, security, and controls.

BRILLIANT HUMAN SERVICES SECURITY CONCERNS

Society's yearning and mechanical ability to use sorting out headways reliably outperform their ability to control the security of that advances. Sorted out remedial devices is not evasion. They give gigantic points of interest to the front line restorative administrations structure, so planners and adopters close their eyes and attempt not to see honest to goodness security gaps in new things. The situation will proceed as previously or break down if security specialists and device makers don't make 46 the required walks now. It could happen that an immense impact of helpful zero-day undertakings and security openings without defend will connect accessible. Along these lines, there are four standard and closed domains of human administrations Internet of Things concern: Accidental disappointments (Changchit and Bagchi, 2017). Ensuring patient's security Intentional disturb, Widespread upset, Accidental frustrations are the most clear issue, which lessens the general trust of customers, in light of the way that if any fantastic disillusionment happens, society will dismiss organized helpful contraptions, putting off the improvement of social protection and pharmaceutical for a significant long time. People can trust in masters, anyway it is continually hard to place stock in the machine if there were some mechanical or programming botch, provoked some irreversible result. Orchestrated therapeutic contraptions are frail against something past criminal reason. Like some other mechanical, automated contraption or development they can isolate absolutely or authentic direct can be changed. It's definitely not a result of uncalled for building or terrible parts; it is an eventual outcome of amassing deserts, programming messes up or other circumstance affected by countless. The multifaceted design of contraptions and operational development which controls physical methodology, for instance, pumps, makes exponential open entryways for surrenders in layout, use, or action, any of which can provoke amazing unintentional disappointment (Baker, Xiang and Atkinson, 2017). The probability of frustration must be nearly nothing (it couldn't be veritable 0 eventually and even on a basic level) concerning restorative devices appeared differently in relation to other sorted out headways.

After contenders' examination and market consideration, the summary of issues to handle and challenges is clear: Avoid using extra devices and use an advanced cell. Make a pleasing gadget. Make one device that fits all parts. Consider the future organic framework and focus on working up a connectable gadget. Make a progressed and stunning gadget. Utilize open models. Make an application profitable and prepared to give data bits of knowledge. Build up a characteristic application and natural contraption controls. Spotlight on security. Spotlight on centered crowd clearly, this summary isn't full; anyway these points of view are crucial. Subsequent to starting inventive work, the likelihood of the arm adornments was imagined. It fulfills the helpful medications (bear is a tolerable place for insulin implantation) and necessities of real sharp social protection wearable. In following segments I will discuss features, specific purposes of intrigue, and model of the wrist knickknack itself.

CONCLUSION

Medicinal services and pharmaceutical are crucial social parts and the necessity for mechanical help there is extending everlastingly as instruments and treatment strategies are ending up additionally created. Introduce day communicate correspondences and machine learning open new routes for symptomatic process and treatment strategies. Web of Things offers the possibility of the interconnected world, where therapeutic organizations are maintained by each piece of being, from sustenance to transportation. Everything considered, the benefits of sharp organizations in individual therapeutic administrations saw through the examination are vanquishing all drawbacks. In any case, security and assurance, customer experience and determination are huge concentrations to be considered and advanced. This examination that by and by completes has focused on singular social protection Internet of Things, which gives the customer electronic restorative and thriving organizations or application. It is the best bit of the whole helpful division, as different strong people are more prominent and it is basic to get their eye and focus it on prosperity before certifiable bothers when remedy starts. In a perfect world, my examination comes about are significant for an extensive variety of associations, anyway it is charming to understand that there is no best quality level for impacting associations, to even in the social protection field, where various controls are associated. The explanation behind my work is to give bits of learning of the sharp human administrations fragment and to give key revelations to IT people who are not prepared to use propels for working up a proper thing and for business professionals who can't relate the possible results of current advances to the necessities of purchasers. This report should close the gap between two solidly related social affairs of people, giving appreciation all in all field and essentials for new things. This is, clearly, only a to a great degree preliminary proposal that has helped me to develop my understanding in different ways: It has empowered me to enter a field of research that was absolutely dark to me already, which is telemedicine, with its mechanical and restorative foundations. It has empowered me to have a first look on how ask about is done around there. It has accustomed with a couple of parts of solution, it has exhibited to me the path for the usage of business looks at for creative undertakings. To complete, should need to express that clearly there are an impressive measure of conduct by which my examination could be widened: Medical IoT could be explored and its association with human administrations could be inquired about. Extraordinary and all the more puzzling examinations could be performed for focused regions, similar to security or gathering of splendid social protection devices elective case things could be produced.

REFERENCES

Abrahamson, K., Myers, J., Arling, G., Davila, H., Mueller, C., Abery, B., & Cai, Y. (2016). Capacity and readiness for quality improvement among home and community-based service providers. *Home Health Care Services Quarterly*, *35*(3-4), 182–196. doi:10.1080/01621424.2016.1264343 PMID:27897462

Al-Taee, M., Al-Nuaimy, W., Muhsin, Z., & Al-Ataby, A. (2017). Robot Assistant in Management of Diabetes in Children Based on the Internet of Things. *IEEE Internet Of Things Journal*, *4*(2), 437–445. doi:10.1109/JIOT.2016.2623767

Al-Turjman, F., Kirsal Ever, Y., Ever, E., Nguyen, H., & David, D. (2017). Seamless Key Agreement Framework for Mobile-Sink in IoT Based Cloud-Centric Secured Public Safety Sensor Networks. *IEEE Access: Practical Innovations, Open Solutions*, *5*, 24617–24631. doi:10.1109/ACCESS.2017.2766090

Alemdar, H., Durmus, Y., & Ersoy, C. (2010). Wireless Healthcare Monitoring with RFID-Enhanced Video Sensor Networks. *International Journal of Distributed Sensor Networks*, *6*(1), 473037. doi:10.1155/2010/473037

Allegretti, M. (2014). Concept for Floating and Submersible Wireless Sensor Network for Water Basin Monitoring. *Wireless Sensor Network*, *6*(6), 104–108. doi:10.4236/wsn.2014.66011

Arbeille, P., Zuj, K., Saccomandi, A., Andre, E., De La Porte, C., & Georgescu, M. (2016). Tele-Operated Echography and Remote Guidance for Performing Tele-Echography on Geographically Isolated Patients. *Journal of Clinical Medicine*, *5*(6), 58. doi:10.3390/jcm5060058 PMID:27304972

Baker, S., Xiang, W., & Atkinson, I. (2017). Internet of Things for Smart Healthcare: Technologies, Challenges, and Opportunities. *IEEE Access: Practical Innovations, Open Solutions*, *5*, 26521–26544. doi:10.1109/ACCESS.2017.2775180

Bera, S., Misra, S., Roy, S., & Obaidat, M. (2016). Soft-WSN: Software-Defined WSN Management System for IoT Applications. *IEEE Systems Journal*, 1–8. doi:10.1109/jsyst.2016.2615761

Berkowitz, C. (2012). Sudden Infant Death Syndrome, Sudden Unexpected Infant Death, and Apparent Life-Threatening Events. *Advances in Pediatrics*, *59*(1), 183–208. doi:10.1016/j.yapd.2012.04.011 PMID:22789579

Bisio, I., Delfino, A., Lavagetto, F., & Sciarrone, A. (2016). Enabling IoT for In-Home Rehabilitation: Accelerometer Signals Classification Methods for Activity and Movement Recognition. *IEEE Internet Of Things Journal*, 1-1. doi:10.1109/jiot.2016.2628938

Buiu, O. (2017). Internet of Things and the Human Body. *Journal Of Nanomedicine Research*, *5*(2). doi:10.15406/jnmr.2017.05.00113

Changchit, C., & Bagchi, K. (2017). Privacy and Security Concerns with Healthcare Data and Social Media Usage. *Journal Of Information Privacy And Security*, *13*(2), 49–50. doi:10.1080/15536548.2017.1322413

Dangerfield, M., Ward, K., Davidson, L., & Adamian, M. (2017). Initial Experience and Usage Patterns With the Owlet Smart Sock Monitor in 47,495 Newborns. *Global Pediatric Health*, *4*. doi:10.1177/2333794x17742751

Dhanalakshmi, & Sam Leni, A. (2017). Instance vehicle monitoring and tracking with internet of things using Arduino. *International Journal on Smart Sensing and Intelligent Systems, 10*(4), 123-135. doi:10.21307/ijssis-2017-240

Duckett, K. (2016). Innovation in Home Healthcare. *Home Healthcare Now*, *34*(7), 403–404. doi:10.1097/NHH.0000000000000394 PMID:27348039

Farris, I., Pizzi, S., Merenda, M., Molinaro, A., Carotenuto, R., & Iera, A. (2017). 6lo-RFID: A Framework for Full Integration of Smart UHF RFID Tags into the Internet of Things. *IEEE Network*, *31*(5), 66–73. doi:10.1109/MNET.2017.1600269

Fattah, S., Sung, N., Ahn, I., Ryu, M., & Yun, J. (2017). Building IoT Services for Aging in Place Using Standard-Based IoT Platforms and Heterogeneous IoT Products. *Sensors (Basel)*, *17*(10), 2311. doi:10.339017102311 PMID:29019964

Fosso Wamba, S., Barjis, J., & Takeoka Chatfield, A. (2010). Business impacts of RFID applications. *Business Process Management Journal*, *16*(6), bpmj.2010.15716faa.001. doi:10.1108/bpmj.2010.15716faa.001

Franckhauser, M. (2013). Rural Healthcare and the Challenges of Home Healthcare and Hospice. *Home Healthcare Nurse*, *31*(4), 227–228. doi:10.1097/NHH.0b013e318289c429 PMID:23549255

Fuji, K., & Abbott, A. (2014). Ensuring Effective Medication Reconciliation in Home Healthcare. *Home Healthcare Nurse*, *32*(9), 516–522. doi:10.1097/NHH.0000000000000136 PMID:25268524

Gao, L. (2016). Building of Smart Home Medical System Based on Internet of Things. *Internet Of Things And Cloud Computing*, *4*(3), 34. doi:10.11648/j.iotcc.20160403.14

Gond, J., Cabantous, L., & Krikorian, F. (2017). How do things become strategic? 'Strategifying' corporate social responsibility. *Strategic Organization*. doi:10.1177/1476127017702819

Hu, Y., Wu, Y., & Wang, H. (2014). Detection of Insider Selective Forwarding Attack Based on Monitor Node and Trust Mechanism in WSN. *Wireless Sensor Network*, *06*(11), 237–248. doi:10.4236/wsn.2014.611023

Internet of Things – Integration and Semantic Interoperability of Sensor Data of Things in Heterogeneous Environments. (2016). Internet of Things – Integration and Semantic Interoperability of Sensor Data of Things in Heterogeneous Environments. *International Journal Of Modern Trends In Engineering & Research*, *3*(12), 174–178. doi:10.21884/IJMTER.2016.3166.Y4XEN

IoT Delegate: Smart Home Framework for Heterogeneous IoT Service Collaboration. (2016). *KSII Transactions On Internet And Information Systems*, *10*(8). doi:10.3837/tiis.2016.08.029

Jepsen, T. (2014). Doctor's Orders: Healthcare Apps and Self-Monitoring. *IT Professional*, *16*(4), 48–49. doi:10.1109/MITP.2014.49

John Livingston, J., & Umamakeswari, A. (2015). Internet of Things Application using IP-enabled Sensor Node and Web Server. *Indian Journal of Science and Technology*, *8*(S9), 207. doi:10.17485/ijst/2015/v8iS9/65577

Kashyap, R. (2019a). Security, Reliability, and Performance Assessment for Healthcare Biometrics. In D. Kisku, P. Gupta, & J. Sing (Eds.), Design and Implementation of Healthcare Biometric Systems (pp. 29-54). Hershey, PA: IGI Global. doi:10.4018/978-1-5225-7525-2.ch002

Kashyap, R. (2019b). Biometric Authentication Techniques and E-Learning. In A. Kumar (Ed.), *Biometric Authentication in Online Learning Environments* (pp. 236–265). Hershey, PA: IGI Global; doi:10.4018/978-1-5225-7724-9.ch010

Kashyap, R. (2019c). Machine Learning for Internet of Things. In I.-S. Comşa & R. Trestian (Eds.), *Next-Generation Wireless Networks Meet Advanced Machine Learning Applications* (pp. 57–83). Hershey, PA: IGI Global; doi:10.4018/978-1-5225-7458-3.ch003

Kashyap, R. (2019d). Geospatial Big Data, Analytics and IoT: Challenges, Applications and Potential. In H. Das, R. Barik, H. Dubey & D. Sinha Roy, Cloud Computing for Geospatial Big Data Analytics (1st ed., pp. 191-213). Switzerland AG: Springer International Publishing.

Kashyap, R., & Gautam, P. (2017). Fast Medical Image Segmentation Using Energy-Based Method. *Biometrics. Concepts, Methodologies, Tools, and Applications*, *3*(1), 1017–1042. doi:10.4018/978-1-5225-0983-7.ch040

Kashyap, R., Gautam, P., & Tiwari, V. (2018). Management and Monitoring Patterns and Future Scope. In Handbook of Research on Pattern Engineering System Development for Big Data Analytics. IGI Global. doi:10.4018/978-1-5225-3870-7.ch014

Kashyap, R., & Piersson, A. (2018a). Big Data Challenges and Solutions in the Medical Industries. In Handbook of Research on Pattern Engineering System Development for Big Data Analytics. IGI Global. doi:10.4018/978-1-5225-3870-7.ch001

Kashyap, R., & Piersson, A. (2018b). Impact of Big Data on Security. In Handbook of Research on Network Forensics and Analysis Techniques (pp. 283–299). IGI Global. doi:10.4018/978-1-5225-4100-4.ch015

Kashyap, R., & Tiwari, V. (2018). Active contours using global models for medical image segmentation. *International Journal of Computational Systems Engineering*, *4*(2/3), 195. doi:10.1504/IJCSYSE.2018.091404

Khan, M., Silva, B., & Han, K. (2017). A Web of Things-Based Emerging Sensor Network Architecture for Smart Control Systems. Sensors (Basel), 17(2), 332. doi:10.339017020332 PMID:28208787.

Khan, M., Silva, B., & Han, K. (2017). A Web of Things-Based Emerging Sensor Network Architecture for Smart Control Systems. *Sensors (Basel)*, *17*(2), 332. doi:10.339017020332 PMID:28208787

Khan, M., Silva, B., & Han, K. (2017). A Web of Things-Based Emerging Sensor Network Architecture for Smart Control Systems. *Sensors (Basel)*, *17*(2), 332. doi:10.339017020332 PMID:28208787

Kim, B., & Mondal, S. (2016). Design of TSV-based Inductors for Internet of Things. *Additional Conferences (Device Packaging, Hitec, Hiten, & CICMT)*. doi: 10.4071/2016dpc-tha34

Kim, J., Kim, M., & Seo, J. (2017). Implementation and Evaluation of IoT Service System for Security Enhancement. *Journal Of The Korea Institute Of Information Security And Cryptology*, *27*(2), 181–192. doi:10.13089/JKIISC.2017.27.2.181

Klumpp, M. (2018). Innovation Potentials and Pathways Merging AI, CPS, and IoT. *Applied System Innovation*, *1*(1), 5. doi:10.3390/asi1010005

Kumar, S., & Chaurasiya, V. (2018). A multisensor data fusion strategy for path selection in Internet-of-Things oriented wireless sensor network (WSN). *Concurrency and Computation*, *e4477*. doi:10.1002/cpe.4477

Lake, D., Milito, R., Morrow, M., & Vargheese, R. (2014). Internet of Things: Architectural Framework for eHealth Security. *Journal Of ICT Standardization*, *1*(3), 301–328. doi:10.13052/jicts2245-800X.133

Lake, D., Milito, R., Morrow, M., & Vargheese, R. (2014). Internet of Things: Architectural Framework for eHealth Security. *Journal Of ICT Standardization*, *1*(3), 301–328. doi:10.13052/jicts2245-800X.133

Lamberts, R., Swart, J., Capostagno, B., Noakes, T., & Lambert, M. (2009). Heart rate recovery as a guide to monitor fatigue and predict changes in performance parameters. *Scandinavian Journal of Medicine & Science in Sports*, *20*(3), 449–457. doi:10.1111/j.1600-0838.2009.00977.x PMID:19558377

Lee, B. (2015). Dynamic Data Binding Protocol between IoT Medical Device and IoT Medical Service for Mobile Healthcare. *International Journal Of Smart Home*, *9*(6), 141–150. doi:10.14257/ijsh.2015.9.6.16

Lingam, M. S. (2017). Transforming Smart Healthcare through the Internet of Things (IoT). *International Journal Of Emerging Trends In Science And Technology*, *4*(9). doi:10.18535/ijetst/v4i9.08

Makushin, M., & Martynov, V. (2018). Problems and prospects for the development of the industrial internet of things. *Electronics: Science, Technology. Business (Atlanta, Ga.)*, (3): 156–168. doi:10.22184/1992-4178.2018.174.3.156.168

Mengden, T., Vetter, H., Tislér, A., & Illyés, M. (2001). Tele-monitoring of home blood pressure. *Blood Pressure Monitoring*, 6(4), 185–189. doi:10.1097/00126097-200108000-00004 PMID:11805466

Mittelstadt, B. (2017). Ethics of the health-related internet of things: A narrative review. *Ethics and Information Technology*, *19*(3), 157–175. doi:10.100710676-017-9426-4

Namatame, N., Nakazawa, J., & Tokuda, H. (2012). Logical Sensor Network: An Abstraction of Sensor Data Processing over Multidomain Sensor Network. *ISRN Sensor Networks*, *2012*, 1–9. doi:10.5402/2012/234251

Navya Teja, Y., Vooha, L., Rohini Priya, A., & Ramesh, N. (2018). IOT Based Smart Health Care. *International Journal Of Engineering & Technology, 7*(2), 470. doi:10.14419/ijet.v7i2.7.10865

Novo, O. (2018). Blockchain Meets IoT: An Architecture for Scalable Access Management in IoT. *IEEE Internet Of Things Journal*, 5(2), 1184–1195. doi:10.1109/JIOT.2018.2812239

Novo, O. (2018). Blockchain Meets IoT: An Architecture for Scalable Access Management in IoT. *IEEE Internet Of Things Journal*, 5(2), 1184–1195. doi:10.1109/JIOT.2018.2812239

Numerical Studies on the Electronic Gadgets in a Personal Computer Using CFD. (n.d.). *International Journal Of Science And Research*, 5(7). doi:10.21275/v5i7.art2016526

O'Neill, M. (2016). Insecurity by Design: Today's IoT Device Security Problem. *Engineering*, 2(1), 48–49. doi:10.1016/J.ENG.2016.01.014

Onyshchenko, K., & Afanasieva, I. (2017). Structured methodology for development of the service for providing remote control of intelligent home devices using Internet of Things solutions. *Sciencerise*, 5(2), 30–33. doi:10.15587/2313-8416.2017.101735

Progress on the development of the MediWatch ambulatory blood pressure monitor and related devices. (2004). *Blood Pressure Monitoring*, 9(6), 327. doi:10.1097/00126097-200412000-00011

Rahman, M., & Hossain, M. (2017). m-Therapy: A Multi-sensor Framework for in-home Therapy Management: A Social Therapy of Things Perspective. *IEEE Internet Of Things Journal*, 1-1. doi:10.1109/jiot.2017.2776150

Salibian, A., & Scholz, T. (2011). Smartphones in Surgery. *Journal of Healthcare Engineering*, *2*(4), 473–486. doi:10.1260/2040-2295.2.4.473

Sensor-embedded wristband uses sweat to monitor wearer's health. (2016). *Physics Today*. doi:10.1063/pt.5.029532

Shukla, R., Gupta, R. K., & Kashyap, R. (2019). A multiphase pre-copy strategy for the virtual machine migration in cloud. In S. Satapathy, V. Bhateja, & S. Das (Eds.), *Smart Intelligent Computing and Applications. Smart Innovation, Systems and Technologies* (Vol. 104). Singapore: Springer.

Singh, M., & Mittal, A. (2016). Internet of Things: Challenges in Web Based Remote Patient Monitoring (RPM). *Scholars Journal Of Applied Medical Sciences*, *4*(7), 2706–2709. doi:10.21276jams.2016.4.7.84

Siryani, J., Tanju, B., & Eveleigh, T. (2017). A Machine Learning Decision-Support System Improves the Internet of Things' Smart Meter Operations. *IEEE Internet Of Things Journal*, *4*(4), 1056–1066. doi:10.1109/JIOT.2017.2722358

Te Lindert, B., & Van Someren, E. (2013). Affordable sleep estimates using micro-electro-mechanical-systems (MEMS) accelerometry. *Sleep Medicine*, *14*, e294–e295. doi:10.1016/j.sleep.2013.11.721

Tiwari, S., Gupta, R. K., & Kashyap, R. (2019). To enhance web response time using agglomerative clustering technique for web navigation recommendation. In H. Behera, J. Nayak, B. Naik, & A. Abraham (Eds.), *Computational Intelligence in Data Mining. Advances in Intelligent Systems and Computing* (Vol. 711). Singapore: Springer.

Tsui, S., Liu, C., & Lin, C. (2017). Modified maternal ECG cancellation for portable fetal heart rate monitor. *Biomedical Signal Processing and Control*, *32*, 76–81. doi:10.1016/j.bspc.2016.11.001

Vukovic, M. (2015). Internet Programmable IoT: On the role of APIs in IoT. *Ubiquity*, *2015*(November), 1–10. doi:10.1145/2822873

Wemple, M., & Luks, A. (2012). Challenges Associated With Central Venous Catheter Placement and Central Venous Oxygen Saturation Monitoring. *Respiratory Care*. doi:10.4187/respcare.01762 PMID:22613046

Yaghmaee Moghaddam, M., & Leon-Garcia, A. (2018). A Fog-Based Internet of Energy Architecture for Transactive Energy Management Systems. *IEEE Internet Of Things Journal*, 5(2), 1055–1069. doi:10.1109/JIOT.2018.2805899

Zhou, W., & Piramuthu, S. (2017). IoT security perspective of a flexible healthcare supply chain. *Information Technology Management*. doi:10.100710799-017-0279-7

Zhou, W., & Piramuthu, S. (2017). IoT security perspective of a flexible healthcare supply chain. *Information Technology Management*. doi:10.100710799-017-0279-7

KEY TERMS AND DEFINITIONS

ACM: Active contour model, also called snakes, is a structure in PC vision for delineating a challenge design from a maybe noisy 2D picture. The snakes show is standard in PC vision, and snakes are fundamentally used as a piece of usages like inquiry following, shape affirmation, division, edge acknowledgment and stereo planning. A snake is an imperativeness restricting, deformable spline influenced by prerequisite and picture controls that draw it towards challenge structures and inside forces that contradict misshaping. Snakes may be fathomed as an extraordinary case of the general arrangement of organizing a deformable model to a photo by techniques for imperativeness minimization. In two estimations, the dynamic shape show addresses a discrete interpretation of this approach, misusing the point dissemination model to keep the shape range to an unequivocal region learnt from an arrangement set.

ECG: Electrocardiography is the route toward recording the electrical development of the heart over some vague time period using cathodes put on the skin. These anodes perceive the little electrical changes on the skin that rises up out of the heart muscle's electrophysiologic case of depolarizing and depolarizing amid each heartbeat. It is customarily performed to recognize any cardiovascular issues.

IHH: In home healthcare service. Human administrations at home is a pioneer in bringing modified and capable home therapeutic administrations benefits in India to allow quick and accommodating recovery inside the comfort of one's home. A part of the critical organizations offered to consolidate setting up ICU at home, giving Cancer Care at home, nursing care, physiotherapy organizations and widely inclusive stroke recuperation close by providing a lot of clinical system at home along these lines passing on pretty much 70% of each clinical organization at home.

IoT: Internet of things (IoT) is the arrangement of physical devices, vehicles, home mechanical assemblies and distinctive things introduced with equipment, programming, sensors, actuators, and accessibility which engages these things to partner and exchange data, making open entryways for more direct coordination of the physical world into pc based systems, achieving capability overhauls, money related points of interest and decreased human intervention.

M2M: M2M advancement was first grasped in amassing and mechanical settings, and later found applications in therapeutic administrations, business, insurance and anything is possible from that point. It is in like manner the foundation for the web of things, the rule inspiration driving machine-to-machine advancement is to exploit sensor data and transmit it to a framework. Not in any manner like SCADA or other remote watching gadgets, m2m structures consistently use open frameworks and access strategies for example, cell or ethernet to make it more cost-effective. The essential parts of a M2M system fuse sensors, RFID, a wi-fi or cell correspondences interface, and autonomic figuring programming modified to help a framework device interpret data and choose. These m2m applications interpret the data, which can trigger prearranged, mechanized exercises.

RFID: Radio-frequency identification is the use of radio waves to examine and get information set away on a name associated with an inquiry. A tag can be scrutinized from up to a couple of feet away and ought not to be inside direct distinguishable pathway of the peruser to be taken after.

Chapter 8
Relevance of Technologies for Smart Cities

Olga Berenice Mora
Universidad de Guadalajara, Mexico

Elsa Julieta Cedillo-Elias
Universidad de Guadalajara, Mexico

Emmanuel Aceves
Universidad de Guadalajara, Mexico

Victor M. Larios
Universidad de Guadalajara, Mexico

ABSTRACT

Most of the work to develop a smart city is how to connect physical urban infrastructure to the digital world to use it as a solution space for citizens and authorities to make best decisions to reach the best quality of life every day. Every city as a complex system needs to adequately manage their different dimensions. This chapter proposes the second approach with a top-down architecture identifying a set of information technologies linked in processes that every city service needs as part of their digital transformation process in their urban space. Hence, this chapter introduces six technological layers in a workflow pipeline that are explained as an approach to develop every smart system of a city. However, in the proposed workflow of technologies to implement, the authors give a central focus to the IoT infrastructure as the base to build information of quality, to have reliable services even after getting insights from analytics to come back to the IoT with their connected actuators to take actions.

DOI: 10.4018/978-1-5225-7811-6.ch008

INTRODUCTION

Smart City is defining as a complex system that involves multiple factors and many interrelated processes that coexist, generating a holistic environment in which interconnected devices interact, providing relevant information that becomes services for human beings and intelligent decision makers. At present, urban areas are growing rapidly, which generates a greater number of interconnected devices, capable of developing and offering efficient services in the different areas that make up the Smart Cities (Schaffers et al., 2011).

The services that a Smart City can generate and deliver to citizens must go hand in hand with solutions that offer technologies capable of optimizing processes and services. All interested parties involved in the development of services require information about what is happening at each point of the city in order to design a customized, adequate and efficient solution for each one of them (Pettit et al., 2017).

Within a Smart City environment, systems that provide services to citizens are prone to be victims of malicious attacks that interfere with the communications of the Control System, for example by inserting data frames and denial of service attacks causing instability in the system, generating faults that can be chaotic when it comes to a traffic light control system.

The sensor networks that depend on data networks, the traffic of data, the capture of this information, the storage in data repositories, and perform an analytical to generate an adequate perception in the data visualization form a technological system complex that serves as the basis of a Smart City in which resilience and interoperability are important challenges to provide citizens with services that can guarantee a better quality of life (V. M. Larios, L. Gomez, O. B. Mora, R. Maciel, 2016).

The IoT had its origin in the manufacturing industry where M2M communication (machine-to-machine) enabled manufacturing with complex devices, later it was expanded to commercial use as device monitoring in a smart home, until now offering services to a city, a new era arises where the modules used provide a high availability of economic sensors and transmitters, standards and communication protocols (TCP/IP), robust infrastructure generating an interconnected and data-rich environment (Pettit et al., 2017).

IoT is defined as a global infrastructure for the information society, which allows advanced services interconnecting things (physical and virtual) based on existing and evolving interoperable information and communication technologies ("Internet of Things Global Standards Initiative," n.d.). The term applies to several areas, some of them are: health, education, environment, etc. To cover the impact of device coverage in Smart Cities, it is necessary for IoT controllers to obtain the data and send it to a server in which they are analyzed and converted into the information required for the actors of the system. This interaction requires a solid, dynamic and reliable transport infrastructure between the IoT devices and the server that processes and stores the information.

Smart Traffic System, the use of IoT technologies generates an intelligent traffic monitoring system providing a good transportation experience by relieving traffic congestion, helping detect thefts, reporting traffic accidents, decreasing environmental pollution, the traffic lighting system can be adaptable to the climate to save energy.

Smart Environment, predicting natural disasters such as floods: fires, earthquakes, etc., will be possible thanks to the innovative technologies of the IoT, monitoring the quality of the air in the environment will generate a better quality of life for citizens.

Smart Home, the IoT provides solutions for home automation that allow remote control of appliances according to the needs of the user. Proper monitoring, the supply of energy and water will help save resources and detect water leaks, unexpected overloads, etc. The aim to reach the establish of a Smart Home is that the environment can be comfortable, have been defined social relationships between IoT's to discover devices, service and resources, these provide distributed solutions effectives and efficient working in a SDN environment. (Kim & Lee, 2015).

Smart Hospitals, hospitals equipped with smart wearable's integrated with RFID tags that are delivered to incoming patients, through which doctors and nurses can monitor heart rate, blood pressure, temperature and other conditions of patients inside or outside the hospital. In the beginning of 2016 in the project ELGA (electronic health record) was established the first phase of an information network between hospitals that allows them to exchange limited patient information. It has the aim to eventually provide doctors, pharmacists, hospitals and care facilities nationwide with access to important patient information, including laboratory results, medical history and current medication regimes.

These works are some of the efforts to implement Smarts Environments to improve Smart Healthcare. (Administration, n. d).

Smart Agriculture, it allows monitoring the nutrition of soil, light, humidity, etc., and improve the experience of ecological life by adjusting some variable to maximize production. The precise irrigation and fertilization will help improve the quality of the product and save water. The Internet of Things (IoT) allows the development of applications for agriculture to the control, the selection of crop growth, support of irrigation decisions, etc. Through the implementation of sensor networks, agriculture can be connected to the IoT, allowing the creation of connections between agronomists, farmers and crops, regardless of their geographic locations to achieve the optimization of the use of fertilizers and water, maximizing the yield of the crops and analyzing the climatic conditions of the field. (Savale, Managave, Ambekar, & Sathe, 2015).

Smart Retailing and supply-chain Management, the IoT with the RFID offers advantages to the retailers, when having products equipped with RFID, a trader can easily track the stock and detect theft of products in stores. You can make a record of all items in a store and to prevent them from running out an order is automatically made, you can even generate sales tables and graphs for effective strategies. (U.Farooq et al. 2015).

We have classified 3 different kinds of technologies according to the implementation that is given to each of them. 1, IoT Controllers; they are the technologies that use the devices in charge of gathering information. 2, Data Networks, these technologies are responsible for the interconnection of devices and the transport of information. 3, Data Servers, this layer is responsible for storing, analyzing and viewing the information collected (Figure 1).

In this work, the terms IoT and Smart City will be used when referring to managing thousands of connected devices that communicate with each other, supporting the monitoring of the city in order to automate with decision makers the processes, reaching services for the construction of more efficient city cities. In the following sections we present some of the most used technological tools and protocols in the field of a Smart City (Madakam, et al., 2015).

TECHNOLOGIES FOR SMART CITIES

Figure 2 shows the layers of a Smart City developed by work groups of IEEE Guadalajara Smart Cities Working Group.

Figure 1. Technological layers implemented at CUCEA Living Lab

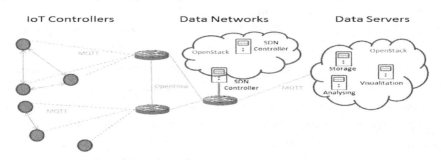

Interconnected Physical Infrastructure

The first layer is responsible for maintaining sensors, actuators, data networks, servers, etc. that allow collecting and storing data. To go to the IoT layer (Jin, et al., 2014), present the IoT infrastructure as the key technological enabler, where IoT is introduced from three different domains: network-centric IoT, Cloud-centric IoT and data-centric IoT, corresponding to communications, management, and computation requirements of Smart City development and deployment.

Internet of Things

The Internet of Things is a system that supports large range of applications with different requirements integrated heterogeneous components. IoT applications maybe include smart infrastructure, smart healthcare, smart governance, smart mobility, smart technology, etc. In addition to complying with these characteristics, IoT must also be modular, scalable, secure and reliable in all the services and applications it is capable of offering to users or citizens of a Smart City. (Datta, Parul, B.S. 2017)

Open Data Repository

Open data have the potential to empower citizens, change how government works and improve the delivery of public services while generating significant economic value. There are some features of open data: Availability and access, reuse and redistribution, universal participation, primacy, machine readability and licensing. (Guardado-Medina, et al., 2015).

Analytics and Information Visualization

The different sensor networks that are implemented in a Smart City must be able to provide a large amount of unstructured data flows. These data flows must be purified and placed in the Open Data Repository before being used for the analysis to obtain information on the dynamism of a Smart City.

This data in the Open Data repository, should be represented in a georeferenced map as part of a dashboard showing the main Smart City Metrics of performance for each service or indicator of the urban environment. (Aceves, E., & Larios, V.M. (2015)

Smart City Metrics

Measurement is a fundamental issue, since it improves the quality of life by understanding the performance of the city in four key areas: talent, innovation, connections and distinctive character.

The metrics of the city require standard specifications; methods and strategies to allow cities to be compared under the same framework. (Castañeda, V., & Guzman, E. 2015)

Education for Smart Cites

The main tool to enable a Smart City are ICTs but are of not useful if the users of smart technology are not able to interact with the smart services. One of the main priorities of smart cities should be to increase access to smart devices and, above all, to educate them about their use, at all levels of income an age groups. (Policy, I.T.U., & Division, T. W., 2015).

IoT CONTROLLERS

At the living Lab, the research group has identified as requirements of these devices an independent Operating System, adaptation to different types and brands of sensors, process automation, resilience capacity and independence, in situations of failure of the global system as well as intercommunication between them.

Figure 2. Technological layers for smart cities

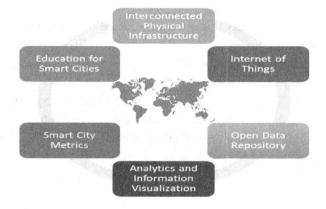

Technologies

Some of the used microcontrollers are Galileo, Raspberry Pi 3. Linux-based Operating Systems are implemented so that the implementation does not depend on special licenses.

ROS

More recently, the implementation of ROS ("ROS.org | Powering the world's robot," n.d) is proposed since it provides controllers with distributed computing, reuse of software as well as the ability to analyze and test quickly. Allowing a modular and scalable development easy to reuse and implement in different heterogeneous devices, generating an integral system.

Protocols

Some of the main protocols (Al-Fuqaha, Guizani, Mohammadi, Aledhari, & Ayyash, 2015) used in the IoT oriented to a smart city are the following:

Constrained Application Protocol (CoAP)

It is a protocol located in the application layer, for IoT applications. CoAP is defined as a web transfer protocol based on REpresentational State Transfer (REST) over HTTP functionalities; REST represents a simple way to exchange data between clients and servers through HTTP. It transmits under UDP. CoAP modifies some HTTP functions to meet IoT requirements, such as low power consumption and operation in the presence of noisy and loss links.

Message Queue Telemetry Transport (MQTT)

The objective of this protocol is to connect devices and integrated networks with middleware applications. It uses a routing mechanism (one to one, one to many, many to many); it is an optimal connection protocol for IoT and M2M applications. It is suitable for devices with limited resources that use unreliable links or low bandwidth, works under the TCP protocol. MQTT is composed of three elements: subscriber, publisher and broker. A device is registered as a subscriber of specific topics for the intermediary to inform when publishers publish topics of interest. Then the editor transmits the information to the interested entities (subscribers) through the broker (OASIS, 2014).

171

Extensible Messaging and Presence Protocol (XMPP)

It is an instant messaging standard that is used for multi-party conversations, voice calls and video calls. It allows users to communicate with each other by sending instant messages on the Internet regardless of which operating system they are using. XMPP connects a client to a server using a sequence of XML stanzas.

Advanced Message Queuing Protocol (AMQP)

It is a protocol located in the standard application layer open for IoT focused on message-oriented environments. Work under TCP to exchange messages. Communications are handled by two main components: exchanges and message queues. Exchanges are used to route messages to appropriate queues. The routing between exchanges and message queues is based on some predefined rules and conditions.

We realized an analysis of these four principal IoT protocols considering their characteristics and we could define the best protocol for implementing in a Smart City. The best protocol for the Smart Cities is MQTT protocol, because it is appropriate for the distributed systems. CoAP is lighter and working with UDP packets, however MQTT work with UDP and TCP, contributing a higher security level to the data.

The AMQP protocol like MQTT protocol work with TCP therefore its implementation could be similar however MQTT has less latency in delivery of packets (Suresh Kumar & Kumar, 2017).

Resilience in an IoT System

Have a fault tolerant system, capable of recovering from an attack of the system itself or external that provides security to system users. Resilience also describes the ability to recover to original status.

In (Huang, Y., et al., 2015), the goal of resilience is to build fault tolerant networks. The strength of a system emphasizes the ability to resist attacks against it, but does not imply the ability to re-establish the error. If the system is robust, that means that the system is very difficult to degrade under several attacks. As for the ability to survive, this indicates that the system is very difficult to damage completely.

Security

There are some issues from security (Lin, et al., 2017)., makes reference to some of the main issues.

Confidentiality

Confidentiality is one of the important principles since most of the devices can be integrated into the IoT, it becomes essential to guarantee that the collected data does not reveal information to neighboring interconnected devices. Confidentiality is intended to ensure that all data is available only to authorized users and can not be intercepted by unauthorized users.

Integrity

Integrity ensures that data can not be altered during data delivery in data networks, keeping accurate data for authorized users. Integrity in the IoT is important since if the applications or services receive falsified data or altered data, the status of the operation can be estimated erroneous and consequently the feedback commands are erroneous, causing failures in the applications or IoT services.

Availability

Availability is to ensure that data and devices are available to authorized users and services whenever services are requested. In IoT, services are commonly requested in real time, and services can not be scheduled or provided if the requested data can not be delivered in a timely manner.

Therefore, availability is also an important security principle.

Identification and Authentication

Identification ensures that unauthorized devices or applications can not connect to IoT, and authentication ensures that the data delivered to data networks is legitimate, and the devices or applications that request the data are also legitimate.

The design of efficient mechanisms to deal with the authentication of objects or things is critical in IoT. (Lin, et al., 2017)

Privacy

IoT is part of different environments: remote monitoring of patients, traffic control, electric power consumption, parking systems, production chains, shopping at the supermarket, etc.

In all these cases the user provides personal information, therefore it is required that the personal information related to their habits, movements and interactions with this protected, that is, their privacy and personal information is guaranteed. (Sicari, et al., 2014)

IoT Challenges

When thousands of interconnected devices are deployed, it becomes a challenge to manage them efficiently, the more numbers of interconnected devices there are, the greater the challenge to be covered.

The main strategy is the implementation of Gateways, where a group of controllers are connected to one under a centralized scheme, the Gateway is the only controller linked to the Data Network. Also is possible implement a direct access to the network, which implies the deployment of a robust, dynamic and innovative infrastructure that is capable of supporting the transfer of information generated and required by the controllers.

DATA NETWORKS INFRASTRUCTURE

When talking about of the Infrastructure of an Intelligent City, it references to the Information and Communication Technology (ICT) physical technology necessary for the functional operation of the Smart City, including buildings, roads, power supply lines and water, among others. The ICT infrastructure is the central component of an Intelligent City that brings together all the others to achieve a joint interaction (Mohanty, 2016).

In the proposed layer model, we define layer 1, IoT Controllers as the one in charge of gathering information and the possible executor of required actions: layer 2, Data Network is responsible for the transport of information and layer 3, Data Servers, where the information analysis is done. In this section we focus on layer 2, with the objective of presenting the options that exist to have a successful communication between devices in addition to the characteristics that the infrastructure must meet to meet the needs of Smart Cities.

To comply with the objective of the proposed layer model, it is necessary that the data network layer be able to carry out efficiently the transfer of information, regardless of whether it travels from the controllers to the servers or the servers to the controller. It must also to able be implemented in any field, Agriculture, Economy, Transit, Health, etc.

The Data Networks operate in layers 0 to 4 of the open systems interconnection model (ISO / IEC 7498-1) OSI for communication (ISO/IEC 7498-1:1994 – Information technology—Open Systems Interconnection--Basic Reference Model: The Basic Model. (n.d) Retrieved June 30, 2018, from: https://www.iso.org/ standard/20269.html). In order for these to be functional in the environment of an Intelligent City, they must be capable of continuing to provide the services to which users are accustomed and must also cover the communication requirements of the sensor networks between the different controllers and the server.

In Table 1 we present some Data Network technologies that are implemented at the level of layer 1 of the OSI model to make information transport in the Smart Cities more efficient.

These are only some physical technologies that have worked efficiently in the data transport between devices, however, it is necessary to analyze how should be the data treated during transport.

Within Layers 2, 3 and 4 Virtualized Network services are implemented through the implementation of SDN and NFV with the objective that Smart Cities have an infrastructure that is dynamic, innovative and reliable. In addition, consideration should be given to the way in which different networks should be interconnected in order to collect information in large geographic areas, considering WAN Networks, the role of 5G communications, as well as access to the cloud and containment in the fog.

Table 1. Some technologies used in smart cities

Technology	Description	Characteristics	Use
Near Filed Communication (NFC)	Wireless technology complementary to Bluetooth and 802.11	Does not require line of sight, simple and simple connection method. Short range of 13.56 MHz, requires a distance of 4 cm.	Simplify transactions, exchange digital content and connect electronic devices with just a touch.
Bluetooth	Economical and short-range radio technology eliminates the need for wiring between devices.	Communication less than 1Mbps, uses the IEEE 802.15.1 standard specification. It has a range of 10 to 100 meters.	Personal area networks (PAN) in a range of 2 to 8 devices to share text, image, video and sound.
Radio Frequency Identification (RFID)	System that transmits the identity of an object or person wirelessly using radio waves.	Reliable, efficient, safe, economical and accurate.	Used in the IoT to solve object identification problems. Wireless applications: distribution, patient monitoring, and military applications.

Sensor Networks

A network of sensors is formed by a set of sensors and requires the transfer of information between them and the devices that collect the information they obtain, in IoT a controller is able to many of sensors and the controller can use the information gathered for these, to make decisions and made an action or send the information to the server layer so that the information will be analyzed and storage. An example of implementation of a sensor network is that of taking a room temperature, there is a group of sensors scattered in the room which take an independent measurement, these measurements be averaged to calculate the general temperature in the room (Kumar and Madria 2013)

SDN Networks

The Smart Cities require an intelligent infrastructure for the Data transport. The conventional Networks present problems about to guarantee the information delivery, for that SDN (Software Defined Networks) have been the option to satisfy the requirements of the Smart Cities

SDN enable a Network Control programmable offering a solution of a great variety of uses case. That was changed the perception of the Data Networks. In (Jarschel et al. 2014) the principles that SDN networks must comply with are presented. These principles are: Separation of control and data plane, Logically centralized control and Open interfaces programmability.

The separation of the control and data plane helps integration of devices from different manufactures, which are very important considering the dimensions of the cities. The logically centralized control permits the concentration of decision making for its greater control. And finally, open interfaces programmability allows a dynamic behavior of the network.

SDN presents the variants in the data networks that provide us with the benefits required for the proper functioning of the sensor and actuator networks that the Internet of Things currently requires to support Smart Cities.

In 2009, Stanford University published version 1.0 of the OpenFlow protocol (Pfaff, Ben and Lantz, B and Heller 2012)[6] with the aim of creating a dynamic, manageable, profitable and, above all, adaptable network architecture, which opened the options for network administrators to manage data traffic in a more efficient and dynamic way through implementation of Software Defined Networks.

NFV

In small cities and metropolitan areas governments have adopted SDN and NFV with the aim of providing flexibility and agility to the adoption of intelligent technologies that improve their ability and work capacity (Daniele Loffreda, 2015).

With the need to implement millions of sensors that can automatically collect data, which must be stored and analyzed to identify current situations and events that may occur in the future. This collection and analysis of data generates an endless list of potential benefits.

It is necessary that the communication networks converge to achieve flexibility and minimize costs. SDN and NFV allow an efficient, fast and virtual implementation of services that support multiple types of priority data traffic. The IoT requires a dynamic connection of the final devices to data centers and services in the cloud; this service is also provided by SDN and NFV.

NFV allows the control of software-based solutions that executed according to the demand that presented.

With virtual network functions (VNF, Virtual Network Functions) the network can react in an agile way to the requirements that arise in an Intelligent City and must able to solve problems in real time.

Together SDN and NFV allow bandwidth balancing, guarantee data security, protect against intrusions to the sensor network and final devices in the Smart Cities; reducing hardware, space, electricity consumption, implementing portable and updatable software applications in the network.

Cloud and Fog Computing

Fog is an architecture that distributes computing, communication, control and storage closer to end users along the continuum from the cloud to things. Sometimes, the term "fog" is used interchangeably with the term "edge", although the fog is broader than the typical notion of edge. The relevance of fog / edge lies both in the inadequacy of the traditional cloud and in the appearance of new opportunities for Internet of Things, 5G and artificial intelligence incorporated. (Chiang, Mung., et al., 2016) shown a table with the main features of Cloud and Fog Computing.

5G Communications

The objective of implementation of the 5G networks is to present a massive coverage for the IoT, with a low latency, high availability, flexibility and a better cost-efficiency on other types of networks. One of the main benefits of 5G networks is that it seeks to provide QoS in the wireless network environment through dynamic control (NGMN Alliance 2015).

Some requirements for the good performance of a 5G network are higher volumes of mobile data, high number of connected devices, low latency and how it focused on mobile devices the battery life must be high.

Network Challenges

In our work we propose the implementation of an SDN and NVF network, is the viable option for the Communications infrastructure locally in a Smart City, however the transport of information generated in remote networks to the cloud becomes complex. The 5G Communications present a global solution regarding the users experience when using their services but the challenge is to satisfy the needs of a Smart City.

DATA SERVERS

One of the technologies that have had the most development in recent years is the Artificial Intelligence (AI) that refers to do certain operations, taking proper measures and identify patterns respect (or in relation) to sensitive electronic environments and receptive to presence of people.

This is compos of following characteristics: Integration, many networked devices are intertwined in the environment. Conscious context, with AI techniques these devices can recognize you and perceive your environment customized, can adapt to your needs. Adaptable, they can change in response to you. Anticipatory, through Machine Learning processes it is possible to anticipate your wishes without a conscious mediation (Benbassat, 2017).

Data Bases Management

IoT devices generate a lot of information so it is necessary to systematically store a large amount of information organized to access it, this in order to manipulate them and then analyze them for decision making, to this end we need basic technologies of data, consisting of information storage, administration, distribution, integration, processing, consulting and related to each other, in an organized manner, thus facilitating their use and manipulation (Garcia-Molina et al., 2010). Mainly we have two types of SQL and NoSQL databases, the former are characterized by being a table-like structure and relate between some link in their data; the second because it has a collection structure, it is not relational and allows it to grow by embedding data without changing its structure, the details are shown below.

We have databases SQL type (Structured Query Language), is a structured programming language used to consult and manipulate a database with a relationship between your data, SQL data declarations are used to store, manipulate and create data. The schemas that SQL uses consist of creating database objects such as indexes, tables and restrictions, where the way in which the datasets can interact is through consultations, conversions and manipulation of data (Beaulieu, 2009).

There are also NoSQL types, in the case of new generation databases, in which they are characterized as non-relational, open source, distributed and scalable (Johannes Zollmann, 2012). These BDs were designed for the data storage requirements of cloud computing and its information processing. The, NoSQL DBs have different characteristics to solve the large quantity data functions that grow rapidly (Deka, 2014). This means that they specialize in large scale and high concurrency data that are capable of storing and processing large volumes of information efficiently, having high performance in writing and reading through fast search engines and queries dynamically (Han, Haihong, Le, & Du, 2011).

Once the types of databases have been assessed, we bear in mind that in the project we will handle large volumes of information for the processing, writing and reading of data. For these databases we will make a comparison between the NoSQL solutions, focusing on three of the most popular solutions for performance, workloads and necessary use cases: MongoDB, Cassandra and CouchBase.

MongoDB it is essential to manage a collection of data for an adequate management of information that allows us to implement different types of IoT devices and different sensors, forming a scalable data system that allows us to include heterogeneous devices. It is necessary to provide adequate maintenance to the MongoDB Databases, so they are automatically stored by means of a program that runs on the server and are stored in Datasets formed by of JSON files that are standard agile formats, easy to read and write how to analyze (JSON.org, 2014), these are formats of light collections for data management. Without neglecting the need to have backup and security systems.

Cassandra, like MongoDB, is very scalable open source and provides a distributed storage mechanism to store a large amount of structured data. Your model provides dynamic control over the design and layout of data. Its architecture is based on a distributed system where all the nodes are equal and the data is distributed among the nodes. It also allows managing high writing performance without sacrificing readings, persistently manages small and large components that make the systems on which this service is based reliable and scalable (Lakshman & Malik, 2010).

Another of the most used NoSQL databases is CouchBase with a distributed architecture for performance, scalability and availability. This DB allows developers to create applications faster and easier with the flexibility of JSON4. It also speeds up queries because your model separates data in a way that facilitates data modeling and streamlines queries (CouchBase, 2011). Next we will observe a table for the comparison of the three databases mentioned: Table 2.

Due to the large amount of information generated by thousands of sensors in a city, the implementation of NoSQL database structures is proposed, which are no-relational systems that provide ease of development, scalable performance, high availability and resilience (Deka, 2014). For this data management Mongo DB is implemented oriented to documents that allow us agility and scalability, giving us a high performance for both reading and writing (Chodorow, 2013).

Georeferenced System

To understand the data, it was proposed to use a graphical interface that allows us to perceive more intuitively what is happening in the city. This is done through a WEB site that allows us to visualize this data in a georeferenced system with important event points and show predictions of what could happen, the graphics are also an important part of the visualization to be able to perceive in a history how it is behaving a Smart City.

Table 2. Comparison of NoSQL databases

Name	Cassandra	CouchBase	MongoDB
Description	Column store based on BigTable ideas	JSON-based document store derived from CouchDB	Stores your data by collection type documents
Database Model	By Column Store	For Documents	For Documents
Web Site	cassandra.apache.org	www.couchbase.com	www.mongodb.com
License	Open Source	Open Source	Open Source
Secondary Indexes	Restricted	Yes	Yes
API's and Other Access Methods	Own Protocol	Memcached Protocol y API HTTP	Own Protocol using JSON
Server-side Scripts	No	JavaScript	JavaScript
Triggers	Yes	Yes	No
Concurrence	Yes	Yes	Yes
Durability	Yes	Yes	Yes

In references to cartographic systems, several platforms are taken that are tools that can be used for this purpose, there are some developments or technologies that allow us to visualize a map and add layers that can show us information about some specific points and assign information. Among them were applications for maps on the Internet that are among the most popular such as the ESRI (Environmental Systems Research Institute) maps and open maps (Open Street Maps / OSM).

ESRI is a company that develops software for geographic information systems (GIS) and has storage of spatial data in geographic systems (ESRI, 1969). One of its main products is ArcGIS being a platform that through GIS connects map maps, data and applications developed in JavaScript 5. This technology is accessible to programmers allowing them to create and manage georeferenced systems, visualization mapping and data analysis (Figure 3).

OpenStreetMap just like Google Maps is a platform for displaying cartographic data and it is also used as a JavaScript development tool to integrate layers into what you want to use. The main advantage of this platform is that it is open source and free access in which a large community of collaborators Figure 4., creates it, which with their contributions to the map add and maintain the novel data (OpenStreetMaps, 2004)

When considering ESRI, it was taken into account that it speeds up the way of working with web programming and also offers an attractive view on maps, allows easy integration into the project and usability. With good support, the obstacle in which it was not used as the main platform was that they have cost of use that when thinking about the future, it is necessary to integrate a completely free platform, but this only limits what could be development and support, and do not rule out where we can use as base layers your maps in which only reference to correspond to an ESRI map allow you to make use of it (ArcGIS, 2012).

Figure 3. ArcGIS of ESRI

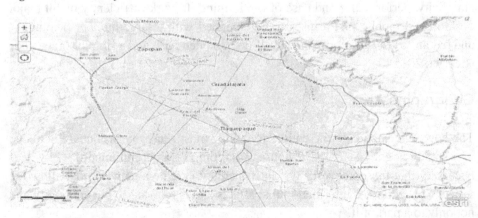

Figure 4. OpenStreetMap

By selecting the cartographic system as a design base layer for implementation, it is necessary to identify what technologies we can use to program the geo-referenced system, locating the IoT devices and showing real-time data of the measurements, as well as identifying technologies for the realization of graphs.

For our web system we have JavaScript is the best option for web interface and application development in the map browser such as OpenLayers (OpenLayers, 2007), we find some APIs in JavaScript or PHP that help us support to develop a geo-referenced system visually, with the existence of these libraries we take some for the development of the application based on its characteristics and what we are looking for we take the best implementation options.

For the development we selected the Leaflet mapping library, these tools support us for the manipulation of data sampling and referencing the position where our measurements are located. Leaflet is developed in JavaScript for the friendly management of interactive maps. With a weight of 33 KB of programming in JavaScript, it has all the mapping that the programmer needs. It is designed with simplicity, performance and ease of use in mind. It works efficiently on all major desktop and mobile platforms, can be extended with a large number of plugins, and has an easy-to-use form and a well-documented API, and a simple source code (Leaflet, 2015).

Geographic Area

The coverage extends to the entire city, today most sensor networks are bounded in a small geographical area, a house, a building or a certain area of a city, it is necessary that these networks can interoperate to create a network that allow the massive collection of information that affects and is relevant to the entire city and not only to a part of it.

Information Analysis

Through the implementation of IoT controllers, the collection of information that allows us to identify the behavior of different elements of the cities is sought with the aim of supporting the decision making of the actors of these, in addition to being able to carry out automations of processes that make life easier for the inhabitants of cities. To know what to do with that information, it is necessary to make an adequate analysis of it.

Machine Learning

With the Datasets we can implement analytics and find correlations in the data sets to detect patterns that allow us to evaluate and extract the most relevant information about critical events, show events in real time and use machine learning through Machine Learning techniques creating valuable information for the decision makers, so that we can find problems in the city and be able to make intelligent decisions (Benbassat, 2017).

Data Servers Challenges

There are some challenges of what we have faced in the development of the project, among them there are compatibility problems of data types between different devices and they send us different readings and information, the storage is limited so you need to have a datasets strategy to maintain the agility and stability in the databases, to share the information, as well as being open data, it is necessary that all the information can be represented correctly and converted into value. We present some points of challenges and in some cases, how they were solved.

- We have a large number of diverse open data repositories and one of the biggest challenges is how to make the compatibility in our systems for its representation.
- Because we have different types of devices that yield different readings of different types and information, it is necessary to generate a structure of data collections, which allows us to accommodate this information and unify the different devices for a more homogeneous reading.
- Compatibility with other data repositories that allow us to interpret and share information, for which an ontology and semantic system was generated in which the keys with value are represented by values that were already defined, seeking interoperability.

- Because the amount of information is limited in our databases that can later lead to information saturation or malfunctioning such as failures or speed, it is necessary to generate consequently send them to a repository, generating an engine backup and debugging of databases to keep it running smoothly, reading and writing quickly.

CONCLUSION

Undoubtedly the IoT and the evolution of software and hardware technology are indispensable elements in the development of a smart city infrastructure. The proper implementation and use of them generate great advances that facilitate the decision-making that affects citizens in different areas. There are different technologies that can cover in a certain way the needs of Smart Cities, however it is necessary to analyze and test them with the aim of identifying those that provide the necessary characteristics in an efficient and economical way at different levels.

This is achieved through the Smart Cities cycle: starting with the implementation of a sensor network, followed by the management of the data and then performing the analysis and visualization, finding points of improvement and thus continue with the improvement cycle.

There are also pilot projects for smart cities that address various challenges, which can only be solved with an interdisciplinary work team working under a holistic environment. In this document we mention the main characteristics of some technologies that have been experienced in a satisfactory manner, and we try to capture the acquired learning, with the aim of shortening the path to experimentation and development of proposals for those who have access to it. The technologies are still in development, so they are always in constant improvement. However, by classifying the technologies that intervene in a Smart City and identify the challenges they have, you can work on the development and experimentation in a specific way to make significant contributions to Smart Cities.

REFERENCES

Aceves, E., & Larios, V. M. (2015). *Data Visualization for Georeferenced IoT Open Data Flows for a GDL Smart City Pilot*. Academic Press.

Administration, I. T. (n.d.). *Smart Cities, Regions & Communities - Export Opportunities*. Academic Press.

Al-Fuqaha, A., Guizani, M., Mohammadi, M., Aledhari, M., & Ayyash, M. (2015). Internet of Things: A Survey on Enabling Technologies, Protocols, and Applications. *IEEE Communications Surveys and Tutorials*, *17*(4), 2347–2376. doi:10.1109/COMST.2015.2444095

ArcGIS. (2012). Retrieved October 24, 2016, from https://developers.arcgis.com/javascript/

Beaulieu, A. (2009). Learning SQL. *Database*. doi:10.1017/CBO9781107415324.004

Benbassat, M. (2017). *Double Deep Machine Learning*. Retrieved from http://search.arxiv.org:8081/paper.jsp?r=1711.06517&qid=1521507142396swap_nCnN_66269 4859&qs=Double+Deep+Machine+Learning

Castañeda, V., & Guzman, E. (2015). Towards the preparation of the Guadalajara's Smart City Metrics Structure. *IEEE-GDL CCD Smart Cities White Paper*, 1–5.

Chiang, M., & Zhang, T. (2016). Fog and IoT. *IEEE Internet of Things Journal*, *3*(6), 854–864. doi:10.1109/JIOT.2016.2584538

Chodorow, K. (2013). MongoDB: The Definitive Guide. *Journal of Infectious Diseases, 203*. doi:10.1093/infdis/jir001

CouchBase. (2011). Retrieved November 21, 2016, from http://www.couchbase.com/

Datta, P., B. S. (2017). A Survey on IoT Architectures, Protocols, Security and Smart City based Applications. *International Conference on Computing, Communications and Networking Technologies*. 10.1109/ICCCNT.2017.8203943

Deka, G. C. (2014). NoSQL databases. Handbook of Research on Cloud Infrastructures for Big Data Analytics. doi:10.4018/978-1-4666-5864-6.ch008

ESRI. (1969). Retrieved October 24, 2016, from http://www.esri.com/about-esri

Garcia-Molina, H., Ullman, J. D., Widom, J., Özsu, M., Valduriez, P., Connolly, T., … Virk, R. (2010). Database Systems: A Practical Approach to Design, Implementation, and Management. *International Journal of Computer Applications*, *49*. doi:10.1007/978-1-4842-0877-9_10

Han, J., Haihong, E., Le, G., & Du, J. (2011). Survey on NoSQL database. In *Proceedings - 2011 6th International Conference on Pervasive Computing and Applications, ICPCA 2011* (pp. 363–366). Academic Press. doi:10.1109/ICPCA.2011.6106531

Huang, Y., Martínez, J.-F., Sendra, J., & López, L. (2015). Resilient Wireless Sensor Networks Using Topology Control: A Review. *Sensors (Basel)*, *15*(10), 24735–24770. doi:10.3390151024735 PMID:26404272

Internet of Things Global Standards Initiative. (n.d.). Retrieved June 29, 2018, from https://www.itu.int/en/ITU-T/gsi/iot/Pages/default.aspx

ISO/IEC 7498-1:1994 - Information technology -- Open Systems Interconnection -- Basic Reference Model: The Basic Model. (n.d.). Retrieved June 30, 2018, from https://www.iso.org/standard/20269.html

Guardado-Medina, Larios, & Patarroyo. (2015). ODF best practices towards a GDL Smart City. *IEEE-GDL CCD Smart Cities White Paper*, 1–6.

Jin, J., Gubbi, J., Marusic, S., & Palaniswami, M. (2014). An Information Framework for Creating a Smart City Through Internet of Things. *IEEE Internet of Things Journal*, *1*(2), 112–121. doi:10.1109/JIOT.2013.2296516

Zollmann, J. (2012). NOSQL Databases. *NoSQL Archive*, 149. Retrieved from http://nosql-database.org/

JSON.org. (2014). *Introducing JSON*. Retrieved from http://www.json.org/

Kim, Y., & Lee, Y. (2015). Automatic Generation of Social Relationships between Internet of Things in Smart Home Using SDN-Based Home Cloud. *Proceedings - IEEE 29th International Conference on Advanced Information Networking and Applications Workshops, WAINA 2015*, 662–667. 10.1109/WAINA.2015.93

Kumar & Sanjai. (2013). Secure Data Aggregation in Wireless Sensor Networks. *2013 12th Annual Mediterranean Ad Hoc Networking Workshop (MED-HOC-NET)*. doi:10.1109/MedHocNet.2013.6767410

Lakshman, A., & Malik, P. (2010). Cassandra. *Operating Systems Review*, *44*(2), 35. doi:10.1145/1773912.1773922

Leaflet. (2015). Retrieved September 12, 2016, from http://leafletjs.com/

Lin, J., Yu, W., Zhang, N., Yang, X., Zhang, H., & Zhao, W. (2017). A Survey on Internet of Things: Architecture, Enabling Technologies, Security and Privacy, and Applications. *IEEE Internet of Things Journal*, 4(5), 1–1. doi:10.1109/JIOT.2017.2683200

Madakam, S., Ramaswamy, R., & Tripathi, S. (2015). Internet of Things (IoT): A Literature Review. *Journal of Computer and Communications*, 3(5), 164–173. doi:10.4236/jcc.2015.35021

Mohanty, S. P., Choppali, U., & Kougianos, E. (2016). Everything You Wanted to Know About Smart Cities. *IEEE Consumer Electronics Magazine*, 5(3), 60–70. doi:10.1109/MCE.2016.2556879

OASIS. (2014). *MQTT Version 3.1.1*. OASIS Standard, (October), 81. Retrieved from http://docs.oasis-open.org/mqtt/mqtt/v3.1.1/os/mqtt-v3.1.1-os.html

OpenLayers. (2007). *OpenLayers 3*. Retrieved November 19, 2016, from https://openlayers.org/

OpenStreetMaps. (2004). Retrieved September 12, 2016, from https://www.openstreetmap.org/about

Pettit, C., Bakelmun, A., Lieske, S. N., Glackin, S., Hargroves, K., Thomson, G., … Newman, P. (2017). Planning support systems for smart cities. *City, Culture and Society*. doi:10.1016/j.ccs.2017.10.002

Policy, I. T. U., & Division, T. W. (2015). *Smart Cities Seoul: A case study*. Academic Press.

ROS.org. (n.d.). *Powering the world's robots*. Retrieved June 30, 2018, from http://www.ros.org/

Savale, O., Managave, A., Ambekar, D., & Sathe, S. (2015). *Internet of Things in Precision Agriculture using Wireless Sensor Networks Introduction: Literature Survey*. Academic Press.

Schaffers, H., Komninos, N., Pallot, M., Trousse, B., Nilsson, M., & Oliveira, A. (2011). Smart cities and the future internet: Towards cooperation frameworks for open innovation. Lecture Notes in Computer Science, 6656, 431–446. doi:10.1007/978-3-642-20898-0_31

Sicari, S., Rizzardi, A., Grieco, L. A., & Coen-Porisini, A. (2014). Security, privacy and trust in Internet of Things: The road ahead. *Computer Networks*, *76*, 146–164. doi:10.1016/j.comnet.2014.11.008

Suresh Kumar, S. S., & Kumar, S. (2017). *A Framework for predicting the performance of IoT protocols, a Use Case based approach*. Academic Press. doi:10.1109/SmartTechCon.2017.8358437

Farooq, M., Waseem, M., Mazhar, S., Khairi, A., & Kamal, T. (2015). A Review on Internet of Things (IoT). *International Journal of Computers and Applications*, *113*(1), 1–7. doi:10.5120/19787-1571

Larios, V. M., Gomez, L., Mora, O. B., & Maciel, R. N. V.-R. (2016). Living labs for smart cities: A use case in Guadalajara city to foster innovation and develop citizen-centered solutions. IEEE.

Chapter 9

Sustainable Smart Farming for Masses Using Modern Ways of Internet of Things (IoT) Into Agriculture

Rahul Singh Chowhan
Agriculture University Jodhpur, India

Purva Dayya
MPUAT, India

ABSTRACT

Modern technologies are revolutionizing the way humans have lived. The world's population is expected to reach 9.6 billion by year 2050 and to serve this much population, the agricultural industries and layman farmers need to embrace IoT and e-agriculture or ICT in agriculture. Feeding the global population is the biggest problem of the world. The terminology has advanced from IIoT (Industrial Internet of Things), IoFT (Internet of Farm Things), IoSFT (Internet of Smart Farming Things), etc. The agriculture industries are open for ideas, advances, and technically trained workforce to help sustain ever increasing needs of food and allocate better choices of resources. Smart farming is less labor intensive and more capital intensive. Smart farming is furthering the Third Green Revolution around the globe by using various ICT technologies in agriculture.

DOI: 10.4018/978-1-5225-7811-6.ch009

INTRODUCTION

Adapting to farming and meeting its requests are extremely challenging in today's time. Farming fills in as the core of Indian economy and half of the populace in India survives on the basis of agriculture. Adapting to farming and meeting its requests are extremely challenging in today's time. Farming fills in as the core of Indian economy and half of the populace in India survives on the basis of agriculture. The technological acceptance in Indian Farming activities is confined to many reasons which may include lack of skilled labor, less trust on technology, etc but IoT is an easy innovation which fills in as an answer for the various issues in agricultural scenarios. It utilizes different sensors which are associated through web and furthermore with the coordination to the satellites it does monitoring of all segments. It is as easy as using smart phones now-a-days. Sometimes the implementation and maintenance cost is also high due to which farmers producing at low scale may hesitate to introduce new technology for farming. IoT has wide range of components comprising of features like high precision, high accuracy, mobility etc. which farmers can use as per need at lower costs (Khattab, 2016). It additionally utilizes different conventions by empowering the IoT to become faster in processing and monitoring capabilities.

The Internet of Things has opened up to a great degree profitable approaches for agriculturists and cultivators to develop soil and raise animals with the utilization of simple to-introduce sensors and a wealth of keen information they offer. Succeeding on this productive develop of the Internet of Things in horticulture, brilliant cultivating applications are making strides with the guarantee to convey day in and day out perceivability into soil and harvest wellbeing, apparatus being used, capacity conditions, animal behavior, and vitality utilization level. The open-source IoT Platform is a significant middleware innovation that permits strolling securely into the IoT enables farms and fields. IoT based smart farming bonds and entwins distinctive sensors, associated gadgets, and cultivating offices by streamlining the advancement of keen cultivating frameworks to the greatest degree conceivable (Kviesis, 2015). This likewise empowers high accuracy crop control, valuable information accumulation and automated cultivating methods. IoT conveys its capacity to improve the scene of current cultivating strategies is completely noteworthy.

IoT sensors are fully equipped to submit agriculturists data about harvest yields, pest infestation, and soil sustenance are significant to generation and offer exact information which can be utilized to enhance cultivating strategies overtime. With a future of proficient, information driven, profoundly exact cultivating techniques, it is certainly to call this kind of cultivating smart. We can expect IoT will always show signs of change the way we develop to grow food with newly generated methods. Regarding natural issues, IoT based smart farming can serve many awesome advantages including more productive water use, or enhancement of available resources. In

IoT-based smart farming, a framework is maintained for checking and monitoring the field with the assistance of sensors (temperature, soil moisture, humidity and so on.) and computerizing the agricultural framework (Azaza, 2016). The agriculturists can inspect the farms from their mobile devices. Smart farming based on IoT is profoundly effective when contrasted with traditional approach.

The uses and application domain of IoT based smart farming is not confined to the large cultivation activities but also extends to inspire other developing basic patterns in horticultural as in organic farming, small space cultivation like kitchen gardening, preservation of quality crops and also helps in upgrading the straightforward cultivation processes. IoT based smart cultivation process can give incredible advantages to deal with natural issues, including more productive water utilization, or streamlining of information sources and optimized treatments. Presently, the talk of town is all about the significant contribution and utilizations of IoT based smart farming that are revolutionizing the conventional way of monitoring farms and increasing income in agri-businesses.

REVITALIZATION OF FARMING WITH IOT

To numerous individuals, IoT summons pictures of most recent contraptions like Google Glass, Apple Watch or self communicating automated systems. Indeed, the most imaginative and daily purpose applications are going on in the industries using Internet of Things like urban communities, savvy horticulture, brilliant manufacturing plants, and so forth. Be that as it may, the utilization of IoT in horticulture can have the best effect. The Internet of Things is changing the horticulture business more than ever by enabling agriculturists and cultivators to manage the colossal difficulties they confront. Till now, farming has been a high-hazard, work serious, low-compensate industry (Silva, 2011). Agriculturists are probably going to be affected by sudden natural changes, monetary downturns, and numerous other hazard factors.

IoT can help reshape agriculture tactics in various ways. At its most essential level, sensors can be sent crosswise over homestead and cultivating hardware so as to empower ranchers to pick up a plenitude of quick information, for example, the temperature of storage, the measure of compost utilized, the measure of underground water, the quantity of seeds planted, capacity conditions, the status of cultivating gear and apparatus being used, and so on. Agriculturists and farmers can monitor without much of a stretch track of an assortment of ecological factors and take educated choices once an IoT-empowered framework is set up in the farms and fields. Smart farming is only a tool for improvement of present strategies but is an important advancement, which if effectively executed could enable farmers to manage every one of the difficulties they to look in cultivating. Besides, the rich bits of knowledge got from savvy sensors could enable ranchers to be more exact in their utilization of pesticides and composts, in this way moderating some ecological effects (Channe, 2015). IoT organization in horticulture can address numerous difficulties and increment the quality, amount, and cost-viability of rural creation.

Agriculture lands are getting up more associated and interconnected as agriculturists and farmers understand the capability of IoT advances in helping them limit activity cost that too accomplishing better outcomes. This incorporates the higher harvest, reduced losses of domesticated animals, and less water consumption. IoT developers and commercial companies keep on developing various devices applicable to development stages to help enhance cultivate execution that can detect, process, and impart accurate ecological information. Behind these IoT lies the stage in a variety of advances that incorporates sensing, microcontrollers, transmitters, vitality gathering, LED lights, automatons, drones and many more.[38]

APPLICATION DOMAINS AND USE CASES OF IOT IN AGRICULTURE

These days, technological innovations play an indispensable part in numerous domains of our lives. While it appears farming would be excluded from thatbut cultivating crops isn't an easy task by just dropping seeds on ground and letting plants grow. As the populace develops at an exponential rate it makes extreme issues for sustaining individuals. More population implies more food should be delivered. Be that as it may, more individuals likewise imply more homes will be build-up and more water will be consumed. That result in significant utilization of land and water assets required for population. Keeping all scenarios modern agriculture has to sustain this developing populace with minimal assets, this also means that the modern farming businesses need to adapt mechanical and technological enhancements for optimal growth and supply of products (Channe, 2015). The technologies and smart farming applications that are helping the modern farmers in cultivation and raising livestock are as under.

Livestock Tracking and Geo-Fencing

Animals and fields are collared with tracking devices and cameras, respectively, to monitor the health of grazing animals directly from smart phone or home computer. This has become possible with IoT based smart tag for tracking livestock. This neckline tracking tag utilizes satellite system to geo-fence domesticated animals, helping ranchers discover animals that are near the edge of a fenced zone or have gotten away. It additionally gives agriculturists the chance to take a more educated and proactive way to deal with herding so they lose lesser animals to predators. When it is evident that a sheep has not moved in some time, the agriculturist is currently ready to send herders to the appropriate location of the lost animal, sparing significant time and assets (Malveaux, 2014). Ranchers conveying the collars have effectively encountered a noteworthy decrease in the quantity of animals lost to ailment or predators, which directly affects their pay. It is also capable of tracking the areas where the cattle often fees themselves. This helps to best utilize and decide the appropriate area for grazing and safe deploying of animals (Chen, 2011). The figure 1 shows the GPS tag based communication that happens among the connected devices.

Internal Sensor for tracking digestion related problems and external sensor can track movement patterns to determine the health, sensing injuries, checking the breeding time, eating habits etc. This data can help in analyzing the overall health patterns of a particular animal. These sensors can also help to monitor heart rate, respiratory rate, blood pressure, digestion and other vitalities on or before time (Zhao, 2010). A few favorable advantages of using this technology for the cattle industry are status covers for cows and their group nutritional information collection, reproduction reports, ailment, fodder quality and area with geo-fencing. Moreover, it will encourage cow roaming in remote regions and will give early burglary notices straightforwardly to the farmer's cell phone. One such technology within the IoT domain is narrowband mobile IoT service which allows more sheep collar devices to be connected to mobile connection or GPS device at very low cost. These narrow bandwidth devices possess longer battery life and sound connection as they are occasionally used and not in constant connection with the device (Zhang, 2012). They are mostly activated when animals are unfenced and free roaming outside the fence often for grazing.

Figure 1. GPS Tag based Communication

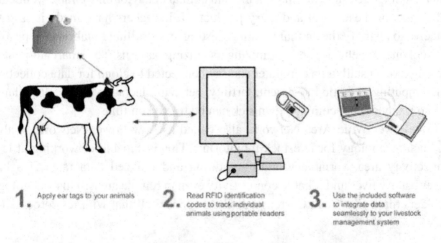

1. Apply ear tags to your animals

2. Read RFID identification codes to track individual animals using portable readers

3. Use the included software to integrate data seamlessly to your livestock management system

Figure 2. GPS Tagging for Geo Fencing

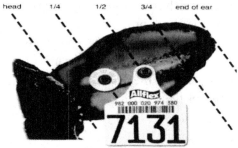

We can use modern technology to make our everyday life easier by digitizing the daily things. These devices can be helpful in dealing with 10% of flocks that is lost or have travelled far from the mentored area. These collar devices have basically three main parts: low cost collar that has inbuilt GPS receiver, communication unit and a rechargeable battery (Jin, 2017). These collars transmit the GPS location which is collected on smart phone installed with app on which a map shows location of all the herds. The collar provides real time monitored data like herd's movement, rumination, temperature, number of chews before regurgitating etc. This gathered information on one device allows farmers to actively take care for each one of animal in the herd. IoT is conveying new levels of productivity to the horticultural part. IoT is required to keep farmers in knowledge of their livestock location. It provides tracking capabilities and committed assurance for roaming animals (Yan, 2011). The blend of microprocessor, microchips and satellite communication has made it reasonable to track domesticated animals, especially dairy cattle, sheep and deer which wander in remote parts of the world. There is a tremendous potential in understanding the effect of reproducing and animal behavior on welfare, wellbeing and items, for meat, wool and dairy products. IoT trackers have made it easy to conceive to quantify the animal is eating, resting and strolling to fabricate a profile of its conduct & behavior and optimizing its grazing patterns. The smart automated tracking tools installed on computer can say connected to cloud for data collection and computing of cattle movement, fertility, behavior, lactation and health related data so if any animal coming down sick can be treated on time.

Low Power Wide Area Network, also called as Low Power Network, is also one such technology for livestock monitoring. This is capable of working at less connectivity area, variable weather condition and reduced data rate. This has longer battery lives and reliable connectivity even in remote areas. This technology considers three C's: Cost, Current and Coverage and all that with less processing power and memory. They are used to form a private wireless sensor network as a service or infrastructure served by third party allowing the farmers to monitor the data locally (TongKe, 2013).

Water Conservation and Irrigation Monitoring

Internet of Things can be utilized for getting the appropriate measure of water at the required destination in correct duration of time. It is essentially a data-driven water conservation move which is made conceivable by the remote correspondence empowered by the addition of Internet of Things. The IoT can be utilized to decide when, where, and how much water is required in scene and agrarian water system. IoT ought to be utilized to rouse the appropriation of innovation based water conservation measures. The IoT can help diminish water deficiencies by giving noteworthy data which empowers utilization be more proficient and less inefficient (Fulton, 2018). AMI or Advanced Metering Infrastructure frameworks are basically the IOT's response to the water meter that any utility uses to quantify a farmer's water utilizes. In the past the meter must be physically & consistently checked for overall water consumption. However, now AMI meters can send a flag to IoT connected water utility revealing how much water has been utilized at regular intervals. This permits water holes to be repaired all the more proficiently, sparing enormous measures of water and it additionally keeps the service organization from losing profitable water, which saves the cash too.

IOT gadgets, for example, cloud-associated meters, stream checking gadgets, and water system frameworks are always gathering information, which can offer building proprietors and tenants phenomenal levels of data about their water utilize. Regardless of whether refreshed hourly or month to month, the capacity to get to use data makes individuals more mindful of their water utilize and the outcome is that water clients are engaged to all the more viably actualize preservation endeavors and screen the accomplishment of those endeavors (Gómez-Candón, 2014).

AMI meters may give extra knowledge into water use without the steady need to peruse physical water meters. AMI frameworks utilize programming to show a property of water utilization rapidly and feature issues so farm proprietors would more be able to effectively screen their utilization. The smart sensors are implanted in the farms that measure the dampness and moisture levels. The sensors at that point transfer this data to the smart sprinkler and the sprinklers make use of only the appropriate measure of water (Sundmaeker, 2016). The sensor based intelligent irrigation technology can curb the overwatering inefficiencies in conventional irrigation system.

Figure 3. Remotely Monitored Data Maps[16]

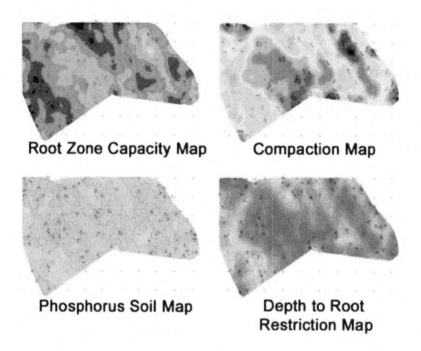

Root Zone Capacity Map   Compaction Map

Phosphorus Soil Map   Depth to Root Restriction Map

Plant and Soil Monitoring

Internet of Things (IoT) innovation has appeared on farm bases as introduction of easy to install soil sensors. Agriculturists are putting specific dampness measuring sensors all through their fields to gauge and offer information about moisture within the farm field. This supportive and real time data is then sent to a central collection point where it can be gathered and examined. At last this gives ranchers a guide decisively demonstrating where water levels are less, ideal, or high (Yong, 2013). Internet of Things in agriculture is making efforts to care for every drop by plotting intelligent and innovative methods of farming. In the most advanced water systems, these sensors are withstanding to convey certain levels of automation reducing mechanization and saving water. After rainfall, they can recommend changing schedules of pre-specified water systems either by holding off, or diminishing the measure of water connected to the field. This significant information empowers ranchers to utilize just what is required and not a drop more (Hedley, 2009).

A standout amongst the most energizing potential outcomes of IoT innovation is the scale at which it can be connected. The costs for IoT sensor equipment have fallen in the course of the most recent decade. Smallholder ranchers in creating farming easier for developing countries like India will acquire access to this effective innovation (Jafar, 2014). A variant of this development is as of now furnishing smallholder ranchers in rising economies with opportune information. At the point when rainfall is lacking, ranchers definitely hope to streams, waterways, groundwater, and lakes to fulfill water requirements. The more weight is put on these environments and the harder it progresses toward becoming to maintain natural water resources. Embracing sensor innovations and technologies can help ranchers to improve freshwater conservation during rainfall and water management during drought. The more efficiently natural resources are treated, the more productive farming becomes as the sensor based technology reduces the overall water dependency on natural resources (Ye, 2013).

Precision Farming

This is the farm management technique, also called as Precision Agriculture, which makes use of various autonomous systems, control systems, hardware, different kinds of sensors and many more. This way of farming provides quite accurate and precise data for livestock and crops (Kaiwartya, 2016). This trend of agriculture adopts the speedy internet connection, reliable network connectivity even with mobile devices, high precision agricultural-technological tools like global positioning system etc.

Figure 4. Sensor Equipment to Measure Soil Moisture (Kumar, 2016)

for purpose of imagery data analysis. The famer's tractor may use GPS-associated controller that can naturally directs the view of the directions and coordinates feed of the field (Khosla, 2002). This decreases controlling blunders by drivers and along these lines any over passes on the field. Thus, this outcome makes appropriate use of seed, compost, fuel, and time. There are various technologies under an umbrella of precision agriculture that are as under.

Variable Rate Irrigation

In the precision agronomics, the most famous precision farming technology is VRI (Variable Rate Irrigation). This system takes care for uneven leveling of farm lands, variable soils and topography by conserving water usage in areas with limited water resources. The uniform fields typically make use of center pivot irrigation methodology which is inefficient for the non-uniform fields (Lecocq, 2015).

VRI defines the site-specific management of water by varying the supply of water used for irrigation in zones within a particular field. The motto of this technology is to avoid overwatering or under-watering tendencies while allowing the farmers

Figure 5. Various Field Data for VRI

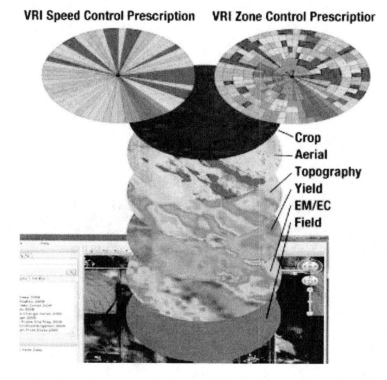

to conserve the water resources with appropriate watering. This is achieved by using the various automated and manual controls that are capable of detecting the dry land areas, non-cropping areas, steep slopes etc. using pulse control system to turn on/off water utility. The basic need for this technology is a computer, VRI software, controller and differential global positioning system (DGPS) (Lei, 2018). This helps in reducing the water application rates, energy conservation, increased pump efficiency, reduces percolation and prevent the yield losses (Dan, 2015). Precision farming is a growing scope in agricultural-technological domain. It may also include high precision positioning systems, automated steering systems, Geo-mapping Systems etc. The others may include integrated communication systems, variable rate technology (VRT) and many more.

Soil Sampling Using GPS

This is another major technology used within the precision farming that is capable of testing the soil various reasons like acknowledging the available nutrients in soil, checking the pH of soil and other vital data that makes the system to take profitable future decisions and required preventions (Mobley, 2013). The soil sampling data can also be fed to Variable Rate Applications that can optimize at time of seeding, composting, watering and using fertilizer. This allows the Hi-tech farmers to take site-specific soil sampling to identify regions with poor or rich soil fertility. It generates individual layers for different nutrients that can help in recognizing deficiency or efficiency of any nutrients within the site-specific area. This makes it more cost-efficient, reduces the impact of chemicals on land and preserves the water.

Remote Sensing

This is the way to getting information about any object or process without being physically in contact with it. Remote sensing is utilized to conjecture the normal yield creation and yield over a given region and decide the amount of the product will be collected under particular conditions. Analysts can have the capacity to anticipate the amount of product that will be delivered in a given farmland over a given timeframe (Mobley, 2016).

This methodology is basically called as Crop Production Forecasting (CPF) in agricultural terminology. In case of losses in harvest or any advances in yield, remote sensing can be utilized to decide precisely the amount of a crop has been damaged and the status of remaining crop. This way it can be used to assess crop damage and progress based on previously recorded data. Remote sensing can also be used to analyzing the flower growth patterns and based on analysis various predictions and

Figure 6. Active and Passive Remote Sensing (Harun, 2015)

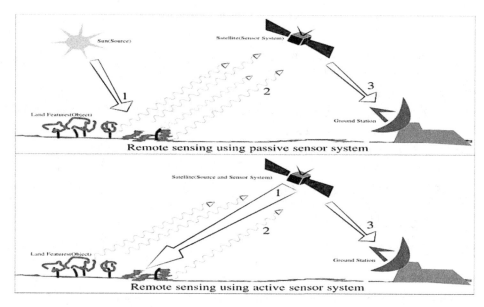

reports can be generated. It also helps in studying and identifying the crop culture for various mysterious species (Ferrández-Pastor, 2016).

Soil Moisture Probes

The soil moisture technology makes use of electromagnetic signals to measure the moisture within the soil. There are many Soil Moisture Probes like Frequency Domain Relflectometry (FDR), Gypsium Blocks, Netron Probes etc. In general this sends the electromagnetic signals that propagate in to soil through the channel of metallic wires. The amplitude of reflected signals are measured and a voltage signal is generated that can be used in mathematical equations to estimate the soil water contents.

Smart Greenhouses

Greenhouses are basically used to enhance yields of veggies, fruits and others. These require manual maintenance for controlling environmental parameters like humidity, temperature etc. This way of dealing with greenhouse is not cost effective as it causes production losses and also requires labors for manual intervention. Smart Greenhouse is an automatic, small scale atmosphere controlled system for ideal plant development. Smart or intelligent greenhouses drastically reduce the manual inspection, improving the model to automatically carry out work under the shed. They are fit with various sensors to monitor soil dampness, humidity in air, temperature, luminosity, ventilation and many more. They also have automatic drip irrigation system that check for requirement of water time to time and regulates the water usage. These all devices within the smart greenhouses are controlled using a Wi-Fi router connected to farmer's smart-phone. The associated software generates a health card for green house including parameters like soil moisture, air humidity, and temperature and water consumption. It reacts to the environmental changes and triggers automatic action plans to actuators. It can pass on the signals to actuators for evaluation of changes and take proper action likewise if sunlight is needed it can instruct windows to open up etc. In general any smart greenhouse can have three major integral parts: greenhouse armed with sensors and actuators, central control hub and a device installed with interactive app for wireless communication (Jayaraman, 2015).

Greenhouse Armed With Sensors and Actuators

The devices that are connected inside the smart greenhouse pass on the messages using two major devices: a sensor hub and an actuator hub. Both communicate based on the data collected on various parameters by the different sensors within the smart greenhouse. The sensor hub signals the actuators hub for any action to be taken associated with that particular measured sensory data. The actuator hub pass on the action to the connected actuators like automated window, ventilator or luminosity controller. This is also called a Microcontroller Unit from which Iot enables devices communicate with each other. With help on various microcontrollers, cameras can be fit in to monitor the real time growth of plants. These are configured with Bluetooth and are fitted either in the stem of plant or in the soil (Satpute, 2014).

Central Controller Hub

It has various parts as controller web application, web server, input functions and others. It is capable of taking inputs from interactive web interface and acting as per given instructions. It also enables web app to display various monitored data from sensors. With this request and response mechanism it also allows valid user authentication that can authenticate an app based controls of smart greenhouse. Its live streaming web server also avails with real time data display of various parameter like humidity, soil moisture etc. on the display to farmer's device. It also tells the current status of actuators such as if a sprinkler is on it could show its state as busy. Though the parameters are monitoring live and there are times when data variation is high. That time it would express too many readings from sensors but this situation must not impact the actuators (Rad, 2015). So there is a lambda function that would take preconfigured based on the average of five latest readings. Like if temperature inside smart greenhouse is being high for too long then it would fire a pre-configured sequence of action, often called as action plan, to open a ventilation window, turn on fan and other required measures.

Interactive Interface

This is a web app or software that can be installed on computer connected with the central controller hub. This provides with a facility of dashboard to interact with smart hub. It also displays the monitored data and statistics. This requires the user authentication for approved access to various controls of smart hub. The farmer can get direct access to control manipulation from which actuators can be instructed with action plans. It is also enables with simple voice command based support to activate or deactivate various actuators (Stojkoska, 2017).

Agricultural Drones

Drones are put to farm fields to ameliorate crop production and monitoring the growth of crop. They have completely revolutionized the way agriculture was growing and farming was carried out. There are various categories of drone technology that contributed by monitoring, fertilizer sprinkling, field investigation, real time data collection and many more applications that are growing day by day. Farmers are continuously embracing the drone technology as they are revolutionizing the food production, increase in productivity, reduced water consumption, and many more benefits to traditional farming techniques. The various uses of agricultural drones in various aspects are as under:

Soil and Farm Analysis

Drones can carry out early soil analysis i.e. before the seeds are going to be planted. They can generate the 3D view in form of maps and help agriculturists for proper plantation. Post-plantation also they can investigate fields for the appropriate irrigation procedure and nitrogen level management.

Plantation

They are capable of planting seeds automatically based on the pre specified arguments for plantation. They have shoot pipes that can plant seeds and that too with appropriate nutritional contents. These are called the seed pods that are filled with nutrients this reduces the scattering of seeds that often happens in aerial spreading. Later on they can be used to monitor plant heath and management of plant related data on collected source (Gebbers, 2010). Automated drones are appropriate for a wide range of complex landscape, products and plantings of differing statures.

Spraying

The use of drones has opened a new possibility of spraying fertilizers and chemicals, though use of chemical in huge amount has caused suffering from land to people but it's the fundamental need for large scale farming. Savvy cultivating drones are decreasing its natural effects by appropriately spraying the chemicals on required area only. These particular UAVs are furnished with sprayers, yet in addition with different sorts of innovation, as ultrasonic resounding gadgets and lasers, which can gauge distance separation with extreme accuracy. The outcome is an immense lessening in spraying with comparison with general spraying resulting in lesser chemicals reaching the groundwater (Santesteban, 2013). Drones are capable of scanning ground and spraying the appropriate fertilizers or water when required. Aerial spraying is efficient in terms of manual spraying as it is faster and only sprays where required. Yield Spraying with an unmanned flying vehicle sprayer does not require a runway as drones are free to fly over the field. Flying at the low height of a few yards, the harvest splashing can be controlled. Exact harvest spraying guarantees the best scope and utilization of composts or pesticides. New age drones are now equipped with ultrasonic echoing technology that can help them hover at appropriate height which results in precision spraying and reduced overspray of chemicals. They are capable of spraying at faster pace than the manual spraying in covering spaces and spraying appropriately.

Figure 7. Seed Capsule Plantation using Drone (Sawant, 2014)

Figure 8. Drone based Field Spraying (Piao, 2010)

Disease Recognition

These are specialized drones that can take various infrared images of the field and can detect changes to evaluate health of crop. This can help in spotting bacterial infection or pest attacks on the farms so appropriate measures can be taken at it earliest. There do exists thermal imaging drones fitted with multispectral sensors that can help in detecting needs of water, fertilizers etc. to specific area in the field and not to the whole farm.

Crop Monitoring

The regular monitoring of large fields is inefficient and man power consuming. Drones can perform aerial mapping, giving a reasonable picture of the aggregate size of a harvest field, and in addition indicating underutilized areas of land. They can likewise, if outfitted with the camera, screen the soundness of plants as far as temperature, chlorophyll levels, attack of pest and even thickness of leaves. This data can enable a rancher to change the vital parameters of their horticultural procedure in order to address the issues previously they turn out to be more far reaching. This brings about higher harvest yields with efficient intervention of drones for farming (Shaughnessy, 2013).

Health Assessment

It is very necessary to evaluate wellbeing and spot bacterial infections of crops on time. By checking a product utilizing both noticeable and close infrared light, drones attached with cameras can distinguish which plants reflect diverse measures of green light and NIR light. This data can deliver multispectral pictures that track changes in plants and demonstrate their wellbeing. Likewise, when an ailment is found, agriculturists can apply and screen cures all the more decisively. This could help whole plantation from getting affected by disease. These two potential outcomes increment a plant's capacity to conquer illness (Singh, 2014).

Irrigation Management

Drones can fly high and can alert for areas have pooled water or insufficient moisture contents. Thermal drones can give better monitoring and management of fields for appropriate and on time requirement of water. This could not only conserve water usage but also helps in pooling or leaks in irrigation. After the growth of crop it can also monitor the vegetation index, heat signature and growth rate of crop. Accomplishing most extreme harvest yield at least cost is one of the objectives of horticultural creation. Early discovery and administration of issues related with trim yield pointers can enable increment to return and ensuing benefit. The planning and amount of compost and herbicide applications in farming frameworks are basic where augmenting power and yield is a definitive objective (Stoces, 2016). While manures and fertilizers are generally used to advance plant development phase and supply appropriate nutrients to growing plants. Herbicides are ordinarily used to control weeds with a specific end goal to decrease the weeds' opposition for supplements. Satellite imaginary is much of the time used to screen horticultural exercises and vegetation indices (VIs) are broadly connected in investigation of harvest status.

Beekeeping Monitoring

For optimized bee colony management precision beekeeping monitoring approaches are required. The automated bee monitoring and management system can keep track of beehive behavior. The hive health status can be remotely monitored and inspected based on various parameters like temperature, humidity, weight of system, disease insurgence, stocked honey and many other parameters are included. The beehive is also fixed with a GPS system that could help locating it in case of theft and vandalism. It is often difficult to predict actually what is happening inside the beehive (Nandyala, 2016). So the monitoring sensor can intimate about increased intake of food or availability of food based on which new servings can be scheduled within the hive. It also considers the weather conditions which would increase in weight parameters for the wooden boxes. Beekeepers are intimated on daily basis about the status report of beehive via cloud server or mobile phone. The weighing systems are the most important role player in beekeeping monitoring as they alerts when the honey is ready for collection based on the previous parameters like weight when hive is empty and other measures.

The user interface available on user end i.e. on PC or smart phone allows showcasing the degree of insight obtained from multiple sensors within the hive. This enables user to monitor colony health and behavior makes its efficient, innovative and productive. The alarming reduction in population of bees has compelled the scientist to rethink over the causes like Colony Collapse Disorder and their remedial solution soonest possible. This easy deployable monitoring system seems a promising solution for investigating bees' behaviors and colony monitoring. Precision apiculture can be used to monitor beehives for research and reducing the resource consumption with delay in production (Thinagaran, 2015).

Apiary boxes are located in fields for purpose of pollination and these are checked using transducers and ultrasonic sensors to keep track of nectar production and bee's input/output activities. They are also connected to microcontroller of IEEE 108 standard for wireless intimation to monitoring unit or on smart phone. Further, the readings gathered from each of the compartment can be stored to cloud or transferred to an online business organization for purchase of selling. There are various other sensors for detecting spectrum of light, honeybee foraging behavior,

Figure 9. Microcontroller for Measuring Various Parameter in Beehive (Perumal 2015)

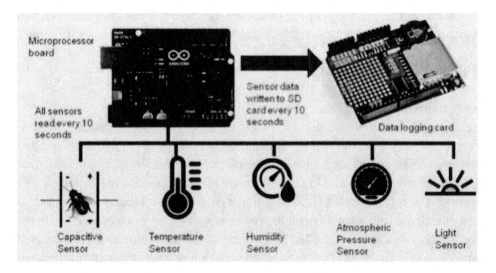

weight gain of hive, detecting quality of air for oxygen and carbon dioxide, diagnosis of disease, sound sensors to predict birth of new bees and monitoring many such activities (Vasisht, 2017).

Sensor Based Field and Resource Mapping

Information technology can help in management of site specific resources for betterment of farming and increase agricultural productivity. The over-stretching of natural resource due to random growth in population has impacted the socio-economic development of country.

GIS

This stands for Global Information System. It has become one of the major tools for management of crops. Geographic data about soil condition causes ranchers to be extra advantageous in sectioning arable land so as to practice differential rates of manure, and estimating to determine when, where, and what to plant in what is acknowledged as accuracy farming. Satellite and airborne symbolism is utilized to break down current states of the land, soil assessments taken from the fields are

Figure 10. Various Monitoring Parameters in Apiary Boxes (Yifan, 2011)

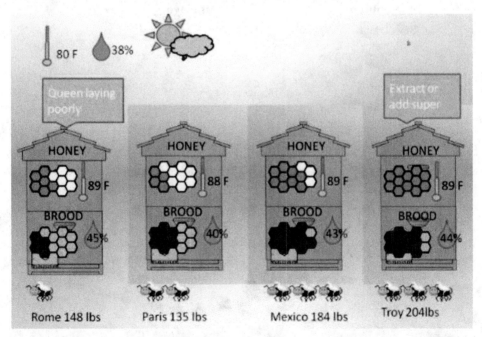

utilized to make an extra exact comprehension of the state of a homestead (Xiaojun, 2012). By understanding the state of farms on a miniaturized scale, ranchers and those in the horticulture field can better oversee manure and water application, bringing about reduced charges and higher product yields. Agricultural Global Information System is capable of mapping water usage, tracking potential plant diseases etc. With the collection of data from the GIS scientists and farmers can collaboratively work to enhance the quality and effectively use the technology. GIS utilities in agriculture has been playing an increasingly vital role in crop production throughout the world by means of supporting farmers in growing production, lowering costs, and managing their land resources more efficiently. GIS application in agriculture such as agricultural mapping plays a imperative role in monitoring and administration of soil and irrigation of any given farm land (Zacepins, 2013). GIS agriculture and agricultural mapping act as critical tools for management of agricultural zone by using obtaining and imposing the correct facts into a mapping environment. GIS utility in agriculture additionally helps in administration and manipulate of agricultural resources. GIS agriculture technological know-how helps in improvement of the existing structures of obtaining and generating GIS agriculture and sources data.

Figure 11. Data Layers of a Field Map (Donatis, 2006)

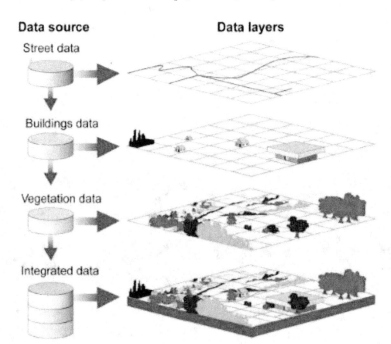

Remote Sensing

It is the science of acquiring knowledge about any object by sensing the reflected energy, processing and analyzing to apply that information for overall farms productivity. Satellite-based optical and radar sensing are utilized generally in checking farming. Radar sensing is specifically used in stormy or rainy season. Integrated utilization of geospatial technologies with edit models can help in organizing auspicious yield creation conjectures and dealing with droughts. Remote sensing also helps researchers to predict the expected production and yield based on forecasted data. This can also help in predicting the crop losses and progress of in farm crops. It can also detect the growing patterns of crops and can make predictions based on the analysis of data. It can determine the quality of crops by capturing the withstanding capacity of a crop in particular stress conditions (Jha, 2007). They can identify plants, harvesting dates, detect diseases and their infestation, soil moisture estimation, predict rainfall patterns, monitor the drought determining the weather patterns, air and soil moisture estimation and many more. It can also help in detecting nutritional deficiencies in crops based on change in color, moisture content and internal structure of leaves based on reflections received. Properties of soil can also be inferred from microwave data using empirical methods. These soil properties may include mineralogy, organic compound in soil, salinity, iron, soil moisture and other contents in the soil (Lefsky, 2002).

Figure 12. Remote Sensing Monitoring (Rogan, 2004)

GPS

The GPS stands for Global Positioning System which serves with many application and benefits in the field of agriculture. The site specific cropping is made possible with combination of GPS and GIS. With the help of global positioning system and analysis of gathered data, GPS can enable farmers to keep on tracking in less visibility conditions like heavy rain, fog and in night time. Precision farming activities allow farmers with productive and efficient GPS-derived tools to map field boundaries, irrigation system and various problem domains like weeds or crop diseases (Neményi, 2003). GPS also allows farmers to navigate between various locations within the field and monitor soil conditions. The various usages of GPS are as under:

Weed Scouting

Field scouting is required everyday for record keeping of real time field conditions. This allows monitoring of every activity from planting to harvesting, soil & compost testing and many other features. GPS weed scouting program let farmers control the weed problems by identifying and dealing with them.

GPS Smart Soil Sampling

GPS is capable of providing appropriate and accurate information of ideal type of soil for a particular variety of crop. Soil sampling data can help determining and distinguishing the quality of soil defining the growth of crops (Katzberg, 2006).

Locating Machinery

GPS trackers are as small as size of coin which can be attached with various farms' equipments and machineries. This way they can be located in vast land areas. The smart phone supports the app that can communicate with the devices with GPS tracker and help them locate. It can not only intimate when the machinery is within the field but also notifies when it moves out of geo-fences. It can also provide real time tracking of speed, status of engine, pre-stored location history, mileage details, vehicle route and many other tracking facilities (Shamshiri, 2013).

Characterized Classification of Field Areas

GPS helps location and terrain mapping of different areas based on the type of soil and cultivation capabilities. It can help in identifying the suitable and unsuitable areas for cultivation so that they can be alienated or developed based on analysis of the data collected (Pike, 2012).

Soil Sampling and Property Control

GPS can help identifying the quality of soil for variability and sustainability of soil. This also helps in applying appropriate use of pesticides reducing the overall amount of over-sprinkling of them by estimating the size of area.

Predictive Analytics for Crop and Livestock

The development of information technology in agriculture allows prediction of crop related information like yield, profit & loss analysis and many more. Agriculture ecosystem deals with various varieties of fields that make use of sensing technology and analytical tools to generate reports for accumulated data. As manual accumulation of information make it troublesome for ranchers to accomplish ideal levels of proficiency, particularly given the geographic dispersal of their agricultural lands.[2] At this place intervention of innovation and technology is making an undeniably essential role. The advancement of the present sensors, web empowered gadgets, programming applications, and cloud information storage are permitting analysis of bulk information to be controlled, analyzed and sustained to be fed into decision systems for better management of objective data. Moisture recognizing sensors installed in the soil can communicate accurately and wirelessly with the farm devices. The predictive analysis can also help in controlling automated irrigation system. This helps in proper usage of water to grow crops under monitored conditions. The modern farming makes use of data mining techniques that includes different classification and clustering techniques. The classification techniques can help in predicting newly obtained unknown data sets based on the information provided in classified samples. These techniques include supervised learning algorithm, linear regression, generalized linear model, structured prediction, and others.[48] The clustering process is begin to compare the benchmark data that may include various factors like time, accuracy, etc. which can help in present predictions as well as future predictions.

Climate Monitoring and Forecasting

The weather conditions directly impact the yield of crops and it's the fundamental parameter for the software to analyze the present data. Real time information of the crop can be collected using various parameters like metrological data, agronomic data, soil water holding capacity etc. Crop forecasting is the technique to know the yields of crop and estimate the production even before the harvesting. Weather and climatic changes are considered the most influencing factor for production of crops. Weather Stations aggregate the weather data and transmit it to local receivers in farm stations which help farmers in scheduling crops (Bolton, 2013). This not only helps

Figure 13. Cattle Data Collection at Cloud Server (Baggio, 2005)

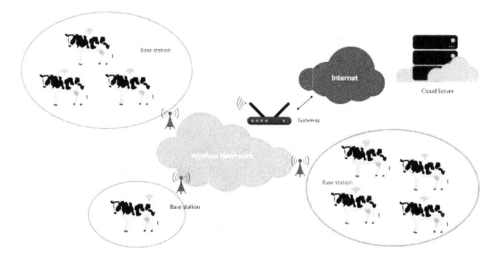

in minimizing the yield loss but also aggravates the produce quality. In this manner harnessing the weather related information and data analysis from decision making can provide an opportunity of transforming the climatic hazards into resources (Guo, 2014). The technology to provide reliable and easy to handle interface has developed with time and use of these technological appliances has increased as they promises to solve the traditional problems like variation in climate, loss of production due to pests and disease, weather unpredictability etc. To feed the increasing population technological advancements to monitor climatic changes can help in reducing the associated losses.

CONCLUSION

Indian agriculture has evolved from a very long manner of manual efforts and mounted several records by surpassing the production and productivity that man has ever imagined in the past years of evolution of agriculture. The growing adoption rate of technology in agriculture is enhancing and encouraging more farmers to learn and adopt innovative ideas for urbanization of farming. Agriculture has been hand-operative, time-consuming and labor-intensive which demands the use of modern technologies for cooperating farming tasks to increase efficiency at reduced costs and available resources. With the effective use of modern IoT, is providing exact information on when to sow the crop, the temperature around their farms, the appropriate blend of fertilizers, how to deal with crop diseases and lastly indicating the correct harvesting time of the crop based on parameters like crop maturity, size and others.

Agriculture technologies have changed and continuously cooperating to change almost all the domains of farming from sowing to harvesting. These technologies are continued to evolve and invent new innovations that act as catalyst to ameliorate farmers' life by increasing incoming and providing the access to research stations and agro-scientists. The interventions of IoT is not only changing the way agriculture has been thriving to survive but also innovate novice ideas by spreading awareness about the pragmatic application of using technology on ground level. The use of technology can make farmers feel more empowered and enable them to adopt required measures in needful time. It has potential capabilities to transform agriculture into a better prospect to get aware of climatic change and appropriate use of limited natural resources in agricultural land. There is a lot of innovation in the Internet of Things, have the potential to make a huge impact on the farm. For example, tracking and Geo-fencing, plant, soil & irrigation monitoring, precision farming, remote sensing and use of GPS etc. are all within reach of even every farmer today.

This chapter projects the present and future insight into use of precision agriculture in current ways of growing crops. It also introduces use of various technologies that will continue enhancing the productivity based on the future needs like water conservation, increased nutritional value of crops etc. This is also an equal contribution of agro-industries and companies to keep on exploring the new possibilities and providing solutions to current challenges and limitations posed by agricultural technologies. To strengthen the supporting framework for growth, it will be important to focus on creating new information products, like the Talking Fields maps, that allows more accurate and on time handling of site-specific farming techniques. Fewer production costs, as resources such as water, seeds, and fertilizer are not wasted. More efficient in the sense of yield per fertilizer or water used. A successful future growth strategy for agriculture will need to perceive agriculture as a sustainable Smart Farming not accept only livelihood enterprise. Ultimately, we think that all of these technologies, when deployed effectively, will work towards achieving long-term objectives of sustainable agriculture.

This chapter projects the present needs and future insight into use of precision agriculture in current ways of growing crops. It also introduces use of various technologies that will continue enhancing the productivity based on the future needs like water conservation, increased nutritional value of crops etc. This is also an equal contribution of agro-industries and companies to keep on exploring the new possibilities and providing solutions to current challenges and limitations posed by agricultural technologies. This way the development of technological agriculture that is soundly capable to satiate the future needs of food to feed on an approx of 9.5 billion populations in the year 2050. To strengthen the supporting framework for growth, it will be important to focus on creating new information products, like the Talking Fields maps, allows the farmer to more accurately react with site-specific farming techniques. Fewer production costs, as resources such as water, seeds, and fertilizer are not wasted. More efficient in the sense of yield per fertilizer or water used. A successful future growth strategy for agriculture will need to perceive agriculture as a sustainable Smart Farming not accept only livelihood enterprise. Ultimately, we think that all of these technologies, when deployed effectively, will work towards achieving long-term objectives of sustainable agriculture.

REFERENCES

Azaza, M., Tanougast, C., Fabrizio, E., & Mami, A. (2016). Smart greenhouse fuzzy logic based control system enhanced with wireless data monitoring. *ISA Transactions*, *61*, 297–307. doi:10.1016/j.isatra.2015.12.006 PMID:26749556

Baggio, A. (2005, June). Wireless sensor networks in precision agriculture. In *ACM Workshop on Real-World Wireless Sensor Networks (REALWSN 2005)* (Vol. 20). ACM.

Bo, Y., & Wang, H. (2011, May). The application of cloud computing and the internet of things in agriculture and forestry. In *2011 International Joint Conference on Service Sciences* (pp. 168-172). IEEE. 10.1109/IJCSS.2011.40

Bolton, D. K., & Friedl, M. A. (2013). Forecasting crop yield using remotely sensed vegetation indices and crop phenology metrics. *Agricultural and Forest Meteorology*, *173*, 74–84. doi:10.1016/j.agrformet.2013.01.007

Channe, H., Kothari, S., & Kadam, D. (2015). Multidisciplinary model for smart agriculture using internet-of-things (IoT), sensors, cloud-computing, mobile-computing & big-data analysis. *Int. J. Computer Technology and Application*, *6*(3), 374–382.

Chen, S. X., Ma, H. T., & Liu, X. (2011). Design of smart greenhouse system. *Hebei Journal of Industrial Science and Technology, 4*.

Dan, L. I. U., Xin, C., Chongwei, H., & Liangliang, J. (2015, December). Intelligent agriculture greenhouse environment monitoring system based on IOT technology. In *2015 International Conference on Intelligent Transportation, Big Data and Smart City* (pp. 487-490). IEEE.

De Donatis, M., & Bruciatelli, L. (2006). MAP IT: The GIS software for field mapping with tablet pc. *Computers & Geosciences, 32*(5), 673–680. doi:10.1016/j.cageo.2005.09.003

Ferrández-Pastor, F., García-Chamizo, J., Nieto-Hidalgo, M., Mora-Pascual, J., & Mora-Martínez, J. (2016). Developing ubiquitous sensor network platform using internet of things: Application in precision agriculture. *Sensors (Basel), 16*(7), 1141. doi:10.339016071141 PMID:27455265

Fulton, J. P., & Port, K. (2018). Precision agriculture data management. *Precision Agriculture Basics*, 169-188.

Gebbers, R., & Adamchuk, V. I. (2010). Precision agriculture and food security. *Science, 327*(5967), 828–831. doi:10.1126cience.1183899 PMID:20150492

Gómez-Candón, D., De Castro, A. I., & Lopez-Granados, F. (2014). Assessing the accuracy of mosaics from unmanned aerial vehicle (UAV) imagery for precision agriculture purposes in wheat. *Precision Agriculture, 15*(1), 44–56. doi:10.100711119-013-9335-4

Guo, W. W., & Xue, H. (2014). Crop yield forecasting using artificial neural networks: A comparison between spatial and temporal models. *Mathematical Problems in Engineering*.

Harun, A. N., Kassim, M. R. M., Mat, I., & Ramli, S. S. (2015, May). Precision irrigation using wireless sensor network. In *2015 International Conference on Smart Sensors and Application (ICSSA)* (pp. 71-75). IEEE. 10.1109/ICSSA.2015.7322513

Hedley, C. B., & Yule, I. J. (2009). Soil water status mapping and two variable-rate irrigation scenarios. *Precision Agriculture, 10*(4), 342–355. doi:10.100711119-009-9119-z

Jafar, I. B., Raihana, K., Bhowmik, S., & Shakil, S. R. (2014, May). Wireless monitoring system and controlling software for Smart Greenhouse Management. In *2014 International Conference on Informatics, Electronics & Vision (ICIEV)* (pp. 1-5). IEEE. 10.1109/ICIEV.2014.6850748

Jayaraman, P. P., Palmer, D., Zaslavsky, A., & Georgakopoulos, D. (2015, April). Do-it-Yourself Digital Agriculture applications with semantically enhanced IoT platform. In *2015 IEEE Tenth International Conference on Intelligent Sensors, Sensor Networks and Information Processing (ISSNIP)* (pp. 1-6). IEEE. 10.1109/ISSNIP.2015.7106951

Jha, M. K., Chowdhury, A., Chowdary, V. M., & Peiffer, S. (2007). Groundwater management and development by integrated remote sensing and geographic information systems: Prospects and constraints. *Water Resources Management, 21*(2), 427–467. doi:10.100711269-006-9024-4

Jin, Z., Prasad, R., Shriver, J., & Zhuang, Q. (2017). Crop model-and satellite imagery-based recommendation tool for variable rate N fertilizer application for the US Corn system. *Precision Agriculture, 18*(5), 779–800. doi:10.100711119-016-9488-z

Kaiwartya, O., Abdullah, A. H., Cao, Y., Raw, R. S., Kumar, S., Lobiyal, D. K., ... Shah, R. R. (2016). T-MQM: Testbed-based multi-metric quality measurement of sensor deployment for precision agriculture—A case study. *IEEE Sensors Journal, 16*(23), 8649–8664.

Katzberg, S. J., Torres, O., Grant, M. S., & Masters, D. (2006). Utilizing calibrated GPS reflected signals to estimate soil reflectivity and dielectric constant: Results from SMEX02. *Remote Sensing of Environment, 100*(1), 17–28. doi:10.1016/j.rse.2005.09.015

Khattab, A., Abdelgawad, A., & Yelmarthi, K. (2016, December). Design and implementation of a cloud-based IoT scheme for precision agriculture. In *28th International Conference on Microelectronics* (pp. 201-204). IEEE. 10.1109/ICM.2016.7847850

Khosla, R., Fleming, K., Delgado, J. A., Shaver, T. M., & Westfall, D. G. (2002). Use of site-specific management zones to improve nitrogen management for precision agriculture. *Journal of Soil and Water Conservation, 57*(6), 513–518.

Kranthi Kumar, M., & Srenivasa Ravi, K. (2016). Automation of irrigation system based on Wi-Fi technology and IOT. *Indian Journal of Science and Technology, 9*(17), 17. doi:10.17485/ijst/2016/v9i17/93048

Kviesis, A., & Zacepins, A. (2015). System architectures for real-time bee colony temperature monitoring. *Procedia Computer Science, 43*, 86–94. doi:10.1016/j.procs.2014.12.012

Lecocq, A., Kryger, P., Vejsnæs, F., & Jensen, A. B. (2015). Weight watching and the effect of landscape on honeybee colony productivity: Investigating the value of colony weight monitoring for the beekeeping industry. *PLoS One, 10*(7), e0132473. doi:10.1371/journal.pone.0132473 PMID:26147392

Lefsky, M. A., Cohen, W. B., Parker, G. G., & Harding, D. J. (2002). Lidar remote sensing for ecosystem studies: Lidar, an emerging remote sensing technology that directly measures the three-dimensional distribution of plant canopies, can accurately estimate vegetation structural attributes and should be of particular interest to forest, landscape, and global ecologists. *Bioscience*, *52*(1), 19–30. doi:10.1641/0006-3568(2002)052[0019:LRSFES]2.0.CO;2

Lei, Z. (2018). Internet of Things Applications for Agriculture. Internet of Things A to Z: Technologies and Applications, 507-528.

Malveaux, C., Hall, S. G., & Price, R. (2014). Using drones in agriculture: unmanned aerial systems for agricultural remote sensing applications. In *2014 Montreal, Quebec Canada July 13–July 16, 2014* (p. 1). American Society of Agricultural and Biological Engineers.

Mobley, T. (2013). Tracking and monitoring of animals with combined wireless technology and geofencing. *U.S. Patent Application, 13*(917), 328.

Mobley, T. (2016). Tracking and monitoring of animals with combined wireless technology and geo-fencing. *U.S. Patent Application 15*(76), 584.

Nandyala, C. S., & Kim, H. K. (2016). Green IoT agriculture and healthcare application (GAHA). *International Journal of Smart Home*, *10*(4), 289–300. doi:10.14257/ijsh.2016.10.4.26

Neményi, M., Mesterházi, P. Á., Pecze, Z., & Stépán, Z. (2003). The role of GIS and GPS in precision farming. *Computers and Electronics in Agriculture*, *40*(1-3), 45–55. doi:10.1016/S0168-1699(03)00010-3

O'Shaughnessy, S. A., Urrego, Y. F., Evett, S. R., Colaizzi, P. D., & Howell, T. A. (2013). Assessing application uniformity of a variable rate irrigation system in a windy location. *Applied Engineering in Agriculture*, *29*(4), 497–510.

Perumal, T., Sulaiman, M. N., & Leong, C. Y. (2015, October). Internet of Things (IoT) enabled water monitoring system. In *2015 IEEE 4th Global Conference on Consumer Electronics (GCCE)* (pp. 86-87). IEEE.

Piao, S., Ciais, P., Huang, Y., Shen, Z., Peng, S., Li, J., ... Fang, J. (2010). The impacts of climate change on water resources and agriculture in China. *Nature*, *467*(7311), 43–51. doi:10.1038/nature09364 PMID:20811450

Pike, A., Muller, T., Rienzi, E. A., Neelakantan, S., Mijatovic, B., Karathanasis, A. D., & Rodrigues, M. (2012). *Terrain analysis for locating erosion channels: Assessing LiDAR data and flow direction algorithm.* Academic Press.

Rad, C. R., Hancu, O., Takacs, I. A., & Olteanu, G. (2015). Smart monitoring of potato crop: A cyber-physical system architecture model in the field of precision agriculture. *Agriculture and Agricultural Science Procedia, 6*, 73–79. doi:10.1016/j.aaspro.2015.08.041

Rogan, J., & Chen, D. (2004). Remote sensing technology for mapping and monitoring land-cover and land-use change. *Progress in Planning, 61*(4), 301–325. doi:10.1016/S0305-9006(03)00066-7

Santesteban, L. G., Guillaume, S., Royo, J. B., & Tisseyre, B. (2013). Are precision agriculture tools and methods relevant at the whole-vineyard scale? *Precision Agriculture, 14*(1), 2–17. doi:10.100711119-012-9268-3

Satpute, P., & Tembhurne, O. (2014). A review of: Cloud centric IoT based framework for supply chain management in precision agriculture. *International Journal of Advance Research in Computer Science and Management Studies, 2*(11), 14–23.

Sawant, S. A., Adinarayana, J., & Durbha, S. S. (2014, July). KrishiSense: A semantically aware web enabled wireless sensor network system for precision agriculture applications. In *2014 IEEE Geoscience and Remote Sensing Symposium* (pp. 4090-4093). IEEE. 10.1109/IGARSS.2014.6947385

Shamshiri, R., & Ismail, W. I. W. (2013). Exploring gps data for operational analysis of farm machinery. *Research Journal of Applied Sciences, Engineering and Technology, 5*(12), 3281–3286. doi:10.19026/rjaset.5.4568

Silva, C. B., de Moraes, M. A. F. D., & Molin, J. P. (2011). Adoption and use of precision agriculture technologies in the sugarcane industry of São Paulo state, Brazil. *Precision Agriculture, 12*(1), 67–81. doi:10.100711119-009-9155-8

Singh, D., Tripathi, G., & Jara, A. J. (2014, March). A survey of Internet-of-Things: Future vision, architecture, challenges and services. In *2014 IEEE World Forum on Internet of Things (WF-IoT)* (pp. 287-292). IEEE.

Stočes, M., Vaněk, J., Masner, J., & Pavlík, J. (2016). Internet of things (iot) in agriculture-selected aspects. *Agris on-line Papers in Economics and Informatics, 8*, 83.

Stojkoska, B. L. R., & Trivodaliev, K. V. (2017). A review of Internet of Things for smart home: Challenges and solutions. *Journal of Cleaner Production, 140*, 1454–1464. doi:10.1016/j.jclepro.2016.10.006

Sundmaeker, H., Verdouw, C., Wolfert, S., & Pérez Freire, L. (2016). Internet of food and farm 2020. Digitising the Industry-Internet of Things connecting physical, digital and virtual worlds, 129-151.

TongKe, F. (2013). Smart agriculture based on cloud computing and IOT. *Journal of Convergence Information Technology, 8*(2).

Vasisht, D., Kapetanovic, Z., Won, J., Jin, X., Chandra, R., Sinha, S., . . . Stratman, S. (2017). Farmbeats: An iot platform for data-driven agriculture. In *14th USENIX Symposium on Networked Systems Design and Implementation* (pp. 515-529). USENIX.

Xiaojun, Y., Weirui, W., & Jianping, L. (2012). Application mode construction of internet of things (IOT) for facility agriculture in Beijing. *Nongye Gongcheng Xuebao (Beijing), 2012*(4).

Yan-e, D. (2011, March). Design of intelligent agriculture management information system based on IoT. In *2011 Fourth International Conference on Intelligent Computation Technology and Automation* (Vol. 1, pp. 1045-1049). IEEE. 10.1109/ICICTA.2011.262

Ye, J., Chen, B., Liu, Q., & Fang, Y. (2013, June). A precision agriculture management system based on Internet of Things and WebGIS. In *2013 21st International Conference on Geoinformatics* (pp. 1-5). IEEE. 10.1109/Geoinformatics.2013.6626173

Yong, H., Pengcheng, N., & Fei, L. (2013). Advancement and trend of internet of things in agriculture and sensing instrument. *Nongye Jixie Xuebao, 44*(10), 216–226.

Zacepins, A., & Karasha, T. (2013, May). Application of temperature measurements for the bee colony monitoring: a review. In *Proceedings of the 12th International Scientific Conference "Engineering for Rural Development* (pp. 126-131). Academic Press.

Zhang, C., & Kovacs, J. M. (2012). The application of small unmanned aerial systems for precision agriculture: A review. *Precision Agriculture, 13*(6), 693–712. doi:10.100711119-012-9274-5

Zhao, J. C., Zhang, J. F., Feng, Y., & Guo, J. X. (2010, July). The study and application of the IOT technology in agriculture. In *2010 3rd International Conference on Computer Science and Information Technology* (Vol. 2, pp. 462-465). IEEE.

Chapter 10
Radio Frequency Identification Systems Security Challenges in Supply Chain Management

Kamalendu Pal
City, University of London, UK

ABSTRACT

The radio frequency idtentification (RFID) is a wireless technology that enable automatic identification and extraction of stored information from any tagged object within a supply chain environment. A simple RFID system uses radio waves to collect and transfer data from a tag attached to an object linked to an RFID reader for identifying, tracking, and data capturing. However, RFID-based systems have numerous security- and privacy-related threats for the deployment of such technology in supply chain automation purpose. This chapter explains the technical fundamentals of RFID systems and its security threats. It also classifies the existing security and privacy threats into those which target the RFID components such as the tag, the communication channel, and the overall system threats. Finally, the chapter discusses the open research challenges that need further investigation, especially with the rapid introduction of diverse RFID applications in supply chain management (SCM).

DOI: 10.4018/978-1-5225-7811-6.ch010

INTRODUCTION

All business today understands the value and importance of building an effective supply chain, as part of organizational growth and profitability (Pal, 2019). A supply chain is a network of business facilities and distribution options that performs key functions: raw material procurement, transformation of these materials into intermediate and finished products, and distribution of these finished products to warehouses; and finally, from warehouses to retail customers (Pal, 2017). Supply chain management (SCM) uses various approaches to integrate suppliers, manufacturers, distributors in performing their functions, and to provide the appropriate strategy to deliver products and services to customers in the right quantities, to the right locations and the right time to meet the required service level with optimal cost. Through collaboration and information sharing SCM system can produce efficient value-added services to its customers and create competitive advantage in the market place. An integrated diagrammatic representation of market specific supply and demand information, warehousing and distribution details along a supply chain, is shown in Figure 1.

Managing a supply chain involves numerous business decisions about the flow of information, product, funds, and their coordination. SCM has been instrumental in connecting and smoothing business activities as well as forming various kinds of business relationships, for example - customer relationship management (CRM), supplier relationship management (SRM), among supply chain stakeholders. In this way, SCM is a complex coordination mechanism to manage the total flow of a distribution channel from supplier level to production, distribution and then ultimately to the end customer. The aim is to achieve goals related to total system performance rather than optimization of a single phase in a logistics chain. The objective of SCM is to enhance productivity by reducing total inventory level and cycle time for orders. It is important for supply chain business-partners to create a network that is agile and able to respond rapidly to unpredictable changes in demand. To achieve these objectives close cooperation among business partners is essential.

SCM system utilizes modern Information and Communication Technologies (ICT) to acquire, interpret, retain, and distribute information. RFID –based technological solution provides a major advantage to SCM. Implementing supply chain collaboration along with RFID technology can enable retailer to achieve the best level of business performance. Retailers can expect extensive inventory and labour-cost savings. In fact, the retail industry (with such major retailers like Walmart and TESCO in the USA, and United Kingdom's Mark & Spencer and Germany's METRO Group) is the initial driver of RFID technology adoption in business operation.

In recent decades, RFID technology has been used in many supply chain coordination activities: manufacturing, transportation and logistics operations. Associated with the integration of RFID technology in business and in the day-to-

Figure 1. A diagrammatic representation of supply chain business processes

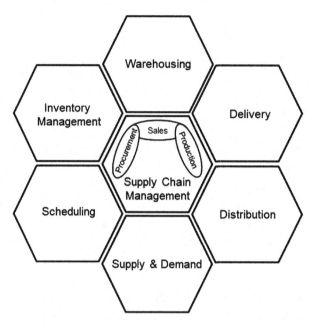

day life of consumers are various security and privacy concerns. The potential to reduce purchase anonymity, embedded tags in products that can reveal sensitive information, violation of location privacy with no-contact, non-line-of-sight through non-conducting material (e.g. cardboard or paper), fast read rate at up to a few meters and invisible identification which can be done indiscriminately has raised privacy concerns.

Security and privacy aspects related to RFID applications are, however, gain significant importance as the absence of good security and privacy is partially responsible for holding back the large-scale implementations that are required for global SCM. Because RFID is a wireless system without any standard security controls, tag can be read, modified, manipulated, or disabled without physical contact. The privacy issues have been frequently hyped in the media by certain individuals and groups that are against the use of RFID technology, particularly in consumer products, as they expect it to violate their privacy. Their primary concern is that RFID tags are not disabled after purchase and can therefore still be scanned and read for unwanted purposes such as obtaining sensitive personal data or locating and tracking very valuable goods. Although the primary focus of RFID issues is on privacy, supply chain businesses that use RFID-based technological solutions must be aware of security as well. Unprotected RFID tags can be scanned to obtain business sensitive information and locate valuable products but can also be disabled to easily steal products or sabotage enterprise supply chains.

Researchers have been trying to find ways to prevent these RFID security and privacy threats. Most of the published academic papers on protection capabilities for RFID are independent studies, each presenting new security and privacy techniques with unique abilities. These independent studies are, however, not very useful for enterprises to determine which threats exist for their RFID implementation and how these threats need to be countered. This chapter therefore analyzed a large sample of academic research works from which it has selected the most common RFID threats.

Although there have been other classifications of RFID threats, these classifications do not include the possible security and privacy measures that can counter these threats. Additionally, there has been very limited research in how these threats relate to the risk management of organizations, which is required to determine that how risks are to be countered. This chapter provides an overview of the well-known privacy and security threats in wireless RFID communication. This chapter consists of seven sections. Section 2 presents the background information of RFID-based technological solution. Section 3 provides the overview of simple RFID-based system. It also includes the purpose of electronic product code (EPC), object name service (ONS), and physical markup language (PML). Section 4 explains the relevance of RFID standards, which consists of international standard organization (ISO) standards and EPC-based standards. Section 5 outlines the security and privacy related issues in RFID-based technological solutions for supply chain management. Section 6 introduces the future research directions. Section 7 concludes with concluding remarks.

BACKGROUND OF RFID-BASED TECHNOLOGY

In today's digital age, real-time data stream is the supply chain's survivable lifeblood. Whether contracting new fleets in London, or recruiting supply chain operation managers in Milan, or looking at adverse weather forecasting services for smooth transportation of goods through Dorah Pass in Hindu Kush area of Asia, data keeps everything running smoothly. In RFID-based applications, data are stored into the tags. A simple RFID tag (or transponder) and its reader (or integrator / scanner) are shown in Figure 2.

RFID tags are attached to objects (e.g. men, machines, and merchandise items) for identification purpose. Each tag typically consists of an antenna constructed from a small coil of wires; a microchip used to store information digitally about the companion object; and encapsulating material to enclose the chip and the coil. Like there are distinct types of barcode, RFID tags are available with different memory sizes and encoding options. These tags can also incorporate sensors to record temperature, vibration, shock, or humidity, for example, providing the ability to track and report on an object's environmental characteristics dynamically.

Figure 2. A basic RFID tag and its interrogator

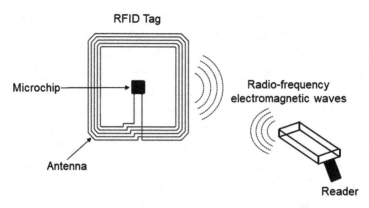

A RFID reader is the device generally used to communicate with the RFID tag(s). It discharges radio frequency (RF) signals to, and receives radio waves from, the tag via an antenna or antennas. The reader converts the received radio waves into digital information that is usually passed to a backend system. Reader, either as stationary or handheld devices, consists of a transmitter, receiver, antenna, microprocessor, controller, memory and power source.

The RFID tag can come in different shapes (e.g. Paper Sticker, Barcode Tags, Plastic Card, Chemical and Heat Resistance Plastic Capsule). The tag might be even powered by very small battery to support local functions such as storing temperature reading or enhancing the reach of the radio communication, and so on. In this way, RFID tags are at the heart of an RFID system, and can be categorized as active, semi-active / semi-passive and passive in relation to power, as well as read / write and read only in terms of their memory.

The major portion of RFID tags produced today are *passive* RFID tags, comprised basically of a micro-circuit and an antenna. They are referred to as passive tags because the only time at which they are actively communicating is when they are within relatively close-proximity of a passive RFID tag reader.

Another type of common RFID tag in the marketplace today is known as the *active* RFID tag, which usually contains a battery that directly powers radio frequency communication. This onboard power source allows an active RFID tag to transmit information about itself at great range, either by constantly *beaconing* this information to a RFID tag reader or by transmitting only when it is prompted to do so. Active tags are usually large in size and can contain substantially more information (because of higher amounts of memory) than do pure passive tag designs. Within these basic categories of RFID tags can be found subcategories such as *semi-passive* RFID tags.

Read-Only vs. Read/Write or Smart Tags

Read-only tags have permanently encoded data set, usually in the form of a serial number. When it is in a reader field it starts to continuously broadcast this number. The flow is only one way, which means that the reader cannot access the transponder, it can only receive the information. It is important to make sure that there is only one transponder in the reader interrogation zone. Otherwise continuously transmit from the transponders creates a data collision and the reader cannot distinct one transponder from another. Read-only tags are much used as a substitute for barcodes in identification of products, containers or in other measures where very small amounts of data is needed. Read/Write-tags are wide diversity of different memory size.

The availability of low-cost RFID technology today allows for wider use beyond its traditional niche applications such as animal tagging and access control. In logistics, RFID competes with the omnipresent bar code in identifying arbitrary physical goods along the entire supply chain. Unlike bar codes, RFID allows for the unique identification of individual items and bulk reading with no line-of-sight required even under harsh environmental conditions. This gives rise to opportunities to collect the kind of fine-granular, real-time information about physical processes in the supply chain which often cannot be monitored using conventional approaches.

Besides its ever-broader diffusion across many industries, RFID has also become a fruitful research topic, not only in electrical engineering and computer science, but also in business management. Specifically, several success stories have recently been developed in the fields of information systems and operations management that not only support designers of RFID-based systems and processes but also explain how RFID can generate business value in organizations (Pal, 2019) (Roussos et al, 2002) (Jones et al, 2004a) (Oghazi, et al., 2018) (Alwadi, et al, 2017) (Choi., et al., 2018). However, most of this work tends to consider RFID as a "next generation data capturing innovative technology" differing only slightly from its predecessor in its enhanced precision and the timeliness of collected data. This narrow view runs the risk of ignoring the various fundamental levels of data quality associated with the RFID-based technologies. However, the RFID-based system's data quality related issues are beyond the scope of this chapter. To initiate the exploration of the main theme of this chapter, the next section provides a basic description of an RFID-based system.

OVERVIEW OF A SIMPLE RFID SYSTEM

An RFID system has three key components: the tag, the reader, and the backend system. RFID tags, also known as transponders, are identification devices that are attached to objects. Each tag typically consists of

A simple RFID-based system solution consists of six main components as shown in Figure 2. These components are:

1. **Tag**: A tag is the data (or information) carrier part of RFID-based business solution. Generally, it contains a unique identification number, and specific *electronic product code* (EPC) programmed into the tag.
2. **Reader and Antenna**: A reader captures the data provided by the tag when tags come in the range of sensing area covered by the specific reader using its antenna (i.e. an electronic *signal receiving special circuit*).
3. **Middleware**: The middleware can be software as well as hardware dedicated to process data captured by the *tag reader*, then dispatch this information to backend servers.
4. **Backend Servers**: The backend servers hold the data collected from RFID-based application systems for processing purpose.
5. **Network Infrastructure**: This part of RFID-based solution infrastructure is basically providing data communication provision. It plays a very important role for RFID-based system solutions security and privacy related issues.
6. **Database for Tags Information**: This is the part of the enterprise information system.

Figure 3. A basic RFID-based solution technology architecture

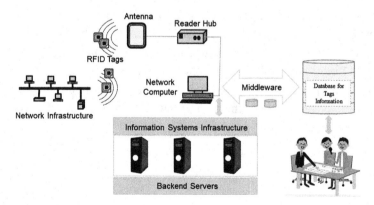

Using an antenna, the information that is stored on the tag can be read or written from the tag. In a typical situation, the antenna is packaged with the transceiver into a larger structure called a reader that oversees the system's data communication and acquisition. The data that is obtained and analyzed by the reader can then be transported to a corporate data storage.

Readers

The reader usually consists of a microcontroller part, an analogue part and an antenna. The analogue part has some sort of bit coding, carrier modulation and a power storage to ensure reception / transmission of signal. To ensure reception it needs reception of the transponders load modulation of the transmitted signal. It also needs to be able to process the signal through amplification, filtering, demodulation and validation of the bits. The microcontroller part ensures anti-collision, manages the encryption algorithm, display information on an LCD screen or ensures connection to the host if needed. A backend system, sometimes referred to as an online database, is needed to collect, filter, process, and manage the RFID data.

Moreover, RFID tags of different frequencies and functionality are used together for supply chain operations management.

RFID Frequency and Uses

An RFID device requires a defined radio frequency and communication protocol to transmit and receive data from RFID tags. The exact frequencies (and power levels) used in RFID systems vary by country or region; however, typical RFID systems utilize the following frequency ranges, as shown in Table 1.

Table 1. Frequency characteristics of RFID systems

Frequency Range	Characteristics	Applications
Low Frequency (LF) 125 ~ 300 KHz	Short range (to 18 inches) Low reading speed	Livestock identification purpose.
High Frequency (HF) 13.56 MHz	Medium range (3 ~ 10 feet) Medium reading speed	Access Control Library automation Mass Transit Ticketing
Ultra High Frequency (UHF) 400 MHz ~ 1 GHz (primarily 860 – 930 MHz)	High range (10 ~ 30 feet) High reading speed Orientation sensitive	Supply chain management Industrial automation Vehicle Identification
Microwave Frequency (MF) > 1 GHz; primarily 2.45 (USA) and 5.8 GHz (Europe)	Maximum range (300+ feet)	Pallet and Container Tracking

Low and High frequency systems are more easily controlled. UHF systems are harder to control as energy is sent over long distance and reading is a challenge around metal and water. However, the benefits include low cost (passive) and high read range. Currently, logistics and supply chain tend to use the UHF band, either between 860 – 930 MHz (Passive).

Comparison of RFID Technology to Bar-Codes

Although it is often thought that RFID and Bar-Codes are competitive technologies, they are in fact complementary in some respects. The primary element of differentiation between the two is that RFID does not require line-of-sight technology. Bar-Codes must be scanned at specific orientation to establish line-of-sight, such as an item in a retail outlet, and RFID tags need only be within range of a reader to be read or scanned.

Both RFID-based applications and Bar-Codes-based information systems deployment share some similarities and they are: (i) act as a support tool to automate processes and improve day-to-day supply chain operations management, (ii) reduce labour cost and eliminate human errors; and (iii) generate a wealth of data for corporate decision-making. However, there are differences in these technological solutions: firstly, RFID tags can be embedded and hidden with no need for line-of-sight. The tags can be read through wood, plastic, carboard, any material except metal. Tags can be reprogrammed on-the-fly. In addition, tags can be used in harsh operational environments, such as outdoors, in the vicinity of toxic chemicals, moisture and very high temperatures.

By comparing the characteristics of RFID against object identification using Bar-Codes, some major advantages can be identified for both technologies. Furthermore, a completely new product identification scheme, the Electronic Product Code (EPC), allows for a massively increased address space.

The Electronic Product Code

May be the most important advantage of RFID over the traditional Bar-Code is the ability to uniquely identify every sole product along with the product class. A new identification scheme for products, the Electronic Product Code (EPC) created by the Auto-ID center, has become one of the dominant RFID standards. The Auto-ID center was established in 1999 at the Massachusetts Institute of Technology (MIT) as a research group consisting of several leading universities and aimed to develop a low-cost, open standard RFID infrastructure for industrial applications. An important feature is its capability to serve as a meta-scheme that integrates with existing numbering schemes, as the serialized Global Trade Item Number (GTIN) standard used in retail.

The EPC is a simple, compact 'license plate' that uniquely identifies objects (items, cases, pallets, locations, etc.) in a supply chain. Like many current numbering schemes used in commerce, the EPC is divided into numbers that identify the manufacturer and product type. But the EPC uses an extra set of digits, a serial number, to identify unique items.

An EPC number contains:

- Header, which identifies the length, type, structure, version and generation of EPC
- Manager Number, which identifies the company or company entity
- Object Class refers to a stock keeping unit or product SKU (Stock Keeping Unit)
- Serial Number, which identifies a specific item of the Object Class being tagged

Additional fields may also be used as part of the EPC in order to properly encode and decode information from different numbering systems into their native (human readable) forms. EPCglobal Network defines a framework that enables immediate, automatic identification and sharing of information on items in the supply chain. The network is comprised of five fundamental elements: The Electronic Product Code (EPC), the ID System (EPC Tags and Readers), Object Name Service (ONS), Physical Markup Language (PML), and Savant software. A reader infrastructure of RFID antenna can identify the tagged items.

The reader then passes the number to a computer or local application system, known as the Object Name Service (ONS). ONS tells where to locate information on the network about the object carrying an EPC, such as when the item was produced. Physical Markup Language (PML) is used as a common language in the EPCglobal Network to describe all product related information. Savant is a software tool that manages the data as it is collected and provides it in real-time to business software systems, e.g. ERP systems. The EPC Global Network can virtually connect physical object and data via the internet. Data about every product – its history or other product related information can be made available through a standardized infrastructure anywhere and anytime.

DIFFERENT TYPES OF RFID STANDARDS

There exists a large variety of RFID systems and their main characteristics are defined by standards. Their air interface (frequency, coding, modulation), communication protocol, bandwidth, anti-collision and security mechanisms are standardized.

RFID is a relatively heterogeneous radio technology with significant number of associated standards. Figure 4 represents the most relevant technology standards, i.e. those standards describing the physical and data link layers (air interface, anti-collision, communication protocols, and security functions). Further RFID standards describe test methods and application data standards (format of the Unique Identifier, data protocol and application programming interfaces).

Contactless integrated circuit cards are special instances of identification cards as defined by International Standard Organization (ISO) in ISO 7810 specification. Specifically, there are three types of contactless cards which can be distinguished in terms of their communication range: close-couple cards (ISO 10536) that operate at a very close distance to the reader (e.g. < 1 centimeter); proximity cards (ISO 14443) operate at approximate 10 centimeters distance from the reader; and vicinity cards (ISO 15693) have a range of up to 1 meter. These cards can be used for identification and simple applications like access control. The standards describe the air interface, anti-collision and the transmission protocol.

Item management RFID tags play an important role in manufacturing and transport management systems in supply chain. ISO 18000 defines the air interface, collision detection mechanism and the communication protocol for item tags in different frequency bands.

Figure 4. RFID technology standards and frequency bands

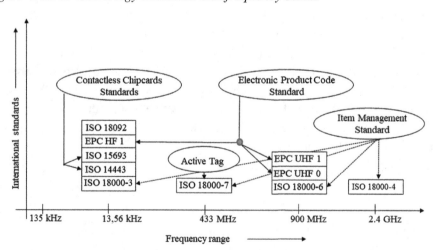

Table 2. RFID standards relevant for supply chain management

Specification	Description	Frequency	Sponsor
ePC HF Class 1	EPC tag class	13.56 MHz	EPC Global
ePC HF Class 2	EPC tag class	860-960 MHz	EPC Global
ePC HF Class 4	EPC tag class	860-960 MHz	EPC Global
ISO 14443/15693	Near Field	13.56 MHz	ISO
ISO 18000-3	RFID Air Interface	13.56 MHz	ISO
ISO 18000-4	RFID Air Interface	2.4 GHz	ISO
ISO 18000-6	RFID Air Interface	860-960 MHz	ISO

There are several existing ISO standards and proposed RFID standards (EPC – Electronic Product Code, Global) that deal with air interface protocol (how tag and readers communicate), data content (how data is organized and formatted), conformance (ways to test that products meet specifications) and applications (how standards are used on shipping labels, and so on). Table 2 shows a summary of RFID standards relevant for SCM applications. Each of these standards provides appropriate security and privacy related implementation frameworks. The following section provides a general overview of RFID-based application systems security and privacy challenges.

SECURITY AND PRIVACY THREATS

In recent years, there have been a number of high-profile security breaches with global supply management. For example, retailer Target experienced a huge corporate data breach incident involving the theft of nearly 110 million customers' data and at least 40 million payment cards (Krebsonsecurity, 1014). In many of the most reported business cases, the attackers have targeted corporate strategic information, financial information, including debit and credit card details. Most of these security breaches initiated through the corporate ICT infrastructures and it includes RFID-based IS systems.

The radio communication between RFID tags and readers raises several security related issues. There are two main classes of RFID-based system's security attacks: privacy infringements and security infringements. In privacy infringements, the conspirator tries to find information from the objects by eavesdropping to the communications between the tagged-object and reader or by tracking them. In security infringements, an adversary counterfeits the behaviour of a tag or a reader for making undesirable communications. Such security attacks may target the physical tag, the communication channel between the tag and the reader, or the application or the system, which employs the RFID technology. This section classifies the existing security risks and threats according to their target into physical threats, channel threats and system threats. However, threats, which supply chain RFID-based systems face today, are not limited to those listed below.

Physical Threats of RFID Systems

Physical threats are those threats that use physical means to attack the RFID-based information system's infrastructure to disable tags, modify their content data, or use these data for espionage purpose. Different types of physical threats for RFID-based system is shown in Table 3.

Table 3. Types of physical threats for RFID systems

Threats Type	Description
Disabling RFID Tags	In these infringements, a predator takes advantage of the wireless nature of RFID systems in order to disable tags temporarily or permanently. To permanently disable a tag, the predator may remove the tag from one item with high price and switch it with a tag of an item with low price. The other way is sending a kill command to erase the memory of the tag. Removing the antenna or giving a high energy wave to a tag will destroy the tag permanently. To disable the tag temporarily, the predator can use a Faraday cage like an aluminum foil-lined bag in order to block electromagnetic waves from it. In other case, the predator may prevent tags from communicating with readers by generating a signal in the same range as the reader which is called active jamming.
Tag Modification	Since most RFID tags us writable memory, an adversary can take advantage of this feature to modify or delete valuable data from the memory of the tag. This information might be critical such as the data about a product's specification which any inconsistency between the data stored on the RFID tag and the corresponding tagged object may result in serious problems. In some cases, the reader may not even notice this inconsistency during the communication and thinks that the content of the tag is unaltered.
Cloning Tags	In these attacks, the attacker clones or imitates the tags after skimming the tag's information. Each RFID tag used for identification has a unique ID number. If the ID information is exposed by the attacker, the tag can easily be copied. Now that a lot of programmable read-write tags are put into use, cloning a tag is not challenging. This new tag can then act as the ordinary tag without being detected. Such cloned tags are used in counterfeiting and spoofing system-level attack.
Reverse Engineering andPhysical Exploration	To maintain the tag cost low, most RFID tags are not equipped with a tamper-resistant mechanism for an estimated long period of time. An attacker with physical access to a tag can duplicate a tag with reverse engineering, and by means of physical probing, the attacker can get confidential information stored within tag. This is different from tag cloning which does not require physical exploration of the tag. However, they also are used in counterfeiting and spoofing system-level attack.

Channel Threats of RFID Systems

Channel threats refer to the attacks targeting the insecure channel between a reader and a tag. Since the RFID technology uses wireless means of communication between the reader and the tag, RFID systems may face eavesdropping, snooping, counterfeiting, playback, tracking threats, and other communication security issues that lead to privacy leaks. Different types of channel threats for RFID-based system is shown in Table 4.

Channel Threats of RFID Systems

System threats mainly refer to the attacks on the flaws existing in the authentication protocol and encryption algorithms. RFID tag data can be sensitive in terms of the security and privacy related issues. Operation managers need to make sure that the system has a proven security protocol to protect all possible security properties before one deploys RFID in a sensitive data exchange chain. Academics are working hard to establish a security standard for all types of RFID uses. To date, RFID industries have several standards applicable to some specific applications. One needs to be aware of these standards so that we can judge before using this technology. There are several well-established RFID security and privacy threats (Rieback, Crispo et al, 2006) such as: counterfeiting and spoofing attacks, tracing and tracking, password decoding, and denial of service (DOS) attacks.

RFID systems also may be subject to Denial of Service (DoS) attacks, which causes the system to not work properly. The attacker targets to block the reader from reading tags by using a blocker tag. Denial of service attacks are the threat to all modern communication systems. A set of mature anti-DoS solutions has developed for such threats. However, many of these solutions cannot be used in RFID systems due to the limited resources of RFID tags. For the RFID system to prevent denial of service attacks is still an area to be studied. Modern readers use anti-collision algorithms to support serving tags within their coverage areas. There are two main ant-collision algorithms; slotted ALOHA and binary search tree.

Security challenges raised by RFID can also be structured according to the traditional dimensions of information security: loss of availability, integrity and confidentiality. Availability, integrity and confidentiality are useful conceptual distinctions, but the separation is often artificial: a failure in one dimension can have consequences in another and therefore the concepts are interdependent and overlapping. Accountability and audit are often associated to these dimensions. They ensure allocation of responsibility for a security control and provide means for monitoring and measuring its effectiveness. Examples below help understand the nature of the general risk associated with each of these security dimensions and

Table 4. Types of channel threats for RFID systems

Threats Type	Description
Eavesdropping	The wireless nature of RFID makes eavesdropping one of the most serious and widely deployment threats in supply chain management applications. In eavesdropping an unauthorized individual uses an antenna in order to record communications between legitimate RFID tags and readers. This type of attack can be performed in both directions tag-to-reader and reader-to-tag. In simple, the communication between reader and transponder via the air interface is monitored by intercepting and decoding the radio signals. The feasibility of this attack depends on many factors, such as the distance of the attacker from the legitimate RFID supply chain applications. This is one of the most important threats to RFID systems.
Snooping	Intruders can create a cloned tag by properly formatting an existing tag which can then be used for identity theft. For example, someone could clone an RFID transponder, using a sniffed and decrypted identifier. Then use that transponder to procure some commodity or service.
Sniffing	RFID tags are designed to be read by any generic reader device which might occur without the knowledge of the tag bearer and/or over a large distance. This could trigger the skimming of contactless identification card information theft.
Skimming	In this attack, the adversary observes the information exchanged between a legitimate tag and legitimate reader. Via the extracted data, the attacker attempts to make a cloned tag which imitates the original RFID tag. To perform this attack, the attacker does not need to have any physical access to the real tag. Skimming attack is precarious when documents like drivers' licenses are authenticated through RFID system. In these situations, the attackers observe the interactions between the RFID tag embedded in the document with the reader to make a fake document.
Replay Attack	One of the most serious threats which RFID systems face is the replay attack. The replay attack is when a malicious node or device replays that key information which is eavesdropped through the communication between reader and tag, in order to achieve deception. A typical application is when the illegal device playback the authentication between the reader and the tags, deceiving readers or tags to pass verification. Solutions to replay attacks include the use of stamp program, a one-time password and using the random number in authentication protocol or updating the ID information dynamically.
Relay Attacks	A relay attack, also known as man-in-the-middle attack, is when an attacker places an illegal device between the reader and the tag such that it can intercept the information between the two nodes and then modify it or forwarded directly to the other end. The information transmitted through illegal deices will encounter some delay, and hence, these attacks are called relay attacks.
Electromagnetic Interference	RFID channels can be the target of an adversary which aims at sabotaging the communication channel to prevent the tags from communicating with the reader. Such a communication channel threat can be either unintentional (passive interference) or intentional (active jamming). Passive Interference: Since RFID systems operate in an inherently unstable and noisy environment, their communication is rendered susceptible to possible interference and collisions from any source of radio interference such as noisy electronic generators and power switching supplies. This interference prevents accurate and efficient communication between the tags and the readers. Active Jamming: Although passive interference is usually unintentional, an attacker can take advantage of the fact that an RFID tag listens indiscriminately to all radio signals in its range. Thus, an adversary may cause electromagnetic jamming by creating a signal in the same range as the reader in order to prevent tags from communicating with readers.
Malware	The RFID tag can store small amount of data; but researchers (Rieback et al, 2006) proved that RFID malware, RFID worms and RFID viruses are a reality. The RFID malware can exploit RFID system components such as back-end databases and generic protocols.
Rogue Reader	Attacks based on malicious RFID readers are also a sincere concern which can manipulate, corrupt and hijack the connection between an authentic reader and a tag (Konidala, 2006). The rogue reader can obtain personal information about a user's performances.

illustrate the potential consequences of attacks. Examples refer to logistic systems (e.g. tracking of containers, pallets and goods), and retail business (e.g. inventory management, check out, warranty services).

Risks Related to Tags and Readers

Many events can disrupt a RFID system. They can be categorized as interface or disruption of either the hardware, or the data components of the system. Interference or disruption to the physical components of readers and tags can be deliberate or accidental. Accidental or deliberate disruption of the radio components can be of the reader or tag or both. Deliberate attacks can be active or passive. Interference or disruption on the data components can be of the tag or reader data or both.

- **Availability**: Availability is the assurance of timely and reliable access to data services for authorized users. It ensures that information or resources are available when required. For instance, Denial of Service (DoS) attacks target the availability of a system. Consequences of disruption of availability of typical RFID systems could be, for example, delays in processing identity document thus preventing individuals to access supply chain operation activity (e.g. warehouse access card) or work premises (e.g. access control cards), preventing automatic processing of international transportation document (e.g. loading control pass).

Threats to the availability of the physical components of a RFID system can be overt or covert. Overt attacks on tags include cutting the electrical circuit on the tag, detaching the tag from the tagged item, discharging the battery on an active tag, or masking the antenna (shielding) with a conductive material or paint. Such strategies could be pursued to evade anti-theft RFID-based systems in retail supply chain. They could also be used for privacy protection purpose: companies have developed RFID blocking wallets (for RFID cards) that is presented as privacy protective purpose.

Covert attacks can be conducted by overloading receiving components to stop them from functioning or to destroy them, for example by subjecting a passive tag to a high energy field in proximity. Hackers have demonstrated that a strong energy field generated by an inexpensive, modified, single-user camera flash light can produce this result.

- **Integrity**: Integrity is the underlying assurance that data has not been altered during a transmission from the point of origin to the point of reception. Consequences of loss of integrity in common RFID systems could include, for example, delays and misdirection in the supply chain or confusion in retail operations due to corrupt or erroneous information. In some cases, loss of integrity generates loss of availability. For example, corrupt access cards would not enable individuals to access the warehouse management system. If track ignition key information is altered, then it is likely that access to the track will be impossible.

A man-made unwanted signal can also be used to inject a false signal, compromising the system's integrity. Reader identity could be falsified to access, modify or kill a tag. For example, a "kill" command could be sent before the tag is read by legitimate reader and lead to fraud in a retail context or disrupt supply chain information. Tag cloning and emulation could be used to falsify the identity of goods, and, for example, replace them with cheaper item identifiers.

- **Confidentiality**: Confidentiality is the assurance that information is accessible only to those who are authorized to have access. When the data relates to an individual, loss of confidentiality results in data protection violations. Consequences of loss of confidentiality in typical RFID systems could include, for example, stealing competitor information in the supply chain or in the retail environment, stealing a track by gaining access to electronic key information and cloning the chip. Unauthorized remote access to data is sometimes also called "skimming".

Any system based on radio technology is susceptible to eavesdropping of the radio signal between transmitter and receiver, thus raising confidentiality challenges (as well as integrity challenges if the data can be reinjected). RFID systems based on magnetic induction also generate radio waves that an attacker equipped with the appropriate radio equipment could, in theory, intercept. However, although theoretically possible, it is practically improbable because the energy levels would be relatively low and would be covered by noise, forcing the attacker to operate at short distance of the rags and reader.

RFID eavesdropping can be both passive and active. The attacker (or "interceptor") may actively send a signal to the tag to get a response, or simply passively listen to the response prompted by a reader activating the tag. Some tags can only reply with data (e.g. an identification number). More "intelligent" tags can send back a processed response akin to being actively interrogated with the objective of exploring a vulnerability.

Eavesdropping on the transmission can reveal the existence of a communication between RFID devices potentially leading to the disclosure of valuable information for the attacker (e.g. the number of goods arriving in a warehouse or the presence of an individual in each area). It enables tracking of the tag and the attached object.

It can also reveal the content of the communications thus enabling unauthorized access to potentially valuable business, competitive or personal information and enabling other attacks such as unwanted modification of the data or "man in the middle attack" (where the interceptor modifies the data exchanged between the tag and the reader).

Moreover, a RFID system is vulnerable to Denial-of-Service (DoS) attack, privacy, and traceability. Applying a combination of these basic threats, offenders can try to clone RFID transponders, to prevent reading processes (e.g. in automated checkout systems), to obscure theft or manipulate data in production or business processes. In order to avoid misuse of RFID technologies, both the system reliability and system security must be optimized. Generally, the following security requirements must be considered in the context of RFID systems: functional reliability, authenticity, confidentiality, integrity, availability, liability, and data privacy.

Currently existing RFID transponders provide just very limited security functionalities. Further definitions of RFID tags as well as data and communication standards (e.g. EPC Class2) will address this issue. Therefore, new methods for authentication and authorization, encryption, integrity protection, pseudonymization, tag deactivation and prevention of unauthorized read/write operations must be addressed in ongoing research. In addition, the middleware must process the incoming RFID data intelligently to integrate into the business application. Major challenges of this layer are collision in singulation, data redundancy and data noise.

Since tag costs (e.g. tag complexity) must be kept in certain limits, new effective methods for mutual authentication of transponders and interrogators need to be developed. In this context the effectiveness of the communication in a limited timeframe must be considered. Classical methods like hased-based authentication demand a lot of computation effort on the reader side and even on the transponder side a comparatively large hardware effort is necessary. Symmetric encryption methods are not suitable, since the effort for a secure key management is comparatively high and not affordable at the required limited transponder complexities / costs. Furthermore, there is a certain risk that secret keys could be revealed by reverse engineering and this in effect would compromise the whole security concept. Therefore, new lightweight cryptography methods are required, including effective methods for the on-tag generation of random numbers and the computation of hash functions. Concepts as physically unclonable functions may show a way out of the security at high implementation cost dilemma.

RESEARCH CHALLENGES IN RFID SYSTEM SECURITY

Even though research on RFID security and privacy protection has advanced in recent years, but it is not still adequate. For practical deployment of RFID in wide scale many issues need to be resolved. Also, there are almost no works done for security in chip-less RFID. The followings are some of the research challenges in RFID security as noted by Duc et al. (2009):

Cryptography plays the core role in security protocol as described above. There are very strong and well-proven cryptographic techniques for wired networks, and in recent times cryptographic algorithms for wireless networks have also been significantly improved. However, RFID tags have very limited processing power and therefore, for practical deployment, one need cryptographic algorithms that are lightweight and fast, but at the same time possess strong cryptographic properties. The lack of the study on light-weight cryptographic primitives includes design of new primitives, analysis of the security of new primitives and their efficient implementation (Duc et al., 2009). Though few lightweight cryptographic algorithms are proposed in literature, much research needs to be done to evaluate them through cryptanalysis and investigate new algorithms for strong protection. As new types of attacks are reported, research need to focus to counter those attacks. Another important aspect that plays vital roles in cryptography is the regeneration of pseudorandom number so that it generation can be predicted. Further research needs to do to generate random number that satisfies the requirement of RFID.

FUTURE RESEARCH DIRECTIONS

In the *physical world*, human beings and animals are adept at sensing the environment. Their ears prick up strange sounds; their body hair gets spiked-up in the sense of danger; their skin tingles when something threatened their security of existence; they notice subtle body language in a stranger that makes them *suspicious* and *venerable*. Human being and intelligent animals are hardwired smartly to recognize the body-language of their neighbors; yet, most of RFID-based supply chain management systems operational environment's object identification occurs digitally, by voice, text, or using other *biometric recognition* technique. In addition, currently most of RFID-based supply chain operational community don't have full solutions when someone tries to extract potential business information by snooping from a distance or sending a group of smart armies of malware or block the whole network by jamming electromagnetically. In future, this research will review most of these challenges and will try bringing together potential solutions for naive operational managers.

CONCLUSION

This chapter focused on the issues and potential solutions for a range of RFID technology have generated significant interest in supply chain management. The use of RFID has grown across a variety of core industries, such as logistics, manufacturing, and retail. Although each application has its own specific requirements, security vulnerability will be always a major concern when deploying RFID applications. Like the Internet or mobile telephony, RFID is a wireless network technology. While the non-contact and non-line-of-sight properties of RFID systems increase the convenience and efficiency of their applications, these properties also increase the system's vulnerability.

With the increasing usages of RFID, such as manufacturing, retail transactions and consumer products, potential security threats and compliance risks in the future are enormous. It is necessary to pay attention to standardization of RFID systems.

Moreover, risk vary according to the type of technology used to perform a specific function. RFID is an umbrella concept for a variety of technologies with distinctive characteristics. The risks mentioned above are theoretically applicable to all RFID systems. However, on a continuum of risks, the likeliness of certain risks is higher in some technical configurations than in others. Parameters such as the use of passive or active tags, of electromagnetic induction or radio-wave communications, of read only or read-write capable memory influence the degree of likeliness that certain risks materialize.

A well-designed RFID policy can reduce the risk of attacks. When dealing with security and risk management, policy decisions also play a significant role in the security of an RFID system. An RFID security policy is a document that states how an organization plans to protect its physical RFID devices and information data assets. Since, sooner or later, new threats will appear, an RFID security policy should be considered a "living" document that needs to be continuously updated as the RFID technology and implementation requirements change. The policy also needs to consider how the users will be trained in the proper use of RFID and explain how security measures will be carried out and enforced.

REFERENCES

Alwadi, A., Gawanmeh, A., Parvin, S., & Al-Karaki, J. N. (2017). Smart Solutions for RFID Based Inventory Management Systems. *Survey (London, England)*, *18*(4), 347–360.

Alwadi, A., Kilby, J., & Gawanmeh, A. (2017). Tracking and Automating a Library System Using Radio Frequency Identification Technology. *International Journal on Smart Sensing and Intelligent Systems, 10*(2), 425–450. doi:10.21307/ijssis-2017-219

Baird, J. L. (1928). Improvements in or relating to apparatus for transmitting views or images to a distance. *Patent, GB292*, 185.

Bansal, R. (2003). Coming Soon to a Wal-Mart Near You. *IEEE Antennas & Propagation Magazine, 45*(6), 105–106. doi:10.1109/MAP.2003.1282186

Choi, T., Wing-Kwan, Y., Cheng, T. C. E., & Yue, X. (2018). Optimal Scheduling, Coordination, and the Value of RFID Technology in Garment Manufacturing Supply Chains. *IEEE Transactions on Engineering Management, 65*(1), 72–84. doi:10.1109/TEM.2017.2739799

Duc, D. N., Lee, H., Konidala, D. M., & Kim, K. (2009). Open issues in RFID security. *Proceedings of the International Conference on Internet Technology and Security Transactions,* 1-5.

Harman, P. M. (1998). *The natural philosophy of James Clerk Maxwell*. Cambridge, UK: Cambridge University Press.

Johnson, D. (2002). RFID tags improve tracking, quality on Ford line in Mexico. *Control Engineering, 49*(11), 16.

Kärkkäinen, M. (2003). Increasing efficiency in the supply chain for short shelf life goods using RFID tagging. *International Journal of Retail & Distribution Management, 31*(10), 529–536. doi:10.1108/09590550310497058

Kinsella, B. (2003). The Wal-Mart factors. *Industrial Engineering (American Institute of Industrial Engineers),* 32–36.

Knospe, H., & Pohl, H. (2004). RFID security. *Information Security Technical Report, 9*(4), 39–50. doi:10.1016/S1363-4127(05)70039-X

Krebsonsecurity (2014). http://krebsonsecurity.com/2014/02/target-hackers-broke-in-via-hvac-company/

Luckett, D. (2004). The supply chain. *BT Technology Journal, 22*(3), 50–55. doi:10.1023/B:BTTJ.0000047119.22852.38

Oghazi, P., Rad, F. F., Karlsson, K., & Haftor, H. (2018). RFID and ERP Systems in Supply Chain Management. *European Journal of Management and Business Economics,* 171-182.

Pal, K. (2017). Supply Chain Coordination Based on Web Services. In H. K. Chan, N. Subraanian, & M. D. Abdulrahman (Eds.), *Supply Chain Management in the Big Data Era* (pp. 137–171). Hershey, PA: IGI Global Publishing. doi:10.4018/978-1-5225-0956-1.ch009

Pal, K. (2019a). Quality Assurance Issues for Big Data Applications in Supply Chain Management, In Predictive Intelligence Using Big Data and Internet of Things. IGI Global Publishing.

Rieback, M. R., Crispo, B., & Tanenbaum, A. S. (2006). Is your cat infected with a computer virus? Proceedings of PerCon, 169-179. doi:10.1109/PERCOM.2006.32

Roberti, M. (2005, December 31). Financing for RFID Prison System. *RFID Journal*.

Sabbaghi, A., & Ganesh, V. (2008). Effectiveness and Efficiency of RFID Technology in Supply Chain Management: Strategic Values and Challenges. *Journal of Theoretical and Applied Electronic Commerce Research*, *3*(2), 71–81. doi:10.4067/S0718-18762008000100007

Stockman, H. (1948). Communication by Means of Reflected Power. *Proceedings of the Institute of Radio Engineers*.

KEY TERMS AND DEFINITIONS-

Active Tag: A tag with its own battery that can initiate communications.

Auto-ID: Automatic identification (Auto-ID) systems automatically identify physical objects through optical, electromagnetic, or chemical means.

EAS: Electronic article surveillance. A radio frequency device that announces its presence but contains no unique identifying data. EAS tags are frequently attached to books or compact discs.

EPC: Electronic product code. A low-cost RFID tag designed for consumer products as a replacement for the UPC (Universal Product Code).

HF: High frequency; 13.56 MHz.

LF: Low frequency; 120-140 KHz.

Linear Barcode: A one-dimensional, optical bar code used for auto-ID.

Passive Tag: A tag with no on-board power source that harvests its energy from a reader-provided RF signal.

Reader: An RFID transceiver, providing real and possible write access to RFID tags.

RF: Radio frequency.

RFID: Radio frequency identification. Describes a broad spectrum of devices and technologies and is used to refer both to individual tags and overall systems.

Semi-Passive Tag: A tag with no on-board power source that is unable to initiate communications with a reader.

Skimming: An attack where an adversary wirelessly reads data from a RFID tag that enables forgery or cloning.

Supply Chain Management: A supply chain consists of a network of *key business processes* and facilities, involving end users and suppliers that provide products, services and information. In this chain management, improving the efficiency of the overall chain is an influential factor; and it needs at least four important strategic issues to be considered: supply chain network design, capacity planning, risk assessment and management, and performances monitoring and measurement. The coordination of these huge business processes and their performance improvement are the main objectives of a supply chain management system.

Tag: An RFID transponder, typically consisting of an RF coupling element and a microchip that carries identifying data. Tag functionality may range from simple identification to being able to form ad hoc networks.

UCC: Uniform code council; a standards committee originally formed by grocery manufacturers and food distributors that designed the UPC barcode.

UHF: Ultra-high frequency, 868-928 MHz.

UPC: Universal product code (UPC) is a one-dimensional, optical barcode found on many consumer products.

UWB: Ultra-wide band (UWB) is a weak communication signal and it is broadcast over a very wide band of frequencies (e.g. 3.1 – 10.6 GHz).

Compilation of References

Abrahamson, K., Myers, J., Arling, G., Davila, H., Mueller, C., Abery, B., & Cai, Y. (2016). Capacity and readiness for quality improvement among home and community-based service providers. *Home Health Care Services Quarterly*, *35*(3-4), 182–196. doi:10.1080/01621424.2016.1264343 PMID:27897462

Abu Alsheikh, M., Lin, S., Niyato, D., & Tan, H. P. (2014). Machine learning in wireless sensor networks: Algorithms, strategies, and applications. *IEEE Communications Surveys and Tutorials*, *16*(4), 1996–2018. doi:10.1109/COMST.2014.2320099

Aceto, G., Botta, A., Donato, W., & Pescape, A. (2013). Cloud monitoring: A survey. *Computer Networks*, *57*(9), 2093–2115. doi:10.1016/j.comnet.2013.04.001

Aceves, E., & Larios, V. M. (2015). *Data Visualization for Georeferenced IoT Open Data Flows for a GDL Smart City Pilot*. Academic Press.

Administration, I. T. (n.d.). *Smart Cities, Regions & Communities - Export Opportunities*. Academic Press.

Advanced Encryption Standard (AES). (2017). *Federal Information Processing Standards Publications (FIPSPUBS)*. doi:10.6028/NIST.FIPS.197

Agren, M., Hell, M., Johansson, T., & Meier, W. (2011). Grain-128a: A new version of Grain-128 with optional authentication. *International Journal of Wireless and Mobile Computing*, *5*(1), 48–59. doi:10.1504/IJWMC.2011.044106

Ahmed, Ramana, & Gajanand. (2015). *Smart Surveillance Image Transmission Using Raspberry PI*. doi:10.4010/2015.480

Akhter, S., Rahman, R., & Islam, A. (2016). Neural network nn based route weight computation for bi-directional traffic management system. *International Journal of Applied Evolutionary Computation*, 45–59.

Alemdar, H., Durmus, Y., & Ersoy, C. (2010). Wireless Healthcare Monitoring with RFID-Enhanced Video Sensor Networks. *International Journal of Distributed Sensor Networks*, *6*(1), 473037. doi:10.1155/2010/473037

Al-Fuqaha, A., Guizani, M., Mohammadi, M., Aledhari, M., & Ayyash, M. (2015). Internet of things: A survey on enabling technologies, protocols and applications. *IEEE Communications Surveys and Tutorials*, *17*(4), 2347–2376. doi:10.1109/COMST.2015.2444095

Allegretti, M. (2014). Concept for Floating and Submersible Wireless Sensor Network for Water Basin Monitoring. *Wireless Sensor Network*, *6*(6), 104–108. doi:10.4236/wsn.2014.66011

Allychevalier. (2017). *What is the Difference Between GPS and RFID Tracking?* Retrieved from http://www.brighthub.com/electronics/gps/articles/60599.aspx

Al-Taee, M., Al-Nuaimy, W., Muhsin, Z., & Al-Ataby, A. (2017). Robot Assistant in Management of Diabetes in Children Based on the Internet of Things. *IEEE Internet Of Things Journal*, *4*(2), 437–445. doi:10.1109/JIOT.2016.2623767

Al-Turjman, F., Kirsal Ever, Y., Ever, E., Nguyen, H., & David, D. (2017). Seamless Key Agreement Framework for Mobile-Sink in IoT Based Cloud-Centric Secured Public Safety Sensor Networks. *IEEE Access: Practical Innovations, Open Solutions*, *5*, 24617–24631. doi:10.1109/ACCESS.2017.2766090

Alwadi, A., Gawanmeh, A., Parvin, S., & Al-Karaki, J. N. (2017). Smart Solutions for RFID Based Inventory Management Systems. *Survey (London, England)*, *18*(4), 347–360.

Alwadi, A., Kilby, J., & Gawanmeh, A. (2017). Tracking and Automating a Library System Using Radio Frequency Identification Technology. *International Journal on Smart Sensing and Intelligent Systems*, *10*(2), 425–450. doi:10.21307/ijssis-2017-219

Anand, M., Cronin, E., Sherr, M., Blaze, M. A., Ives, Z. G., & Lee, I. (2006). Sensor network security: more interesting than you think. In *1st USENIX Workshop on Hot Topics in Security*. USENIX Association.

Andrea, I., Chrysostomou, C., & Hadjichristofi, G. (2015). Internet of Things: Security vulnerabilities and challenges. *IEEE Symposium on Computers and Communications*, 180–187. 10.1109/ISCC.2015.7405513

Ansari, Sedkyl, Sharma, & Tyagi. (2015). An internet of things approach for motion detection using raspberry Pi. In *International conference on intelligent computing and internet of things (ICIT)*. IEEE.

Arampatzis & Manesis. (2005). A Survey of Applications of Wireless Sensors and Wireless Sensor Networks. *Proceedings of the 2005 IEEE International Symposium on, Mediterrean Conference on Control and Automation Intelligent Control, 2005.* 10.1109/.2005.1467103

Arbeille, P., Zuj, K., Saccomandi, A., Andre, E., De La Porte, C., & Georgescu, M. (2016). Tele-Operated Echography and Remote Guidance for Performing Tele-Echography on Geographically Isolated Patients. *Journal of Clinical Medicine, 5*(6), 58. doi:10.3390/jcm5060058 PMID:27304972

ArcGIS. (2012). Retrieved October 24, 2016, from https://developers.arcgis.com/javascript/

Arduino Board Uno. (2017). Retrieved from https://www.arduino.cc/en/Main/ArduinoBoardUno

Arduino Rain Sensor Module Guide and Tutorial capnfatz. (n.d.). Retrieved from https://henrysbench.capnfatz.com/henrys-bench/arduino-sensors-and-input/arduino-rain-sensor-module-guide-and-tutorial/

Aref, M. A., Jayaweera, S. K., & Machuzak, S. (2017). Multi-agent reinforcement learning based cognitive anti jamming. *IEEE Wireless Communication and Networking Conference*, 1–6. 10.1109/WCNC.2017.7925694

Asadullah, M., & Raza, A. (2016). An overview of home automation systems. In *2nd International Conference on Robotics and Artificial Intelligence (ICRAI)* (pp. 27-31). Rawalpindi, Pakistan: IEEE.

Ashraf, Q. M., & Habaebi, M. H. (2015). Autonomic schemes for threat mitigation in Internet of Things, *Elsevier. Journal of Network and Computer Applications, 49*(1), 112–127. doi:10.1016/j.jnca.2014.11.011

Ashraf, Q. M., Habaebi, M. H., Sinniah, G. R., & Chebil, J. (2014). Broadcast based registration technique for heterogenous nodes in the IoT. *International Conference on Control, Engineering, and Information Technology*.

Aumasson, J. P., Henzen, L., Meier, W., & Naya-Plasencia, M. (2013). Quark: A lightweight hash. *Journal of Cryptology, 26*(2), 313–339. doi:10.100700145-012-9125-6

Ayed, Elkosantini, & Abid. (2017). An Automated Surveillance System based on Multi-Processor System-On-Chip and Hardware Accelerator. *International Journal of Advanced Computer Science and Applications.*, *8*(9), 59.

Azaza, M., Tanougast, C., Fabrizio, E., & Mami, A. (2016). Smart greenhouse fuzzy logic based control system enhanced with wireless data monitoring. *ISA Transactions*, *61*, 297–307. doi:10.1016/j.isatra.2015.12.006 PMID:26749556

Babbage, S., & Dodd, M. (2008). The MICKEY stream ciphers. In M. Robshaw & O. Billet (Eds.), *New stream cipher designs*. Berlin: Springer. doi:10.1007/978-3-540-68351-3_15

Baggio, A. (2005, June). Wireless sensor networks in precision agriculture. In *ACM Workshop on Real-World Wireless Sensor Networks (REALWSN 2005)* (Vol. 20). ACM.

Baird, J. L. (1928). Improvements in or relating to apparatus for transmitting views or images to a distance. *Patent, GB292*, 185.

Baker, S., Xiang, W., & Atkinson, I. (2017). Internet of Things for Smart Healthcare: Technologies, Challenges, and Opportunities. *IEEE Access: Practical Innovations, Open Solutions*, *5*, 26521–26544. doi:10.1109/ACCESS.2017.2775180

Bansal, R. (2003). Coming Soon to a Wal-Mart Near You. *IEEE Antennas & Propagation Magazine*, *45*(6), 105–106. doi:10.1109/MAP.2003.1282186

Bashal, Jilani, & Arun. (2016). An Intelligent Door System using Raspberry Pi and Amazon Web Services IoT. *International Journal of Engineering Trends and Technology*.

Basyal, Kaushal, & Singh. (2018). Voice Recognition Robot with Real Time Surveillance and Automation. *International Journal of Creative Research Thoughts*, *6*(1), 2320–2882.

Beaulieu, A. (2009). Learning SQL. *Database*. doi:10.1017/CBO9781107415324.004

Benbassat, M. (2017). *Double Deep Machine Learning*. Retrieved from http://search.arxiv.org:8081/paper.jsp?r=1711.06517&qid=1521507142396swap_nCnN_662694859&qs=Double+Deep+Machine+Learning

Bera, S., Misra, S., Roy, S., & Obaidat, M. (2016). Soft-WSN: Software-Defined WSN Management System for IoT Applications. *IEEE Systems Journal*, 1–8. doi:10.1109/jsyst.2016.2615761

Berkowitz, C. (2012). Sudden Infant Death Syndrome, Sudden Unexpected Infant Death, and Apparent Life-Threatening Events. *Advances in Pediatrics, 59*(1), 183–208. doi:10.1016/j.yapd.2012.04.011 PMID:22789579

Bharanialankar & ManikandaBabu. (2014). Intelligent Home Appliance Status Intimation Control and System Using GSM. *International Journal of Advanced Research in Computer Science and Software Engineering, 4*(4).

Bhatkule, Shinde, & Zanwar. (2016). Home Based Security Control System using Raspberry Pi and GSM. *International Journal of Innovative Research in Computer and Communication Engineering, 4*(9).

Bisio, I., Delfino, A., Lavagetto, F., & Sciarrone, A. (2016). Enabling IoT for In-Home Rehabilitation: Accelerometer Signals Classification Methods for Activity and Movement Recognition. *IEEE Internet Of Things Journal*, 1-1. doi:10.1109/jiot.2016.2628938

Bogdanov, A., Knudsen, L., Leander, G., Paar, C., Poschmann, A., Robshaw, M., . . . Vikkelsoe, C. (2007). PRESENT: An ultra-lightweight block cipher. In *International Workshop on Cryptographic Hardware and Embedded Systems* (pp. 450-466). Vienna, Austria: Springer.

Bogdanov, A., Knezevic, M., Leander, G., Toz, D., Varici, K., & Verbauwhede, I. (2011). SPONGENT: A lightweight hash function. In *International Workshop on Cryptographic Hardware and Embedded Systems* (pp. 312-325). Berlin: Springer.

Bolton, D. K., & Friedl, M. A. (2013). Forecasting crop yield using remotely sensed vegetation indices and crop phenology metrics. *Agricultural and Forest Meteorology, 173*, 74–84. doi:10.1016/j.agrformet.2013.01.007

Bouwmans, T. (2011). Recent Advanced Statistical Background Modeling for Foreground Detection: A Systematic Survey. *Recent Patents on Computer Science, 4*(3), 147–176.

Bovet, G., Ridi, A., & Hennebert, J. (2014). Toward Web Enhanced Building Automation System, in Eds. N. Bessis & C. Dobre - Big Data and Internet of Things: A Roadmap for Smart Environments. *Studies in Computational Intelligence, 546*, 259–283.

Bo, Y., & Wang, H. (2011, May). The application of cloud computing and the internet of things in agriculture and forestry. In *2011 International Joint Conference on Service Sciences* (pp. 168-172). IEEE. 10.1109/IJCSS.2011.40

Bozdogan, Z., & Kara, R. (2015). Layered model architecture for internet of things. *Jouranl of Engineering Research and Applied Science*, *4*(1), 260–264.

Brutze, S., Hoferlin, B., & Heidemann, G. (2011). Evaluation of background subtraction techniques for video surveillance. *IEEE Conference on Computer Vision and Pattern Recognition (CVPR)*, 1937–1944.

Buczak, A. L., & Guven, E. (2015). A survey of data mining and machine learning methods for cyber security intrusion detection. *IEEE Communications Surveys and Tutorials*, *18*(2), 1153–1176. doi:10.1109/COMST.2015.2494502

Buiu, O. (2017). Internet of Things and the Human Body. *Journal Of Nanomedicine Research*, *5*(2). doi:10.15406/jnmr.2017.05.00113

Burlina, P., & Chellappa, R. (1998). Temporal analysis of motion in video sequences through predictive operators. *International Journal of Computer Vision*, *28*(2), 175–192. doi:10.1023/A:1008067101494

Castañeda, V., & Guzman, E. (2015). Towards the preparation of the Guadalajara's Smart City Metrics Structure. *IEEE-GDL CCD Smart Cities White Paper*, 1–5.

Castro, C., & Rodriguez, C. (2017). Wearable-Based Human Activity Recognition Using an IoT Approach. *Journal Sensor and Actuator Networks, 6*(28).

Changchit, C., & Bagchi, K. (2017). Privacy and Security Concerns with Healthcare Data and Social Media Usage. *Journal Of Information Privacy And Security*, *13*(2), 49–50. doi:10.1080/15536548.2017.1322413

Channe, H., Kothari, S., & Kadam, D. (2015). Multidisciplinary model for smart agriculture using internet-of-things (IoT), sensors, cloud-computing, mobile-computing & big-data analysis. *Int. J. Computer Technology and Application*, *6*(3), 374–382.

Chen, Q., Sun, Q. S., Heng, P. A., & Xia, S. (2010). Two-Stage Object Tracking Method Based on Kernel and Active Contour. IEEE Transactions on Circuits and Systems for Video Technology, 605-609. doi:10.1109/TCSVT.2010.2041819

Chen, S. X., Ma, H. T., & Liu, X. (2011). Design of smart greenhouse system. *Hebei Journal of Industrial Science and Technology, 4*.

Chen, B., Wu, M., Yao, S., & Ni, B. (2006). ZigBee Technology and Its Application on Wireless Meter-reading System. In *IEEE International Conference on Industrial Informatics (INDIN 06)*. IEEE Press. 10.1109/INDIN.2006.275820

Chen, T. (2009). Object Tracking Based on Active Contour Model by Neural Fuzzy Network. *IITA International Conference on Control Automation and Systems Engineering*, 570-574. 10.1109/CASE.2009.165

Cheung, G. K. M., Kanade, T., Bouguet, J. Y., & Holler, M. (2000). *Real time system for robust 3 D voxel reconstruction of human motions*. CVPR. doi:10.1109/CVPR.2000.854944

Cheung, S. C., & Kamath, C. (2004). Robust techniques for background subtraction in urban traffic video. *Video Communications and Image Processing*, *5308*(1), 881–892.

Chhaya, L., Sharma, P., Bhagwatikar, G., & Kumar, A. (2017). Communication theories and protocols for smart grid hierarchical network. *Journal of Electrical and Electronics Engineering (Oradea)*, *10*(1), 43–48.

Chhaya, L., Sharma, P., Bhagwatikar, G., & Kumar, A. (2017). Wireless Sensor Network Based Smart Grid Communications: Cyber Attacks, Intrusion Detection System and Topology Control. *Electronics (Basel)*, *6*(1), 5. doi:10.3390/electronics6010005

Chiang, M., & Zhang, T. (2016). Fog and IoT. *IEEE Internet of Things Journal*, *3*(6), 854–864. doi:10.1109/JIOT.2016.2584538

Chiu, Ku, & Wang. (2010). Automatic Traffic Surveillance System for Vision-Based Vehicle Recognition and Tracking. *Journal of Information Science and Engineering*, *26*, 611–629.

Chodorow, K. (2013). MongoDB: The Definitive Guide. *Journal of Infectious Diseases*, *203*. doi:10.1093/infdis/jir001

Choi, T., Wing-Kwan, Y., Cheng, T. C. E., & Yue, X. (2018). Optimal Scheduling, Coordination, and the Value of RFID Technology in Garment Manufacturing Supply Chains. *IEEE Transactions on Engineering Management*, *65*(1), 72–84. doi:10.1109/TEM.2017.2739799

Christin, D., Mogre, D. S., & Hollick, M. (2010). Survey on wireless sensor network technologies for industrial automation: The security and quality of service perspectives. *Future Internet*, *2*(2), 96–125. doi:10.3390/fi2020096

Collins, R., & Liu, Y. (2001). Online Selection of Discriminative Tracking Feature. *IEEE Transactions on Pattern Analysis and Machine Intelligence*, *27*(10), 1631–1643. doi:10.1109/TPAMI.2005.205 PMID:16237997

Comaniciu, D., Ramesh, V., & Meer, P. (2000). Real time tracking of non-rigid objects using mean shift. *IEEE Conference on Computer Vision and Pattern Recognition (CVPR '00)*, 2, 142-149. 10.1109/CVPR.2000.854761

Comaniciu, D., Ramesh, V., & Meer, P. (2003). Kernal Based Object Tracking. *IEEE Transactions on Pattern Analysis and Machine Intelligence*, 25(5), 564–577. doi:10.1109/TPAMI.2003.1195991

CouchBase. (2011). Retrieved November 21, 2016, from http://www.couchbase.com/

Cucchiara, R., Grana, C., Neri, G., Piccardi, M., & Prati, A. (2001). The sakbot system for moving object detection and tracking. *European Workshop on Advanced Video-Based Surveillance Systems*, 171, 159.

Cucchiara, R., Grana, C., Piccardi, M., & Prati, A. (2003). Detecting moving objects, ghosts, and shadows in video streams. *IEEE Transactions on Pattern Analysis and Machine Intelligence*, 25(10), 1337–1347. doi:10.1109/TPAMI.2003.1233909

Danelljan, M., Khan, F. S., Felsberg, M., & Weijer, J. V. D. (2014). *Adaptive Color Attributes for Real-Time Visual Tracking*. CVPR. doi:10.1109/CVPR.2014.143

Dangerfield, M., Ward, K., Davidson, L., & Adamian, M. (2017). Initial Experience and Usage Patterns With the Owlet Smart Sock Monitor in 47,495 Newborns. *Global Pediatric Health, 4*. doi:10.1177/2333794x17742751

Dan, L. I. U., Xin, C., Chongwei, H., & Liangliang, J. (2015, December). Intelligent agriculture greenhouse environment monitoring system based on IOT technology. In *2015 International Conference on Intelligent Transportation, Big Data and Smart City* (pp. 487-490). IEEE.

Datta, P., B. S. (2017). A Survey on IoT Architectures, Protocols, Security and Smart City based Applications. *International Conference on Computing, Communications and Networking Technologies*. 10.1109/ICCCNT.2017.8203943

De Canniere, C., & Preneel, B. (2008). Trivium specifications. In M. Robshaw, & O. Billet (Eds.), New Stream Cipher Designs. Springer.

De Canniere, C., Dunkelman, O., & Knezevic, M. (2009). KATAN and KTANTAN - A family of small and efficient hardware-oriented block ciphers. In *International Workshop on Cryptographic Hardware and Embedded Systems* (pp. 272-288). Berlin: Springer. 10.1007/978-3-642-04138-9_20

De Donatis, M., & Bruciatelli, L. (2006). MAP IT: The GIS software for field mapping with tablet pc. *Computers & Geosciences, 32*(5), 673–680. doi:10.1016/j.cageo.2005.09.003

Deka, G. C. (2014). NoSQL databases. Handbook of Research on Cloud Infrastructures for Big Data Analytics. doi:10.4018/978-1-4666-5864-6.ch008

Deng, J., Han, R., & Mishra, S. (2006). Countermeasures against traffic analysis attacks in wireless sensor networks. In *First International Conference on Security and Privacy for Emerging Areas in Communications Networks* (pp. 113-126). Athens, Greece: IEEE.

Desima, M., Ramli, P., Ramdani, D., & Rahman, S. (2017). Alarm system to detect the location of IOT-based public vehicle accidents. *International Conference on Computing, Engineering, and Design (ICCED), 1 – 5*. 10.1109/CED.2017.8308118

Dhanalakshmi, & Sam Leni, A. (2017). Instance vehicle monitoring and tracking with internet of things using Arduino. *International Journal on Smart Sensing and Intelligent Systems, 10*(4), 123-135. doi:10.21307/ijssis-2017-240

Domadia & Mehta. (2014). Automated Video Surveillance System for Human Motion Detection with Face Detection. *International Journal of Advance Engineering and Research Development, 1*(5).

Duc, D. N., Lee, H., Konidala, D. M., & Kim, K. (2009). Open issues in RFID security. *Proceedings of the International Conference on Internet Technology and Security Transactions, 1*-5.

Duckett, K. (2016). Innovation in Home Healthcare. *Home Healthcare Now, 34*(7), 403–404. doi:10.1097/NHH.0000000000000394 PMID:27348039

Dujovne, D., Watteyne, T., Vilajosana, X., & Thubert, P. (2014). 6TiSCH: Deterministic IP-enabled industrial internet (of things). *IEEE Communications Magazine, 52*(12), 36-41.

Elgammal, A., Harwood, D., & Davis, L. (2000). Non-parametric Model for Background Subtraction. *European Conference on Computer Vision, 2*, 751-767.

Elgammal, A., Harwood, D., & Davis, L. (2004). *Non-parametric model for background subtraction* (Vol. 4). IEEE FRAME-RATE Workshop, Springe on Systems, Man and Cybernetics.

EMC & IDC. (2014). *The Internet of Things: Data from embedded systems will account for 10% of the digital universe by 2020: In The digital universe of opportunities: rich data and increasing value of the Internet of Things.* EMC & IDC White Paper.

Erasala, N., & Yen, D. C. (2002). Bluetooth technology: A strategic analysis of its role in global 3G wireless communication era. *Computer Standards & Interfaces, 24*(3), 193–206. doi:10.1016/S0920-5489(02)00018-1

Erol-Kantarci, M., & Mouftah, H. (2011). Wireless multimedia sensor and actor networks for the next generation power grid. *Ad Hoc Networks, 9*(4), 542–551. doi:10.1016/j.adhoc.2010.08.005

ESRI. (1969). Retrieved October 24, 2016, from http://www.esri.com/about-esri

Evans, D. (2011). *The Internet of Things - How the Next Evolution of the Internet Is Changing Everything.* CISCO White Paper.

Evans, D. (2011). *The Internet of Things How the Next Evolution of the Internet Is Changing Everything.* Cisco.

Farooq, M., Waseem, M., Mazhar, S., Khairi, A., & Kamal, T. (2015). A Review on Internet of Things (IoT). *International Journal of Computers and Applications, 113*(1), 1–7. doi:10.5120/19787-1571

Farooq, H., & Jung, L. (2014). Choices available for implementing Smart Grid communication network. In *Computer and Information Sciences* (Vol. 5). Kuala Lumpur: ICCOINS.

Farooq, M. U., Waseem, M., Khairi, A., & Mazhar, S. (2015). A critical analysis on the security concerns of Internet of Things. *International Journal of Computers and Applications, 111*(7), 1–6. doi:10.5120/19547-1280

Farris, I., Pizzi, S., Merenda, M., Molinaro, A., Carotenuto, R., & Iera, A. (2017). 6lo-RFID: A Framework for Full Integration of Smart UHF RFID Tags into the Internet of Things. *IEEE Network, 31*(5), 66–73. doi:10.1109/MNET.2017.1600269

Fattah, S., Sung, N., Ahn, I., Ryu, M., & Yun, J. (2017). Building IoT Services for Aging in Place Using Standard-Based IoT Platforms and Heterogeneous IoT Products. *Sensors (Basel), 17*(10), 2311. doi:10.339017102311 PMID:29019964

Federal Trade Commission (FTC). (2015). *Internet of Things Privacy & Security in a Connected World.* FTC White Paper.

Fernandez-Caballero, A., Gomez, F. J., & Lopez-Lopez, J. (2008). Road-traffic monitoring by knowledge-driven static and dynamic image analysis. *Expert Systems with Applications*, *35*(3), 701–719. doi:10.1016/j.eswa.2007.07.017

Ferrández-Pastor, F., García-Chamizo, J., Nieto-Hidalgo, M., Mora-Pascual, J., & Mora-Martínez, J. (2016). Developing ubiquitous sensor network platform using internet of things: Application in precision agriculture. *Sensors (Basel)*, *16*(7), 1141. doi:10.339016071141 PMID:27455265

Foresti, M., & Snidaro, R. (2005). Active video-based surveillance system: The low-level image and video processing techniques needed for implementation. *IEEE Signal Processing Magazine*, *22*(2), 25–37. doi:10.1109/MSP.2005.1406473

Fosso Wamba, S., Barjis, J., & Takeoka Chatfield, A. (2010). Business impacts of RFID applications. *Business Process Management Journal*, *16*(6), bpmj.2010.15716faa.001. doi:10.1108/bpmj.2010.15716faa.001

Franckhauser, M. (2013). Rural Healthcare and the Challenges of Home Healthcare and Hospice. *Home Healthcare Nurse*, *31*(4), 227–228. doi:10.1097/NHH.0b013e318289c429 PMID:23549255

Fuji, K., & Abbott, A. (2014). Ensuring Effective Medication Reconciliation in Home Healthcare. *Home Healthcare Nurse*, *32*(9), 516–522. doi:10.1097/NHH.0000000000000136 PMID:25268524

Fulton, J. P., & Port, K. (2018). Precision agriculture data management. *Precision Agriculture Basics*, 169-188.

Gama & Gaber. (2007). *Learning from Data Streams Processing Techniques in Sensor Networks*. Springer.

Ganek, A. G. & Corbi, T. A. (2003). The dawning of the autonomic computing era. *IBM Systems Journal*, *42*(1), 5-18.

Gao, L. (2016). Building of Smart Home Medical System Based on Internet of Things. *Internet Of Things And Cloud Computing*, *4*(3), 34. doi:10.11648/j.iotcc.20160403.14

Garcia-Molina, H., Ullman, J. D., Widom, J., Özsu, M., Valduriez, P., Connolly, T., ... Virk, R. (2010). Database Systems: A Practical Approach to Design, Implementation, and Management. *International Journal of Computer Applications*, *49*. doi:10.1007/978-1-4842-0877-9_10

Gebbers, R., & Adamchuk, V. I. (2010). Precision agriculture and food security. *Science*, *327*(5967), 828–831. doi:10.1126cience.1183899 PMID:20150492

Ghosh, R., Pragathi, R., Ullas, S., & Borra, S. (2017). Intelligent transportation systems: A survey. In *International Conference on Circuits, Controls, and Communications* (pp. 160-165). Bangalore, India: IEEE.

Goldman Sachs. (2014). *Making sense of the next mega-trend*. Goldman Sachs Global Investment Research Report.

Gómez-Candón, D., De Castro, A. I., & Lopez-Granados, F. (2014). Assessing the accuracy of mosaics from unmanned aerial vehicle (UAV) imagery for precision agriculture purposes in wheat. *Precision Agriculture*, *15*(1), 44–56. doi:10.100711119-013-9335-4

Gond, J., Cabantous, L., & Krikorian, F. (2017). How do things become strategic? 'Strategifying' corporate social responsibility. *Strategic Organization*. doi:10.1177/1476127017702819

GPRS GSM GPS Bluetooth All in one SIM808 Shield for Arduino. (n.d.). Retrieved from https://store.roboticsbd.com/arduino-shield/322-gprs-gsm-gps-bluetooth-all-in-one-sim808-shield-for-arduino.html

Granjal, J., Monteiro, E., & Sa Silva, J. (2015). Security for the internet of things: A survey of existing protocols and open research issues. *IEEE Communications Surveys and Tutorials*, *17*(3), 1294–1312. doi:10.1109/COMST.2015.2388550

Grindvoll, H., Vermesan, O., Crosbie, T., Bahr, R., Dawood, N., & Revel, G. M. (2012). A wireless sensor network for intelligent building energy management based on multi communication standards – a case study. *ITcon*, *17*, 43–62.

Guardado-Medina, Larios, & Patarroyo. (2015). ODF best practices towards a GDL Smart City. *IEEE-GDL CCD Smart Cities White Paper*, 1–6.

Gunge, Y. (2016). Smart Home Automation: A Literature Review. *International Journal of Computer Applications*.

Gungor, V., Lu, B., & Hancke, G. (2010). Opportunities and Challenges of Wireless Sensor Networks in Smart Grid. *IEEE Transactions on Industrial Electronics*, *57*(10), 3557–3564. doi:10.1109/TIE.2009.2039455

Guo, J. J., Peyrin, T., & Poschmann, A. (2011). The PHOTON family of lightweight hash functions. In *Annual Cryptology Conference* (pp. 222-239). Berlin: Springer. 10.1007/978-3-642-22792-9_13

Guo, W. W., & Xue, H. (2014). Crop yield forecasting using artificial neural networks: A comparison between spatial and temporal models. *Mathematical Problems in Engineering*.

Guo, X., Wang, Z., & Zhao, L. (2013). Intelligent Industrial Park based on Internet of Things. *Advanced Materials Research*, *722*, 486–490. doi:10.4028/www.scientific.net/AMR.722.486

Gürel & Erden (2012). Design of Face Recognition System. In The 15th International Conference on Machine Design and Production, Pamukkale, Denizli, Turkey.

Hampapur, B., & Connell, P. (2004). Smart Surveillance: Applications, Technologies and Implications. *ETP '04 Proceedings of the 2004 ACM SIGMM workshop on Effective telepresence*, 59-62.

Han, J., Haihong, E., Le, G., & Du, J. (2011). Survey on NoSQL database. In *Proceedings - 2011 6th International Conference on Pervasive Computing and Applications, ICPCA 2011* (pp. 363–366). Academic Press. doi:10.1109/ICPCA.2011.6106531

Han, G., Xiao, L., & Poor, H. V. (2017). Two-dimensional anti-jamming communication based on deep reinforcement learning. *IEEE Int'l Conf. Acoustics, Speech and Signal Processing*, 2087–2091. 10.1109/ICASSP.2017.7952524

Harman, P. M. (1998). *The natural philosophy of James Clerk Maxwell*. Cambridge, UK: Cambridge University Press.

Harun, A. N., Kassim, M. R. M., Mat, I., & Ramli, S. S. (2015, May). Precision irrigation using wireless sensor network. In *2015 International Conference on Smart Sensors and Application (ICSSA)* (pp. 71-75). IEEE. 10.1109/ICSSA.2015.7322513

Hatzivasilis, G., Fysarakisloannis, K., Papaefstathiou, I., & Manifavas, C. (2018). A review of lightweight block ciphers. *Journal of Cryptographic Engineering*, *8*(2), 141–184. doi:10.100713389-017-0160-y

Hedley, C. B., & Yule, I. J. (2009). Soil water status mapping and two variable-rate irrigation scenarios. *Precision Agriculture*, *10*(4), 342–355. doi:10.100711119-009-9119-z

Hell, M., Johansson, T., & Meier, W. (2007). Grain - A stream cipher for constrained environments. *International Journal of Wireless and Mobile Computing*, *2*(1), 86–93. doi:10.1504/IJWMC.2007.013798

Hoffstein, J., Pipher, J., & Silverman, J. H. (1998). NTRU: A ring-based public key cryptosystem. In *International Algorithmic Number Theory Symposium* (pp. 267-288). Berlin: Springer-Verlag. 10.1007/BFb0054868

Hossain, M. D., & George, F. (2018). IOT Based Real-Time Drowsy Driving Detection System for the Prevention of Road Accidents. In International Conference on Intelligent Informatics and Biomedical Sciences (Vol. 3, pp. 190–195). ICIIBMS. http://i21www.ira.uka.de/image_sequences

Hsia, K.-H., & Gu, J.-H. (2017). Fusion-Algorithm-Based Security System with Multiple Sensors. *Sensors and Materials*, *29*(7), 1069–1080.

Huang, Y., Martínez, J.-F., Sendra, J., & López, L. (2015). Resilient Wireless Sensor Networks Using Topology Control: A Review. *Sensors (Basel)*, *15*(10), 24735–24770. doi:10.3390151024735 PMID:26404272

Hung, M. (2018). *Leading the IoT.* Gartner White Paper.

Hu, Y., Wu, Y., & Wang, H. (2014). Detection of Insider Selective Forwarding Attack Based on Monitor Node and Trust Mechanism in WSN. *Wireless Sensor Network*, *06*(11), 237–248. doi:10.4236/wsn.2014.611023

Internet of Things – Integration and Semantic Interoperability of Sensor Data of Things in Heterogeneous Environments. (2016). Internet of Things – Integration and Semantic Interoperability of Sensor Data of Things in Heterogeneous Environments. *International Journal Of Modern Trends In Engineering & Research*, *3*(12), 174–178. doi:10.21884/IJMTER.2016.3166.Y4XEN

Internet of Things Global Standards Initiative. (n.d.). Retrieved June 29, 2018, from https://www.itu.int/en/ITU-T/gsi/iot/Pages/default.aspx

IoT Delegate: Smart Home Framework for Heterogeneous IoT Service Collaboration. (2016). *KSII Transactions On Internet And Information Systems*, *10*(8). doi:10.3837/tiis.2016.08.029

ISO/IEC 7498-1:1994 - Information technology -- Open Systems Interconnection -- Basic Reference Model: The Basic Model. (n.d.). Retrieved June 30, 2018, from https://www.iso.org/standard/20269.html

Jafar, I. B., Raihana, K., Bhowmik, S., & Shakil, S. R. (2014, May). Wireless monitoring system and controlling software for Smart Greenhouse Management. In *2014 International Conference on Informatics, Electronics & Vision (ICIEV)* (pp. 1-5). IEEE. 10.1109/ICIEV.2014.6850748

James, M., Stephen, J., & Anthony, D. (2000). Visual surveillance for moving vehicles. *International Journal of Computer Vision, 37*(2), 187–197. doi:10.1023/A:1008155721192

Jan. (2004). Neural Network Based Threat Assessment for Automated Visual Surveillance. *Neural Networks, 2004. Proceedings. 2004 IEEE International Joint Conference on.* Doi:10.1109/IJCNN.2004.1380133

Jaouedi, Zaghbani, Boujnah, & Bouhlel. (2017). Human Motion Detection and Tracking. *Proceedings Ninth International Conference on Machine Vision.*

Jayaraman, P. P., Palmer, D., Zaslavsky, A., & Georgakopoulos, D. (2015, April). Do-it-Yourself Digital Agriculture applications with semantically enhanced IoT platform. In *2015 IEEE Tenth International Conference on Intelligent Sensors, Sensor Networks and Information Processing (ISSNIP)* (pp. 1-6). IEEE. 10.1109/ISSNIP.2015.7106951

Jepsen, T. (2014). Doctor's Orders: Healthcare Apps and Self-Monitoring. *IT Professional, 16*(4), 48–49. doi:10.1109/MITP.2014.49

Jerkins, J. A. (2017). Motivating a market or regulatory solution to IoT insecurity with the Mirai botnet code. In *7th Annual Computing and Communication Workshop and Conference.* Las Vegas, NV: IEEE. 10.1109/CCWC.2017.7868464

Jeyabharathi, D., & Dejey, D (2016). A novel Rotational Symmetry Dynamic Texture (RSDT) based sub space construction and SCD (Similar-Congruent-Dissimilar) based scoring model for background subtraction in real time videos. *Multimedia Tools and Applications, 75*(16), 1-29. doi:). doi:10.100711042-016-3772-9

Jeyabharathi, D., & Dr Dejey, D. (2016). Vehicle Tracking and Speed Measurement System (VTSM) Based on Novel Feature Descriptor: Diagonal Hexadecimal Pattern (DHP). *International Journal of Visual Communication and Image Representation, 40*, 816–830. doi:10.1016/j.jvcir.2016.08.011

Jeyabharathi, D., & Dr Dejey, D. (2018). Cut set-based Dynamic Key frame selection and Adaptive Layer-based Background Modeling for Background Subtraction. *Journal of Visual Communication and Image Representation, 55*, 434–446. doi:10.1016/j.jvcir.2018.06.024

Jeyabharathi, D., & Dr Dejey, D. (2018). Efficient background subtraction for thermal images using reflectional symmetry pattern (RSP). *Multimedia Tools and Applications, 77*(17), 22567–22586. doi:10.100711042-018-6220-1

Jha, M. K., Chowdhury, A., Chowdary, V. M., & Peiffer, S. (2007). Groundwater management and development by integrated remote sensing and geographic information systems: Prospects and constraints. *Water Resources Management*, *21*(2), 427–467. doi:10.100711269-006-9024-4

Jin, J., Gubbi, J., Marusic, S., & Palaniswami, M. (2014). An Information Framework for Creating a Smart City Through Internet of Things. *IEEE Internet of Things Journal*, *1*(2), 112–121. doi:10.1109/JIOT.2013.2296516

Jin, Y., Tomoishi, M., & Yamai, N. (2017). A secure and lightweight IoT device remote monitoring and control mechanism using DNS. In *41st Annual Computer Software and Applications Conference* (pp. 282-283). Turin, Italy: IEEE. 10.1109/COMPSAC.2017.33

Jin, Z., Prasad, R., Shriver, J., & Zhuang, Q. (2017). Crop model-and satellite imagery-based recommendation tool for variable rate N fertilizer application for the US Corn system. *Precision Agriculture*, *18*(5), 779–800. doi:10.100711119-016-9488-z

John Livingston, J., & Umamakeswari, A. (2015). Internet of Things Application using IP-enabled Sensor Node and Web Server. *Indian Journal of Science and Technology*, *8*(S9), 207. doi:10.17485/ijst/2015/v8iS9/65577

Johnson, D. (2002). RFID tags improve tracking, quality on Ford line in Mexico. *Control Engineering*, *49*(11), 16.

JSON.org. (2014). *Introducing JSON*. Retrieved from http://www.json.org/

Kadu, Dekhane, Dhanwala, & Awate. (2015). Real Time Monitoring and Controlling System. *International Journal of Engineering and Science*, *4*(2), 15-18.

Kaiwartya, O., Abdullah, A. H., Cao, Y., Raw, R. S., Kumar, S., Lobiyal, D. K., ... Shah, R. R. (2016). T-MQM: Testbed-based multi-metric quality measurement of sensor deployment for precision agriculture—A case study. *IEEE Sensors Journal*, *16*(23), 8649–8664.

Kärkkäinen, M. (2003). Increasing efficiency in the supply chain for short shelf life goods using RFID tagging. *International Journal of Retail & Distribution Management*, *31*(10), 529–536. doi:10.1108/09590550310497058

Kashyap, R. (2019a). Security, Reliability, and Performance Assessment for Healthcare Biometrics. In D. Kisku, P. Gupta, & J. Sing (Eds.), Design and Implementation of Healthcare Biometric Systems (pp. 29-54). Hershey, PA: IGI Global. doi:10.4018/978-1-5225-7525-2.ch002

Kashyap, R. (2019d). Geospatial Big Data, Analytics and IoT: Challenges, Applications and Potential. In H. Das, R. Barik, H. Dubey & D. Sinha Roy, Cloud Computing for Geospatial Big Data Analytics (1st ed., pp. 191-213). Switzerland AG: Springer International Publishing.

Kashyap, R., & Piersson, A. (2018a). Big Data Challenges and Solutions in the Medical Industries. In Handbook of Research on Pattern Engineering System Development for Big Data Analytics. IGI Global. doi:10.4018/978-1-5225-3870-7.ch001

Kashyap, R., & Piersson, A. (2018b). Impact of Big Data on Security. In Handbook of Research on Network Forensics and Analysis Techniques (pp. 283–299). IGI Global. doi:10.4018/978-1-5225-4100-4.ch015

Kashyap, R., Gautam, P., & Tiwari, V. (2018). Management and Monitoring Patterns and Future Scope. In Handbook of Research on Pattern Engineering System Development for Big Data Analytics. IGI Global. doi:10.4018/978-1-5225-3870-7.ch014

Kashyap, R. (2019b). Biometric Authentication Techniques and E-Learning. In A. Kumar (Ed.), *Biometric Authentication in Online Learning Environments* (pp. 236–265). Hershey, PA: IGI Global; doi:10.4018/978-1-5225-7724-9.ch010

Kashyap, R. (2019c). Machine Learning for Internet of Things. In I.-S. Comşa & R. Trestian (Eds.), *Next-Generation Wireless Networks Meet Advanced Machine Learning Applications* (pp. 57–83). Hershey, PA: IGI Global; doi:10.4018/978-1-5225-7458-3.ch003

Kashyap, R., & Gautam, P. (2017). Fast Medical Image Segmentation Using Energy-Based Method. *Biometrics. Concepts, Methodologies, Tools, and Applications*, *3*(1), 1017–1042. doi:10.4018/978-1-5225-0983-7.ch040

Kashyap, R., & Tiwari, V. (2018). Active contours using global models for medical image segmentation. *International Journal of Computational Systems Engineering*, *4*(2/3), 195. doi:10.1504/IJCSYSE.2018.091404

Kastrinaki, V., Zervakis, M., & Kalaitzakis, K. (2003). A survey of video processing techniques for traffic applications. *Image and Vision Computing*, *21*(4), 359–381. doi:10.1016/S0262-8856(03)00004-0

Katzberg, S. J., Torres, O., Grant, M. S., & Masters, D. (2006). Utilizing calibrated GPS reflected signals to estimate soil reflectivity and dielectric constant: Results from SMEX02. *Remote Sensing of Environment*, *100*(1), 17–28. doi:10.1016/j.rse.2005.09.015

Kechao, Xiangmin, Zhifei, Zongfu, & Jingwei (2011). Design and implementation of embedded network video monitoring terminal. In *IEEE conference on computer science and automation engineering (CSAE)*. IEEE.

Kephart, J., & Chess, D. (2003). The vision of autonomic computing. *Computer*, *36*(1), 41–50. doi:10.1109/MC.2003.1160055

Khan, M., Silva, B., & Han, K. (2017). A Web of Things-Based Emerging Sensor Network Architecture for Smart Control Systems. Sensors (Basel), 17(2), 332. doi:10.339017020332 PMID:28208787.

Khan, M., Silva, B., & Han, K. (2017). A Web of Things-Based Emerging Sensor Network Architecture for Smart Control Systems. *Sensors (Basel)*, *17*(2), 332. doi:10.339017020332 PMID:28208787

Khan, R., Khan, S. U., Zaheer, R., & Khan, S. (2012). Future Internet: The Internet of Things Architecture, Possible Applications and Key Challenges. In *10th International Conference on Frontiers of Information Technology* (pp. 257-260). Islamabad, India: IEEE. 10.1109/FIT.2012.53

Kharat, Kharat, & Kharat. (2014). Wireless Intrusion Detection System Using Wireless Sensor Network: A Conceptual Framework. *International Journal of Electronics and Electrical Engineering*, *2*(2).

Kharik, Chaudhuri, & Bhambare. (2014). A Smart Home Security System Based On Arm7 Processor. *International Journal of Engineering and Computer Science*, *3*(4), 5283-5287.

Khattab, A., Abdelgawad, A., & Yelmarthi, K. (2016, December). Design and implementation of a cloud-based IoT scheme for precision agriculture. In *28th International Conference on Microelectronics* (pp. 201-204). IEEE. 10.1109/ICM.2016.7847850

Khemapech, Duncan, & Miller. (2014). *A Survey of Wireless Sensor Network Technology*. Academic Press.

Khosla, R., Fleming, K., Delgado, J. A., Shaver, T. M., & Westfall, D. G. (2002). Use of site-specific management zones to improve nitrogen management for precision agriculture. *Journal of Soil and Water Conservation*, *57*(6), 513–518.

Khurana. (2017). IoT Based Safety and Security System. *International Journal of Advance Research, Ideas and Innovations in Technology, 3*(3).

Kim, B., & Mondal, S. (2016). Design of TSV-based Inductors for Internet of Things. *Additional Conferences (Device Packaging, Hitec, Hiten, & CICMT).* doi: 10.4071/2016dpc-tha34

Kim, Y., & Lee, Y. (2015). Automatic Generation of Social Relationships between Internet of Things in Smart Home Using SDN-Based Home Cloud. *Proceedings - IEEE 29th International Conference on Advanced Information Networking and Applications Workshops, WAINA 2015,* 662–667. 10.1109/WAINA.2015.93

Kim, J., Kim, M., & Seo, J. (2017). Implementation and Evaluation of IoT Service System for Security Enhancement. *Journal Of The Korea Institute Of Information Security And Cryptology, 27*(2), 181–192. doi:10.13089/JKIISC.2017.27.2.181

Kinsella, B. (2003). The Wal-Mart factors. *Industrial Engineering (American Institute of Industrial Engineers), 32–36.*

Klumpp, M. (2018). Innovation Potentials and Pathways Merging AI, CPS, and IoT. *Applied System Innovation, 1*(1), 5. doi:10.3390/asi1010005

Knospe, H., & Pohl, H. (2004). RFID security. *Information Security Technical Report, 9*(4), 39–50. doi:10.1016/S1363-4127(05)70039-X

Ko & Lee. (2015). Stereo Camera-based Intelligence Surveillance System. *Journal of Automation and Control Engineering, 3*(3), 2015. doi:10.12720/joace.3.3.253-257

Koblitz, N. (1987). Elliptic curve cryptosystems. *Mathematics of Computation, 48*(177), 203–209. doi:10.1090/S0025-5718-1987-0866109-5

Kodali, Bose, & Boppana. (2016). IoT Based Smart Security and Home Automation System. *In: International Conference on Computing, Communication and Automation (ICCCA2016).*

Kolias, V., Stavrou, A., Voas, J., Bojanova, I., & Kuhn, R. (2016). Learning Internet-of-Things Security "Hands-On". *IEEE Security and Privacy, 14*(1), 37–46. doi:10.1109/MSP.2016.4

Kranthi Kumar, M., & Srenivasa Ravi, K. (2016). Automation of irrigation system based on Wi-Fi technology and IOT. *Indian Journal of Science and Technology, 9*(17), 17. doi:10.17485/ijst/2016/v9i17/93048

Krebsonsecurity (2014). http://krebsonsecurity.com/2014/02/target-hackers-broke-in-via-hvac-company/

Kumar & Sanjai. (2013). Secure Data Aggregation in Wireless Sensor Networks. *2013 12th Annual Mediterranean Ad Hoc Networking Workshop (MED-HOC-NET)*. doi:10.1109/MedHocNet.2013.6767410

Kumar, J. S. & Patel, D. R. (2014). A Survey on Internet of Things: Security and Privacy Issues. *International Journal of Computer Applications*, *90*(11), 20-25.

Kumar, H., & Singh, A. (2016). Internet of Things: A comprehensive analysis and security implementation through elliptic curve cryptography. *International Journal of Current Engineering and Technology*, *6*(2), 498–502.

Kumari, G., & Reddy (2009). PiCam: IoT based Wireless Alert System for Deaf and Hard of Hearing. *International Conference on Advanced Computing and Communication*.

Kumar, S., & Chaurasiya, V. (2018). A multisensor data fusion strategy for path selection in Internet-of-Things oriented wireless sensor network (WSN). *Concurrency and Computation, e4477*. doi:10.1002/cpe.4477

Kumar, S., & Sharma, P. (2007). Home Automation System Using Android via Bluetooth. *International Journal of Advanced Research in Electrical Electronics and Instrumentation Engineering*, *6*(4), 3297.

Kviesis, A., & Zacepins, A. (2015). System architectures for real-time bee colony temperature monitoring. *Procedia Computer Science*, *43*, 86–94. doi:10.1016/j.procs.2014.12.012

Lake, D., Milito, R., Morrow, M., & Vargheese, R. (2014). Internet of Things: Architectural Framework for eHealth Security. *Journal Of ICT Standardization*, *1*(3), 301–328. doi:10.13052/jicts2245-800X.133

Lakshman, A., & Malik, P. (2010). Cassandra. *Operating Systems Review*, *44*(2), 35. doi:10.1145/1773912.1773922

Lamaazi, H., Benamar, N., Jara, A. J., Ladid, L., & El Ouadghiri, D. (2014). Challenges of the Internet of Things: IPv6 and Network Management. *Eighth International Conference on Innovative Mobile and Internet Services in Ubiquitous Computing*.

Lamberts, R., Swart, J., Capostagno, B., Noakes, T., & Lambert, M. (2009). Heart rate recovery as a guide to monitor fatigue and predict changes in performance parameters. *Scandinavian Journal of Medicine & Science in Sports*, *20*(3), 449–457. doi:10.1111/j.1600-0838.2009.00977.x PMID:19558377

Larios, V. M., Gomez, L., Mora, O. B., & Maciel, R. N. V.-R. (2016). Living labs for smart cities: A use case in Guadalajara city to foster innovation and develop citizen-centered solutions. IEEE.

Leaflet. (2015). Retrieved September 12, 2016, from http://leafletjs.com/

Lecocq, A., Kryger, P., Vejsnæs, F., & Jensen, A. B. (2015). Weight watching and the effect of landscape on honeybee colony productivity: Investigating the value of colony weight monitoring for the beekeeping industry. *PLoS One*, *10*(7), e0132473. doi:10.1371/journal.pone.0132473 PMID:26147392

Lee, B. (2015). Dynamic Data Binding Protocol between IoT Medical Device and IoT Medical Service for Mobile Healthcare. *International Journal Of Smart Home*, *9*(6), 141–150. doi:10.14257/ijsh.2015.9.6.16

Lefsky, M. A., Cohen, W. B., Parker, G. G., & Harding, D. J. (2002). Lidar remote sensing for ecosystem studies: Lidar, an emerging remote sensing technology that directly measures the three-dimensional distribution of plant canopies, can accurately estimate vegetation structural attributes and should be of particular interest to forest, landscape, and global ecologists. *Bioscience*, *52*(1), 19–30. doi:10.1641/0006-3568(2002)052[0019:LRSFES]2.0.CO;2

Lei, Z. (2018). Internet of Things Applications for Agriculture. Internet of Things A to Z: Technologies and Applications, 507-528.

Lin & Kung. (1997). Face Recognition/Detection by Probabilistic Decision-Based Neural Network. *IEEE Transactions on Neural Networks*, *8*(1), 1045–9227. PMID:18255615

Li, N., Liu, D., & Nepal, S. (2017). Lightweight mutual authentication for IoT and its applications. *IEEE Transactions on Sustainable Computing*, *2*(4), 359–370. doi:10.1109/TSUSC.2017.2716953

Lingam, M. S. (2017). Transforming Smart Healthcare through the Internet of Things (IoT). *International Journal Of Emerging Trends In Science And Technology*, *4*(9). doi:10.18535/ijetst/v4i9.08

Lin, J., Yu, W., Zhang, N., Yang, X., Zhang, H., & Zhao, W. (2017). A Survey on Internet of Things: Architecture, Enabling Technologies, Security and Privacy, and Applications. *IEEE Internet of Things Journal*, *4*(5), 1–1. doi:10.1109/JIOT.2017.2683200

Liu, G. X., Xu, J. L., & Hong, X. B. (2013). Internet of Things Sensor Node Information Scheduling Model and Energy Saving Strategy. *Advanced Materials Research*, *773*, 215–220. doi:10.4028/www.scientific.net/AMR.773.215

Liu, X., Zhao, M., Li, S., Zhang, F., & Trappe, W. (2017). A security framework for the Internet of Things in the future Internet architecture. *Future Internet*, *9*(3), 1–28. doi:10.3390/fi9030027

Li, Y., Quevedo, D., Dey, E. S., & Shi, L. (2016). SINR-based DoS attack on remote state estimation: A game-theoretic approach, *IEEE Trans. Control of Network Systems*, *4*(3), 632–642. doi:10.1109/TCNS.2016.2549640

Lopez. (2013). *An Introduction to the Internet of Things (IoT)*. Lopez Research Report.

Lu, L. (2017). *Wise-paas introduction Advantech*. Retrieved from http://www2. advantech.com.tw/embcore/promotions/whitepaper/WISE-PaaS

Luckett, D. (2004). The supply chain. *BT Technology Journal*, *22*(3), 50–55. doi:10.1023/B:BTTJ.0000047119.22852.38

Lumpkins, W. (2013). The internet of things meets cloud computing. *IEEE Consumer Electronics Magazine*, *2*(2), 47–51. doi:10.1109/MCE.2013.2240615

Lynggaard, P. (2017). *Artificial intelligence and Internet of Things in a "smart home" context: A Distributed System Architecture*. Retrieved from vbn.aau.dk

Madakam, S., Ramaswamy, R., & Tripathi, S. (2015). Internet of Things (IoT): A Literature Review. *Journal of Computer and Communications*, *3*(5), 164–173. doi:10.4236/jcc.2015.35021

Maddalena & Petrosino. (2008). A Self-Organizing Approach to Background Subtraction for Visual Surveillance Applications. *IEEE Transactions on Image Processing*, *17*(7), 2008. PMID:18586624

Maene, P., Gotzfried, J., de Clercq, R., M̈uller, T., Freiling, F., & Verbauwhede, I. (2017). Hardware-Based Trusted Computing Architectures for Isolation and Attestation. *IEEE Transactions on Computers*, *67*(3), 361–374. doi:10.1109/TC.2017.2647955

Mahmood, A., Javaid, N., & Razzaq, S. (2015). A review of wireless communications for smart grid. *Renewable & Sustainable Energy Reviews*, *41*, 248–260. doi:10.1016/j.rser.2014.08.036

Makushin, M., & Martynov, V. (2018). Problems and prospects for the development of the industrial internet of things. *Electronics: Science, Technology. Business (Atlanta, Ga.)*, (3): 156–168. doi:10.22184/1992-4178.2018.174.3.156.168

Malveaux, C., Hall, S. G., & Price, R. (2014). Using drones in agriculture: unmanned aerial systems for agricultural remote sensing applications. In *2014 Montreal, Quebec Canada July 13–July 16, 2014* (p. 1). American Society of Agricultural and Biological Engineers.

Mandrupkar & Mane. (2013). Smart Video Security Surveillance with Mobile Remote Control. *International Journal of Advanced Research in Computer Science and Software Engineering Research Paper*, *3*(3).

Mashal, I., Alsaryrah, O., Chung, T. Y., Yang, C. Z., Kuo, W. H., & Agrawal, D. P. (2015). Choices for interaction with things on Internet and underlying isssues. *Ad Hoc Networks*, *28*, 68–90. doi:10.1016/j.adhoc.2014.12.006

Mell, P., & Grance, T. (2011). The NIST Definition of Cloud Computing. *NIST Special Publication*, 800-145. Retrieved from https://csrc.nist.gov/publications/detail/sp/800-145/final

Mengden, T., Vetter, H., Tislér, A., & Illyés, M. (2001). Tele-monitoring of home blood pressure. *Blood Pressure Monitoring*, *6*(4), 185–189. doi:10.1097/00126097-200108000-00004 PMID:11805466

Messelodi, S., & Modena, C. (1999). Automatic identification and skew estimation of text lines in real scene images. *Pattern Recognition*, *32*(5), 791–810. doi:10.1016/S0031-3203(98)00108-3

Mittelstadt, B. (2017). Ethics of the health-related internet of things: A narrative review. *Ethics and Information Technology*, *19*(3), 157–175. doi:10.100710676-017-9426-4

Mobley, T. (2013). Tracking and monitoring of animals with combined wireless technology and geofencing. *U.S. Patent Application, 13*(917), 328.

Mobley, T. (2016). Tracking and monitoring of animals with combined wireless technology and geo-fencing. *U.S. Patent Application 15*(76), 584.

Moghaddam & Pentland. (1995). Probabilistic Visual Learning for Object Detection. *IEEE Transactions on Pattern Analysis and Machine Intelligence*, *19*(7).

Mohanty, S. P., Choppali, U., & Kougianos, E. (2016). Everything You Wanted to Know About Smart Cities. *IEEE Consumer Electronics Magazine, 5*(3), 60–70. doi:10.1109/MCE.2016.2556879

Nagarajan & Surendran. (2015). A High End Building Automation and Online Video Surveillance Security System. *International Journal of Engineering and Technology, 7*(1).

Namatame, N., Nakazawa, J., & Tokuda, H. (2012). Logical Sensor Network: An Abstraction of Sensor Data Processing over Multidomain Sensor Network. *ISRN Sensor Networks, 2012*, 1–9. doi:10.5402/2012/234251

Nandyala, C. S., & Kim, H. K. (2016). Green IoT agriculture and healthcare application (GAHA). *International Journal of Smart Home, 10*(4), 289–300. doi:10.14257/ijsh.2016.10.4.26

Nasim. (2012). Security Threats Analysis. *International Journal of Network Security & Its Applications, 4*(3). doi: 41 doi:10.5121/ijnsa.2012.4303

Navya Teja, Y., Vooha, L., Rohini Priya, A., & Ramesh, N. (2018). IOT Based Smart Health Care. *International Journal Of Engineering & Technology, 7*(2), 470. doi:10.14419/ijet.v7i2.7.10865

Nawrin, S., Rahman, M. R., & Akhter, S. (2017). Exploreing k-means with internal validity indexes for data clustering in traffic management system. *International Journal of Advanced Computer Science and Applications, 8*(3), 264–268. doi:10.14569/IJACSA.2017.080337

Neményi, M., Mesterházi, P. Á., Pecze, Z., & Stépán, Z. (2003). The role of GIS and GPS in precision farming. *Computers and Electronics in Agriculture, 40*(1-3), 45–55. doi:10.1016/S0168-1699(03)00010-3

Nguyen, Loan, & Huh. (2017). Low Cost Real-Time System Monitoring Using Raspberry Pi. *Innovations in Electronics and Communication Engineering*.

Novo, O. (2018). Blockchain Meets IoT: An Architecture for Scalable Access Management in IoT. *IEEE Internet Of Things Journal, 5*(2), 1184–1195. doi:10.1109/JIOT.2018.2812239

Numerical Studies on the Electronic Gadgets in a Personal Computer Using CFD. (n.d.). *International Journal Of Science And Research, 5*(7). doi:10.21275/v5i7.art2016526

O'Neill, M. (2016). Insecurity by Design: Today's IoT Device Security Problem. *Engineering*, *2*(1), 48–49. doi:10.1016/J.ENG.2016.01.014

O'Shaughnessy, S. A., Urrego, Y. F., Evett, S. R., Colaizzi, P. D., & Howell, T. A. (2013). Assessing application uniformity of a variable rate irrigation system in a windy location. *Applied Engineering in Agriculture*, *29*(4), 497–510.

OASIS. (2014). *MQTT Version 3.1.1*. OASIS Standard, (October), 81. Retrieved from http://docs.oasis-open.org/mqtt/mqtt/v3.1.1/os/mqtt-v3.1.1-os.html

Oghazi, P., Rad, F. F., Karlsson, K., & Haftor, H. (2018). RFID and ERP Systems in Supply Chain Management. *European Journal of Management and Business Economics*, 171-182.

Oludele, Avodele, Oladele, & Olurotimi. (2009). Design of an Automated Intrusion Detection System incorporating an Alarm. *Journal of Computers*, *1*(1), 2151–9617.

Ondrej, T., & Milos. (2009). Neural Network Based Intrusion Detection System for Critical Infrastructures. *Proceedings of International Joint Conference on Neural Networks*.

Onyshchenko, K., & Afanasieva, I. (2017). Structured methodology for development of the service for providing remote control of intelligent home devices using Internet of Things solutions. *Sciencerise*, *5*(2), 30–33. doi:10.15587/2313-8416.2017.101735

OpenLayers. (2007). *OpenLayers 3*. Retrieved November 19, 2016, from https://openlayers.org/

OpenStreetMaps. (2004). Retrieved September 12, 2016, from https://www.openstreetmap.org/about

Opoku. (2011). *An Indoor Tracking System Based On Bluetooth Technology*. Academic Press.

Over, P., Awad, G., & Fiscus, J. (2009). *Goals, Tasks, Data, Evaluation Mechanisms and Metrics* (Vol. 16). TRECVID-NIST.

Padgette, J., Bahr, J., & Batra, M. (2012). *Guide to bluetooth security*. NIST Special Publication, 800-121. 1 doi:0.6028/NIST.SP.800-121r2

Pal, K. (2019a). Quality Assurance Issues for Big Data Applications in Supply Chain Management, In Predictive Intelligence Using Big Data and Internet of Things. IGI Global Publishing.

Pal, K. (2017). Supply Chain Coordination Based on Web Services. In H. K. Chan, N. Subraanian, & M. D. Abdulrahman (Eds.), *Supply Chain Management in the Big Data Era* (pp. 137–171). Hershey, PA: IGI Global Publishing. doi:10.4018/978-1-5225-0956-1.ch009

Pang, Z., Chen, O., Tian, J., Zheng, L., & Dubrova, E. (2013). Ecosystem analysis in the design of open platform-based in home healthcare terminals towards the internet-of-things. In *15th International Conference on Advanced Communications Technology* (pp. 529-534). PyeongChang, South Korea: IEEE.

Parvin, S., Gawanmeh, A., Venkatraman, S., Alwadi, A., & Al-Karak, J. (2018). Efficient Lightweight Mechanism for Node Authentication in WBSN. Advances in Engineering Technology & Sciences Multi-Conferences.

Parvin, S., Gawanmeh, A., & Venkatraman, S. (2018). Optimised Sensor Based Smart System for Efficient Monitoring of Grain Storage. *IEEE International Conference on Communications Workshops*. 10.1109/ICCW.2018.8403537

Parvin, S., Gawanmeh, A., Venkatraman, S., Alwadi, A., & Al-Karak, J. (2018). Trust-based Authentication Framework for Enhanced Security of WPAN/WBAN Networks, Forthcoming paper. *Journal of Communications and Networks (Seoul)*.

Patel, A., Aparicio, J., Tas, N., Loiacono, M., & Rosca, J. (2011). *Assessing communications technology options for Smart Grid applications*. IEEE Press. doi:10.1109/SmartGridComm.2011.6102303

Patel, Vallabhbhai, & Choksi, Bhaskaracharya, & Jadhav. (2016). Smart Motion Detection System using Raspberry Pi. *International Journal of Applied Information Systems. Foundation of Computer Science, 10*.

Perera, C., Zaslavsky, A., Christen, P., & Georakopoulus, D. (2013). Context aware computing for the Internet of Things: A survey. *IEEE Communications Surveys and Tutorials, 16*(1), 414–454. doi:10.1109/SURV.2013.042313.00197

Peris-Lopez, P., Hernandez-Castro, J. C., Estevez-Tapiador, J. M., & Ribagorda, A. (2009). Cryptanalysis of a novel authentication protocol conforming to epc-c1g2 standard. *Computer Standards & Interfaces, 31*(2), 372–380. doi:10.1016/j.csi.2008.05.012

Perumal, T., Sulaiman, M. N., & Leong, C. Y. (2015, October). Internet of Things (IoT) enabled water monitoring system. In *2015 IEEE 4th Global Conference on Consumer Electronics (GCCE)* (pp. 86-87). IEEE.

Pettit, C., Bakelmun, A., Lieske, S. N., Glackin, S., Hargroves, K., Thomson, G., ... Newman, P. (2017). Planning support systems for smart cities. *City, Culture and Society*. doi:10.1016/j.ccs.2017.10.002

Piao, S., Ciais, P., Huang, Y., Shen, Z., Peng, S., Li, J., ... Fang, J. (2010). The impacts of climate change on water resources and agriculture in China. *Nature*, *467*(7311), 43–51. doi:10.1038/nature09364 PMID:20811450

Pike, A., Muller, T., Rienzi, E. A., Neelakantan, S., Mijatovic, B., Karathanasis, A. D., & Rodrigues, M. (2012). *Terrain analysis for locating erosion channels: Assessing LiDAR data and flow direction algorithm*. Academic Press.

Policy, I. T. U., & Division, T. W. (2015). *Smart Cities Seoul: A case study*. Academic Press.

Power, P., & Schoonees, J. (2002). Understand background mixture models for foreground Segmentation. *Proc. Image and Vision Computing*, 267–271.

Progress on the development of the MediWatch ambulatory blood pressure monitor and related devices. (2004). *Blood Pressure Monitoring, 9*(6), 327. doi:10.1097/00126097-200412000-00011

Qin, E., Long, Y., Zhang, C., & Huang L. (2013). Human Interface and the Management of Information. *Information and Interaction for Health, Safety, Mobility and Complex Environments*, 173-180.

Rad, C. R., Hancu, O., Takacs, I. A., & Olteanu, G. (2015). Smart monitoring of potato crop: A cyber-physical system architecture model in the field of precision agriculture. *Agriculture and Agricultural Science Procedia*, *6*, 73–79. doi:10.1016/j.aaspro.2015.08.041

Rahman, M. R., & Akhter, S. (2015). Bi-directional traffic management support system with decision tree based dynamic routing. *2015 10th International Conference for Internet Technology and Secured Transactions (ICITST)*, 170-178.

Rahman, M. R., & Akhter, S. (2015). Real Time Bi-directional Traffic Management Support System with GPS and WebSocket. *2015 IEEE International Conference on Computer and Information Technology; Ubiquitous Computing and Communications; Dependable, Autonomic and Secure Computing; Pervasive Intelligence and Computing*, 959-964.

Rahman, M., & Hossain, M. (2017). m-Therapy: A Multi-sensor Framework for in-home Therapy Management: A Social Therapy of Things Perspective. *IEEE Internet Of Things Journal*, 1-1. doi:10.1109/jiot.2017.2776150

Rahman, M. R., & Akhter, S. (2016). Bi-directional traffic management with multiple data feeds for dynamic route computation and prediction system. *International Journal of Intelligent Computing Research*, *7*(2), 720–727. doi:10.20533/ijicr.2042.4655.2016.0088

Ramlee, L., Singh, I., Othman, S., & Misran, M. (2013). Bluetooth Remote Home Automation System Using Android Application. *International Journal of Engineering and Science*, *1*, 149-153.

Rao, S.K. (2015). Raspberry pi home automation with wireless sensors using smart phone. *International Journal of Computer Science and Mobile Computing*, *4*, 797 – 803.

Raza, S., Trabalza, D., & Voigt, T. (2012). 6LoWPAN compressed DTLS for CoAP. *IEEE 8th International Conference on Distributed Computing in Sensor Systems*, 287–289.

Raza, S., Shafagh, H., Hewage, R., Hummen, K., & Voigt, T. (2013). Lithe: Lightweight Secure CoAP for the Internet of Things. *Sensors Journal, IEEE*, *13*(10), 3711–3720. doi:10.1109/JSEN.2013.2277656

Rhodes. (2006). *Bluetooth Security*. Retrieved from www.infosecwriters.com

Rieback, M. R., Crispo, B., & Tanenbaum, A. S. (2006). Is your cat infected with a computer virus? Proceedings of PerCon, 169-179. doi:10.1109/PERCOM.2006.32

Rieck, K. (2011). Self-Learning Network Intrusion Detection. *Information Technology*, *53*(3), 152-156.

Rieck, K., Trinius, P., Willems, C., & Holz, T. (2011). Automatic analysis of malware behavior using machine learning. *Journal of Computer Security*, *19*(4), 639–668. doi:10.3233/JCS-2010-0410

Rivest, R., Shamir, A., & Adleman, L. (1978). A method for obtaining digital signatures and public-key cryptosystems. *Communications of the ACM*, *21*(2), 120–126. doi:10.1145/359340.359342

Roberti, M. (2005, December 31). Financing for RFID Prison System. *RFID Journal*.

Rogan, J., & Chen, D. (2004). Remote sensing technology for mapping and monitoring land-cover and land-use change. *Progress in Planning, 61*(4), 301–325. doi:10.1016/S0305-9006(03)00066-7

Roman, R., Lopez, J., & Mambo, M. (2018). Mobile edge computing, Fog et al.: A survey and analysis of security threats and challenges. *Future Generation Computer Systems, 78*(3), 680–698. doi:10.1016/j.future.2016.11.009

Roman, R., Zhou, J., & Lopez, J. (2013). On the features and challenges of security and privacy in distributed internet of things. *Computer Networks, 57*(10), 2266–2279. doi:10.1016/j.comnet.2012.12.018

ROS.org. (n.d.). *Powering the world's robots*. Retrieved June 30, 2018, from http://www.ros.org/

Rose, K., Eldridge, S., & Chapin, L. (2015). *The Internet of Things: An Overview Understanding the Issues and Challenges of a More Connected World*. ISOC.

Russell, S. J., & Norvig, P. (1995). *Artificial Intelligence a Modern Approach*. Prentice Hall.

S., & G. (2016). Motion Detection Using IoT and Embedded System Concepts. *International Journal of Advanced Research in Electrical, Electronics and Instrumentation, 5*(10).

Sabbaghi, A., & Ganesh, V. (2008). Effectiveness and Efficiency of RFID Technology in Supply Chain Management: Strategic Values and Challenges. *Journal of Theoretical and Applied Electronic Commerce Research, 3*(2), 71–81. doi:10.4067/S0718-18762008000100007

Said, O., & Masud, M. (2013). Towards internet of things: Survey and future vision. *International Journal of Computer Networks, 5*(1), 1–17.

Salibian, A., & Scholz, T. (2011). Smartphones in Surgery. *Journal of Healthcare Engineering, 2*(4), 473–486. doi:10.1260/2040-2295.2.4.473

Santesteban, L. G., Guillaume, S., Royo, J. B., & Tisseyre, B. (2013). Are precision agriculture tools and methods relevant at the whole-vineyard scale? *Precision Agriculture, 14*(1), 2–17. doi:10.100711119-012-9268-3

Saputro, N., Akkaya, K., & Uludag, S. (2012). A survey of routing protocols for smart grid communications. *Computer Networks*, *56*(11), 2742–2771. doi:10.1016/j.comnet.2012.03.027

Satpute, P., & Tembhurne, O. (2014). A review of: Cloud centric IoT based framework for supply chain management in precision agriculture. *International Journal of Advance Research in Computer Science and Management Studies*, *2*(11), 14–23.

Savale, O., Managave, A., Ambekar, D., & Sathe, S. (2015). *Internet of Things in Precision Agriculture using Wireless Sensor Networks Introduction: Literature Survey*. Academic Press.

Sawant, S. A., Adinarayana, J., & Durbha, S. S. (2014, July). KrishiSense: A semantically aware web enabled wireless sensor network system for precision agriculture applications. In *2014 IEEE Geoscience and Remote Sensing Symposium* (pp. 4090-4093). IEEE. 10.1109/IGARSS.2014.6947385

Schaffers, H., Komninos, N., Pallot, M., Trousse, B., Nilsson, M., & Oliveira, A. (2011). Smart cities and the future internet: Towards cooperation frameworks for open innovation. Lecture Notes in Computer Science, 6656, 431–446. doi:10.1007/978-3-642-20898-0_31

Sensor-embedded wristband uses sweat to monitor wearer's health. (2016). *Physics Today*. doi:10.1063/pt.5.029532

Serrano, M., Barnaghi, P., Carrez, F., Cousin, P., Vermesan, O., & Friess, P. (2015). Internet of Things Semantic Interoperability: Research Challenges, Best Practices, Recommendations and Next Steps. In European research cluster on the internet of things. IERC.

Sethi, P., & Sarangi, S. R. (2017). Internet of Things: Architectures, Protocols, and Applications. *Journal of Electrical and Computer Engineering*, *2017*, 1–25. doi:10.1155/2017/9324035

Shah, Omar, & Khurram. (2007). Automated Visual Surveillance in realistic Scenarios. *IEEE Computer Society*.

Shaik & D. (2016). IoT based Smart Home Security System with Alert and Door Access Control using Smart Phone. *International Journal of Engineering Research & Technology*, *5*(12).

Shamshiri, R., & Ismail, W. I. W. (2013). Exploring gps data for operational analysis of farm machinery. *Research Journal of Applied Sciences, Engineering and Technology*, 5(12), 3281–3286. doi:10.19026/rjaset.5.4568

Sharma & Sarma. (2016). Soft-Computational Techniques and Spectro-Temporal Features for Telephonic Speech Recognition: An Overview and Review of Current State of the Art. Handbook of Research on Advanced Hybrid Intelligent Techniques and Applications.

Sharma & Tiwari. (2016). A review paper on "IOT" & It's Smart Applications. *International Journal of Science, Engineering and Technology Research*, 5(2).

Shelbyand, Z., & Bormann, C. (2009). *6LoWPAN: The Wireless Embedded Internet*. Wiley. doi:10.1002/9780470686218

Sherly, J., & Somasundareswari, D. (2015). Internet of things based smart transportation systems. *International Research Journal of Engineering and Technology*, 2(7), 1207–1210.

Shi, C., Liu, J., Liu, H., & Chen, Y. (2017). Smart user authentication through actuation of daily activities leveraging WiFi-enabled IoT. *ACM Int Symposium on Mobile Ad Hoc Networking and Computing*, 1–10. 10.1145/3084041.3084061

Shukla, R., Gupta, R. K., & Kashyap, R. (2019). A multiphase pre-copy strategy for the virtual machine migration in cloud. In S. Satapathy, V. Bhateja, & S. Das (Eds.), *Smart Intelligent Computing and Applications. Smart Innovation, Systems and Technologies* (Vol. 104). Singapore: Springer.

Sicari, S., Rizzardi, A., Grieco, L. A., & Coen-Porisini, A. (2014). Security, privacy and trust in Internet of Things: The road ahead. *Computer Networks*, 76, 146–164. doi:10.1016/j.comnet.2014.11.008

Silva, C. B., de Moraes, M. A. F. D., & Molin, J. P. (2011). Adoption and use of precision agriculture technologies in the sugarcane industry of São Paulo state, Brazil. *Precision Agriculture*, 12(1), 67–81. doi:10.100711119-009-9155-8

Singh & Verma. (2012). Tracking of Moving object in Video scene using Neural Network. *International Journal of Advanced Research in Computer Engineering & Technology*, 1(10), 2278–1323.

Singh, D., Tripathi, G., & Jara, A. J. (2014, March). A survey of Internet-of-Things: Future vision, architecture, challenges and services. In *2014 IEEE World Forum on Internet of Things (WF-IoT)* (pp. 287-292). IEEE.

Singh, D., & Mandal, S. (2010). Moving Object Tracking Using Object Segmentation. *International Conference on Advances in Information and Communication Technologies ICT 2010: Information and Communication Technologies*, 691-694.

Singh, M., & Mittal, A. (2016). Internet of Things: Challenges in Web Based Remote Patient Monitoring (RPM). *Scholars Journal Of Applied Medical Sciences*, 4(7), 2706–2709. doi:10.21276jams.2016.4.7.84

Sinha, A., Kumar, P., Rana, N., Islam, R., & Dwivedi, Y. (2017). Impact of internet of things (IoT) in disaster management: A task-technology fit perspective. *Annals of Operations Research*, 1–36.

Siryani, J., Tanju, B., & Eveleigh, T. (2017). A Machine Learning Decision-Support System Improves the Internet of Things' Smart Meter Operations. *IEEE Internet Of Things Journal*, 4(4), 1056–1066. doi:10.1109/JIOT.2017.2722358

Slama, D., Puhlmann, F., Morrish, J., & Bhatnagar, R. (2015). Enterprise IoT. Strategies and best practices for connected products and services. Sebastopol, CA: O'Reilly Media.

Standaert, F. X., Piret, G., Gershenfeld, N., & Quisquater, J. J. (2006). SEA: A scalable encryption algorithm for small embedded applications. In *International Conference on Smart Card Research and Advanced Applications* (pp. 222-236). Berlin: Springer. 10.1007/11733447_16

Stauffer & Grimson. (1999). Adaptive background mixture models for real-time tracking. *Proc. IEEE Conf. CVPR*, 2246–2252.

Stočes, M., Vaněk, J., Masner, J., & Pavlík, J. (2016). Internet of things (iot) in agriculture-selected aspects. *Agris on-line Papers in Economics and Informatics, 8*, 83.

Stockman, H. (1948). Communication by Means of Reflected Power. *Proceedings of the Institute of Radio Engineers*.

Stojkoska, B. L. R., & Trivodaliev, K. V. (2017). A review of Internet of Things for smart home: Challenges and solutions. *Journal of Cleaner Production, 140,* 1454–1464. doi:10.1016/j.jclepro.2016.10.006

Sumit, S. H., & Akhter, S. (2018). C-means clustering and deep-neuro-fuzzy classification for road weight measurement in traffic management system. Soft Computing [Internet]. Springer Nature; 2018 Feb 21; Available from: http://dx.doi.org/10.1007/s00500-018-3086-0.

Sundmaeker, H., Verdouw, C., Wolfert, S., & Pérez Freire, L. (2016). Internet of food and farm 2020. Digitising the Industry-Internet of Things connecting physical, digital and virtual worlds, 129-151.

Sun, Z., Zhao, T., & Che, N. (2009). Design of electric power monitoring system based on ZigBee and GPRS. In *1st International Symposium on Computer Network and Multimedia Technology (CNMT 2009).* IEEE Press. 10.1109/CNMT.2009.5374624

Suresh Kumar, S. S., & Kumar, S. (2017). *A Framework for predicting the performance of IoT protocols, a Use Case based approach.* Academic Press. doi:10.1109/SmartTechCon.2017.8358437

Tai, J., Tseng, S., Lin, C., & Song, K. (2004). Real-time image tracking for automatic traffic monitoring and enforcement applications. *Image and Vision Computing, 22*(6), 485–501. doi:10.1016/j.imavis.2003.12.001

Takahashi, M., Kawai, Y., Fujii, M., Shibata, M., Babaguchi, N., & Satoh, S. (2009). *NHK STRL at TRECVID 2009: Surveillance Event Detection and High-Level Feature Extraction* (Vol. 17). TRECVID.

Te Lindert, B., & Van Someren, E. (2013). Affordable sleep estimates using micro-electro-mechanical-systems (MEMS) accelerometry. *Sleep Medicine, 14,* e294–e295. doi:10.1016/j.sleep.2013.11.721

Tendulkar, N., Sonawane, K., Vakte, D., Pujari, D., & Dhomase, G. (2016). A review of traffic management system using IoT. *International Journal of Modern Trends in Engineering and Research,* 247-249.

Tennenhouse, D. (2001). Proactive computing. *Communications of the ACM, 43*(5), 43–50. doi:10.1145/332833.332837

Teschioni, Oberti, & Regazzoni. (1991). *A Neural-Network Approach for Moving Objects Recognition in Color Image Sequences for Surveillance Applications.* Academic Press.

Thingom, I. (2015). Internet of Things: design of a new layered architecture and study of some exisiting issues. *IOSR Journal of Computer Engineering*, 26-30.

Tiwari, S., Gupta, R. K., & Kashyap, R. (2019). To enhance web response time using agglomerative clustering technique for web navigation recommendation. In H. Behera, J. Nayak, B. Naik, & A. Abraham (Eds.), *Computational Intelligence in Data Mining. Advances in Intelligent Systems and Computing* (Vol. 711). Singapore: Springer.

TongKe, F. (2013). Smart agriculture based on cloud computing and IOT. *Journal of Convergence Information Technology*, 8(2).

Tsui, S., Liu, C., & Lin, C. (2017). Modified maternal ECG cancellation for portable fetal heart rate monitor. *Biomedical Signal Processing and Control*, *32*, 76–81. doi:10.1016/j.bspc.2016.11.001

Turaga & Chellappa. (2008). Machine Recognition of Human Activities. *Survey (London, England)*.

Tuscano, L., & Machado, R. (2013). Smart Web Cam Detection Surveillance System. *International Journal of Modern Engineering Research*, *3*(2), 1169-1171.

U.S. Department of Energy. (2009). *Smart Grid System Report*. Author.

Umetani, T., Ishii, M., Tamura, Y., & Saiwaki, N. (2018). Change Detection of Sleeping Conditions based on Multipoint Ambient Sensing of Comforter on Bed. *40th Annual International Conference of the IEEE Engineering in Medicine and Biology Society (EMBC)*, 4997 - 5001. 10.1109/EMBC.2018.8513477

Valera & Velastin. (2004). Intelligent distributed surveillance systems: a review. *Intelligent Distributed Surveillance Systems, IEEE Proceedings*. doi: 10.1049/ip-vis:20041147

Vasisht, D., Kapetanovic, Z., Won, J., Jin, X., Chandra, R., Sinha, S., . . . Stratman, S. (2017). Farmbeats: An iot platform for data-driven agriculture. In *14th USENIX Symposium on Networked Systems Design and Implementation* (pp. 515-529). USENIX.

Venkatraman, S. (2010). Self-Learning framework for intrusion detection. *International Congress on Computer Applications and Computational Science (CACS)*.

Venkatraman, S. (2017). Autonomic Framework for IT Security Governance. *International Journal of Managing Information Technology, 9*(3), 1–14. doi:10.5121/ijmit.2017.9301

Venkatraman, S., & Alazab, M. (2017). Classification of Malware Using Visualisation of Similarity Matrices, IEEE Xplore. *Cybersecurity and Cyberforensics Conference,* 21-23.

Vermesan, O., & Friess, P. (2014). Internet of Things Strategic Research and Innovation Agenda. In O. Vermesan & P. Friess (Eds.), *Internet of Things–From Research and Innovation to Market Deployment* (pp. 7–122). River Publishers Series in Communications.

Vukovic, M. (2015). Internet Programmable IoT: On the role of APIs in IoT. *Ubiquity, 2015*(November), 1–10. doi:10.1145/2822873

Wemple, M., & Luks, A. (2012). Challenges Associated With Central Venous Catheter Placement and Central Venous Oxygen Saturation Monitoring. *Respiratory Care*. doi:10.4187/respcare.01762 PMID:22613046

What is Cloud Computing? (2017). Retrieved from https://azure.microsoft.com/en-in/overview/what-is-cloud-computing/

What is iaas? (2017). Retrieved from https://azure.microsoft.com/en-us/overview/what-is-iaas/

Xiao, L., Li, Y., Han, G., Liu, G. & Zhuang, W. (2016). PHY-layer spoofing detection with reinforcement learning in wireless networks. *IEEE Trans. Vehicular Technology, 65*(12), 10037–10047.

Xiaojun, Y., Weirui, W., & Jianping, L. (2012). Application mode construction of internet of things (IOT) for facility agriculture in Beijing. *Nongye Gongcheng Xuebao (Beijing), 2012*(4).

Xiao, L., Li, Y., Huang, X., & Du, X. J. (2017). Cloud-based malware detection game for mobile devices with offloading. *IEEE Transactions on Mobile Computing, 16*(10), 2742–2750. doi:10.1109/TMC.2017.2687918

Xu, Y., Cui, W., & Peinado, M. (2015). Controlled-channel attacks: Deterministic side channels for untrusted operating systems. In *IEEE Symposium on Security and Privacy*. IEEE.

Xu, Z., Xue, Y., & Wong, K. (2014). Recent Advancements on Smart Grids in China. *Electric Power Components and Systems, 42*(3-4), 251–261. doi:10.1080/1 5325008.2013.862327

Yaghmaee Moghaddam, M., & Leon-Garcia, A. (2018). A Fog-Based Internet of Energy Architecture for Transactive Energy Management Systems. *IEEE Internet Of Things Journal, 5*(2), 1055–1069. doi:10.1109/JIOT.2018.2805899

Yan, C., Xie, H., Yang, D., Yin, Y., & Zhang, Q. (2017). Supervised hash coding with deep neural network for environment perception of intelligent vehicles. *IEEE Transactions on Intelligent Transportation Systems*, 1–12.

Yan-e, D. (2011, March). Design of intelligent agriculture management information system based on IoT. In *2011 Fourth International Conference on Intelligent Computation Technology and Automation* (Vol. 1, pp. 1045-1049). IEEE. 10.1109/ ICICTA.2011.262

Yan, Z., Zhang, P., & Vasilakos, A. V. (2014). A survey on trust management for Internet of Things. *Journal of Network and Computer Applications, 42*(3), 120–134. doi:10.1016/j.jnca.2014.01.014

Ye, J., Chen, B., Liu, Q., & Fang, Y. (2013, June). A precision agriculture management system based on Internet of Things and WebGIS. In *2013 21st International Conference on Geoinformatics* (pp. 1-5). IEEE. 10.1109/Geoinformatics.2013.6626173

Yokoi, K., & Watanabe. (2009). Surveillance Event Detection Task. *TRECVID, 17*.

Yong, H., Pengcheng, N., & Fei, L. (2013). Advancement and trend of internet of things in agriculture and sensing instrument. *Nongye Jixie Xuebao, 44*(10), 216–226.

Yu, Liu, & Li. (2011). Review of Intelligent Video Surveillance Technology Research. *International Conference on Electronic & Mechanical Engineering and Information Technology*.

Yu, X., Sun, F., & Cheng, X. (2012). Intelligent urban traffic management system based on cloud computing and internet of things. *2012 International Conference on Computer Science and Service System, 31*(2), 2169-2172. 10.1109/CSSS.2012.539

Zacepins, A., & Karasha, T. (2013, May). Application of temperature measurements for the bee colony monitoring: a review. In *Proceedings of the 12th International Scientific Conference "Engineering for Rural Development* (pp. 126-131). Academic Press.

Zhang, W., Bao, Z., Lin, D., Rijmen, V., & Yang, B. (2014). RECTANGLE: A bit-slice ultra-lightweight block cipher suitable for multiple platforms. *Cryptology ePrint Archive*. Retrieved from https://eprint.iacr.org/2014/084.pdf

Zhang, C., & Kovacs, J. M. (2012). The application of small unmanned aerial systems for precision agriculture: A review. *Precision Agriculture, 13*(6), 693–712. doi:10.100711119-012-9274-5

Zhang, T., Ghanem, B., Liu, S., & Ahuja, N. (2013). Robust visual tracking vis structured multi-task spare learning. *International Journal of Computer Vision, 101*(2), 367–383. doi:10.100711263-012-0582-z

Zhao, J. C., Zhang, J. F., Feng, Y., & Guo, J. X. (2010, July). The study and application of the IOT technology in agriculture. In *2010 3rd International Conference on Computer Science and Information Technology* (Vol. 2, pp. 462-465). IEEE.

Zhao, G., Barnard, M., & Pietikainen, M. (2009). Lipreading with local spatial temporal descriptor. *IEEE Transactions on Multimedia, 11*(7), 1254–1265. doi:10.1109/TMM.2009.2030637

Zhao, T., & Nevatia, R. (2004). Tracking Multiple Humans in Crowed Environment. *IEEE Computer Society Conference on Computer Vision and Pattern Recognition (CVPR'04)*, 2, 406.

Zhao, Y., Gong, H., Lin, L., & Jia, Y. (2008). *Spatio-temporal patches for night background modeling by subspace learning*. IEEE ICPR.

Zhong, W., Lu, H., & Yang, M. (2012). Robust Object Tracking via Sparsity-based Collaborative Model. *IEEE International Conference on Computer Vision and Pattern Recognition*. 10.1109/CVPR.2012.6247882

Zhou, H., Yuan, Y., & Shi, C. (2009). Object tracking using SIFT features and mean shift. *Computer Vision and Image Understanding, 113*(3), 345–352. doi:10.1016/j.cviu.2008.08.006

Zhou, J., Cao, Z., Dong, X., & Vasilakos, A. V. (2017). Security and privacy for cloud-based IoT: Challenges. *IEEE Communications Magazine, 55*(1), 26–33. doi:10.1109/MCOM.2017.1600363CM

Zhou, W., & Piramuthu, S. (2017). IoT security perspective of a flexible healthcare supply chain. *Information Technology Management*. doi:10.100710799-017-0279-7

Zhu, Z., Xu, G., Yang, B., Shi, D., & Lin, X. (2000). Visatram: a real-time vision system for automatic traffic monitoring. *Image and Vision Computing*, *18*(10), 781-794.

Zollmann, J. (2012). NOSQL Databases. *NoSQL Archive*, 149. Retrieved from http://nosql-database.org/

Related References

To continue our tradition of advancing information science and technology research, we have compiled a list of recommended IGI Global readings. These references will provide additional information and guidance to further enrich your knowledge and assist you with your own research and future publications.

Aasi, P., Rusu, L., & Vieru, D. (2017). The Role of Culture in IT Governance Five Focus Areas: A Literature Review. *International Journal of IT/Business Alignment and Governance, 8*(2), 42-61. doi:10.4018/IJITBAG.2017070103

Abdrabo, A. A. (2018). Egypt's Knowledge-Based Development: Opportunities, Challenges, and Future Possibilities. In A. Alraouf (Ed.), *Knowledge-Based Urban Development in the Middle East* (pp. 80–101). Hershey, PA: IGI Global. doi:10.4018/978-1-5225-3734-2.ch005

Abu Doush, I., & Alhami, I. (2018). Evaluating the Accessibility of Computer Laboratories, Libraries, and Websites in Jordanian Universities and Colleges. *International Journal of Information Systems and Social Change, 9*(2), 44–60. doi:10.4018/IJISSC.2018040104

Adeboye, A. (2016). Perceived Use and Acceptance of Cloud Enterprise Resource Planning (ERP) Implementation in the Manufacturing Industries. *International Journal of Strategic Information Technology and Applications, 7*(3), 24–40. doi:10.4018/IJSITA.2016070102

Adegbore, A. M., Quadri, M. O., & Oyewo, O. R. (2018). A Theoretical Approach to the Adoption of Electronic Resource Management Systems (ERMS) in Nigerian University Libraries. In A. Tella & T. Kwanya (Eds.), *Handbook of Research on Managing Intellectual Property in Digital Libraries* (pp. 292–311). Hershey, PA: IGI Global. doi:10.4018/978-1-5225-3093-0.ch015

Adhikari, M., & Roy, D. (2016). Green Computing. In G. Deka, G. Siddesh, K. Srinivasa, & L. Patnaik (Eds.), *Emerging Research Surrounding Power Consumption and Performance Issues in Utility Computing* (pp. 84–108). Hershey, PA: IGI Global. doi:10.4018/978-1-4666-8853-7.ch005

Afolabi, O. A. (2018). Myths and Challenges of Building an Effective Digital Library in Developing Nations: An African Perspective. In A. Tella & T. Kwanya (Eds.), *Handbook of Research on Managing Intellectual Property in Digital Libraries* (pp. 51–79). Hershey, PA: IGI Global. doi:10.4018/978-1-5225-3093-0.ch004

Agarwal, R., Singh, A., & Sen, S. (2016). Role of Molecular Docking in Computer-Aided Drug Design and Development. In S. Dastmalchi, M. Hamzeh-Mivehroud, & B. Sokouti (Eds.), *Applied Case Studies and Solutions in Molecular Docking-Based Drug Design* (pp. 1–28). Hershey, PA: IGI Global. doi:10.4018/978-1-5225-0362-0.ch001

Ali, O., & Soar, J. (2016). Technology Innovation Adoption Theories. In L. Al-Hakim, X. Wu, A. Koronios, & Y. Shou (Eds.), *Handbook of Research on Driving Competitive Advantage through Sustainable, Lean, and Disruptive Innovation* (pp. 1–38). Hershey, PA: IGI Global. doi:10.4018/978-1-5225-0135-0.ch001

Alsharo, M. (2017). Attitudes Towards Cloud Computing Adoption in Emerging Economies. *International Journal of Cloud Applications and Computing*, *7*(3), 44–58. doi:10.4018/IJCAC.2017070102

Amer, T. S., & Johnson, T. L. (2016). Information Technology Progress Indicators: Temporal Expectancy, User Preference, and the Perception of Process Duration. *International Journal of Technology and Human Interaction*, *12*(4), 1–14. doi:10.4018/IJTHI.2016100101

Amer, T. S., & Johnson, T. L. (2017). Information Technology Progress Indicators: Research Employing Psychological Frameworks. In A. Mesquita (Ed.), *Research Paradigms and Contemporary Perspectives on Human-Technology Interaction* (pp. 168–186). Hershey, PA: IGI Global. doi:10.4018/978-1-5225-1868-6.ch008

Anchugam, C. V., & Thangadurai, K. (2016). Introduction to Network Security. In D. G., M. Singh, & M. Jayanthi (Eds.), Network Security Attacks and Countermeasures (pp. 1-48). Hershey, PA: IGI Global. doi:10.4018/978-1-4666-8761-5.ch001

Anchugam, C. V., & Thangadurai, K. (2016). Classification of Network Attacks and Countermeasures of Different Attacks. In D. G., M. Singh, & M. Jayanthi (Eds.), Network Security Attacks and Countermeasures (pp. 115-156). Hershey, PA: IGI Global. doi:10.4018/978-1-4666-8761-5.ch004

Anohah, E. (2016). Pedagogy and Design of Online Learning Environment in Computer Science Education for High Schools. *International Journal of Online Pedagogy and Course Design*, 6(3), 39–51. doi:10.4018/IJOPCD.2016070104

Anohah, E. (2017). Paradigm and Architecture of Computing Augmented Learning Management System for Computer Science Education. *International Journal of Online Pedagogy and Course Design*, 7(2), 60–70. doi:10.4018/IJOPCD.2017040105

Anohah, E., & Suhonen, J. (2017). Trends of Mobile Learning in Computing Education from 2006 to 2014: A Systematic Review of Research Publications. *International Journal of Mobile and Blended Learning*, 9(1), 16–33. doi:10.4018/IJMBL.2017010102

Assis-Hassid, S., Heart, T., Reychav, I., & Pliskin, J. S. (2016). Modelling Factors Affecting Patient-Doctor-Computer Communication in Primary Care. *International Journal of Reliable and Quality E-Healthcare*, 5(1), 1–17. doi:10.4018/IJRQEH.2016010101

Bailey, E. K. (2017). Applying Learning Theories to Computer Technology Supported Instruction. In M. Grassetti & S. Brookby (Eds.), *Advancing Next-Generation Teacher Education through Digital Tools and Applications* (pp. 61–81). Hershey, PA: IGI Global. doi:10.4018/978-1-5225-0965-3.ch004

Balasubramanian, K. (2016). Attacks on Online Banking and Commerce. In K. Balasubramanian, K. Mala, & M. Rajakani (Eds.), *Cryptographic Solutions for Secure Online Banking and Commerce* (pp. 1–19). Hershey, PA: IGI Global. doi:10.4018/978-1-5225-0273-9.ch001

Baldwin, S., Opoku-Agyemang, K., & Roy, D. (2016). Games People Play: A Trilateral Collaboration Researching Computer Gaming across Cultures. In K. Valentine & L. Jensen (Eds.), *Examining the Evolution of Gaming and Its Impact on Social, Cultural, and Political Perspectives* (pp. 364–376). Hershey, PA: IGI Global. doi:10.4018/978-1-5225-0261-6.ch017

Banerjee, S., Sing, T. Y., Chowdhury, A. R., & Anwar, H. (2018). Let's Go Green: Towards a Taxonomy of Green Computing Enablers for Business Sustainability. In M. Khosrow-Pour (Ed.), *Green Computing Strategies for Competitive Advantage and Business Sustainability* (pp. 89–109). Hershey, PA: IGI Global. doi:10.4018/978-1-5225-5017-4.ch005

Basham, R. (2018). Information Science and Technology in Crisis Response and Management. In M. Khosrow-Pour, D.B.A. (Ed.), Encyclopedia of Information Science and Technology, Fourth Edition (pp. 1407-1418). Hershey, PA: IGI Global. doi:10.4018/978-1-5225-2255-3.ch121

Batyashe, T., & Iyamu, T. (2018). Architectural Framework for the Implementation of Information Technology Governance in Organisations. In M. Khosrow-Pour, D.B.A. (Ed.), Encyclopedia of Information Science and Technology, Fourth Edition (pp. 810-819). Hershey, PA: IGI Global. doi:10.4018/978-1-5225-2255-3.ch070

Bekleyen, N., & Çelik, S. (2017). Attitudes of Adult EFL Learners towards Preparing for a Language Test via CALL. In D. Tafazoli & M. Romero (Eds.), *Multiculturalism and Technology-Enhanced Language Learning* (pp. 214–229). Hershey, PA: IGI Global. doi:10.4018/978-1-5225-1882-2.ch013

Bennett, A., Eglash, R., Lachney, M., & Babbitt, W. (2016). Design Agency: Diversifying Computer Science at the Intersections of Creativity and Culture. In M. Raisinghani (Ed.), *Revolutionizing Education through Web-Based Instruction* (pp. 35–56). Hershey, PA: IGI Global. doi:10.4018/978-1-4666-9932-8.ch003

Bergeron, F., Croteau, A., Uwizeyemungu, S., & Raymond, L. (2017). A Framework for Research on Information Technology Governance in SMEs. In S. De Haes & W. Van Grembergen (Eds.), *Strategic IT Governance and Alignment in Business Settings* (pp. 53–81). Hershey, PA: IGI Global. doi:10.4018/978-1-5225-0861-8.ch003

Bhatt, G. D., Wang, Z., & Rodger, J. A. (2017). Information Systems Capabilities and Their Effects on Competitive Advantages: A Study of Chinese Companies. *Information Resources Management Journal*, *30*(3), 41–57. doi:10.4018/IRMJ.2017070103

Bogdanoski, M., Stoilkovski, M., & Risteski, A. (2016). Novel First Responder Digital Forensics Tool as a Support to Law Enforcement. In M. Hadji-Janev & M. Bogdanoski (Eds.), *Handbook of Research on Civil Society and National Security in the Era of Cyber Warfare* (pp. 352–376). Hershey, PA: IGI Global. doi:10.4018/978-1-4666-8793-6.ch016

Boontarig, W., Papasratorn, B., & Chutimaskul, W. (2016). The Unified Model for Acceptance and Use of Health Information on Online Social Networks: Evidence from Thailand. *International Journal of E-Health and Medical Communications*, *7*(1), 31–47. doi:10.4018/IJEHMC.2016010102

Brown, S., & Yuan, X. (2016). Techniques for Retaining Computer Science Students at Historical Black Colleges and Universities. In C. Prince & R. Ford (Eds.), *Setting a New Agenda for Student Engagement and Retention in Historically Black Colleges and Universities* (pp. 251–268). Hershey, PA: IGI Global. doi:10.4018/978-1-5225-0308-8.ch014

Burcoff, A., & Shamir, L. (2017). Computer Analysis of Pablo Picasso's Artistic Style. *International Journal of Art, Culture and Design Technologies*, *6*(1), 1–18. doi:10.4018/IJACDT.2017010101

Related References

Byker, E. J. (2017). I Play I Learn: Introducing Technological Play Theory. In C. Martin & D. Polly (Eds.), *Handbook of Research on Teacher Education and Professional Development* (pp. 297–306). Hershey, PA: IGI Global. doi:10.4018/978-1-5225-1067-3.ch016

Calongne, C. M., Stricker, A. G., Truman, B., & Arenas, F. J. (2017). Cognitive Apprenticeship and Computer Science Education in Cyberspace: Reimagining the Past. In A. Stricker, C. Calongne, B. Truman, & F. Arenas (Eds.), *Integrating an Awareness of Selfhood and Society into Virtual Learning* (pp. 180–197). Hershey, PA: IGI Global. doi:10.4018/978-1-5225-2182-2.ch013

Carlton, E. L., Holsinger, J. W. Jr, & Anunobi, N. (2016). Physician Engagement with Health Information Technology: Implications for Practice and Professionalism. *International Journal of Computers in Clinical Practice, 1*(2), 51–73. doi:10.4018/IJCCP.2016070103

Carneiro, A. D. (2017). Defending Information Networks in Cyberspace: Some Notes on Security Needs. In M. Dawson, D. Kisku, P. Gupta, J. Sing, & W. Li (Eds.), Developing Next-Generation Countermeasures for Homeland Security Threat Prevention (pp. 354-375). Hershey, PA: IGI Global. doi:10.4018/978-1-5225-0703-1.ch016

Cavalcanti, J. C. (2016). The New "ABC" of ICTs (Analytics + Big Data + Cloud Computing): A Complex Trade-Off between IT and CT Costs. In J. Martins & A. Molnar (Eds.), *Handbook of Research on Innovations in Information Retrieval, Analysis, and Management* (pp. 152–186). Hershey, PA: IGI Global. doi:10.4018/978-1-4666-8833-9.ch006

Chase, J. P., & Yan, Z. (2017). Affect in Statistics Cognition. In *Assessing and Measuring Statistics Cognition in Higher Education Online Environments: Emerging Research and Opportunities* (pp. 144–187). Hershey, PA: IGI Global. doi:10.4018/978-1-5225-2420-5.ch005

Chen, C. (2016). Effective Learning Strategies for the 21st Century: Implications for the E-Learning. In M. Anderson & C. Gavan (Eds.), *Developing Effective Educational Experiences through Learning Analytics* (pp. 143–169). Hershey, PA: IGI Global. doi:10.4018/978-1-4666-9983-0.ch006

Chen, E. T. (2016). Examining the Influence of Information Technology on Modern Health Care. In P. Manolitzas, E. Grigoroudis, N. Matsatsinis, & D. Yannacopoulos (Eds.), *Effective Methods for Modern Healthcare Service Quality and Evaluation* (pp. 110–136). Hershey, PA: IGI Global. doi:10.4018/978-1-4666-9961-8.ch006

Cimermanova, I. (2017). Computer-Assisted Learning in Slovakia. In D. Tafazoli & M. Romero (Eds.), *Multiculturalism and Technology-Enhanced Language Learning* (pp. 252–270). Hershey, PA: IGI Global. doi:10.4018/978-1-5225-1882-2.ch015

Cipolla-Ficarra, F. V., & Cipolla-Ficarra, M. (2018). Computer Animation for Ingenious Revival. In F. Cipolla-Ficarra, M. Ficarra, M. Cipolla-Ficarra, A. Quiroga, J. Alma, & J. Carré (Eds.), *Technology-Enhanced Human Interaction in Modern Society* (pp. 159–181). Hershey, PA: IGI Global. doi:10.4018/978-1-5225-3437-2. ch008

Cockrell, S., Damron, T. S., Melton, A. M., & Smith, A. D. (2018). Offshoring IT. In M. Khosrow-Pour, D.B.A. (Ed.), Encyclopedia of Information Science and Technology, Fourth Edition (pp. 5476-5489). Hershey, PA: IGI Global. doi:10.4018/978-1-5225-2255-3.ch476

Coffey, J. W. (2018). Logic and Proof in Computer Science: Categories and Limits of Proof Techniques. In J. Horne (Ed.), *Philosophical Perceptions on Logic and Order* (pp. 218–240). Hershey, PA: IGI Global. doi:10.4018/978-1-5225-2443-4.ch007

Dale, M. (2017). Re-Thinking the Challenges of Enterprise Architecture Implementation. In M. Tavana (Ed.), *Enterprise Information Systems and the Digitalization of Business Functions* (pp. 205–221). Hershey, PA: IGI Global. doi:10.4018/978-1-5225-2382-6.ch009

Das, A., Dasgupta, R., & Bagchi, A. (2016). Overview of Cellular Comnputing-Basic Principles and Applications. In J. Mandal, S. Mukhopadhyay, & T. Pal (Eds.), *Handbook of Research on Natural Computing for Optimization Problems* (pp. 637–662). Hershey, PA: IGI Global. doi:10.4018/978-1-5225-0058-2.ch026

De Maere, K., De Haes, S., & von Kutzschenbach, M. (2017). CIO Perspectives on Organizational Learning within the Context of IT Governance. *International Journal of IT/Business Alignment and Governance, 8*(1), 32-47. doi:10.4018/IJITBAG.2017010103

Demir, K., Çaka, C., Yaman, N. D., İslamoğlu, H., & Kuzu, A. (2018). Examining the Current Definitions of Computational Thinking. In H. Ozcinar, G. Wong, & H. Ozturk (Eds.), *Teaching Computational Thinking in Primary Education* (pp. 36–64). Hershey, PA: IGI Global. doi:10.4018/978-1-5225-3200-2.ch003

Deng, X., Hung, Y., & Lin, C. D. (2017). Design and Analysis of Computer Experiments. In S. Saha, A. Mandal, A. Narasimhamurthy, S. V, & S. Sangam (Eds.), Handbook of Research on Applied Cybernetics and Systems Science (pp. 264-279). Hershey, PA: IGI Global. doi:10.4018/978-1-5225-2498-4.ch013

Related References

Denner, J., Martinez, J., & Thiry, H. (2017). Strategies for Engaging Hispanic/ Latino Youth in the US in Computer Science. In Y. Rankin & J. Thomas (Eds.), *Moving Students of Color from Consumers to Producers of Technology* (pp. 24–48). Hershey, PA: IGI Global. doi:10.4018/978-1-5225-2005-4.ch002

Devi, A. (2017). Cyber Crime and Cyber Security: A Quick Glance. In R. Kumar, P. Pattnaik, & P. Pandey (Eds.), *Detecting and Mitigating Robotic Cyber Security Risks* (pp. 160–171). Hershey, PA: IGI Global. doi:10.4018/978-1-5225-2154-9.ch011

Dores, A. R., Barbosa, F., Guerreiro, S., Almeida, I., & Carvalho, I. P. (2016). Computer-Based Neuropsychological Rehabilitation: Virtual Reality and Serious Games. In M. Cruz-Cunha, I. Miranda, R. Martinho, & R. Rijo (Eds.), *Encyclopedia of E-Health and Telemedicine* (pp. 473–485). Hershey, PA: IGI Global. doi:10.4018/978-1-4666-9978-6.ch037

Doshi, N., & Schaefer, G. (2016). Computer-Aided Analysis of Nailfold Capillaroscopy Images. In D. Fotiadis (Ed.), *Handbook of Research on Trends in the Diagnosis and Treatment of Chronic Conditions* (pp. 146–158). Hershey, PA: IGI Global. doi:10.4018/978-1-4666-8828-5.ch007

Doyle, D. J., & Fahy, P. J. (2018). Interactivity in Distance Education and Computer-Aided Learning, With Medical Education Examples. In M. Khosrow-Pour, D.B.A. (Ed.), Encyclopedia of Information Science and Technology, Fourth Edition (pp. 5829-5840). Hershey, PA: IGI Global. doi:10.4018/978-1-5225-2255-3.ch507

Elias, N. I., & Walker, T. W. (2017). Factors that Contribute to Continued Use of E-Training among Healthcare Professionals. In F. Topor (Ed.), *Handbook of Research on Individualism and Identity in the Globalized Digital Age* (pp. 403–429). Hershey, PA: IGI Global. doi:10.4018/978-1-5225-0522-8.ch018

Eloy, S., Dias, M. S., Lopes, P. F., & Vilar, E. (2016). Digital Technologies in Architecture and Engineering: Exploring an Engaged Interaction within Curricula. In D. Fonseca & E. Redondo (Eds.), *Handbook of Research on Applied E-Learning in Engineering and Architecture Education* (pp. 368–402). Hershey, PA: IGI Global. doi:10.4018/978-1-4666-8803-2.ch017

Estrela, V. V., Magalhães, H. A., & Saotome, O. (2016). Total Variation Applications in Computer Vision. In N. Kamila (Ed.), *Handbook of Research on Emerging Perspectives in Intelligent Pattern Recognition, Analysis, and Image Processing* (pp. 41–64). Hershey, PA: IGI Global. doi:10.4018/978-1-4666-8654-0.ch002

Filipovic, N., Radovic, M., Nikolic, D. D., Saveljic, I., Milosevic, Z., Exarchos, T. P., ... Parodi, O. (2016). Computer Predictive Model for Plaque Formation and Progression in the Artery. In D. Fotiadis (Ed.), *Handbook of Research on Trends in the Diagnosis and Treatment of Chronic Conditions* (pp. 279–300). Hershey, PA: IGI Global. doi:10.4018/978-1-4666-8828-5.ch013

Fisher, R. L. (2018). Computer-Assisted Indian Matrimonial Services. In M. Khosrow-Pour, D.B.A. (Ed.), Encyclopedia of Information Science and Technology, Fourth Edition (pp. 4136-4145). Hershey, PA: IGI Global. doi:10.4018/978-1-5225-2255-3.ch358

Fleenor, H. G., & Hodhod, R. (2016). Assessment of Learning and Technology: Computer Science Education. In V. Wang (Ed.), *Handbook of Research on Learning Outcomes and Opportunities in the Digital Age* (pp. 51–78). Hershey, PA: IGI Global. doi:10.4018/978-1-4666-9577-1.ch003

García-Valcárcel, A., & Mena, J. (2016). Information Technology as a Way To Support Collaborative Learning: What In-Service Teachers Think, Know and Do. *Journal of Information Technology Research*, *9*(1), 1–17. doi:10.4018/JITR.2016010101

Gardner-McCune, C., & Jimenez, Y. (2017). Historical App Developers: Integrating CS into K-12 through Cross-Disciplinary Projects. In Y. Rankin & J. Thomas (Eds.), *Moving Students of Color from Consumers to Producers of Technology* (pp. 85–112). Hershey, PA: IGI Global. doi:10.4018/978-1-5225-2005-4.ch005

Garvey, G. P. (2016). Exploring Perception, Cognition, and Neural Pathways of Stereo Vision and the Split–Brain Human Computer Interface. In A. Ursyn (Ed.), *Knowledge Visualization and Visual Literacy in Science Education* (pp. 28–76). Hershey, PA: IGI Global. doi:10.4018/978-1-5225-0480-1.ch002

Ghafele, R., & Gibert, B. (2018). Open Growth: The Economic Impact of Open Source Software in the USA. In M. Khosrow-Pour (Ed.), *Optimizing Contemporary Application and Processes in Open Source Software* (pp. 164–197). Hershey, PA: IGI Global. doi:10.4018/978-1-5225-5314-4.ch007

Ghobakhloo, M., & Azar, A. (2018). Information Technology Resources, the Organizational Capability of Lean-Agile Manufacturing, and Business Performance. *Information Resources Management Journal*, *31*(2), 47–74. doi:10.4018/IRMJ.2018040103

Related References

Gianni, M., & Gotzamani, K. (2016). Integrated Management Systems and Information Management Systems: Common Threads. In P. Papajorgji, F. Pinet, A. Guimarães, & J. Papathanasiou (Eds.), *Automated Enterprise Systems for Maximizing Business Performance* (pp. 195–214). Hershey, PA: IGI Global. doi:10.4018/978-1-4666-8841-4.ch011

Gikandi, J. W. (2017). Computer-Supported Collaborative Learning and Assessment: A Strategy for Developing Online Learning Communities in Continuing Education. In J. Keengwe & G. Onchwari (Eds.), *Handbook of Research on Learner-Centered Pedagogy in Teacher Education and Professional Development* (pp. 309–333). Hershey, PA: IGI Global. doi:10.4018/978-1-5225-0892-2.ch017

Gokhale, A. A., & Machina, K. F. (2017). Development of a Scale to Measure Attitudes toward Information Technology. In L. Tomei (Ed.), *Exploring the New Era of Technology-Infused Education* (pp. 49–64). Hershey, PA: IGI Global. doi:10.4018/978-1-5225-1709-2.ch004

Grace, A., O'Donoghue, J., Mahony, C., Heffernan, T., Molony, D., & Carroll, T. (2016). Computerized Decision Support Systems for Multimorbidity Care: An Urgent Call for Research and Development. In M. Cruz-Cunha, I. Miranda, R. Martinho, & R. Rijo (Eds.), *Encyclopedia of E-Health and Telemedicine* (pp. 486–494). Hershey, PA: IGI Global. doi:10.4018/978-1-4666-9978-6.ch038

Gupta, A., & Singh, O. (2016). Computer Aided Modeling and Finite Element Analysis of Human Elbow. *International Journal of Biomedical and Clinical Engineering*, 5(1), 31–38. doi:10.4018/IJBCE.2016010104

H., S. K. (2016). Classification of Cybercrimes and Punishments under the Information Technology Act, 2000. In S. Geetha, & A. Phamila (Eds.), *Combating Security Breaches and Criminal Activity in the Digital Sphere* (pp. 57-66). Hershey, PA: IGI Global. doi:10.4018/978-1-5225-0193-0.ch004

Hafeez-Baig, A., Gururajan, R., & Wickramasinghe, N. (2017). Readiness as a Novel Construct of Readiness Acceptance Model (RAM) for the Wireless Handheld Technology. In N. Wickramasinghe (Ed.), *Handbook of Research on Healthcare Administration and Management* (pp. 578–595). Hershey, PA: IGI Global. doi:10.4018/978-1-5225-0920-2.ch035

Hanafizadeh, P., Ghandchi, S., & Asgarimehr, M. (2017). Impact of Information Technology on Lifestyle: A Literature Review and Classification. *International Journal of Virtual Communities and Social Networking*, 9(2), 1–23. doi:10.4018/IJVCSN.2017040101

Harlow, D. B., Dwyer, H., Hansen, A. K., Hill, C., Iveland, A., Leak, A. E., & Franklin, D. M. (2016). Computer Programming in Elementary and Middle School: Connections across Content. In M. Urban & D. Falvo (Eds.), *Improving K-12 STEM Education Outcomes through Technological Integration* (pp. 337–361). Hershey, PA: IGI Global. doi:10.4018/978-1-4666-9616-7.ch015

Haseski, H. İ., Ilic, U., & Tuğtekin, U. (2018). Computational Thinking in Educational Digital Games: An Assessment Tool Proposal. In H. Ozcinar, G. Wong, & H. Ozturk (Eds.), *Teaching Computational Thinking in Primary Education* (pp. 256–287). Hershey, PA: IGI Global. doi:10.4018/978-1-5225-3200-2.ch013

Hee, W. J., Jalleh, G., Lai, H., & Lin, C. (2017). E-Commerce and IT Projects: Evaluation and Management Issues in Australian and Taiwanese Hospitals. *International Journal of Public Health Management and Ethics*, 2(1), 69–90. doi:10.4018/IJPHME.2017010104

Hernandez, A. A. (2017). Green Information Technology Usage: Awareness and Practices of Philippine IT Professionals. *International Journal of Enterprise Information Systems*, 13(4), 90–103. doi:10.4018/IJEIS.2017100106

Hernandez, A. A., & Ona, S. E. (2016). Green IT Adoption: Lessons from the Philippines Business Process Outsourcing Industry. *International Journal of Social Ecology and Sustainable Development*, 7(1), 1–34. doi:10.4018/IJSESD.2016010101

Hernandez, M. A., Marin, E. C., Garcia-Rodriguez, J., Azorin-Lopez, J., & Cazorla, M. (2017). Automatic Learning Improves Human-Robot Interaction in Productive Environments: A Review. *International Journal of Computer Vision and Image Processing*, 7(3), 65–75. doi:10.4018/IJCVIP.2017070106

Horne-Popp, L. M., Tessone, E. B., & Welker, J. (2018). If You Build It, They Will Come: Creating a Library Statistics Dashboard for Decision-Making. In L. Costello & M. Powers (Eds.), *Developing In-House Digital Tools in Library Spaces* (pp. 177–203). Hershey, PA: IGI Global. doi:10.4018/978-1-5225-2676-6.ch009

Hossan, C. G., & Ryan, J. C. (2016). Factors Affecting e-Government Technology Adoption Behaviour in a Voluntary Environment. *International Journal of Electronic Government Research*, 12(1), 24–49. doi:10.4018/IJEGR.2016010102

Hu, H., Hu, P. J., & Al-Gahtani, S. S. (2017). User Acceptance of Computer Technology at Work in Arabian Culture: A Model Comparison Approach. In M. Khosrow-Pour (Ed.), *Handbook of Research on Technology Adoption, Social Policy, and Global Integration* (pp. 205–228). Hershey, PA: IGI Global. doi:10.4018/978-1-5225-2668-1.ch011

Huie, C. P. (2016). Perceptions of Business Intelligence Professionals about Factors Related to Business Intelligence input in Decision Making. *International Journal of Business Analytics*, *3*(3), 1–24. doi:10.4018/IJBAN.2016070101

Hung, S., Huang, W., Yen, D. C., Chang, S., & Lu, C. (2016). Effect of Information Service Competence and Contextual Factors on the Effectiveness of Strategic Information Systems Planning in Hospitals. *Journal of Global Information Management*, *24*(1), 14–36. doi:10.4018/JGIM.2016010102

Ifinedo, P. (2017). Using an Extended Theory of Planned Behavior to Study Nurses' Adoption of Healthcare Information Systems in Nova Scotia. *International Journal of Technology Diffusion*, *8*(1), 1–17. doi:10.4018/IJTD.2017010101

Ilie, V., & Sneha, S. (2018). A Three Country Study for Understanding Physicians' Engagement With Electronic Information Resources Pre and Post System Implementation. *Journal of Global Information Management*, *26*(2), 48–73. doi:10.4018/JGIM.2018040103

Inoue-Smith, Y. (2017). Perceived Ease in Using Technology Predicts Teacher Candidates' Preferences for Online Resources. *International Journal of Online Pedagogy and Course Design*, *7*(3), 17–28. doi:10.4018/IJOPCD.2017070102

Islam, A. A. (2016). Development and Validation of the Technology Adoption and Gratification (TAG) Model in Higher Education: A Cross-Cultural Study Between Malaysia and China. *International Journal of Technology and Human Interaction*, *12*(3), 78–105. doi:10.4018/IJTHI.2016070106

Islam, A. Y. (2017). Technology Satisfaction in an Academic Context: Moderating Effect of Gender. In A. Mesquita (Ed.), *Research Paradigms and Contemporary Perspectives on Human-Technology Interaction* (pp. 187–211). Hershey, PA: IGI Global. doi:10.4018/978-1-5225-1868-6.ch009

Jamil, G. L., & Jamil, C. C. (2017). Information and Knowledge Management Perspective Contributions for Fashion Studies: Observing Logistics and Supply Chain Management Processes. In G. Jamil, A. Soares, & C. Pessoa (Eds.), *Handbook of Research on Information Management for Effective Logistics and Supply Chains* (pp. 199–221). Hershey, PA: IGI Global. doi:10.4018/978-1-5225-0973-8.ch011

Jamil, G. L., Jamil, L. C., Vieira, A. A., & Xavier, A. J. (2016). Challenges in Modelling Healthcare Services: A Study Case of Information Architecture Perspectives. In G. Jamil, J. Poças Rascão, F. Ribeiro, & A. Malheiro da Silva (Eds.), *Handbook of Research on Information Architecture and Management in Modern Organizations* (pp. 1–23). Hershey, PA: IGI Global. doi:10.4018/978-1-4666-8637-3.ch001

Janakova, M. (2018). Big Data and Simulations for the Solution of Controversies in Small Businesses. In M. Khosrow-Pour, D.B.A. (Ed.), Encyclopedia of Information Science and Technology, Fourth Edition (pp. 6907-6915). Hershey, PA: IGI Global. doi:10.4018/978-1-5225-2255-3.ch598

Jha, D. G. (2016). Preparing for Information Technology Driven Changes. In S. Tiwari & L. Nafees (Eds.), *Innovative Management Education Pedagogies for Preparing Next-Generation Leaders* (pp. 258–274). Hershey, PA: IGI Global. doi:10.4018/978-1-4666-9691-4.ch015

Jhawar, A., & Garg, S. K. (2018). Logistics Improvement by Investment in Information Technology Using System Dynamics. In A. Azar & S. Vaidyanathan (Eds.), *Advances in System Dynamics and Control* (pp. 528–567). Hershey, PA: IGI Global. doi:10.4018/978-1-5225-4077-9.ch017

Kalelioğlu, F., Gülbahar, Y., & Doğan, D. (2018). Teaching How to Think Like a Programmer: Emerging Insights. In H. Ozcinar, G. Wong, & H. Ozturk (Eds.), *Teaching Computational Thinking in Primary Education* (pp. 18–35). Hershey, PA: IGI Global. doi:10.4018/978-1-5225-3200-2.ch002

Kamberi, S. (2017). A Girls-Only Online Virtual World Environment and its Implications for Game-Based Learning. In A. Stricker, C. Calongne, B. Truman, & F. Arenas (Eds.), *Integrating an Awareness of Selfhood and Society into Virtual Learning* (pp. 74–95). Hershey, PA: IGI Global. doi:10.4018/978-1-5225-2182-2.ch006

Kamel, S., & Rizk, N. (2017). ICT Strategy Development: From Design to Implementation – Case of Egypt. In C. Howard & K. Hargiss (Eds.), *Strategic Information Systems and Technologies in Modern Organizations* (pp. 239–257). Hershey, PA: IGI Global. doi:10.4018/978-1-5225-1680-4.ch010

Kamel, S. H. (2018). The Potential Role of the Software Industry in Supporting Economic Development. In M. Khosrow-Pour, D.B.A. (Ed.), Encyclopedia of Information Science and Technology, Fourth Edition (pp. 7259-7269). Hershey, PA: IGI Global. doi:10.4018/978-1-5225-2255-3.ch631

Karon, R. (2016). Utilisation of Health Information Systems for Service Delivery in the Namibian Environment. In T. Iyamu & A. Tatnall (Eds.), *Maximizing Healthcare Delivery and Management through Technology Integration* (pp. 169–183). Hershey, PA: IGI Global. doi:10.4018/978-1-4666-9446-0.ch011

Related References

Kawata, S. (2018). Computer-Assisted Parallel Program Generation. In M. Khosrow-Pour, D.B.A. (Ed.), Encyclopedia of Information Science and Technology, Fourth Edition (pp. 4583-4593). Hershey, PA: IGI Global. doi:10.4018/978-1-5225-2255-3.ch398

Khanam, S., Siddiqui, J., & Talib, F. (2016). A DEMATEL Approach for Prioritizing the TQM Enablers and IT Resources in the Indian ICT Industry. *International Journal of Applied Management Sciences and Engineering, 3*(1), 11–29. doi:10.4018/IJAMSE.2016010102

Khari, M., Shrivastava, G., Gupta, S., & Gupta, R. (2017). Role of Cyber Security in Today's Scenario. In R. Kumar, P. Pattnaik, & P. Pandey (Eds.), *Detecting and Mitigating Robotic Cyber Security Risks* (pp. 177–191). Hershey, PA: IGI Global. doi:10.4018/978-1-5225-2154-9.ch013

Khouja, M., Rodriguez, I. B., Ben Halima, Y., & Moalla, S. (2018). IT Governance in Higher Education Institutions: A Systematic Literature Review. *International Journal of Human Capital and Information Technology Professionals, 9*(2), 52–67. doi:10.4018/IJHCITP.2018040104

Kim, S., Chang, M., Choi, N., Park, J., & Kim, H. (2016). The Direct and Indirect Effects of Computer Uses on Student Success in Math. *International Journal of Cyber Behavior, Psychology and Learning, 6*(3), 48–64. doi:10.4018/IJCBPL.2016070104

Kiourt, C., Pavlidis, G., Koutsoudis, A., & Kalles, D. (2017). Realistic Simulation of Cultural Heritage. *International Journal of Computational Methods in Heritage Science, 1*(1), 10–40. doi:10.4018/IJCMHS.2017010102

Korikov, A., & Krivtsov, O. (2016). System of People-Computer: On the Way of Creation of Human-Oriented Interface. In V. Mkrttchian, A. Bershadsky, A. Bozhday, M. Kataev, & S. Kataev (Eds.), *Handbook of Research on Estimation and Control Techniques in E-Learning Systems* (pp. 458–470). Hershey, PA: IGI Global. doi:10.4018/978-1-4666-9489-7.ch032

Köse, U. (2017). An Augmented-Reality-Based Intelligent Mobile Application for Open Computer Education. In G. Kurubacak & H. Altinpulluk (Eds.), *Mobile Technologies and Augmented Reality in Open Education* (pp. 154–174). Hershey, PA: IGI Global. doi:10.4018/978-1-5225-2110-5.ch008

Lahmiri, S. (2018). Information Technology Outsourcing Risk Factors and Provider Selection. In M. Gupta, R. Sharman, J. Walp, & P. Mulgund (Eds.), *Information Technology Risk Management and Compliance in Modern Organizations* (pp. 214–228). Hershey, PA: IGI Global. doi:10.4018/978-1-5225-2604-9.ch008

Landriscina, F. (2017). Computer-Supported Imagination: The Interplay Between Computer and Mental Simulation in Understanding Scientific Concepts. In I. Levin & D. Tsybulsky (Eds.), *Digital Tools and Solutions for Inquiry-Based STEM Learning* (pp. 33–60). Hershey, PA: IGI Global. doi:10.4018/978-1-5225-2525-7.ch002

Lau, S. K., Winley, G. K., Leung, N. K., Tsang, N., & Lau, S. Y. (2016). An Exploratory Study of Expectation in IT Skills in a Developing Nation: Vietnam. *Journal of Global Information Management, 24*(1), 1–13. doi:10.4018/JGIM.2016010101

Lavranos, C., Kostagiolas, P., & Papadatos, J. (2016). Information Retrieval Technologies and the "Realities" of Music Information Seeking. In I. Deliyannis, P. Kostagiolas, & C. Banou (Eds.), *Experimental Multimedia Systems for Interactivity and Strategic Innovation* (pp. 102–121). Hershey, PA: IGI Global. doi:10.4018/978-1-4666-8659-5.ch005

Lee, W. W. (2018). Ethical Computing Continues From Problem to Solution. In M. Khosrow-Pour, D.B.A. (Ed.), Encyclopedia of Information Science and Technology, Fourth Edition (pp. 4884-4897). Hershey, PA: IGI Global. doi:10.4018/978-1-5225-2255-3.ch423

Lehto, M. (2016). Cyber Security Education and Research in the Finland's Universities and Universities of Applied Sciences. *International Journal of Cyber Warfare & Terrorism, 6*(2), 15–31. doi:10.4018/IJCWT.2016040102

Lin, C., Jalleh, G., & Huang, Y. (2016). Evaluating and Managing Electronic Commerce and Outsourcing Projects in Hospitals. In A. Dwivedi (Ed.), *Reshaping Medical Practice and Care with Health Information Systems* (pp. 132–172). Hershey, PA: IGI Global. doi:10.4018/978-1-4666-9870-3.ch005

Lin, S., Chen, S., & Chuang, S. (2017). Perceived Innovation and Quick Response Codes in an Online-to-Offline E-Commerce Service Model. *International Journal of E-Adoption, 9*(2), 1–16. doi:10.4018/IJEA.2017070101

Liu, M., Wang, Y., Xu, W., & Liu, L. (2017). Automated Scoring of Chinese Engineering Students' English Essays. *International Journal of Distance Education Technologies, 15*(1), 52–68. doi:10.4018/IJDET.2017010104

Luciano, E. M., Wiedenhöft, G. C., Macadar, M. A., & Pinheiro dos Santos, F. (2016). Information Technology Governance Adoption: Understanding its Expectations Through the Lens of Organizational Citizenship. *International Journal of IT/Business Alignment and Governance, 7*(2), 22-32. doi:10.4018/IJITBAG.2016070102

Related References

Mabe, L. K., & Oladele, O. I. (2017). Application of Information Communication Technologies for Agricultural Development through Extension Services: A Review. In T. Tossy (Ed.), *Information Technology Integration for Socio-Economic Development* (pp. 52–101). Hershey, PA: IGI Global. doi:10.4018/978-1-5225-0539-6.ch003

Manogaran, G., Thota, C., & Lopez, D. (2018). Human-Computer Interaction With Big Data Analytics. In D. Lopez & M. Durai (Eds.), *HCI Challenges and Privacy Preservation in Big Data Security* (pp. 1–22). Hershey, PA: IGI Global. doi:10.4018/978-1-5225-2863-0.ch001

Margolis, J., Goode, J., & Flapan, J. (2017). A Critical Crossroads for Computer Science for All: "Identifying Talent" or "Building Talent," and What Difference Does It Make? In Y. Rankin & J. Thomas (Eds.), *Moving Students of Color from Consumers to Producers of Technology* (pp. 1–23). Hershey, PA: IGI Global. doi:10.4018/978-1-5225-2005-4.ch001

Mbale, J. (2018). Computer Centres Resource Cloud Elasticity-Scalability (CRECES): Copperbelt University Case Study. In S. Aljawarneh & M. Malhotra (Eds.), *Critical Research on Scalability and Security Issues in Virtual Cloud Environments* (pp. 48–70). Hershey, PA: IGI Global. doi:10.4018/978-1-5225-3029-9.ch003

McKee, J. (2018). The Right Information: The Key to Effective Business Planning. In *Business Architectures for Risk Assessment and Strategic Planning: Emerging Research and Opportunities* (pp. 38–52). Hershey, PA: IGI Global. doi:10.4018/978-1-5225-3392-4.ch003

Mensah, I. K., & Mi, J. (2018). Determinants of Intention to Use Local E-Government Services in Ghana: The Perspective of Local Government Workers. *International Journal of Technology Diffusion*, 9(2), 41–60. doi:10.4018/IJTD.2018040103

Mohamed, J. H. (2018). Scientograph-Based Visualization of Computer Forensics Research Literature. In J. Jeyasekar & P. Saravanan (Eds.), *Innovations in Measuring and Evaluating Scientific Information* (pp. 148–162). Hershey, PA: IGI Global. doi:10.4018/978-1-5225-3457-0.ch010

Moore, R. L., & Johnson, N. (2017). Earning a Seat at the Table: How IT Departments Can Partner in Organizational Change and Innovation. *International Journal of Knowledge-Based Organizations*, 7(2), 1–12. doi:10.4018/IJKBO.2017040101

Mtebe, J. S., & Kissaka, M. M. (2016). Enhancing the Quality of Computer Science Education with MOOCs in Sub-Saharan Africa. In J. Keengwe & G. Onchwari (Eds.), *Handbook of Research on Active Learning and the Flipped Classroom Model in the Digital Age* (pp. 366–377). Hershey, PA: IGI Global. doi:10.4018/978-1-4666-9680-8.ch019

Mukul, M. K., & Bhattaharyya, S. (2017). Brain-Machine Interface: Human-Computer Interaction. In E. Noughabi, B. Raahemi, A. Albadvi, & B. Far (Eds.), *Handbook of Research on Data Science for Effective Healthcare Practice and Administration* (pp. 417–443). Hershey, PA: IGI Global. doi:10.4018/978-1-5225-2515-8.ch018

Na, L. (2017). Library and Information Science Education and Graduate Programs in Academic Libraries. In L. Ruan, Q. Zhu, & Y. Ye (Eds.), *Academic Library Development and Administration in China* (pp. 218–229). Hershey, PA: IGI Global. doi:10.4018/978-1-5225-0550-1.ch013

Nabavi, A., Taghavi-Fard, M. T., Hanafizadeh, P., & Taghva, M. R. (2016). Information Technology Continuance Intention: A Systematic Literature Review. *International Journal of E-Business Research*, *12*(1), 58–95. doi:10.4018/IJEBR.2016010104

Nath, R., & Murthy, V. N. (2018). What Accounts for the Differences in Internet Diffusion Rates Around the World? In M. Khosrow-Pour, D.B.A. (Ed.), Encyclopedia of Information Science and Technology, Fourth Edition (pp. 8095-8104). Hershey, PA: IGI Global. doi:10.4018/978-1-5225-2255-3.ch705

Nedelko, Z., & Potocan, V. (2018). The Role of Emerging Information Technologies for Supporting Supply Chain Management. In M. Khosrow-Pour, D.B.A. (Ed.), Encyclopedia of Information Science and Technology, Fourth Edition (pp. 5559-5569). Hershey, PA: IGI Global. doi:10.4018/978-1-5225-2255-3.ch483

Ngafeeson, M. N. (2018). User Resistance to Health Information Technology. In M. Khosrow-Pour, D.B.A. (Ed.), Encyclopedia of Information Science and Technology, Fourth Edition (pp. 3816-3825). Hershey, PA: IGI Global. doi:10.4018/978-1-5225-2255-3.ch331

Nozari, H., Najafi, S. E., Jafari-Eskandari, M., & Aliahmadi, A. (2016). Providing a Model for Virtual Project Management with an Emphasis on IT Projects. In C. Graham (Ed.), *Strategic Management and Leadership for Systems Development in Virtual Spaces* (pp. 43–63). Hershey, PA: IGI Global. doi:10.4018/978-1-4666-9688-4.ch003

Nurdin, N., Stockdale, R., & Scheepers, H. (2016). Influence of Organizational Factors in the Sustainability of E-Government: A Case Study of Local E-Government in Indonesia. In I. Sodhi (Ed.), *Trends, Prospects, and Challenges in Asian E-Governance* (pp. 281–323). Hershey, PA: IGI Global. doi:10.4018/978-1-4666-9536-8.ch014

Odagiri, K. (2017). Introduction of Individual Technology to Constitute the Current Internet. In *Strategic Policy-Based Network Management in Contemporary Organizations* (pp. 20–96). Hershey, PA: IGI Global. doi:10.4018/978-1-68318-003-6.ch003

Related References

Okike, E. U. (2018). Computer Science and Prison Education. In I. Biao (Ed.), *Strategic Learning Ideologies in Prison Education Programs* (pp. 246–264). Hershey, PA: IGI Global. doi:10.4018/978-1-5225-2909-5.ch012

Olelewe, C. J., & Nwafor, I. P. (2017). Level of Computer Appreciation Skills Acquired for Sustainable Development by Secondary School Students in Nsukka LGA of Enugu State, Nigeria. In C. Ayo & V. Mbarika (Eds.), *Sustainable ICT Adoption and Integration for Socio-Economic Development* (pp. 214–233). Hershey, PA: IGI Global. doi:10.4018/978-1-5225-2565-3.ch010

Oliveira, M., Maçada, A. C., Curado, C., & Nodari, F. (2017). Infrastructure Profiles and Knowledge Sharing. *International Journal of Technology and Human Interaction*, *13*(3), 1–12. doi:10.4018/IJTHI.2017070101

Otarkhani, A., Shokouhyar, S., & Pour, S. S. (2017). Analyzing the Impact of Governance of Enterprise IT on Hospital Performance: Tehran's (Iran) Hospitals – A Case Study. *International Journal of Healthcare Information Systems and Informatics*, *12*(3), 1–20. doi:10.4018/IJHISI.2017070101

Otunla, A. O., & Amuda, C. O. (2018). Nigerian Undergraduate Students' Computer Competencies and Use of Information Technology Tools and Resources for Study Skills and Habits' Enhancement. In M. Khosrow-Pour, D.B.A. (Ed.), Encyclopedia of Information Science and Technology, Fourth Edition (pp. 2303-2313). Hershey, PA: IGI Global. doi:10.4018/978-1-5225-2255-3.ch200

Özçınar, H. (2018). A Brief Discussion on Incentives and Barriers to Computational Thinking Education. In H. Ozcinar, G. Wong, & H. Ozturk (Eds.), *Teaching Computational Thinking in Primary Education* (pp. 1–17). Hershey, PA: IGI Global. doi:10.4018/978-1-5225-3200-2.ch001

Pandey, J. M., Garg, S., Mishra, P., & Mishra, B. P. (2017). Computer Based Psychological Interventions: Subject to the Efficacy of Psychological Services. *International Journal of Computers in Clinical Practice*, *2*(1), 25–33. doi:10.4018/IJCCP.2017010102

Parry, V. K., & Lind, M. L. (2016). Alignment of Business Strategy and Information Technology Considering Information Technology Governance, Project Portfolio Control, and Risk Management. *International Journal of Information Technology Project Management*, *7*(4), 21–37. doi:10.4018/IJITPM.2016100102

Patro, C. (2017). Impulsion of Information Technology on Human Resource Practices. In P. Ordóñez de Pablos (Ed.), *Managerial Strategies and Solutions for Business Success in Asia* (pp. 231–254). Hershey, PA: IGI Global. doi:10.4018/978-1-5225-1886-0.ch013

Patro, C. S., & Raghunath, K. M. (2017). Information Technology Paraphernalia for Supply Chain Management Decisions. In M. Tavana (Ed.), *Enterprise Information Systems and the Digitalization of Business Functions* (pp. 294–320). Hershey, PA: IGI Global. doi:10.4018/978-1-5225-2382-6.ch014

Paul, P. K. (2016). Cloud Computing: An Agent of Promoting Interdisciplinary Sciences, Especially Information Science and I-Schools – Emerging Techno-Educational Scenario. In L. Chao (Ed.), *Handbook of Research on Cloud-Based STEM Education for Improved Learning Outcomes* (pp. 247–258). Hershey, PA: IGI Global. doi:10.4018/978-1-4666-9924-3.ch016

Paul, P. K. (2018). The Context of IST for Solid Information Retrieval and Infrastructure Building: Study of Developing Country. *International Journal of Information Retrieval Research*, 8(1), 86–100. doi:10.4018/IJIRR.2018010106

Paul, P. K., & Chatterjee, D. (2018). iSchools Promoting "Information Science and Technology" (IST) Domain Towards Community, Business, and Society With Contemporary Worldwide Trend and Emerging Potentialities in India. In M. Khosrow-Pour, D.B.A. (Ed.), Encyclopedia of Information Science and Technology, Fourth Edition (pp. 4723-4735). Hershey, PA: IGI Global. doi:10.4018/978-1-5225-2255-3.ch410

Pessoa, C. R., & Marques, M. E. (2017). Information Technology and Communication Management in Supply Chain Management. In G. Jamil, A. Soares, & C. Pessoa (Eds.), *Handbook of Research on Information Management for Effective Logistics and Supply Chains* (pp. 23–33). Hershey, PA: IGI Global. doi:10.4018/978-1-5225-0973-8.ch002

Pineda, R. G. (2016). Where the Interaction Is Not: Reflections on the Philosophy of Human-Computer Interaction. *International Journal of Art, Culture and Design Technologies*, 5(1), 1–12. doi:10.4018/IJACDT.2016010101

Pineda, R. G. (2018). Remediating Interaction: Towards a Philosophy of Human-Computer Relationship. In M. Khosrow-Pour (Ed.), *Enhancing Art, Culture, and Design With Technological Integration* (pp. 75–98). Hershey, PA: IGI Global. doi:10.4018/978-1-5225-5023-5.ch004

Poikela, P., & Vuojärvi, H. (2016). Learning ICT-Mediated Communication through Computer-Based Simulations. In M. Cruz-Cunha, I. Miranda, R. Martinho, & R. Rijo (Eds.), *Encyclopedia of E-Health and Telemedicine* (pp. 674–687). Hershey, PA: IGI Global. doi:10.4018/978-1-4666-9978-6.ch052

Qian, Y. (2017). Computer Simulation in Higher Education: Affordances, Opportunities, and Outcomes. In P. Vu, S. Fredrickson, & C. Moore (Eds.), *Handbook of Research on Innovative Pedagogies and Technologies for Online Learning in Higher Education* (pp. 236–262). Hershey, PA: IGI Global. doi:10.4018/978-1-5225-1851-8.ch011

Radant, O., Colomo-Palacios, R., & Stantchev, V. (2016). Factors for the Management of Scarce Human Resources and Highly Skilled Employees in IT-Departments: A Systematic Review. *Journal of Information Technology Research*, *9*(1), 65–82. doi:10.4018/JITR.2016010105

Rahman, N. (2016). Toward Achieving Environmental Sustainability in the Computer Industry. *International Journal of Green Computing*, *7*(1), 37–54. doi:10.4018/IJGC.2016010103

Rahman, N. (2017). Lessons from a Successful Data Warehousing Project Management. *International Journal of Information Technology Project Management*, *8*(4), 30–45. doi:10.4018/IJITPM.2017100103

Rahman, N. (2018). Environmental Sustainability in the Computer Industry for Competitive Advantage. In M. Khosrow-Pour (Ed.), *Green Computing Strategies for Competitive Advantage and Business Sustainability* (pp. 110–130). Hershey, PA: IGI Global. doi:10.4018/978-1-5225-5017-4.ch006

Rajh, A., & Pavetic, T. (2017). Computer Generated Description as the Required Digital Competence in Archival Profession. *International Journal of Digital Literacy and Digital Competence*, *8*(1), 36–49. doi:10.4018/IJDLDC.2017010103

Raman, A., & Goyal, D. P. (2017). Extending IMPLEMENT Framework for Enterprise Information Systems Implementation to Information System Innovation. In M. Tavana (Ed.), *Enterprise Information Systems and the Digitalization of Business Functions* (pp. 137–177). Hershey, PA: IGI Global. doi:10.4018/978-1-5225-2382-6.ch007

Rao, Y. S., Rauta, A. K., Saini, H., & Panda, T. C. (2017). Mathematical Model for Cyber Attack in Computer Network. *International Journal of Business Data Communications and Networking*, *13*(1), 58–65. doi:10.4018/IJBDCN.2017010105

Rapaport, W. J. (2018). Syntactic Semantics and the Proper Treatment of Computationalism. In M. Danesi (Ed.), *Empirical Research on Semiotics and Visual Rhetoric* (pp. 128–176). Hershey, PA: IGI Global. doi:10.4018/978-1-5225-5622-0.ch007

Raut, R., Priyadarshinee, P., & Jha, M. (2017). Understanding the Mediation Effect of Cloud Computing Adoption in Indian Organization: Integrating TAM-TOE- Risk Model. *International Journal of Service Science, Management, Engineering, and Technology*, *8*(3), 40–59. doi:10.4018/IJSSMET.2017070103

Regan, E. A., & Wang, J. (2016). Realizing the Value of EHR Systems Critical Success Factors. *International Journal of Healthcare Information Systems and Informatics*, *11*(3), 1–18. doi:10.4018/IJHISI.2016070101

Rezaie, S., Mirabedini, S. J., & Abtahi, A. (2018). Designing a Model for Implementation of Business Intelligence in the Banking Industry. *International Journal of Enterprise Information Systems*, *14*(1), 77–103. doi:10.4018/IJEIS.2018010105

Rezende, D. A. (2016). Digital City Projects: Information and Public Services Offered by Chicago (USA) and Curitiba (Brazil). *International Journal of Knowledge Society Research*, *7*(3), 16–30. doi:10.4018/IJKSR.2016070102

Rezende, D. A. (2018). Strategic Digital City Projects: Innovative Information and Public Services Offered by Chicago (USA) and Curitiba (Brazil). In M. Lytras, L. Daniela, & A. Visvizi (Eds.), *Enhancing Knowledge Discovery and Innovation in the Digital Era* (pp. 204–223). Hershey, PA: IGI Global. doi:10.4018/978-1-5225-4191-2.ch012

Riabov, V. V. (2016). Teaching Online Computer-Science Courses in LMS and Cloud Environment. *International Journal of Quality Assurance in Engineering and Technology Education*, *5*(4), 12–41. doi:10.4018/IJQAETE.2016100102

Ricordel, V., Wang, J., Da Silva, M. P., & Le Callet, P. (2016). 2D and 3D Visual Attention for Computer Vision: Concepts, Measurement, and Modeling. In R. Pal (Ed.), *Innovative Research in Attention Modeling and Computer Vision Applications* (pp. 1–44). Hershey, PA: IGI Global. doi:10.4018/978-1-4666-8723-3.ch001

Rodriguez, A., Rico-Diaz, A. J., Rabuñal, J. R., & Gestal, M. (2017). Fish Tracking with Computer Vision Techniques: An Application to Vertical Slot Fishways. In M. S., & V. V. (Eds.), Multi-Core Computer Vision and Image Processing for Intelligent Applications (pp. 74-104). Hershey, PA: IGI Global. doi:10.4018/978-1-5225-0889-2.ch003

Romero, J. A. (2018). Sustainable Advantages of Business Value of Information Technology. In M. Khosrow-Pour, D.B.A. (Ed.), Encyclopedia of Information Science and Technology, Fourth Edition (pp. 923-929). Hershey, PA: IGI Global. doi:10.4018/978-1-5225-2255-3.ch079

Romero, J. A. (2018). The Always-On Business Model and Competitive Advantage. In N. Bajgoric (Ed.), *Always-On Enterprise Information Systems for Modern Organizations* (pp. 23–40). Hershey, PA: IGI Global. doi:10.4018/978-1-5225-3704-5.ch002

Rosen, Y. (2018). Computer Agent Technologies in Collaborative Learning and Assessment. In M. Khosrow-Pour, D.B.A. (Ed.), Encyclopedia of Information Science and Technology, Fourth Edition (pp. 2402-2410). Hershey, PA: IGI Global. doi:10.4018/978-1-5225-2255-3.ch209

Rosen, Y., & Mosharraf, M. (2016). Computer Agent Technologies in Collaborative Assessments. In Y. Rosen, S. Ferrara, & M. Mosharraf (Eds.), *Handbook of Research on Technology Tools for Real-World Skill Development* (pp. 319–343). Hershey, PA: IGI Global. doi:10.4018/978-1-4666-9441-5.ch012

Roy, D. (2018). Success Factors of Adoption of Mobile Applications in Rural India: Effect of Service Characteristics on Conceptual Model. In M. Khosrow-Pour (Ed.), *Green Computing Strategies for Competitive Advantage and Business Sustainability* (pp. 211–238). Hershey, PA: IGI Global. doi:10.4018/978-1-5225-5017-4.ch010

Ruffin, T. R. (2016). Health Information Technology and Change. In V. Wang (Ed.), *Handbook of Research on Advancing Health Education through Technology* (pp. 259–285). Hershey, PA: IGI Global. doi:10.4018/978-1-4666-9494-1.ch012

Ruffin, T. R. (2016). Health Information Technology and Quality Management. *International Journal of Information Communication Technologies and Human Development*, 8(4), 56–72. doi:10.4018/IJICTHD.2016100105

Ruffin, T. R., & Hawkins, D. P. (2018). Trends in Health Care Information Technology and Informatics. In M. Khosrow-Pour, D.B.A. (Ed.), Encyclopedia of Information Science and Technology, Fourth Edition (pp. 3805-3815). Hershey, PA: IGI Global. doi:10.4018/978-1-5225-2255-3.ch330

Safari, M. R., & Jiang, Q. (2018). The Theory and Practice of IT Governance Maturity and Strategies Alignment: Evidence From Banking Industry. *Journal of Global Information Management*, 26(2), 127–146. doi:10.4018/JGIM.2018040106

Sahin, H. B., & Anagun, S. S. (2018). Educational Computer Games in Math Teaching: A Learning Culture. In E. Toprak & E. Kumtepe (Eds.), *Supporting Multiculturalism in Open and Distance Learning Spaces* (pp. 249–280). Hershey, PA: IGI Global. doi:10.4018/978-1-5225-3076-3.ch013

Sanna, A., & Valpreda, F. (2017). An Assessment of the Impact of a Collaborative Didactic Approach and Students' Background in Teaching Computer Animation. *International Journal of Information and Communication Technology Education*, *13*(4), 1–16. doi:10.4018/IJICTE.2017100101

Savita, K., Dominic, P., & Ramayah, T. (2016). The Drivers, Practices and Outcomes of Green Supply Chain Management: Insights from ISO14001 Manufacturing Firms in Malaysia. *International Journal of Information Systems and Supply Chain Management*, *9*(2), 35–60. doi:10.4018/IJISSCM.2016040103

Scott, A., Martin, A., & McAlear, F. (2017). Enhancing Participation in Computer Science among Girls of Color: An Examination of a Preparatory AP Computer Science Intervention. In Y. Rankin & J. Thomas (Eds.), *Moving Students of Color from Consumers to Producers of Technology* (pp. 62–84). Hershey, PA: IGI Global. doi:10.4018/978-1-5225-2005-4.ch004

Shahsavandi, E., Mayah, G., & Rahbari, H. (2016). Impact of E-Government on Transparency and Corruption in Iran. In I. Sodhi (Ed.), *Trends, Prospects, and Challenges in Asian E-Governance* (pp. 75–94). Hershey, PA: IGI Global. doi:10.4018/978-1-4666-9536-8.ch004

Siddoo, V., & Wongsai, N. (2017). Factors Influencing the Adoption of ISO/IEC 29110 in Thai Government Projects: A Case Study. *International Journal of Information Technologies and Systems Approach*, *10*(1), 22–44. doi:10.4018/IJITSA.2017010102

Sidorkina, I., & Rybakov, A. (2016). Computer-Aided Design as Carrier of Set Development Changes System in E-Course Engineering. In V. Mkrttchian, A. Bershadsky, A. Bozhday, M. Kataev, & S. Kataev (Eds.), *Handbook of Research on Estimation and Control Techniques in E-Learning Systems* (pp. 500–515). Hershey, PA: IGI Global. doi:10.4018/978-1-4666-9489-7.ch035

Sidorkina, I., & Rybakov, A. (2016). Creating Model of E-Course: As an Object of Computer-Aided Design. In V. Mkrttchian, A. Bershadsky, A. Bozhday, M. Kataev, & S. Kataev (Eds.), *Handbook of Research on Estimation and Control Techniques in E-Learning Systems* (pp. 286–297). Hershey, PA: IGI Global. doi:10.4018/978-1-4666-9489-7.ch019

Simões, A. (2017). Using Game Frameworks to Teach Computer Programming. In R. Alexandre Peixoto de Queirós & M. Pinto (Eds.), *Gamification-Based E-Learning Strategies for Computer Programming Education* (pp. 221–236). Hershey, PA: IGI Global. doi:10.4018/978-1-5225-1034-5.ch010

Sllame, A. M. (2017). Integrating LAB Work With Classes in Computer Network Courses. In H. Alphin Jr, R. Chan, & J. Lavine (Eds.), *The Future of Accessibility in International Higher Education* (pp. 253–275). Hershey, PA: IGI Global. doi:10.4018/978-1-5225-2560-8.ch015

Smirnov, A., Ponomarev, A., Shilov, N., Kashevnik, A., & Teslya, N. (2018). Ontology-Based Human-Computer Cloud for Decision Support: Architecture and Applications in Tourism. *International Journal of Embedded and Real-Time Communication Systems*, 9(1), 1–19. doi:10.4018/IJERTCS.2018010101

Smith-Ditizio, A. A., & Smith, A. D. (2018). Computer Fraud Challenges and Its Legal Implications. In M. Khosrow-Pour, D.B.A. (Ed.), Encyclopedia of Information Science and Technology, Fourth Edition (pp. 4837-4848). Hershey, PA: IGI Global. doi:10.4018/978-1-5225-2255-3.ch419

Sohani, S. S. (2016). Job Shadowing in Information Technology Projects: A Source of Competitive Advantage. *International Journal of Information Technology Project Management*, 7(1), 47–57. doi:10.4018/IJITPM.2016010104

Sosnin, P. (2018). Figuratively Semantic Support of Human-Computer Interactions. In *Experience-Based Human-Computer Interactions: Emerging Research and Opportunities* (pp. 244–272). Hershey, PA: IGI Global. doi:10.4018/978-1-5225-2987-3.ch008

Spinelli, R., & Benevolo, C. (2016). From Healthcare Services to E-Health Applications: A Delivery System-Based Taxonomy. In A. Dwivedi (Ed.), *Reshaping Medical Practice and Care with Health Information Systems* (pp. 205–245). Hershey, PA: IGI Global. doi:10.4018/978-1-4666-9870-3.ch007

Srinivasan, S. (2016). Overview of Clinical Trial and Pharmacovigilance Process and Areas of Application of Computer System. In P. Chakraborty & A. Nagal (Eds.), *Software Innovations in Clinical Drug Development and Safety* (pp. 1–13). Hershey, PA: IGI Global. doi:10.4018/978-1-4666-8726-4.ch001

Srisawasdi, N. (2016). Motivating Inquiry-Based Learning Through a Combination of Physical and Virtual Computer-Based Laboratory Experiments in High School Science. In M. Urban & D. Falvo (Eds.), *Improving K-12 STEM Education Outcomes through Technological Integration* (pp. 108–134). Hershey, PA: IGI Global. doi:10.4018/978-1-4666-9616-7.ch006

Stavridi, S. V., & Hamada, D. R. (2016). Children and Youth Librarians: Competencies Required in Technology-Based Environment. In J. Yap, M. Perez, M. Ayson, & G. Entico (Eds.), *Special Library Administration, Standardization and Technological Integration* (pp. 25–50). Hershey, PA: IGI Global. doi:10.4018/978-1-4666-9542-9.ch002

Sung, W., Ahn, J., Kai, S. M., Choi, A., & Black, J. B. (2016). Incorporating Touch-Based Tablets into Classroom Activities: Fostering Children's Computational Thinking through iPad Integrated Instruction. In D. Mentor (Ed.), *Handbook of Research on Mobile Learning in Contemporary Classrooms* (pp. 378–406). Hershey, PA: IGI Global. doi:10.4018/978-1-5225-0251-7.ch019

Syväjärvi, A., Leinonen, J., Kivivirta, V., & Kesti, M. (2017). The Latitude of Information Management in Local Government: Views of Local Government Managers. *International Journal of Electronic Government Research, 13*(1), 69–85. doi:10.4018/IJEGR.2017010105

Tanque, M., & Foxwell, H. J. (2018). Big Data and Cloud Computing: A Review of Supply Chain Capabilities and Challenges. In A. Prasad (Ed.), *Exploring the Convergence of Big Data and the Internet of Things* (pp. 1–28). Hershey, PA: IGI Global. doi:10.4018/978-1-5225-2947-7.ch001

Teixeira, A., Gomes, A., & Orvalho, J. G. (2017). Auditory Feedback in a Computer Game for Blind People. In T. Issa, P. Kommers, T. Issa, P. Isaías, & T. Issa (Eds.), *Smart Technology Applications in Business Environments* (pp. 134–158). Hershey, PA: IGI Global. doi:10.4018/978-1-5225-2492-2.ch007

Thompson, N., McGill, T., & Murray, D. (2018). Affect-Sensitive Computer Systems. In M. Khosrow-Pour, D.B.A. (Ed.), Encyclopedia of Information Science and Technology, Fourth Edition (pp. 4124-4135). Hershey, PA: IGI Global. doi:10.4018/978-1-5225-2255-3.ch357

Trad, A., & Kalpić, D. (2016). The E-Business Transformation Framework for E-Commerce Control and Monitoring Pattern. In I. Lee (Ed.), *Encyclopedia of E-Commerce Development, Implementation, and Management* (pp. 754–777). Hershey, PA: IGI Global. doi:10.4018/978-1-4666-9787-4.ch053

Triberti, S., Brivio, E., & Galimberti, C. (2018). On Social Presence: Theories, Methodologies, and Guidelines for the Innovative Contexts of Computer-Mediated Learning. In M. Marmon (Ed.), *Enhancing Social Presence in Online Learning Environments* (pp. 20–41). Hershey, PA: IGI Global. doi:10.4018/978-1-5225-3229-3.ch002

Related References

Tripathy, B. K. T. R., S., & Mohanty, R. K. (2018). Memetic Algorithms and Their Applications in Computer Science. In S. Dash, B. Tripathy, & A. Rahman (Eds.), Handbook of Research on Modeling, Analysis, and Application of Nature-Inspired Metaheuristic Algorithms (pp. 73-93). Hershey, PA: IGI Global. doi:10.4018/978-1-5225-2857-9.ch004

Turulja, L., & Bajgoric, N. (2017). Human Resource Management IT and Global Economy Perspective: Global Human Resource Information Systems. In M. Khosrow-Pour (Ed.), *Handbook of Research on Technology Adoption, Social Policy, and Global Integration* (pp. 377–394). Hershey, PA: IGI Global. doi:10.4018/978-1-5225-2668-1.ch018

Unwin, D. W., Sanzogni, L., & Sandhu, K. (2017). Developing and Measuring the Business Case for Health Information Technology. In K. Moahi, K. Bwalya, & P. Sebina (Eds.), *Health Information Systems and the Advancement of Medical Practice in Developing Countries* (pp. 262–290). Hershey, PA: IGI Global. doi:10.4018/978-1-5225-2262-1.ch015

Vadhanam, B. R. S., M., Sugumaran, V., V., V., & Ramalingam, V. V. (2017). Computer Vision Based Classification on Commercial Videos. In M. S., & V. V. (Eds.), Multi-Core Computer Vision and Image Processing for Intelligent Applications (pp. 105-135). Hershey, PA: IGI Global. doi:10.4018/978-1-5225-0889-2.ch004

Valverde, R., Torres, B., & Motaghi, H. (2018). A Quantum NeuroIS Data Analytics Architecture for the Usability Evaluation of Learning Management Systems. In S. Bhattacharyya (Ed.), *Quantum-Inspired Intelligent Systems for Multimedia Data Analysis* (pp. 277–299). Hershey, PA: IGI Global. doi:10.4018/978-1-5225-5219-2.ch009

Vassilis, E. (2018). Learning and Teaching Methodology: "1:1 Educational Computing. In K. Koutsopoulos, K. Doukas, & Y. Kotsanis (Eds.), *Handbook of Research on Educational Design and Cloud Computing in Modern Classroom Settings* (pp. 122–155). Hershey, PA: IGI Global. doi:10.4018/978-1-5225-3053-4.ch007

Wadhwani, A. K., Wadhwani, S., & Singh, T. (2016). Computer Aided Diagnosis System for Breast Cancer Detection. In Y. Morsi, A. Shukla, & C. Rathore (Eds.), *Optimizing Assistive Technologies for Aging Populations* (pp. 378–395). Hershey, PA: IGI Global. doi:10.4018/978-1-4666-9530-6.ch015

Wang, L., Wu, Y., & Hu, C. (2016). English Teachers' Practice and Perspectives on Using Educational Computer Games in EIL Context. *International Journal of Technology and Human Interaction, 12*(3), 33–46. doi:10.4018/IJTHI.2016070103

Watfa, M. K., Majeed, H., & Salahuddin, T. (2016). Computer Based E-Healthcare Clinical Systems: A Comprehensive Survey. *International Journal of Privacy and Health Information Management, 4*(1), 50–69. doi:10.4018/IJPHIM.2016010104

Weeger, A., & Haase, U. (2016). Taking up Three Challenges to Business-IT Alignment Research by the Use of Activity Theory. *International Journal of IT/Business Alignment and Governance, 7*(2), 1-21. doi:10.4018/IJITBAG.2016070101

Wexler, B. E. (2017). Computer-Presented and Physical Brain-Training Exercises for School Children: Improving Executive Functions and Learning. In B. Dubbels (Ed.), *Transforming Gaming and Computer Simulation Technologies across Industries* (pp. 206–224). Hershey, PA: IGI Global. doi:10.4018/978-1-5225-1817-4.ch012

Williams, D. M., Gani, M. O., Addo, I. D., Majumder, A. J., Tamma, C. P., Wang, M., ... Chu, C. (2016). Challenges in Developing Applications for Aging Populations. In Y. Morsi, A. Shukla, & C. Rathore (Eds.), *Optimizing Assistive Technologies for Aging Populations* (pp. 1–21). Hershey, PA: IGI Global. doi:10.4018/978-1-4666-9530-6.ch001

Wimble, M., Singh, H., & Phillips, B. (2018). Understanding Cross-Level Interactions of Firm-Level Information Technology and Industry Environment: A Multilevel Model of Business Value. *Information Resources Management Journal, 31*(1), 1–20. doi:10.4018/IRMJ.2018010101

Wimmer, H., Powell, L., Kilgus, L., & Force, C. (2017). Improving Course Assessment via Web-based Homework. *International Journal of Online Pedagogy and Course Design, 7*(2), 1–19. doi:10.4018/IJOPCD.2017040101

Wong, Y. L., & Siu, K. W. (2018). Assessing Computer-Aided Design Skills. In M. Khosrow-Pour, D.B.A. (Ed.), Encyclopedia of Information Science and Technology, Fourth Edition (pp. 7382-7391). Hershey, PA: IGI Global. doi:10.4018/978-1-5225-2255-3.ch642

Wongsurawat, W., & Shrestha, V. (2018). Information Technology, Globalization, and Local Conditions: Implications for Entrepreneurs in Southeast Asia. In P. Ordóñez de Pablos (Ed.), *Management Strategies and Technology Fluidity in the Asian Business Sector* (pp. 163–176). Hershey, PA: IGI Global. doi:10.4018/978-1-5225-4056-4.ch010

Yang, Y., Zhu, X., Jin, C., & Li, J. J. (2018). Reforming Classroom Education Through a QQ Group: A Pilot Experiment at a Primary School in Shanghai. In H. Spires (Ed.), *Digital Transformation and Innovation in Chinese Education* (pp. 211–231). Hershey, PA: IGI Global. doi:10.4018/978-1-5225-2924-8.ch012

Yilmaz, R., Sezgin, A., Kurnaz, S., & Arslan, Y. Z. (2018). Object-Oriented Programming in Computer Science. In M. Khosrow-Pour, D.B.A. (Ed.), Encyclopedia of Information Science and Technology, Fourth Edition (pp. 7470-7480). Hershey, PA: IGI Global. doi:10.4018/978-1-5225-2255-3.ch650

Yu, L. (2018). From Teaching Software Engineering Locally and Globally to Devising an Internationalized Computer Science Curriculum. In S. Dikli, B. Etheridge, & R. Rawls (Eds.), *Curriculum Internationalization and the Future of Education* (pp. 293–320). Hershey, PA: IGI Global. doi:10.4018/978-1-5225-2791-6.ch016

Yuhua, F. (2018). Computer Information Library Clusters. In M. Khosrow-Pour, D.B.A. (Ed.), Encyclopedia of Information Science and Technology, Fourth Edition (pp. 4399-4403). Hershey, PA: IGI Global. doi:10.4018/978-1-5225-2255-3.ch382

Zare, M. A., Taghavi Fard, M. T., & Hanafizadeh, P. (2016). The Assessment of Outsourcing IT Services using DEA Technique: A Study of Application Outsourcing in Research Centers. *International Journal of Operations Research and Information Systems*, 7(1), 45–57. doi:10.4018/IJORIS.2016010104

Zhao, J., Wang, Q., Guo, J., Gao, L., & Yang, F. (2016). An Overview on Passive Image Forensics Technology for Automatic Computer Forgery. *International Journal of Digital Crime and Forensics*, 8(4), 14–25. doi:10.4018/IJDCF.2016100102

Zimeras, S. (2016). Computer Virus Models and Analysis in M-Health IT Systems: Computer Virus Models. In A. Moumtzoglou (Ed.), *M-Health Innovations for Patient-Centered Care* (pp. 284–297). Hershey, PA: IGI Global. doi:10.4018/978-1-4666-9861-1.ch014

Zlatanovska, K. (2016). Hacking and Hacktivism as an Information Communication System Threat. In M. Hadji-Janev & M. Bogdanoski (Eds.), *Handbook of Research on Civil Society and National Security in the Era of Cyber Warfare* (pp. 68–101). Hershey, PA: IGI Global. doi:10.4018/978-1-4666-8793-6.ch004

About the Contributors

Joel J. P. C. Rodrigues (S'01, M'06, SM'06) is a professor and senior researcher at the National Institute of Telecommunications (Inatel), Brazil, senior researcher at the Instituto de Telecomunicações, Portugal, and Senior Visiting Professor at the Federal University of Piauí, Brazil. He received the Academic Title of Aggregated Professor in informatics engineering from UBI, the Habilitation in computer science and engineering from the University of Haute Alsace, France, a PhD degree in informatics engineering and an MSc degree from the UBI, and a five-year BSc degree (licentiate) in informatics engineering from the University of Coimbra, Portugal. His main research interests include e-health, sensor networks and IoT, vehicular communications, and mobile and ubiquitous computing. Prof. Rodrigues is the leader of the Internet of Things research group (CNPq), Director for Conference Development - IEEE ComSoc Board of Governors, IEEE Distinguished Lecturer, the President of the scientific council at ParkUrbis – Covilhã Science and Technology Park, the Past-Chair of the IEEE ComSoc Technical Committee on eHealth, the Past-chair of the IEEE ComSoc Technical Committee on Communications Software, Steering Committee member of the IEEE Life Sciences Technical Community and Publications co-Chair, and Member Representative of the IEEE Communications Society on the IEEE Biometrics Council. He is the editor-in-chief of the International Journal on E-Health and Medical Communications and editorial board member of several high-reputed journals. He has been general chair and TPC Chair of many international conferences, including IEEE ICC, IEEE GLOBECOM, and IEEE HEALTHCOM. He is a member of many international TPCs and participated in several international conferences organization. He has authored or coauthored over 700 papers in refereed international journals and conferences, 3 books, and 2 patents. He had been awarded several Outstanding Leadership and Outstanding Service Awards by IEEE Communications Society and several best papers awards. Prof. Rodrigues is a licensed professional engineer (as senior member), member of the Internet Society, and a senior member ACM and IEEE.

Amjad Gawanmeh (Senior Member IEEE) is an assistant professor at the Department of Electrical and Computer Engineering at Khalifa University since 2010. He is also an affiliate Assistant professor, Concordia University Montreal, Canada since 2015. He received the M.S. and the Ph.D degrees from Concordia University, Montreal, Canada, 2003 and 2008. He worked as a researcher for the Hardware Verification Group at Concordia University between 2000 and 2008. He worked for Applied Science University in Jordan from 2008 until 2010 as an assistant professor. He has co-authored two edited books, 3 book chapters, more than 20 peer reviewed journal papers, and around 50 peer reviewed conference papers. He was visiting scholar at Syracuse University in June/July 2015, and University of Quebec in June/July 2017. His research interests are verification of hardware systems, security systems, and healthcare systems, modeling and analysis of complex systems such as CPS, performance analysis of complex systems, reliability of as medical system, and Energy efficient algorithms design in CPS. He is the Editor in Chief for the International Journal of Cyber-Physical Systems (IJCPS) IGI, an associate editor for IEEE Access Journal, and for Human-centric Computing and Information Sciences Journal, Springer. He acted as guest editor for several special issues. He is on the reviewer board for several journals in IEEE, Elsevier, Wiley, and many others. He is a member of the executive committee for IPCCC conference. He has co-chaired several conferences and chaired several workshops organized in key conferences including ICC, ICDCS, IPCCC, Healthcom, and WiMob. Has served on the TPC for key conference such as Globecom, ICC, PIMRC, ICCVE, WCNC, and Infocom workshops. He is a senior IEEE member since 2017.

Kashif Saleem is currently working as Assistant Professor at Center of Excellence in Information Assurance (CoEIA), King Saud University. He received his Ph.D. (Electrical Engineering) and M.E. (Electrical Engineering - Electronics & Telecommunication) from Universiti Teknologi Malaysia in 2007 and 2011, respectively. P.G.D. (Computer Technology & Communication) from Government College University, Lahore, Pakistan in 2004 and B.Sc. (Computer Science) from Allama Iqbal Open University, Islamabad, Pakistan in 2002. His research interests Includes Ubiquitous Computing, Mobile Computing, Internet of Things (IoT), Machine to Machine (M2M) Communication, Wireless Mesh Networks (WMNs), Wireless Sensor Networks (WSNs) & Mobile Adhoc Networks (MANETs), Intelligent Autonomous Systems, Information Security, Biological Inspired Optimization Algorithms. Dr. Kashif Saleem has authored several research publications and handling ICT related funded research projects in Saudi Arabia and EU.

* * *

Emmanuel Aceves is a Master of Information Technologies, Computer Engineer and a fulltime student at the PhD of Information Technologies at CUCEA UDG. His work is focused on developing Analytics, Data Visualization and Open Data repositories and developing an algorithm that displays the sensor data in layers inside of a georeferenced map. Emmanuel Aceves has been an IEEE Student member since 2014 and was selected for the IEEE Smart Cities Student Grant.

Shamim Akhter is working as Associate Professor, Department of Computer Science and Engineering (CSE), East West University (EWU), Bangladesh. He received his Ph.D. in Information Processing from Tokyo Institute of Technology (TokyoTech), M.Sc. in Computer Science and Information Management from Asian Institute of Technology (AIT) and B.Sc. in Computer Science from American International University Bangladesh (AIUB) in 2009, 2005 and 2002 respectively. He was also a JSPS Post Doctoral Research Fellow in National Institute of Informatics (NII) from FY 2009-2011, Visiting Researcher in Tokyo Institute of Technology, Japan from FY 2009-2011, Research Associate at the RS and GIS FoS, Asian Institute of Technology, Thailand in 2005, Global COE Research Assistant from Sep 2007~ Aug 2009 in Tokyo Institute of Technology, Japan and full time contact faculty at Thompson Rivers University, CANADA in 2013. He was awarded "The Excellent Student of The Year, FY2008", Global COE Program, Photonics Integration-Core Electronics (PICE), Tokyo Institute of Technology, Japan and Magna-Cum Laude for academic excellence from American International University Bangladesh in 2002. Dr. Akhter has around 50 research publications in renowned journals and conferences. His research interests are Artificial Intelligent, Evolutionary Algorithms and Models for their Parallelization, Remote Sensing (RS) and GIS applications, High Performance Computing (HPC), Algorithm and Complexity Analysis. He is a senior member of IEEE, member of JARC-Net and a member of IEEE CS technical committee for intelligence informatics and parallel processing. He serves as a reviewer of various renowned journals and numerous international conferences.

Samed Bajrić received the Ph.D. degree in mathematics from University of Primorska, Koper, Slovenia, in 2014. From 2017 he is with the Laboratory for Open Systems and Networks, Jožef Stefan Institute, Ljubljana, Slovenia. His research area includes the symmetric key encryption - in particular the design of cryptographic Boolean functions and encryption algorithms for IoT.

Jutika Borah is a final year Master's candidate in the Dept. of Electronics and Communication Technology (ECT) at the Gauhati University, Assam, India. Her areas of working includes surveillance based system design for remote monitoring, face detection and recognition using soft computational techniques, developing learning computational tool. She strongly believes the fact "Leadership and Competence has no gender" and a scientific temper and passion and a keen desire to serve the society and the nation with the potentials through wisdom.

Elsa Cedillo is a PhD Student in information technologies at University of Guadalajara, who belongs to the group of researchers of the Innovation Center of Smart Cities of the U de G. She has been the administrator of the Data Network of a University Center with more than 14,000 students; during the last 11 years she has performing innovative actions, as they were at the time, the installation of WiFi in the 24 buildings of the campus and configuration of the IPv6 protocol. Currently, it promotes implementation of SDN Networks for development of Smart Cities. Her areas of interest are Network Communications, SDN, NFV, Cloud and Fog Computing, 5G Communications.

Kesavaraja D. has completed his B.E (CSE) from Jayaraj Annapackiam CSI College of Engineering, Nazareth under Anna University Chennai in 2005 and M.E (CSE) from Manonmaniam Sundaranar University, Tirunelveli in 2010. He is currently pursuing Ph.D. (I&CE) in Anna University, Chennai. He is a co-author of a book titled "Fundamentals of Computing and Programming" and "Fundamentals of LaTeX Programming". He is currently working as an Assistant Professor, Department of CSE, Dr. Sivanthi Aditanar College of Engineering, Tiruchendur. He has 12 years and 5 months of Teaching Experience. He received SAP Award of Excellence from IIT Bombay. He has published many National and International Journal and conference papers. He has acted as an Associate Faculty of IIT Bombay for conducting online FDPs. He has served as a reviewer for scientific journals such as Springer, Elsevier, IET and Technical Programme Committee Member for many International Conferences. He has guided a student R&D Project Sponsored by IE (I), Kolkatta. His research interests include Cloud Computing.

Sasireka D. has completed her MTech in MS University, Tirunelveli 20111. Her Teaching experience 5 years 8 months in Jayamatha Engineering College, Nagercoil. She is currently doing her full time PhD under Anna University Chennai.

Jeyabharathi Duraipandy has completed her B.E degree in the department of computer science and Engineering from Jayaraj Annapackiam CSI College of Engineering, Nazareth, India, under Anna University Chennai in 2009. She has completed her M.E degree in the department of computer science and Engineering from Manonmaniam Sundaranar University, Tirunelveli, in 2013. She is completed her doctorate from Anna Regional Campus – Tirunelveli, Tirunelveli, in the field of video processing. She is working as an Assistant Professor in the department of Information Technology, Sri Krishna College of Technology, Coimbatore.Her research interests include Image processing, Network security.

Md Abdullah al Forhad is an experienced Graduate Teaching Assistant with a demonstrated history of working in the education management industry. Skilled in Cloud Computing, Internet of Things, C, C++, and Embedded Systems. Strong research professional with a Bachelor's degree focused in Computer Science and Engineering from East West University (EWU), Bangladesh.

Pulak Jyoti Gohain received his B.Sc degree in Electronics from the Dibrugarh University, Assam, India, in 2016 and is currently pursuing M.Sc degree in Electronics and Communication Technology from the Gauhati University. His interests are coding in Python, IoT.

Ramgopal Kashyap's areas of interest are image processing, pattern recognition and machine learning. He has published more than 30 research papers, and book chapters in international journals and conferences like Springer, Inderscience, Elsevier, ACM and IGI-Global indexed by Science Citation Index (SCI) and Scopus (Elsevier).He has Reviewed Research Papers in the Science Citation Index Expanded, Springer Journals and Editorial Board Member and conferences programme committee member of the IEEE, Springer international conferences and journals held in countries: Czech Republic, Switzerland, UAE, Australia, Hungary, Poland, Taiwan, Denmark, India, USA, UK, Austria, and Turkey. He has written many book chapters published by IGI Global, USA.

Victor Larios followed higher education degree programs at the ITESO University in Mexico BSc in Electronics Engineering and the University de Technology de Compiegne in France, Msc and Ph.D. He is a Full Professor at the Information Systems Department at the University of Guadalajara, and he is the Director of the Smart Cities Innovation Center and leads a group of researchers in Smart Cities. His primary research interests are in Smart Cities, IoT Distributed Systems,

Networking, Multiagent Systems and Data Visualization. He has published more than 50 papers in international refereed journals and conferences and published a book in Serios Games. He is also a continuous collaboration with the industry and government in projects using design thinking and agile methodologies to accelerate technology transfer in living labs. He also contributed and coordinated international projects with France, U.S., and ONGs as IEEE where he is a technical advisor for the Guadalajara Smart City project.

Olga Mora is an IoT Research at the Smart Cities Innovation Center since January 2015 and PhD Student in Information Technologies at the Universidad de Guadalajara. Her areas of interest are the IoT, Sensor Networks, Smart Cities and Artificial Intelligence. MS in Electronic Engineering, Instituto Tecnologico de Ciudad Guzman, Mexico, 2013, where she researched embedded systems. Olga has been a member of IEEE since 2015.

Kamalendu Pal is with the Department of Computer Science, School of Mathematics, Computer Science and Engineering, City University of London. Kamalendu received his BSc (Hons) degree in Physics from Calcutta University, India, Postgraduate Diploma in Computer Science from Pune, India; MSc degree in Software Systems Technology from Sheffield University, Postgraduate Diploma in Artificial Intelligence from Kingston University, MPhil degree in Computer Science from University College London, and MBA degree from University of Hull, United Kingdom. He has published dozens of research papers in international journals and conferences. His research interests include knowledge-based systems, decision support systems, computer integrated design, software engineering, and service-oriented computing. He is on the editorial board of international computer science journals. He is a member of the British Computer Society, the Institution of Engineering and Technology, and the IEEE Computer Society.

Kandarpa Kumar Sarma (S'04-M'09, SM '12) is presently with the department of Electronics and Communication Engineering, Gauhati University, India as Professor and Head. He completed his MTech degree in Digital Signal Processing from IIT Guwahati, India, in 2005 and PhD degree from the same institution. His areas of interest include applications of soft-computational tools, mobile communication, pattern recognition and language technology. He is a senior member of IEEE (USA), Fellow IETE (India) and has authored ten books and several research papers.

Sitalakshmi Venkatraman earned her PhD in Computer Science, with a doctoral thesis titled "Efficient Parallel Algorithms for Pattern Recognition", from National Institute of Industrial Engineering in 1993. Prior to that she was awarded MSc (Mathematics) in 1985 and MTech (Computer Science) in 1987, both from Indian Institute of Technology (Madras) and subsequently MEd from University of Sheffield in 2001. Sita has about 30 years of work experience both in industry and academics - developing turnkey projects for IT industry and teaching a variety of IT courses for tertiary institutions, in India, Singapore, New Zealand, and more recently in Australia since 2007. She is currently the Information Technology Lecturer and Discipline Leader for Business Information Systems at Melbourne Polytechnic. She specialises in applying efficient computing models and data mining techniques for various industry problems and recently in the e-health, e-security and e-business domains through collaborations with industry and universities in Australia. She has published seven book chapters and more than 130 research papers in internationally well-known refereed journals and conferences. She is a Senior Member of professional societies and editorial boards of international journals and serves as Program Committee Member of several international conferences every year.

Index

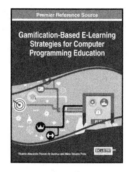
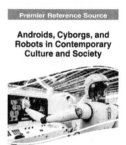

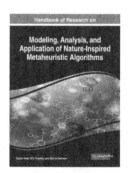

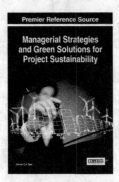

Printed in the United States
By Bookmasters